$10^{00}$

# WHAT VEBLEN TAUGHT

# BY AND ABOUT VEBLEN
*Available in Reprints of Economic Classics*

## IMPERIAL GERMANY
*And the Industrial Revolution (1915). With an Introduction by Joseph Dorfman (1939)*

## AN INQUIRY
## INTO THE NATURE OF PEACE
*And the Terms of Its Perpetuation (1917)*

## THE VESTED INTERESTS
*And the Common Man. "The Modern Point of View and the New Order"*

## THE INSTINCT OF WORKMANSHIP
*And the State of the Industrial Arts (1922) With an Introductory Note by Joseph Dorfman*

## ABSENTEE OWNERSHIP
*And Business Enterprise in Recent Times The Case of America (1923)*

## ESSAYS IN OUR CHANGING ORDER
*(A Posthumous Collection of Papers from Periodicals) Edited by Leon Ardzrooni (1934)*

## WHAT VEBLEN TAUGHT
*Selected Writings of Thorstein Veblen with an Introduction by Wesley C. Mitchell (1936)*

---

## THORSTEIN VEBLEN AND HIS AMERICA
*By Joseph Dorfman (1934)*

## VEBLEN
*By John A. Hobson (1936)*

# WHAT VEBLEN TAUGHT

*Selected Writings*

*of*

THORSTEIN VEBLEN

Edited

With an Introduction

By

WESLEY C. MITCHELL

REPRINTS OF ECONOMIC CLASSICS

*Augustus M. Kelley, Bookseller*
*New York 1964*

*Reprinted 1964 by special arrangement with Viking Press*

Library of Congress Catalogue Card Number
*63 - 23517*

PRINTED IN THE UNITED STATES OF AMERICA
*by* SENTRY PRESS, NEW YORK, N. Y. 10019

# CONTENTS

✿

vi                    Contents

# THORSTEIN VEBLEN

## BY WESLEY C. MITCHELL

"To explain the characteristic animus for which Hume
stands, on grounds that might appeal to Hume, we should
have to inquire into the peculiar circumstances—ultimately material circumstances—that have gone to shape
the habitual view of things within the British community." [1] Thus Thorstein Veblen formulates the problem of
accounting for the preconceptions of another "placid unbeliever."

To explain the characteristic animus for which Veblen
stands, on grounds that might appeal to Veblen, we need
a similar inquiry into the peculiar circumstances that
have gone to shape the habitual view of things within the
American community of his own day. That need is readily met—Veblen has made the inquiry for us. By logical
implication, his explanation of the preconceptions of modern science is an explanation of his own characteristic
animus. Though there is scarcely a word about himself
in all his writings, we can piece together from various
books and essays his account of those elements in his

---

[1] "The Preconceptions of Economic Science," 1899. See p. 56
below.

thinking which he deems it feasible and interesting to explain.

But this explanation will not satisfy our "idle curiosity" about Thorstein Veblen. There are other elements in the make-up of a thinker besides the habitual view of things which prevails in the community from which he springs. For example, note what further Veblen says about Hume:

> Hume was not gifted with a facile acceptance of the group inheritance that made the habit of mind of his generation. Indeed, he was gifted with an alert, though somewhat histrionic, scepticism touching everything that was well received. . . .
>
> There is in Hume . . . an insistence on the prosy, not to say the seamy, side of human affairs. . . . He insists, in season and out of season, on an exhibition of the efficient causes engaged in any sequence of phenomena; and he is sceptical—irreverently sceptical—as to the need or the use of any formulation of knowledge that outruns the reach of his own matter-of-fact, step-by-step argument from cause to effect.
>
> In short, he is too modern to be wholly intelligible to those of his contemporaries who are most neatly abreast of their time. He out-Britishes the British; and, in his footsore quest for a perfectly tame explanation of things, he finds little comfort, and indeed scant courtesy, at the hands of his own

generation. He is not in sufficiently naïve accord with the range of preconceptions then in vogue.

These comments have a double interest. If one knows Veblen, what jumps to mind is that his characterization of Hume might pass as a characterization of himself. Veblen, too, is unable to accept his group inheritance; he is sceptical, he has a histrionic bent, he insists on the seamy side of life, he practises an irreverent neglect of all theories not cast in the matter-of-fact mould. Hence, like Hume, he has not been wholly intelligible to his contemporaries, and he has received scant courtesy at their hands.

A second impression is that Veblen seems to contradict himself. Hume was and was not the child of his time. He was more British than the British, yet he did not accept the habit of mind of his generation. Of course the contradiction is one in seeming only. Human culture is a crazy-quilt of durable patches from the spiritual garments man has worn at successive ages in the past, pieced out by a few patches sewed on recently. Hence the quilt has many patterns; which one a thinker will prefer depends upon his taste. Hume's contemporaries who treated him with scant courtesy were likewise legitimate children of their time. They liked the older patterns in the crazy-quilt—the relics of their ancestors' clothing. Yet a man in advance of the age, repudiated by his generation, may appear in historical perspective to have been the most authentic spokesman for what that generation was adding to culture. He may be typical, for all that he is unique.

This solution of the seeming contradiction throws the problem of the thinker's personality into higher relief. To explain Hume's work, we need not only an inquiry into the peculiar circumstances that shaped the habitual view of things within the British community, but also an inquiry into the circumstances that shaped David Hume into the individual he became, and set him in opposition to his age.

These two inquiries run on different lines and encounter different hazards. One is a venture in cultural history, the other is a venture in psychological biography. It is hard enough to demonstrate an explanation of cultural developments. It is impossible to demonstrate an explanation of personal idiosyncrasies. Veblen, who dealt so confidently with mass habits of thought, left the individual out, or took him for granted. The part of prudence is to follow his example. But Veblen's personality is too intriguing a problem for my prudence. I shall sketch the circumstances of his early years and add a few conjectures, wrested from his own writings, concerning the way in which these circumstances contributed to his characteristics. All of which will do but little to dispel the mystery.


## II

The son of Norwegian immigrants, Veblen was born on a Wisconsin farm July 30, 1857. When he was eight years old, his parents moved to a larger farm in Minnesota. There he grew up in a frontier settlement with eight brothers and sisters who continued to speak Norwegian at home while they learned English in school. The Veblens prospered as efficient farmers may, and gave their children better educational opportunities than most native American farmers have thought worth while. An intellectual drive seems to characterize the family. An elder brother of Thorstein became a professor of physics and one of his nephews is a distinguished mathematician.

At seventeen Veblen entered the academy of Carleton College; at twenty he entered the college, and at twenty-three he graduated with the class of 1880. Carleton was then a small Congregational school which gave a youth predisposed to scepticism abundant provocation to amuse himself with the infirmities of traditional wisdom. By all accounts, the undergraduate impressed his college circle much as the adult was to impress the reading public. But however gravely folk might reprobate his views, everyone acknowledged his extraordinary capacity for assimilating knowledge and putting it to strange uses.

John Bates Clark, later to win fame as one of the foremost economic theoreticians of his generation, was teaching in Carleton in the late 1870's. Thus Veblen was introduced early to the subject about which he finally organized his interests. But for the time being he was engrossed by classical philology, natural history, and philosophy. When he went to Johns Hopkins University in 1881, philosophy was his major subject and economics his minor. Not finding what he wanted, Veblen transferred to Yale, where he took a doctor's degree in philosophy in 1884, with a dissertation entitled "Ethical Grounds of a Doctrine of Retribution." In that same year he published a paper on "Kant's Critique of Judgment" [2] in *The Journal of Speculative Philosophy*.

All this looked like the fair beginning of an academic career. But in those days there were not many openings for young philosophers whose preconceptions resembled Hume's. Veblen was never one who could "sell himself," as advertisers have taught us to say. So he returned to Minnesota, presently married a classmate of literary gifts, and entered on a desultory course of life with wide reading, some writing, and a bit of nondescript office work. This period of incubation lasted some six or seven years. Doubtless the difficulty of obtaining an academic appointment reinforced Veblen's critical attitude toward American "seminaries of the higher learning." Hope deferred is a bitter diet. But the lack of regular occupation and of intellectual companions other than his wife gave Veblen long hours to follow his own thoughts wherever they led. He became more detached than ever from conventional viewpoints and more firmly rooted in his own habit of mind.

A new phase of Veblen's life began in 1891, when he entered Cornell as a graduate student of the social sciences. While there he published a paper called "Some

---

[2] Republished in *Essays in Our Changing Order*, 1934.

Neglected Points in the Theory of Socialism." [3] It was
"offered in the spirit of the disciple" to Herbert Spencer
—in the spirit of the disciple who demonstrated that his
master misconceived the grounds of popular dissatisfaction with economic "freedom." Professor J. Laurence
Laughlin, then at Cornell, appreciated the quality of this
essay. When asked to take charge of the department of
economics at the newly founded University of Chicago,
Laughlin invited Veblen to go with him. Thus Veblen
became one of that extraordinary faculty which President
Harper gathered about him—perhaps the most stimulating group of scholars in the country, certainly the group
with the most varied traditions.

Teaching courses on agricultural economics, socialism,
and the history of economic theory, plus managing *The
Journal of Political Economy*, was a heavy load for one
of Veblen's physique and temperament. But he seems to
have worked best under pressure. In 1898 he published
his first critique of economic theory, "Why Is Economics
Not an Evolutionary Science?" [4] and in 1899 brought out
his first book, *The Theory of the Leisure Class*. From
that year he was a man of mark, known as widely to the
intelligentsia as to his professional brethren.[5]

[3] *The Annals of the American Academy of Political and Social
Science;* reprinted in *The Place of Science in Modern Civilisation*,
1919.
[4] *The Quarterly Journal of Economics;* reprinted in *The Place of
Science in Modern Civilisation*, 1919.
[5] Dr. Joseph Dorfman has given a full account of Veblen's life and
an admirable analysis of his work in *Thorstein Veblen and His America*, New York, The Viking Press, 1934.

## III

The essence of Veblen's critical work and the type of his constructive efforts, as we have known them since, are revealed in the article of 1898 (which was elaborated in "The Preconceptions of Economic Science," 1899–1900) and the book of 1899. It is time to see what account we can make his writings yield of their author's viewpoint.

In that effort my bald sketch of his early life gives a hint. It suggests that as an observer of social behaviour in the American field, Veblen had the initial advantage of coming from a different culture. In his essay on "The Intellectual Pre-eminence of Jews in Modern Europe," [6] Veblen explains how such an experience fits a youth for scientific inquiry.

> The first requisite for constructive work in modern science, and indeed for any work of inquiry that shall bring enduring results, is a sceptical frame of mind. . . .
>
> The young Jew who is at all gifted with a taste for knowledge will unavoidably go afield into that domain of learning where the gentile interests dominate and the gentile orientation gives the outcome. There is nowhere else to go on this quest. . . .
>
> Now it happens that the home-bred Jewish scheme of things, human and divine . . . all bears

---

[6] *Political Science Quarterly*, March 1919, vol. xxxiv; reprinted in *Essays in Our Changing Order*, 1934, pp. 226–30.

the datemark, "B.C." . . . it runs on a logic of personal and spiritual traits, qualities and relations, a
class of imponderables which are no longer of the
substance of those things that are inquired into by
men to whom the ever increasingly mechanistic
orientation of the modern times becomes habitual.

When the gifted young Jew, still flexible in respect of his mental habits, is set loose among the iron
pots of this mechanistic orientation, the clay vessel of
Jewish archaism suffers that fortune which is due
and coming to clay vessels among the iron pots. . . .
He is divested of those archaic conventional preconceptions which will not comport with the intellectual
environment in which he finds himself. But he is not
thereby invested with the gentile's peculiar heritage
of conventional preconceptions which have stood
over, by inertia of habit, out of the gentile past,
which go, on the one hand, to make the safe and
sane gentile conservative and complacent, and which
conduce also, on the other hand, to blur the safe and
sane gentile's intellectual vision, and to leave him
intellectually sessile. . . .

By consequence [the young Jew] is in a peculiar
degree exposed to the unmediated facts of the current situation; and in a peculiar degree, therefore,
he takes his orientation from the run of the facts as
he finds them, rather than from the traditional interpretation of analogous facts in the past. In short,
he is a sceptic by force of circumstances over which

he has no control. Which comes to saying that he is
in line to become a guide and leader of men in that
intellectual enterprise out of which comes the increase and diffusion of knowledge among men, provided always that he is by native gift endowed with
that net modicum of intelligence which takes effect
in the play of the idle curiosity.

Now a Norwegian family of farmer folk is like an
orthodox Jewish family at least in one respect: it also has
a culture which differs widely from the culture of modern
America. The Norwegian brand is not date-marked
"B.C.," but it savours of the Sagas. There is less of business in the Norwegian than in the Jewish heritage, and
the former is by so much the more remote in spirit from
today. A boy brought up in such a family, largely sufficient unto itself, acquires an outlook upon life unlike that
of the son of thoroughly acclimated parents. As he ven-
tures into the world, he finds much strange which those
to the manor born take for granted. If endowed with
curiosity, he wonders both about the notions that his
parents cherish and about the notions that his mates accept. That was Thorstein Veblen's case. And he was in-
satiably curious about everything he encountered—min-
erals, plants, and animals, the tongues men speak, the
arts they practise, the faiths they venerate, and the proofs
they find convincing. He had no collection of established
truths to check his questioning; for the truths taken for
granted at home and the truths taken for granted in

school raised doubts about one another. Thus he, like the Jewish boy of his analysis, became "a sceptic by force of circumstances over which he had no control." . . . On some such lines, the creature of these circumstances might explain his own preparation for scientific inquiry.

But scientific inquiry does not exhaust itself in asking questions; it seeks also to find answers. Veblen's constructive bent is not less marked than his scepticism, though of course it is more specialized. An inquisitive youth may come to doubt all things on principle; but when he begins to contrive explanations, he must limit himself within a range that he can study intensively. What fixed Veblen's choice of problems?

All I can say in answer is that, given his temperament, Veblen's final choice seems a natural outcome of his circumstances. A son of immigrant farmers must wonder about differences among people. That theme is both obvious and subtle; it is beset by prejudices, difficult to treat objectively, fascinating and slippery. Veblen found its dangers, open and concealed, alluring; for in the realm of thought he was bold as a Viking, and as fond of wiles. Yet differences among people are manifold; no one can explore and explain them all. Veblen might have held fast to his early philological interest, fed by his bilingual upbringing. He might have stuck to his first "major," philosophy. Perhaps he would have done so, had he secured a position in that department of learning. He might have pushed deeper into biology, which in the days of Darwinian speculation seemed neatly fitted to his talents. In the end, he found for himself a field more attractive than any one of these. He could fuse his leading interests by studying human cultures. That large venture gave scope to his double heritage from home and school, to his linguistic equipment and facility, to his inveterate scepticism, to his liking for organized systems of thought, to his interest in biology. Also it gave free play to another set of impulses which were as much a part of him as curiosity.

Veblen loved to play with the feelings of people not less than he loved to play with ideas. Now there are few objects of scientific scrutiny more exciting to our feelings than cultural differences. These differences touch our dear selves. Recall how fond we are of making invidious comparisons between people of our own kind and others. We feel magnanimous if we let the comparisons turn to our disadvantage; we feel resentful if others point out inferiorities in us. However objectively our traits are analysed, we react emotionally. The delicate nature of this subject must repel men who dislike complex and ambiguous situations; it attracted Veblen. He usually wrote with one eye on the scientific merits of his analysis, and his other eye fixed on the squirming reader. To him, this reader is the creature of cultural circumstances that have produced standard habits of feeling as well as norms of thinking. Veblen practises vivisection upon his contemporaries; he uses no anæsthetic; he has his notions about what emotional reactions each type will exhibit. Instead of seeking to facilitate the reception of his analysis

by minimizing the reader's emotions, he artfully stimu-
lates them for his own delectation.

Of course most critics of modern culture have strong
feelings of their own, which they strive to impart to their
readers. Moral indignation is the commonest note, and
the one to which we respond most readily. We get a
certain satisfaction from being preached at; even when
we think the preacher bears down rather hard upon our
amiable weaknesses, we respect his zeal. Also we are
used to the open satirist who seeks to laugh us out of our
follies. Veblen repudiates preaching. As an evolutionist
his office is to understand; not to praise, or blame, or
lead us into righteousness. From his point of view, any notions he may entertain concerning what is right and wrong
are vestiges of the cultural environment to which he has
been exposed. They have no authority, and it would be a
futile impertinence to try to impose them upon others.
There is much of the satirist in him; but it is satire of
an unfamiliar and a disconcerting kind. Professedly, he
seeks merely to describe and to explain our cultural traits
in plain terms. But he likes to put his explanations in a
form that will make the commonplaces of our daily lives
startling and ridiculous to us. It is this histrionic foible
which gives his writing its peculiar flavour.

Veblen is an inveterate phrase-maker, and he designs
his phrases to get under our skins. "Conspicuous waste"
fits our habits of consumption like a whiplash. Our philan-
thropies are "essays in pragmatic romance." Modern industry is so "inordinately productive" that prosperity

requires "a conscientious withdrawal of efficiency" by the business men in control—their chief service to production is to practise "capitalistic sabotage." The common stock of trusts formed by combining companies that had competed with one another represents "defunct good-will." As individuals, we find our places either in the "kept classes" or among the "underlying population"—and either ranking makes us wince. His wit spares nothing and no one. If the pulpit is "the accredited vent for the exudation of effete matter from the cultural organism," the scientist is a "finikin sceptic," an "animated slide-rule," "machine made."

To explain this quirk in Veblen's humour would require the assurance of an amateur psycho-analyst. One who lacks that qualification must take the trait for granted, and merely register its consequences. I think Veblen's fondness for quizzing folk helped to determine his choice of problems and to shape the course of his analysis. I am sure it has been largely responsible for the reactions of readers, both professional and lay, to his work. One must be highly sophisticated to enjoy his books.

Within the field of human culture, an investigator must make a more definite choice of themes. Anthropology, history, sociology, economics, political science, social psychology, all deal with culture. A worker in that field must know something of all these disciplines, and Veblen knew much. In the end he organized his inquiries about economics. Perhaps his early contact with an original, though widely different, thinker in that line had some influence upon his choice. But there is an explanation in terms of logic which carries more conviction than psychological conjectures.

Darwin tells what stimulation he received from reflecting upon Malthus's theory of population when he was groping after his own theory of natural selection. An instalment upon this debt of biology to economics was paid by the stimulation which Darwin's doctrines gave to Veblen's theory of cultures. Cultures are complexes of "prevalent habits of thought with respect to particular relations and particular functions of the individual and of the community." [7] The significant question about these habits is the question which Darwin asked about animal species: How did they develop into the forms that we can observe?

The biological view of man's evolution suggests that habits of thought are formed by the activities in which individuals engage. The activities that occupy most hours are likely to exercise most influence in making the mind. The task of getting a living has busied incomparably more men and women for more time than any other task. Hence economic factors have had and still have a major share in shaping mass habits of thought; that is, in making human culture what is has been under varying circumstances in the past, and what it is today. Other types of activity get whatever time and attention the peremp-

[7] *The Theory of the Leisure Class*, p. 190.

tory job of finding food and shelter leaves free. Where
the economic activities themselves are efficient, this margin for indulging such human propensities as emulation,
propitiation, predation, and idle curiosity becomes appreciable. A good many individuals can spend most of
their time in other tasks than making a living, and so
can build up a considerable body of habits not drilled in
by the exigencies of humdrum work. Yet there is perforce a certain congruence among all the mental habits
formed in any single brain, and even among the habits
prevalent in any community at a given time. So the
emancipation even of our religious, æsthetic, and scientific
notions from economic determination is but partial.

Only one other factor can conceivably rival the influence of getting a living in shaping culture. That is the
strictly biological factor of breeding. Veblen thinks, however, that the evidence is all against supposing that *homo
sapiens* has undergone any substantial change in anatomy
or physiology for thousands of years. Our brains are about
as efficient organs as were the brains of neolithic men.
Selective breeding under stress of changing circumstances
doubtless tends to lower the reproduction rate of individuals whose propensities run toward violence in exceptional degree. Perhaps other generalizations of that
type may be made. But the effects of the breeding factor
are slight and dubious in comparison with the effects of
cumulative changes in habits of thinking under the discipline of cumulative changes in modes of getting a living. That the lives we live today are so vastly different

from the lives lived by our ancestors who left their
sketches on the walls of caves and lost their stone implements in the kitchen middens is due in but minor measure
to bodily modifications. The theory of evolution begun
by biologists must be continued by students of culture,
and primarily by economists.

## IV

Needless to say, economists found this a novel conception of their office when Veblen began writing. The
"science of wealth," as they commonly defined their
subject, dealt with production, exchange, and distribution
as these processes run in modern times. About the way in
which the modern scheme of institutions has evolved, the
professed theorists knew little and cared little, for they
did not see that such knowledge would help to solve what
they took to be their central problem—how prices are
determined now, particularly the prices that effect the
distribution of income.

Veblen does not claim that genetic studies will answer
the questions that economists have posed in the form
they have chosen. His fundamental criticism is that economists have asked the wrong questions. Their conception
of science and its problems is antiquated, pre-Darwinian.

The sciences which are in any peculiar sense modern take as an (unavowed) postulate the fact of consecutive change. Their inquiry always centres upon

some manner of process. This notion of process about
which the researches of modern science cluster, is a
notion of a sequence, or complex, of consecutive
change in which the nexus of the sequence, that by
virtue of which the change inquired into is consecutive, is the relation of cause and effect.[8]

Neither the theory of value and distribution as worked
out by Ricardo, nor the refined form of this theory presented by Veblen's teacher, J. B. Clark, deals with consecutive change in any sustained fashion. The more classical political economy was purified, the more strictly was
it limited to what happens in an imaginary "static state."
Hence orthodox economics belongs to the "taxonomic"
stage of inquiry represented, say, by the pre-Darwinian
botany of Asa Gray. Therefore it possesses but meagre
scientific interest. If political economy is to modernize
itself, it must become "an evolutionary science," and it
can become an evolutionary science only by addressing
itself to the problem: How do economic institutions
evolve?

In so far as modern science inquires into the phenomena of life, whether inanimate, brute, or human,
it is occupied about questions of genesis and cumulative change, and it converges upon a theoretical

---

[8] "The Evolution of the Scientific Point of View." Read before the
Kosmos Club, at the University of California, May 4, 1908; first
published in *The University of California Chronicle*, vol. X, no. 4;
reprinted in *The Place of Science in Modern Civilisation*, 1919, p. 32.

formulation in the shape of a life-history drawn in causal terms. In so far as it is a science in the current sense of the term, any science, such as economics, which has to do with human conduct, becomes a genetic inquiry into the human scheme of life; and where, as in economics, the subject of inquiry is the conduct of man in his dealings with the material means of life, the science is necessarily an inquiry into the life-history of material civilization, on a more or less extended or restricted plan. . . . Like all human culture this material civilization is a scheme of institutions—institutional fabric and institutional growth.[9]

Associated with this fundamental charge, that economists have mistaken their chief problem, is a second criticism, that they have worked with an antiquated conception of human nature.

In all the received formulations of economic theory . . . the human material with which the inquiry is concerned is conceived in hedonistic terms; that is to say, in terms of a passive and substantially inert and immutably given human nature. The psychological and anthropological preconceptions of the economists have been those which were accepted by the psychological and social sciences some generations ago. The hedonistic conception of man is that of a

---

[9] "The Limitations of Marginal Utility," 1909. See below, pp. 162–3.

lightning calculator of pleasures and pains, who oscil-
lates like a homogeneous globule of desire of happiness under the impulse of stimuli that shift him
about the area, but leave him intact.[10]

Veblen moulded his own notions of human nature on
Darwin, William James, and anthropological records.
To the biologist and the open-eyed observer, man is essentially active. He is not placed "under the governance
of two sovereign masters, pain and pleasure," as Jeremy
Bentham held; on the contrary he is for ever doing something on his own initiative. Instead of studying pleasures
and pains, or satisfactions and sacrifices, on the supposition
that these "real forces" determine what men do, economists should study the processes of human behaviour at
first hand. For this purpose, the important psychological
categories are not the felicific calculus and the association
of ideas, but propensities and habits. The human individual is born with a vaguely known equipment of tropisms and instincts. Instincts differ from tropisms in that
they involve an element of intelligence; in other words,
they are susceptible of modification by experience. What
modifications instincts will undergo, into what habits they
will develop, depends upon the nature of the experience
encountered, and that depends in turn upon the environment, especially the human environment, in which the
individual grows up. The human environment is of critical

---

[10] "Why Is Economics Not an Evolutionary Science?" 1898; reprinted in *The Place of Science in Modern Civilisation*, p. 73.

importance because through tradition, training, and education "the young acquire what the old have learned."

Cumulatively, therefore, habit creates usages, customs, conventions, preconceptions, composite principles of conduct that run back only indirectly to the native predispositions of the race, but that may affect the working out of any given line of endeavour in much the same way as if these habitual elements were of the nature of a native bias. Along with this body of derivative standards and canons of conduct, and handed on by the same discipline of habituation, goes a cumulative body of knowledge, made up in part of matter-of-fact acquaintance with phenomena and in greater part of conventional wisdom embodying certain acquired predilections and preconceptions current in the community.[11]

This emphasis upon the cumulative character of cultural changes takes us back to Veblen's conception of what constitute the problems of science and to his fundamental criticism of economics. The distinctively modern sciences, we have found him contending, deal with consecutive change. He might have added, though I do not recall his doing so, that the consecutive changes studied by different sciences appear to be cumulative in varying degree. Even physics and chemistry, when applied to the history of

---

[11] *The Instinct of Workmanship*, 1914, p. 39.

the cosmos, are concerned with a situation which develops from millennium to millennium. Biology has its branches that deal with processes conceived to repeat themselves over and over without marked alteration in the total situation to be accounted for; but the problems in which cumulative change is prominent bulk larger in biological than in physico-chemical theory. Cumulation rises to its highest pitch, however, in the social sciences, because the behaviour of men changes in the course of experience far more rapidly than does the behaviour of stars and infra-human species. For that reason, the major explanation of human behaviour at any point in the life-history of our race must be sought in the preceding instalments of the story. As Veblen put it: "Each new situation is a variation of what has gone before it and embodies as causal factors all that has been effected by what went before." [12] To take economic institutions as they stand at a given moment for granted, and merely to inquire into their working, cuts out of economics that behaviour trait which differentiates human activities most clearly from all other subjects of scientific inquiry.

Yet Veblen might have admitted that the quasi-mechanical economics, which takes existing institutions for granted and inquires how they work, has a certain value. This type of inquiry may be regarded as elaborating the logic implicit in the institutions of which it takes cognizance, usually without recognizing their transient

---

[12] "The Limitations of Marginal Utility." See below, p. 164.

character in the life-history of mankind. For example, pecuniary institutions are a prominent feature of current life in the western world. Most of us make money incomes and buy what we want at money prices. To some extent all of us are drilled by experience into the habit of thinking in dollars; all of us acquire some skill in "the exact science of making change"; all of us accept in part "the private and acquisitive point of view." Now a theory such as Veblen's warm admirer Herbert J. Davenport developed on the express assumption that all men are animated by the desire for gain throws light on our economic behaviour just to the extent that men are perfect products of the counting house. The logician who excogitates this mechanical system is prone to exaggerate its adequacy as an account of contemporary behaviour. But Veblen would be the last to deny the importance of pecuniary institutions in modern culture. He does not, in fact, hold that work such as Davenport has done is wrong, or wholly futile. Yet he inclines to take what is valuable in it for granted, much as Davenport takes for granted the existing scheme of institutions. For Veblen is impatient of the well known and eager to develop aspects of the modern situation about which more orthodox types of economic theory have little to say. Men whose conception of what is "scientific" has been moulded by mechanics, criticize his precipitate neglect of their problems, much as Veblen, who builds upon Darwinian biology, criticizes them for their precipitate neglect of evolutionary problems.

One more characteristic of Veblen's procedure must be noted. Representatives of the "exact" sciences stress the importance of measurement. There are those, indeed, who go so far as to claim that the outstanding characteristic of scientific thought is its quantitative precision. Now Darwinian biology was not an exact science; it made but slight use of measurements in any form; it confined itself mainly to "qualitative analysis," supplemented by a recognition that certain factors have played major and other factors minor roles in the development of species. In comparison with Darwin's method, Mendel's experiments in heredity seem precise, and we all know what an impetus the rediscovery of Mendel's work gave to biological research.[13]

Veblen was a good Darwinian in this respect also. His native bent was toward speculation of a philosophical

---

[13] That Veblen grasped the significance of Mendel's work and of the experiments to which it led is shown by his paper on "The Mutation Theory and the Blond Race," reprinted in *The Place of Science in Modern Civilisation*, pp. 457–76. See also his references to "the Mendelian rules of hybridization" in *The Instinct of Workmanship*, pp. 21–5, and in *Imperial Germany and the Industrial Revolution*, pp. 277–8. But this appreciation, supplemented by his admiration for the experiments of Jacques Loeb, did not induce him to attempt close quantitative work of his own. Two early articles on the price of wheat and "A Schedule of Prices for the Staple Foodstuffs" drawn up for the Food Administration in 1918 are the only papers I recall in which Veblen made detailed statistical inquiries. The articles appeared in *The Journal of Political Economy*, Dec. 1892 and June 1893, vol. I, pp. 68–103, 156–61, and 365–79; the memorandum for the Food Administration was unearthed by Dr. Dorfman and may be found, minus the statistics, in *Essays in Our Changing Order*, 1934, pp. 347–54.

sort. No one had keener insight or nicer subtlety in dealing with ideas, and like all efficient inquirers he used the
tools of which he was master. Further, the statistical
invasion of the biological and social sciences was but just
starting in Veblen's youth. Galton was not then recognized as a figure of the first magnitude; Pearson's and
Edgeworth's work on quantitative methods lay in the
future. It was easy for one who had little liking for
mathematical procedures to overlook the promise of
statistics. Finally and most important, problems of cumulative change in "life-history" are exceedingly difficult to
treat by any method of measurement. Each change is by
hypothesis a unique event, begotten by an indefinite number of causes. To disentangle the tangled skein is impossible. Without the aid of an elaborate technique it is hard
to do more with such problems than what Darwin and
Veblen have done—that is, to study the evidence and
select for particular attention what seem to be the salient
factors. That might go without saying concerning all parts
of man's history before social statistics were collected on
a liberal scale and preserved for analysis. It is only when
he comes to recent changes that an investigator has tolera-
bly accurate data. These materials Veblen did not reject;
but he made no great effort to exploit them. In this respect, at least, his practice resembled that of most orthodox economists.

While not addicted to the quantitative method, Veblen
was a keen observer. Having climbed to Darwin's moun-

tain peak, his eyes ranged over a vast stretch of human
experience. About many matters quite invisible to economists immersed in the nineteenth century he thought intensively. The neolithic age in Europe, the feudal system
in Japan, the lives of the Australian blackfellows, and a
thousand things equally remote in time or space from
present-day America seemed strictly pertinent to his problem. Even what he saw of his immediate surroundings
differed from what was patent to his contemporaries.

"All perception," said William James, "is apperception." Every scientific inquirer sees what his mind is prepared to see, and preparation of the mind is a compound
of previous experiences and the thoughts to which they
have given rise. Recall how Darwin's vision was clarified
when, after long fumbling with a mass of observations,
he hit upon the idea of natural selection.

What Veblen saw when he looked at man's activities
differed from what other economists saw because his mind
was equipped with later psychological notions. How
widely Veblen's conception of human nature departed
from that which he imputed to his predecessors has been
remarked. It remains to show how his ideas upon "original
nature" and "culture" controlled the larger issues of his
theorizing, just as notions concerning man's substantial
rationality controlled the larger issues of earlier speculation.

There are two ways of studying behaviour. One may
observe men "objectively," as an experimental psychologist observes animals, and try to form generalizations

concerning their activities without pretending to know what goes on inside their heads. Or one may take his stand inside human consciousness and think how that organ works. If the latter method is chosen, the results arrived at depend upon the thinker's notions about consciousness. Logically, these notions form one premise—usually tacit—in a syllogism. The procedure at this stage is "deductive," though it may have been preceded by an "inductive" derivation of the psychological premise, and it may be followed by an "inductive" testing of the conclusions.

Veblen adhered to the standard practice of the classical masters—he chose to reason out human behaviour. But he sought to explain actual behaviour, not what men will "normally" do; his conclusions are supposed to conform to "facts" and to be open to testing by observation in a directer fashion than are most expositions of "economic laws." Also Veblen gave closer attention than his predecessors to the character of his psychological premise and made it explicit. Profiting by two generations of active research in biology and anthropology as well as in psychology, he could reach what is certainly a later, and presumably a juster, conception of human nature. In so far as his economic theories rest upon the psychological premise, they may be rated a more "scientific" account of human behaviour than theories which rest upon what latter-day writers call the "intellectualist fallacy of the nineteenth century." Yet in so far as any theories of behaviour are conclusions deduced from some conception of human nature, they must be subject to change as knowledge of human nature grows.

Veblen's dealings with psychology, however, are not confined to borrowing ideas from other sciences for use as premises in economics. Anyone who gives an enlightening account of any phase of human behaviour is himself contributing toward our understanding of ourselves. By working with psychological conceptions he develops them, and makes their value and limitations clearer. Thus Jevons contributed to the breakdown of hedonism by applying Bentham's felicific calculus in good faith to explain how exchange value is determined. His literal exposition helped economists to realize the artificiality of ideas which seem plausible so long as they remain vague. The more clearly a social scientist sees that he is dealing with human behaviour, and the more explicit he is about the conceptions of human nature with which he works, the larger the service which he can render to our self-knowledge. Veblen's service in this direction is that he has applied the instinct-habit psychology of Darwin and William James to explain a wide range of human activities. The nascent science of social psychology owes him a heavy debt of gratitude for this accomplishment—a debt which will be all the heavier if his work helps future investigators to do something better than he accomplished.

One of the ways to press forward along Veblen's path is to turn back and test for conformity to "fact" our plausible reasonings about how men behave—that is, to see how our theories about what men do agree with what we can observe. Of course what we can observe is not wholly objective. As recalled above, it depends upon what we are mentally prepared to see, and also upon our techniques. Yet when we can apply them, factual tests of ideas are one of our most effective ways of promoting knowledge. The men who laid the foundations of economics recognized this point, and in their writings upon method admitted the desirability of "inductive verification." But in practice they spent little effort upon this desideratum—it seemed too hopeless a task as matters stood. The notion that inquiries should be framed from the start in such a way as to permit of testing the hypothetical conclusions was not common property in their time. Unless such plans are laid in advance, and laid with skill, it is more than likely that the results attained by reasoning will be in such form that no inquirer can either confirm or refute them by an appeal to facts. Observing this run of affairs, the classical methodologists spoke disparagingly of induction in general and of statistical induction in particular: it seemed to them a tool limited to a narrow range of uses in economics.

Veblen's case is not so very different, except that he deals with actual as distinguished from "normal" behaviour. He does not plan in advance for testing his conclusions. Of course he is bound to be sceptical about them —that attitude is not merely logical in him, but also congenial to his temperament. There is always an aura of playfulness about his attitude toward his own work in

marked contrast to the deadly seriousness of most economists. Yet, when the opportunity offers, he will cite
evidence to support a contention. Usually it is evidence
of a sweeping sort which those who do not agree with his
viewpoint can interpret in a different sense. Sometimes the
evidence is an illustrative case, and the question remains
open how representative the case may be. Rarely does
he undertake a factual survey. Many of his propositions
are not of the type that can be tested objectively with the
means now at our disposal. His work as a whole is like
Darwin's—a speculative system uniting a vast range of
observations into a thoroughly consistent whole, extraordinarily stimulating both to the layman and to the investigator, but waiting for its ultimate validation upon
more intensive and tamer inquiries.


### V

All this about the man, his problems, his viewpoint and
methods of work. What constructive results did he reach?
Veblen's studies in the life-history of mankind range
over the whole interval between "the origin of the blond
type" and the future prospects of business enterprise.
Into this range he has dipped at will, preferring always
the little-known features of the story. He has never
written a systematic treatise upon economics; instead he
has produced numerous essays and ten monographs. An
adequate summary of the ideas he has contributed to the
social sciences would fill another volume as large as *Ab-*

*sentee Ownership.* All that is feasible here is to select topics illustrative of his conclusions. The whole body of writing is so much of one piece that almost any of his disquisitions would serve as an introduction to the whole. Doubtless it is best to take discussions of matters with which everyone is familiar.

Looking over the modern world, Veblen marked a difference between industrial and pecuniary employments; that is, between the work of making goods and the work of making money; in still other terms, between the machine process and business enterprise. No fact of daily life is more commonplace than this difference; neither men on the street nor economic theorists see in it anything exciting or novel. What comments it seems to call for have been made long since. Adam Smith pointed out in the *Wealth of Nations* that division of labour requires exchange of products and that exchange is greatly facilitated by money. But money is merely an intermediary; we must not exaggerate its importance, as the mercantilists did. Bentham's psychology reinforced this view. Pleasures and pains are the only things that really matter to men; commodities and services are important as instruments of pleasures and pains; money stands at a further remove—it is a means of getting commodities and services. The prevalent common-sense on the subject was summed up by John Stuart Mill in a famous passage:

There cannot, in short, be intrinsically a more insignificant thing in the economy of society, than

money; except in the character of a contrivance for
sparing time and labour. It is a machine for doing
quickly and commodiously, what would be done,
though less quickly and commodiously, without it;
and like many other kinds of machinery, it only
exerts a distinct and independent influence of its own
when it gets out of order.[14]

Acting on this conviction, economists have paid a great
deal of attention to the monetary mechanism—the best
ways of designing it and of keeping it in order. But they
treat this problem as a specialty, which has little to do
with general economic theory. In discussing value and
distribution they take money as a tool for investigating
more important matters. Thus Alfred Marshall declares
that money

is the centre around which economic science clusters
. . . not because money or material wealth is regarded as the main aim of human effort, nor even as
affording the main subject-matter for the study of
the economist, but because in this world of ours it is
the one convenient means of measuring human motive on a large scale.[15]

The "real forces" which control behaviour, on Marshall's
showing, are satisfactions and sacrifices. It is these real
forces, and the balancing of one set of them against the

[14] *Principles of Political Economy*, Book III, chap. vii, p. 3. Ashley's edition, p. 488.
[15] *Principles of Economics*, 6th ed., 1910, p. 22.

other set, that require analysis. Money is an indispensable tool for measuring the force of opposing motives; but it remains merely a tool so far as the fundamental principles of economics are concerned.

This view of the place of money in economic theory is perfectly consistent with the conception of human nature entertained by Marshall. Despite his substitution of less colourful terms for "pleasure" and "pain," he thought after Bentham's fashion. Men practise a sort of double-entry bookkeeping, satisfactions on the credit and sacrifices on the debit side of the account; they discount for futurity and for uncertainty; they are ready reckoners. To tell what they will do, one needs to know the motive force of the satisfactions and sacrifices promised by alternative lines of action. That force can best be expressed in terms of money; but the use of money does not alter the substantial character of economic behaviour.[16]

Shift from Marshall's psychological notions to Veblen's, and the whole picture changes. Money becomes a most significant thing in the economy of society, because it shapes the habits of thought into which our native propensities grow. Instead of being "a machine for doing quickly and commodiously what would be done, though less quickly and commodiously, without it," the use of money "exerts a distinct and independent influence of its own" upon our wants as consumers, upon our skill as

[16] In fairness it should be noted that Marshall's discussions of economic behaviour are far more realistic than this schematic framework seems to promise.

planners, upon our methods as producers, and upon our ideals as citizens. And since the discipline which the use of money imposes upon our minds affects some classes far more than it does others, this institution produces social stresses—stresses that may disrupt the present polity.

To begin where Veblen began: In a society where money-making is the commonly accepted test of success in life, our native propensity toward emulation takes on a pecuniary twist. We wish to seem well-to-do, and to attain that agreeable rating we cultivate an air of care-less affluence as much as our means permit. We like goods that look expensive, we keep up with the changing styles however uncomfortable they may be, we subject ourselves to inane and fatiguing social frivolities, we teach our children accomplishments that are elegant because they are costly. Our sense of beauty is stamped with the dollar sign. We stand in awe of the very rich, and approach as close to their reputed manner of life as we can. Though born with an instinct of workmanship which makes futility disagreeable, we get satisfaction from conspicuous waste. Though active creatures, we practise conspicuous leisure, or make our wives and menials do it for us. The higher modern technology raises our standards of living above the "minimum of subsistence," the wider the scope of our invidious consumption. Money cannot be intrinsically insignificant in the economy of a society whose inner cravings bear so deep an impress of pecuniary standards. All this and much more was set forth in Veblen's first volume, *The Theory of the Leisure Class*.

Secondly, money-making drills into us a certain type of rationality—the type that reaches its flower in modern accounting. The monetary unit provides us with a common denominator in terms of which the best drilled among us can express all values, not excepting the value of human lives. However vagrant our fancies, we are all forced by the environment of prices to be somewhat systematic in planning. We learn to reckon costs and income, to make change, to compare the advantages of different types of expenditure. It is the habit of mind begotten by the use of money which makes the pleasure-pain calculus plausible as an account of our own functioning. Thus the use of money lays the psychological basis for that philosophy of human behaviour which Bentham and Mill, Marshall and Clark, represent—a philosophy which, ignorant of its origins, treats money as a thing of slight moment except in facilitating trade and research. As pointed out above, economic theory written from the private and acquisitive viewpoint becomes a system of pecuniary logic that exaggerates the importance of one institutional factor in behaviour to the neglect of others.

Thirdly, money-making both promotes and obstructs the fundamental task of getting a living. Veblen pictures two sets of economic activities running side by side through the life of a modern community. One set is concerned with producing raw materials, working them up into serviceable goods, transporting and distributing the things men desire to use. The other set is the endless series of concatenated bargains by which men determine how much each individual can take to himself of what others have made. The material welfare of the community as a whole depends solely upon the quantity and quality of the goods brought to consumers by the first set of activities. Money-making conduces to material well-being just in so far as it enlarges the quantity or improves the quality of the serviceable goods obtained from a given expenditure of energy. From a common-sense viewpoint, therefore, money-making is a means to getting goods. But in practice, we reverse the relation. We make goods in order to make money. Veblen never wearies of expounding that central paradox and of developing its consequences.

He grants the commonplaces about the economic advantages of this scheme of organization. Adam Smith was right: industrial efficiency requires division of labour, division of labour requires exchange, and exchange requires money. No other scheme of organization which men have tried out in practice yields so large a per-capita flow of goods to consumers as the current scheme of making goods for profit. Business accounting is a marvellous device for controlling complicated undertakings. Industry requires capital and credit, and, as matters now stand, who can supply capital and credit but the capitalist and the banker? The business man is the central figure in modern economic life, the prime mover, what you will. There is no call to quarrel with encomiums of this sort which anyone is moved to pronounce upon the present order. But it is interesting to reflect upon certain features of the situation that are less obvious to business-trained eyes.

One is that the recurrent crises and depressions which ever and again reduce the flow of goods to consumers are due to business, not to industry. There is no technological reason why every few years we should have idle factories and unemployed men walking the streets, while thousands lack the goods employers and men would like to supply. The trouble is that business enterprises are run for profit, not to meet human needs. When times are good, prices rise, profits are high, business men borrow freely and enlarge their output. But such prosperity works its own undoing. The substantial security behind the loans is prospective net earnings capitalized at the current rate of interest. When the rate of interest rises, as it does during prosperity, the capitalized value of a given net income declines, and the loans become less safe. More than that, net earnings in many cases prove less than had been expected in the optimistic days of the nascent boom. Prices cannot be pushed up indefinitely; the costs of doing business rise and encroach upon profits; bank reserves fall and it becomes difficult to get additional credit. When fading profits are added to high interest, creditors become nervous. In such a strained situation, the embarrassment of a few conspicuous concerns will bring down the unstable structure which had seemed so imposing. A demand for liquidation starts and spreads rapidly, for the enterprises pressed for payment put pressure upon their debtors to pay up. So prosperity ends in a crisis, followed by depression. In short, business enterprises cannot prosper without committing business errors which bring on a crisis, and from these errors the whole community suffers.

More serious in the long run than these acute fits of indigestion is a chronic malady of the present order. Business men seek to fix their selling prices at the maximum net-revenue point. There is always danger that an over-supply of products will reduce prices more than the increased turnover will compensate for. This danger is peculiarly great because of the "inordinate" productivity of the modern machine process. Give the engineers their heads and the markets might be swamped by a flood of goods. Business men are constantly on their guard against this peril. It is their office to adjust supply to demand; that is, to prevent an unprofitable rate of output; that is, to keep industrial efficiency "sub-normal"; that is, to practise "capitalistic sabotage."

Indeed, by their very training, business men are incompetent to serve as captains of industry. Technology is becoming more and more an affair of applied science. We have elaborate schools for engineers in which mathematics, physics, chemistry, and electrical theory are the basic subjects of instruction. The graduates from these schools are the men who know how to make goods. If permitted to organize production on a continental scale, they might, with their present knowledge, double or triple the current output of industry. That they will not be suffered to do, so long as they are subject to the higher authority of business men, who do not understand technology and who distrust the vaulting plans of their own engineers. And this distrust is well founded, so long as business enterprise is organized in many units. To set engineering science free from business shackles would smash the independent enterprises of today, and lay out the process of making goods on much broader lines. In the early days of the Industrial Revolution, the business man was an industrial leader; in these later days the development of technology has turned him into an industrial incubus.

Yet the situation of business enterprise which seems so firmly entrenched is becoming precarious, because the habits of thinking engendered in men by modern life are undermining the habits of thinking on which business traffic rests. If business men do not speak the same language as engineers, or enter into their thoughts, neither do engineers speak the language or share the ideas of business men. The one group talks in terms of physical science, the other talks in terms of natural rights, particularly the right of ownership. It is increasingly difficult for the engineer to see why he should not be allowed to develop his plans for increasing output to the limit. He asks why the pecuniary interests of a handful of families should stand in the way of a doubled per-capita income for the community as a whole. Demonstrations that absentee owners have a perfect right to draw dividends from industry without contributing personal service leave him cold. What is more threatening than this doubting mood of the technologists is a growing disaffection among the masses of factory hands. Though not schooled in physical science, these people fall into a somewhat similar habit of thought. Their daily work with materials and machines teaches them to seek an explanation of all things in terms of cause and effect. They tend to become sceptical, matter-of-fact, materialistic, unmoral, unpatriotic, undevout, blind to the metaphysical niceties of natural rights. And nothing effective can be done to check the spread of these subversive habits of thought so long as the workers must be kept at their machines. So it appears that the time is coming when the present order of society, dominated by business enterprise in the interests of absentee ownership, will no longer seem right and good to the mass of mankind.

Veblen has no definite specifications for the new structure of institutions that will grow up in place of the present one, beyond an expectation that technically qualified engineers will have a larger share in managing industry. His evolutionary theory forbids him to anticipate a cataclysm, or to forecast a millennium. What will happen in the inscrutable future is what has been happening since the origin of man. As ways of working shift, they will engender new habits of thinking, which will crystal lize into new institutions, which will form the cultural

setting for further cumulative changes in ways of working, world without end.

## VI

If Veblen has descried aright the trend of cultural
change, his economic theories will commend themselves
to a wider circle in the next generation than in his own.
For on his showing, science, like all other cultural ex-
crescences, is a by-product of the kind of work folk do.
Circumstances made a certain Thorstein Veblen one of
the early recruits in the growing army of men who will
look at all social conventions with sceptical, matter-of-
fact eyes. Just before his time the German historical
school had perceived the relativity of orthodox economics; but they had not produced a scientific substitute for
the doctrine they belittled or discarded. Karl Marx had
been more constructive. In Veblen's view, Marx had
made a brave beginning in cultural analysis, though
handicapped by a superficial psychology derived from
Bentham and by a romantic metaphysics derived from
Hegel. Bentham's influence led Marx to develop a commonplace theory of class interests that overlooked the
way in which certain habits of thought are drilled into
business men by their pecuniary occupations and quite
different habits of thought are drilled into wage earners
by the machine process in which they are caught. Hegel's
influence made the Marxian theory of social evolution
essentially an intellectual sequence that tends to a goal,

"the classless economic structure of the socialistic final
term," whereas the Darwinian scheme of thought en-
visages a "blindly cumulative causation, in which there
is no trend, no final term, no consummation." Hence
Marx strayed from the narrow trail of scientific analysis
appropriate to a mechanistic age and attained an optimistic vision of the future which fulfilled his wish for
a socialist revolution.[17] The Darwinian viewpoint, which
supplies the needed working programme, will spread
among social scientists, not because it is less metaphysical
than its predecessors or nearer the truth (whatever that
may mean), but because it harmonizes better with the
thoughts begotten by daily work in the twentieth century. That the majority of economists still cling to their
traditional analysis is to Veblen merely the latest illustration of the cultural lag in social theory—a lag readily
accounted for by the institutional approach.

Yet Veblen remains an inveterate doubter even of his
own work. The Darwinian viewpoint is due to be superseded in men's minds; the instinct-habit psychology will

---

[17] See Veblen's two papers on "The Socialist Economics of Karl
Marx and his Followers," originally published in *The Quarterly
Journal of Economics*, August, 1906 and February, 1907; reprinted
in *The Place of Science in Modern Civilisation and Other Essays*,
1919, pp. 409–56. The phrases quoted are from pp. 417, 436.
  After dilating upon the "disparity between Marxism and Dar-
winism," Veblen points out that "the socialists of today" have shifted
from "the Marxism of Marx" to "the materialism of Darwin,"
though "of course" without admitting that "any substantial change
or departure from the original position has taken place." See pp.
417, 432, 433.

yield to some other conception of human nature. The body of factual knowledge will continue its cumulative growth, and idle curiosity will find new ways of organizing the data. His own view of the world is date-marked "A.D. 1880–1930," as definitely as Jewish culture is date-marked "B.C."

A heretic needs a high heart, though sustained by faith that he is everlastingly right and sure of his reward hereafter. The heretic who views his own ideas as but to-morrow's fashion in thought needs still firmer courage. Such courage Veblen had. All his uneasy life, he faced outer hostility and inner doubt with a quizzical smile. Uncertain what the future has in store, he did the day's work as best he might, getting a philosopher's pleasures from playing with ideas and exercising "his swift wit and his slow irony" upon his fellows. However matters went with him, and often they went ill, he made no intellectual compromises. In his retreat among the lovely coast hills of California, he died on August 3, 1929, a "placid unbeliever" to the end.

# DATED LIST OF VEBLEN'S BOOKS

✿

The Theory of the Leisure Class, 1899

The Theory of Business Enterprise, 1904

The Instinct of Workmanship and the State of the Industrial Arts, 1914

Imperial Germany and the Industrial Revolution, 1915

An Inquiry into the Nature of Peace and the Terms of Its Perpetuation, 1917

The Higher Learning in America. A Memorandum on the Conduct of Universities by Business Men, 1918

The Vested Interests and the Common Man, 1919

The Place of Science in Modern Civilisation and Other Essays, 1919

The Engineers and the Price System, 1921

Absentee Ownership and Business Enterprise in Recent Times: The Case of America, 1923

The Laxdæla Saga. *Translated from the Icelandic, with an Introduction,* 1925

Essays in Our Changing Order, 1934 (*A posthumous collection of papers from periodicals.*)

## See also

Thorstein Veblen and His America, by Joseph Dorfman, 1934

# WHAT
# VEBLEN
## TAUGHT

# THE PLACE OF SCIENCE IN
# MODERN CIVILIZATION[1]

✿

I T is commonly held that modern Christendom is superior to any and all other systems of civilized life. Other ages and other cultural regions are by contrast spoken of as lower, or more archaic, or less mature. The claim is that the modern culture is superior on the whole, not that it is the best or highest in all respects and at every point. It has, in fact, not an all-around superiority, but a superiority within a closely limited range of intellectual activities, while outside this range many other civilizations surpass that of the modern occidental peoples. But the peculiar excellence of the modern culture is of such a nature as to give it a decisive practical advantage over all other cultural schemes that have gone before or that have come into competition with it. It has proved itself fit to survive in a struggle for existence as against those civilizations which differ from it in respect of its distinctive traits.

Modern civilization is peculiarly matter-of-fact. It contains many elements that are not of this character, but these other elements do not belong exclusively or characteristically to it. The modern civilized peoples are in a peculiar degree capable of an impersonal, dispassionate

---

[1] Reprinted from *The Place of Science in Modern Civilisation and Other Essays*, 1919, pp. 1–31; originally published in *The American Journal of Sociology*, vol. XI, March 1906.

3

insight into the material facts with which mankind has to deal. The apex of cultural growth is at this point. Compared with this trait the rest of what is comprised in the cultural scheme is adventitious, or at the best it is a by-product of this hard-headed apprehension of facts. This quality may be a matter of habit or of racial endowment, or it may be an outcome of both; but whatever be the explanation of its prevalence, the immediate consequence is much the same for the growth of civilization. A civilization which is dominated by this matter-of-fact insight must prevail against any cultural scheme that lacks this element. This characteristic of western civilization comes to a head in modern science, and it finds its highest material expression in the technology of the machine industry. In these things modern culture is creative and self-sufficient; and these being given, the rest of what may seem characteristic in western civilization follows by easy consequence. The cultural structure clusters about this body of matter-of-fact knowledge as its substantial core. Whatever is not consonant with these opaque creations of science is an intrusive feature in the modern scheme, borrowed or standing over from the barbarian past.

Other ages and other peoples excel in other things and are known by other virtues. In creative art, as well as in critical taste, the faltering talent of Christendom can at the best follow the lead of the ancient Greeks and the Chinese. In deft workmanship the handicraftsmen of the middle Orient, as well as of the Far East, stand on a level securely above the highest European achievement, old or new. In myth-making, folklore, and occult symbolism many of the lower barbarians have achieved things beyond what the latter-day priests and poets know how to propose. In metaphysical insight and dialectical versatility many orientals, as well as the Schoolmen of the Middle Ages, easily surpass the highest reaches of the New Thought and the Higher Criticism. In a shrewd sense of the religious verities, as well as in an unsparing faith in devout observances, the people of India or Tibet, or even the medieval Christians, are past-masters in comparison even with the select of the faith of modern times. In political finesse, as well as in unreasoning, brute loyalty, more than one of the ancient peoples give evidence of a capacity to which no modern civilized nation may aspire. In warlike malevolence and abandon the hosts of Islam, the Sioux Indian, and the "heathen of the northern sea" have set the mark above the reach of the most strenuous civilized warlord.

To modern civilized men, especially in their intervals of sober reflection, all these things that distinguish the barbarian civilizations seem of dubious value and are required to show cause why they should not be slighted. It is not so with the knowledge of facts. The making of states and dynasties, the founding of families, the prosecution of feuds, the propagation of creeds and the creation of sects, the accumulation of fortunes, the consumption of superfluities—these have all in their time been felt to justify themselves as an end of endeavour; but in the eyes of modern civilized men all these things seem futile in comparison with the achievements of science. They dwindle in men's esteem as time passes, while the achievements of science are held higher as time passes. This is the one secure holding-ground of latter-day conviction, that "the increase and diffusion of knowledge among men" is indefeasibly right and good. When seen in such perspective as will clear it of the trivial perplexities of workday life, this proposition is not questioned within the horizon of the western culture, and no other cultural ideal holds a similar unquestioned place in the convictions of civilized mankind.

On any large question which is to be disposed of for good and all the final appeal is by common consent taken to the scientist. The solution offered in the name of science is decisive so long as it is not set aside by a still more searching scientific inquiry. This state of things may not be altogether fortunate, but such is the fact. There are other, older grounds of finality that may conceivably be better, nobler, worthier, more profound, more beautiful. It might conceivably be preferable, as a matter of cultural ideals, to leave the last word with the lawyer, the duelist, the priest, the moralist, or the college of heraldry. In past times people have been content to leave their weightiest questions to the decision of some one or other of these tribunals, and, it cannot be denied, with very happy results in those respects that were then looked to with the greatest solicitude. But whatever the common-sense of earlier generations may have held in this respect, modern common-sense holds that the scientist's answer is the

only ultimately true one. In the last resort enlightened
common-sense sticks by the opaque truth and refuses to
go behind the returns given by the tangible facts.

*Quasi lignum vitae in paradiso Dei, et quasi lucerna
fulgoris in domo Domini,* such is the place of science in
modern civilization. This latter-day faith in matter-of-
fact knowledge may be well grounded or it may not. It
has come about that men assign it this high place, perhaps
idolatrously, perhaps to the detriment of the best and
most intimate interests of the race. There is room for
much more than a vague doubt that this cult of science
is not altogether a wholesome growth—that the unmitigated quest of knowledge, of this matter-of-fact kind,
makes for race-deterioration and discomfort on the whole,
both in its immediate effects upon the spiritual life of
mankind, and in the material consequences that follow
from a great advance in matter-of-fact knowledge.

But we are not here concerned with the merits of the
case. The question here is: How has this cult of science
arisen? What are its cultural antecedents? How far is it
in consonance with hereditary human nature? and, What
is the nature of its hold on the convictions of civilized
men?

In dealing with pedagogical problems and the theory
of education, current psychology is nearly at one in saying that all learning is of a "pragmatic" character; that
knowledge is inchoate action inchoately directed to an
end; that all knowledge is "functional"; that it is of the

nature of use. This, of course, is only a corollary under
the main postulate of the latter-day psychologists, whose
catchword is that the Idea is essentially active. There is
no need of quarrelling with this "pragmatic" school of
psychologists. Their aphorism may not contain the whole
truth, perhaps, but at least it goes nearer to the heart of
the epistemological problem than any earlier formulation.
It may confidently be said to do so because, for one thing,
its argument meets the requirements of modern science.
It is such a concept as matter-of-fact science can make
effective use of; it is drawn in terms which are, in the
last analysis, of an impersonal, not to say tropismatic,
character; such as is demanded by science, with its insistence on opaque cause and effect. While knowledge is
construed in teleological terms, in terms of personal interest and attention, this teleological aptitude is itself reducible to a product of unteleological natural selection.
The teleological bent of intelligence is an hereditary trait
settled upon the race by the selective action of forces that
look to no end. The foundations of pragmatic intelligence
are not pragmatic, nor even personal or sensible.

This impersonal character of intelligence is, of course,
most evident on the lower levels of life. If we follow
Mr. Loeb, e.g., in his inquiries into the psychology of
that life that lies below the threshold of intelligence, what
we meet with is an aimless but unwavering motor response
to stimulus.[2] The response is of the nature of motor im-

---

[2] Jacques Loeb, *Heliotropismus der Thiere,* and *Comparative Psychology and Physiology of the Brain.*

pulse, and in so far it is "pragmatic," if that term may fairly be applied to so rudimentary a phase of sensibility. The responding organism may be called an "agent" in so far. It is only by a figure of speech that these terms are made to apply to tropismatic reactions. Higher in the scale of sensibility and nervous complication instincts work to a somewhat similar outcome. On the human plane, intelligence (the selective effect of inhibitive complication) may throw the response into the form of a reasoned line of conduct looking to an outcome that shall be expedient for the agent. This is naïve pragmatism of the developed kind. There is no longer a question but that the responding organism is an "agent" and that his intelligent response to stimulus is of a teleological character. But that is not all. The inhibitive nervous complication may also detach another chain of response to the given stimulus, which does not spend itself in a line of motor conduct and does not fall into a system of uses. Pragmatically speaking, this outlying chain of response is unintended and irrelevant. Except in urgent cases, such an idle response seems commonly to be present as a subsidiary phenomenon. If credence is given to the view that intelligence is, in its elements, of the nature of an inhibitive selection, its seems necessary to assume some such chain of idle and irrelevant response to account for the further course of the elements eliminated in giving the motor response the character of a reasoned line of conduct. So that associated with the pragmatic attention there is found more or less of an irrelevant attention, or idle curiosity. This is more particularly the case where a higher range of intelligence is present. This idle curiosity is, perhaps, closely related to the aptitude for play observed both in man and in the lower animals.[3] The aptitude for play, as well as the functioning of idle curiosity, seems peculiarly lively in the young, whose aptitude for sustained pragmatism is at the same time relatively vague and unreliable.

This idle curiosity formulates its response to stimulus, not in terms of an expedient line of conduct, nor even necessarily in a chain of motor activity, but in terms of the sequence of activities going on in the observed phenomena. The "interpretation" of the facts under the guidance of this idle curiosity may take the form of anthropomorphic or animistic explanations of the "conduct" of the objects observed. The interpretation of the facts takes a dramatic form. The facts are conceived in an animistic way, and a pragmatic animus is imputed to them. Their behaviour is construed as a reasoned procedure on their part looking to the advantage of these animistically conceived objects, or looking to the achievement of some end which these objects are conceived to have at heart for reasons of their own.

Among the savage and lower barbarian peoples there is commonly current a large body of knowledge organized

[3] Cf. Gross, *Spiele der Thiere*, chap. 2 (esp. pp. 65–76) and chap. 5; *The Play of Man*, part III, sec. 3; Spencer, *Principles of Psychology*, secs. 533–5.

in this way into myths and legends, which need have no pragmatic value for the learner of them and no intended bearing on his conduct of practical affairs. They may come to have a practical value imputed to them as a ground of superstitious observances, but they may also not.[4] All students of the lower cultures are aware of the dramatic character of the myths current among these peoples, and they are also aware that, particularly among the peaceable communities, the great body of mythical lore is of an idle kind, as having very little intended bearing on the practical conduct of those who believe in these myth-dramas. The myths on the one hand, and the workday knowledge of uses, materials, appliances, and expedients on the other hand, may be nearly independent of one another. Such is the case in an especial degree among those peoples who are prevailingly of a peaceable habit of life, among whom the myths have not in any great measure been canonized into precedents of divine malevolence.

The lower barbarian's knowledge of the phenomena of nature, in so far as they are made the subject of deliberate speculation and are organized into a consistent body, is of the nature of life-histories. This body of knowledge is in the main organized under the guidance of an

---

[4] The myths and legendary lore of the Eskimo, the Pueblo Indians, and some tribes of the northwest coast afford good instances of such idle creations. Cf. various *Reports* of the Bureau of American Ethnology; also, e.g., Tylor, *Primitive Culture*, esp. the chapters on "Mythology" and "Animism."

idle curiosity. In so far as it is systematized under the canons of curiosity rather than of expediency, the test of truth applied throughout this body of barbarian knowledge is the test of dramatic consistency. In addition to their dramatic cosmology and folk legends, it is needless to say, these peoples have also a considerable body of worldly wisdom in a more or less systematic form. In this the test of validity is usefulness.[5]

The pragmatic knowledge of the early days differs scarcely at all in character from that of the maturest phases of culture. Its highest achievements in the direction of systematic formulation consist of didactic exhortations to thrift, prudence, equanimity, and shrewd management—a body of maxims of expedient conduct. In this field there is scarcely a degree of advance from Confucius to Samuel Smiles. Under the guidance of the idle curiosity, on the other hand, there has been a continued advance toward a more and more comprehensive system of knowledge. With the advance in intelligence and experience there come closer observation and more

---

[5] "Pragmatic" is here used in a more restricted sense than the distinctively pragmatic school of modern psychologists would commonly assign the term. "Pragmatic," "teleological," and the like terms have been extended to cover imputation of purpose as well as conversion to use. It is not intended to criticize this ambiguous use of terms, nor to correct it; but the terms are here used only in the latter sense, which alone belongs to them by force of early usage and etymology. "Pragmatic" knowledge, therefore, is such as is designed to serve an expedient end for the knower, and is here contrasted with the imputation of expedient conduct to the facts observed. The reason for preserving this distinction is simply the present need of a simple term by which to mark the distinction between worldly wisdom and idle learning.

detailed analysis of facts.[6] The dramatization of the sequence of phenomena may then fall into somewhat less personal, less anthropomorphic formulations of the processes observed; but at no stage of its growth—at least at no stage hitherto reached—does the output of this work of the idle curiosity lose its dramatic character. Comprehensive generalizations are made and cosmologies are built up, but always in dramatic form. General principles of explanation are settled on, which in the earlier days of theoretical speculation seem invariably to run back to the broad vital principle of generation. Procreation, birth, growth, and decay constitute the cycle of postulates within which the dramatized processes of natural phenomena run their course. Creation is procreation in these archaic theoretical systems, and causation is gestation and birth. The archaic cosmological schemes of Greece, India, Japan, China, Polynesia, and America all run to the same general effect on this head.[7] The like seems true for the Elohistic elements in the Hebrew scriptures.

Throughout this biological speculation there is present, obscurely in the background, the tacit recognition of a material causation, such as conditions the vulgar operations of workday life from hour to hour. But this causal relation between vulgar work and product is vaguely taken for granted and not made a principle for comprehensive generalizations. It is overlooked as a trivial

[6] Cf. Ward, *Pure Sociology*, esp. pp. 437–48.
[7] Cf., e.g., Tylor, *Primitive Culture*, chap. 8.

matter of course. The higher generalizations take their colour from the broader features of the current scheme of life. The habits of thought that rule in the working-out of a system of knowledge are such as are fostered by the more impressive affairs of life, by the institutional structure under which the community lives. So long as the ruling institutions are those of blood-relationship, descent, and clannish discrimination, so long the canons of knowledge are of the same complexion.

When presently a transformation is made in the scheme of culture from peaceable life with sporadic predation to a settled scheme of predaceous life, involving mastery and servitude, gradations of privilege and honour, co-ercion and personal dependence, then the scheme of knowledge undergoes an analogous change. The pre-daceous, or higher barbarian, culture is, for the present purpose, peculiar in that it is ruled by an accentuated pragmatism. The institutions of this cultural phase are conventionalized relations of force and fraud. The questions of life are questions of expedient conduct as carried on under the current relations of mastery and subservi-ence. The habitual distinctions are distinctions of personal force, advantage, precedence, and authority. A shrewd adaptation to this system of graded dignity and servitude becomes a matter of life and death, and men learn to think in these terms as ultimate and definitive. The system of knowledge, even in so far as its motives are of a dis-passionate or idle kind, falls into the like terms, because

such are the habits of thought and the standards of discrimination enforced by daily life.[8]

The theoretical work of such a cultural era as, for instance, the Middle Ages still takes the general shape of dramatization, but the postulates of the dramaturgic theories and the tests of theoretic validity are no longer the same as before the scheme of graded servitude came to occupy the field. The canons which guide the work of the idle curiosity are no longer those of generation, blood-relationship, and homely life, but rather those of graded dignity, authenticity, and dependence. The higher generalizations take on a new complexion, it may be without formally discarding the older articles of belief. The cosmologies of these higher barbarians are cast in terms of a feudalistic hierarchy of agents and elements, and the causal nexus between phenomena is conceived animistically after the manner of sympathetic magic. The laws that are sought to be discovered in the natural universe are sought in terms of authoritative enactment. The relation in which the deity, or deities, are conceived to stand to facts is no longer the relation of progenitor, so much as that of suzerainty. Natural laws are corollaries under the arbitrary rules of status imposed on the natural universe by an all-powerful Providence with a view to the maintenance of his own prestige. The science that grows in such a spiritual environment is of the class

---

[8] Cf. James, *Psychology*, chap. 9, esp. sec. 5.

represented by alchemy and astrology, in which the imputed degree of nobility and prepotency of the objects and the symbolic force of their names are looked to for an explanation of what takes place.

The theoretical output of the Schoolmen has necessarily an accentuated pragmatic complexion, since the whole cultural scheme under which they lived and worked was of a strenuously pragmatic character. The current concepts of things were then drawn in terms of expediency, personal force, exploit, prescriptive authority, and the like, and this range of concepts was by force of habit employed in the correlation of facts for purposes of knowledge even where no immediate practical use of the knowledge so gained was had in view. At the same time a very large proportion of the scholastic researches and speculations aimed directly at rules of expedient conduct, whether it took the form of a philosophy of life under temporal law and custom, or of a scheme of salvation under the decrees of an autocratic Providence. A naïve apprehension of the dictum that all knowledge is pragmatic would find more satisfactory corroboration in the intellectual output of scholasticism than in any system of knowledge of an older or a later date.

With the advent of modern times a change comes over the nature of the inquiries and formulations worked out under the guidance of the idle curiosity—which from this epoch is often spoken of as the scientific spirit. The change in question is closely correlated with an analogous change in institutions and habits of life, particularly with

the changes which the modern era brings in industry and
in the economic organization of society. It is doubtful
whether the characteristic intellectual interests and teachings of the new era can properly be spoken of as less
"pragmatic," as that term is sometimes understood, than
those of the scholastic times; but they are of another
kind, being conditioned by a different cultural and industrial situation.[9] In the life of the new era conceptions
of authentic rank and differential dignity have grown
weaker in practical affairs, and notions of preferential
reality and authentic tradition similarly count for less in
the new science. The forces at work in the external world
are conceived in a less animistic manner, although anthropomorphism still prevails, at least to the degree required in order to give a dramatic interpretation of the
sequence of phenomena.

The changes in the cultural situation which seem to
have had the most serious consequences for the methods
and animus of scientific inquiry are those changes that
took place in the field of industry. Industry in early
modern times is a fact of relatively greater preponderance, more of a tone-giving factor, than it was under the
regime of feudal status. It is the characteristic trait of

[9] As currently employed, the term "pragmatic" is made to cover
both conduct looking to the agent's preferential advantage, expedient
conduct, and workmanship directed to the production of things that
may or may not be of advantage to the agent. If the term be taken in
the latter meaning, the culture of modern times is no less "pragmatic"
than that of the Middle Ages. It is here intended to be used in the
former sense.

the modern culture, very much as exploit and fealty were
the characteristic cultural traits of the earlier time. This
early-modern industry is, in an obvious and convincing
degree, a matter of workmanship. The same has not been
true in the same degree either before or since. The workman, more or less skilled and with more or less specialized
efficiency, was the central figure in the cultural situation
of the time; and so the concepts of the scientists came to
be drawn in the image of the workman. The dramatiza-
tions of the sequence of external phenomena worked out
under the impulse of the idle curiosity were then conceived in terms of workmanship. Workmanship gradually
supplanted differential dignity as the authoritative canon
of scientific truth, even on the higher levels of speculation and research. This, of course, amounts to saying in
other words that the law of cause and effect was given the
first place, as contrasted with dialectical consistency and
authentic tradition. But this early-modern law of cause
and effect—the law of efficient causes—is of an anthropomorphic kind. "Like causes produce like effects," in much
the same sense as the skilled workman's product is like
the workman; "nothing is found in the effect that was not
contained in the cause," in much the same manner.

These dicta are, of course, older than modern science,
but it is only in the early days of modern science that they
come to rule the field with an unquestioned sway and
to push the higher grounds of dialectical validity to one
side. They invade even the highest and most recondite
fields of speculation, so that at the approach to the transi-

tion from the early-modern to the late-modern period, in the eighteenth century, they determine the outcome even in the counsels of the theologians. The deity, from having been in medieval times primarily a suzerain concerned with the maintenance of his own prestige, becomes primarily a creator engaged in the workmanlike occupation of making things useful for man. His relation to man and the natural universe is no longer primarily that of a progenitor, as it is in the lower barbarian culture, but rather that of a talented mechanic. The "natural laws" which the scientists of that era make so much of are no longer decrees of a preternatural legislative authority, but rather details of the workshop specifications handed down by the master-craftsman for the guidance of handicraftsmen working out his designs. In the eighteenth-century science these natural laws are laws specifying the sequence of cause and effect, and will bear characterization as a dramatic interpretation of the activity of the causes at work, and these causes are conceived in a quasi-personal manner. In later modern times the formulations of causal sequence grow more impersonal and more objective, more matter-of-fact; but the imputation of activity to the observed objects never ceases, and even in the latest and maturest formulations of scientific research the dramatic tone is not wholly lost. The causes at work are conceived in a highly impersonal way, but hitherto no science (except ostensibly mathematics) has been content to do its theoretical work in terms of inert magnitude alone. Activity continues to be imputed to the phenomena with which science deals; and activity is, of course, not a fact of observation, but is imputed to the phenomena by the observer.[10] This is, also of course, denied by those who insist on a purely mathematical formulation of scientific theories, but the denial is maintained only at the cost of consistency. Those eminent authorities who speak for a colourless mathematical formulation invariably and necessarily fall back on the (essentially metaphysical) preconception of causation as soon as they go into the actual work of scientific inquiry.[11]

Since the machine technology has made great advances, during the nineteenth century, and has become a cultural force of wide-reaching consequence, the formulations of science have made another move in the direction of impersonal matter-of-fact. The machine process has displaced the workman as the archetype in whose image causation is conceived by the scientific investigators. The dramatic interpretation of natural phenomena has thereby become less anthropomorphic; it no longer constructs the life-history of a cause working to produce a given effect—after the manner of a skilled workman producing a piece of wrought goods—but it con-

---

[10] Epistemologically speaking, activity is imputed to phenomena for the purpose of organizing them into a dramatically consistent system.

[11] Cf., e.g., Karl Pearson, *Grammar of Science*, and compare his ideal of inert magnitudes as set forth in his exposition with his actual work as shown in chaps. 9, 10, and 12, and more particularly in his discussions of "Mother Right" and related topics in *The Chances of Death*.

structs the life-history of a process in which the distinction between cause and effect need scarcely be observed in an itemized and specific way, but in which the run of causation unfolds itself in an unbroken sequence of cumulative change. By contrast with the pragmatic formulations of worldly wisdom these latter-day theories of the scientists appear highly opaque, impersonal, and matter-of-fact; but taken by themselves they must be admitted still to show the constraint of the dramatic pre-possessions that once guided the savage myth-makers.

In so far as touches the aims and the animus of scientific inquiry, as seen from the point of view of the scientist, it is a wholly fortuitous and insubstantial coincidence that much of the knowledge gained under machine-made canons of research can be turned to practical account. Much of this knowledge is useful, or may be made so, by applying it to the control of the processes in which natural forces are engaged. This employment of scientific knowledge for useful ends is technology, in the broad sense in which the term includes, besides the machine industry proper, such branches of practice as engineering, agriculture, medicine, sanitation, and economic reforms. The reason why scientific theories can be turned to account for these practical ends is not that these ends are included in the scope of scientific inquiry. These useful purposes lie outside the scientist's interest. It is not that he aims, or can aim, at technological improvements. His inquiry is as "idle" as that of the Pueblo myth-maker. But the canons of validity under whose guidance he works are those imposed by the modern technology, through habituation to its requirements; and therefore his results are available for the technological purpose. His canons of validity are made for him by the cultural situation; they are habits of thought imposed on him by the scheme of life current in the community in which he lives; and under modern conditions this scheme of life is largely machine-made. In the modern culture, industry, industrial processes, and industrial products have progressively gained upon humanity, until these creations of man's ingenuity have latterly come to take the dominant place in the cultural scheme; and it is not too much to say that they have become the chief force in shaping men's daily life, and therefore the chief factor in shaping men's habits of thought. Hence men have learned to think in the terms in which the technological processes act. This is particularly true of those men who by virtue of a peculiarly strong susceptibility in this direction become addicted to that habit of matter-of-fact inquiry that constitutes scientific research.

Modern technology makes use of the same range of concepts, thinks in the same terms, and applies the same tests of validity as modern science. In both, the terms of standardization, validity, and finality are always terms of impersonal sequence, not terms of human nature or of preternatural agencies. Hence the easy copartnership between the two. Science and technology play into one another's hands. The processes of nature with which science deals and which technology turns to account, the sequence of changes in the external world, animate and inanimate, run in terms of brute causation, as do the theories of science. These processes take no thought of human expediency or inexpediency. To make use of them they must be taken as they are, opaque and unsympathetic. Technology, therefore, has come to proceed on an interpretation of these phenomena in mechanical terms, not in terms of imputed personality nor even of workmanship. Modern science, deriving its concepts from the same source, carries on its inquiries and states its conclusions in terms of the same objective character as those employed by the mechanical engineer.

So it has come about, through the progressive change of the ruling habits of thought in the community, that the theories of science have progressively diverged from the formulations of pragmatism, ever since the modern era set in. From an organization of knowledge on the basis of imputed personal or animistic propensity the theory has changed its base to an imputation of brute activity only, and this latter is conceived in an increasingly matter-of-fact manner; until, latterly, the pragmatic range of knowledge and the scientific are more widely out of touch than ever, differing not only in aim, but in matter as well. In both domains knowledge runs in terms of activity, but it is on the one hand knowledge of what had best be done, and on the other hand knowledge of what takes place; on the one hand knowledge of ways and means, on the other hand knowledge without any ulterior purpose. The latter range of knowledge may serve the ends of the former, but the converse does not hold true.

These two divergent ranges of inquiry are to be found together in all phases of human culture. What distinguishes the present phase is that the discrepancy between the two is now wider than ever before. The present is nowise distinguished above other cultural eras by any exceptional urgency or acumen in the search for pragmatic expedients. Neither is it safe to assert that the present excels all other civilizations in the volume or the workmanship of that body of knowledge that is to be credited to the idle curiosity. What distinguishes the present in these premises is (1) that the primacy in the cultural scheme has passed from pragmatism to a disinterested inquiry whose motive is idle curiosity, and (2) that in the domain of the latter the making of myths and legends in terms of imputed personality, as well as the construction of dialectical systems in terms of differential reality, has yielded the first place to the making of theories in terms of matter-of-fact sequence.[12]

Pragmatism creates nothing but maxims of expedient conduct. Science creates nothing but theories.[13] It knows nothing of policy or utility, of better or worse. None of all that is comprised in what is today accounted scientific knowledge. Wisdom and proficiency of the pragmatic sort does not contribute to the advance of a knowledge

---

[12] Cf. James, *Psychology*, vol. II, chap. 28, pp. 633–71, esp. p. 640 note.

[13] Cf. Ward, *Principles of Psychology*, pp. 439–43.

of fact. It has only an incidental bearing on scientific research, and its bearing is chiefly that of inhibition and mis-
direction. Wherever canons of expediency are intruded
into or are attempted to be incorporated in the inquiry,
the consequence is an unhappy one for science, however
happy it may be for some other purpose extraneous to
science. The mental attitude of worldly wisdom is at
cross-purposes with the disinterested scientific spirit, and
the pursuit of it induces an intellectual bias that is incompatible with scientific insight. Its intellectual output
is a body of shrewd rules of conduct, in great part designed to take advantage of human infirmity. Its habitual
terms of standardization and validity are terms of human
nature, of human preference, prejudice, aspiration, endeavour, and disability, and the habit of mind that goes
with it is such as is consonant with these terms. No doubt,
the all-pervading pragmatic animus of the older and non-
European civilizations has had more than anything else
to do with their relatively slight and slow advance in
scientific knowledge. In the modern scheme of knowledge it holds true, in a similar manner and with analogous
effect, that training in divinity, in law, and in the related
branches of diplomacy, business tactics, military affairs,
and political theory is alien to the sceptical scientific spirit
and subversive of it.

The modern scheme of culture comprises a large body
of worldly wisdom, as well as of science. This pragmatic
lore stands over against science with something of a jealous reserve. The pragmatists value themselves somewhat

on being useful as well as being efficient for good and evil. They feel the inherent antagonism between themselves and the scientists, and look with some doubt on the latter as being merely decorative triflers, although they sometimes borrow the prestige of the name of science—as is only good and well, since it is of the essence of worldly wisdom to borrow anything that can be turned to account. The reasoning in these fields turns about questions of personal advantage of one kind or another, and the merits of the claims canvassed in these discussions are decided on grounds of authenticity. Personal claims make up the subject of the inquiry, and these claims are construed and decided in terms of precedent and choice, use and wont, prescriptive authority, and the like. The higher reaches of generalization in these pragmatic inquiries are of the nature of deductions from authentic tradition, and the training in this class of reasoning gives discrimination in respect of authenticity and expediency. The resulting habit of mind is a bias for substituting dialectical distinctions and decisions *de jure* in the place of explanations *de facto*. The so-called "sciences" associated with these pragmatic disciplines, such as jurisprudence, political science, and the like, are a taxonomy of credenda. Of this character was the greater part of the "science" cultivated by the Schoolmen, and large remnants of the same kind of authentic convictions are, of course, still found among the tenets of the scientists, particularly in the social sciences, and no small solicitude is still given to their cultivation. Substantially

the same value as that of the temporal pragmatic inquiries belongs also, of course, to the "science" of divinity.
Here the questions to which an answer is sought, as well
as the aim and method of inquiry, are of the same pragmatic character, although the argument runs on a higher
plane of personality, and seeks a solution in terms of a
remoter and more metaphysical expediency.

In the light of what has been said above, the questions
recur: How far is the scientific quest of matter-of-fact
knowledge consonant with the inherited intellectual aptitudes and propensities of the normal man? and, What
foothold has science in the modern culture? The former
is a question of the temperamental heritage of civilized
mankind, and therefore it is in large part a question of
the circumstances which have in the past selectively
shaped the human nature of civilized mankind. Under
the barbarian culture, as well as on the lower levels of
what is currently called civilized life, the dominant note
has been that of competitive expediency for the individual
or the group, great or small, in an avowed struggle for
the means of life. Such is still the ideal of the politician
and business man, as well as of other classes whose habits
of life lead them to cling to the inherited barbarian traditions. The upper-barbarian and lower-civilized culture,
as has already been indicated, is pragmatic, with a thoroughness that nearly bars out any non-pragmatic ideal of
life or of knowledge. Where this tradition is strong, there
is but a precarious chance for any consistent effort to

formulate knowledge in other terms than those drawn from the prevalent relations of personal mastery and subservience and the ideals of personal gain.

During the Dark and Middle Ages, for instance, it is true in the main that any movement of thought not controlled by considerations of expediency and conventions of status is to be found only in the obscure depths of vulgar life, among those neglected elements of the population that lived below the reach of the active class struggle. What there is surviving of this vulgar, non-pragmatic intellectual output takes the form of legends and folk-tales, often embroidered on the authentic documents of the Faith. These are less alien to the latest and highest culture of Christendom than are the dogmatic, dialectical, and chivalric productions that occupied the attention of the upper classes in medieval times. It may seem a curious paradox that the latest and most perfect flower of the western civilization is more nearly akin to the spiritual life of the serfs and villeins than it is to that of the grange or the abbey. The courtly life and the chivalric habits of thought of that past phase of culture have left as nearly no trace in the cultural scheme of later modern times as could well be. Even the romancers who ostensibly rehearse the phenomena of chivalry unavoidably make their knights and ladies speak the language and the sentiments of the slums of that time, tempered with certain schematized modern reflections and speculations. The gallantries, the genteel inanities and devout imbecilities, of medieval high-life would be insufferable even to the meanest and most romantic modern intelligence. So that in a later, less barbarian age the precarious remnants of folklore that have come down through that vulgar channel—half savage and more than half pagan—are treasured as containing the largest spiritual gains which the barbarian ages of Europe have to offer.

The sway of barbarian pragmatism has, everywhere in the western world, been relatively brief and relatively light; the only exceptions would be found in certain parts of the Mediterranean seaboard. But wherever the barbarian culture has been sufficiently long-lived and unmitigated to work out a thoroughly selective effect in the human material subjected to it, there the pragmatic animus may be expected to have become supreme and to inhibit all movement in the direction of scientific inquiry and eliminate all effective aptitude for other than worldly wisdom. What the selective consequences of such a protracted regime of pragmatism would be for the temper of the race may be seen in the human flotsam left by the great civilizations of antiquity, such as Egypt, India, and Persia. Science is not at home among these leavings of barbarism. In these instances of its long and unmitigated dominion the barbarian culture has selectively worked out a temperamental bias and a scheme of life from which objective, matter-of-fact knowledge is virtually excluded in favour of pragmatism, secular and religious. But for the greater part of the race, at least for the greater part of civilized mankind, the regime of the mature barbarian culture has been of relatively short duration, and has had a correspondingly superficial and transient selective effect. It has not had force and time to eliminate certain elements of human nature handed down from an earlier phase of life, which are not in full consonance with the barbarian animus or with the demands of the pragmatic scheme of thought. The barbarian-pragmatic habit of mind, therefore, is not properly speaking a temperamental trait of the civilized peoples, except possibly within certain class limits (as, e.g., the German nobility). It is rather a tradition, and it does not constitute so tenacious a bias as to make head against the strongly materialistic drift of modern conditions and set aside that increasingly urgent resort to matter-of-fact conceptions that makes for the primacy of science. Civilized mankind does not in any great measure take back atavistically to the upper-barbarian habit of mind. Barbarism covers too small a segment of the life-history of the race to have given an enduring temperamental result. The unmitigated discipline of the higher barbarism in Europe fell on a relatively small proportion of the population, and in the course of time this select element of the population was crossed and blended with the blood of the lower elements whose life always continued to run in the ruts of savagery rather than in those of the high-strung, finished barbarian culture that gave rise to the chivalric scheme of life.

Of the several phases of human culture the most protracted, and the one which has counted for most in shaping the abiding traits of the race, is unquestionably that of savagery. With savagery, for the purpose in hand, is to be classed that lower, relatively peaceable barbarism that is not characterized by wide and sharp class discrepancies or by an unremitting endeavour of one individual or group to get the better of another. Even under the full-grown barbarian culture—as, for instance, during the Middle Ages—the habits of life and the spiritual interests of the great body of the population continue in large measure to bear the character of savagery. The savage phase of culture accounts for by far the greater portion of the life-history of mankind, particularly if the lower barbarism and the vulgar life of later barbarism be counted in with savagery, as in a measure they properly should. This is particularly true of those racial elements that have entered into the composition of the leading peoples of Christendom.

The savage culture is characterized by the relative absence of pragmatism from the higher generalizations of its knowledge and beliefs. As has been noted above, its theoretical creations are chiefly of the nature of mythology shading off into folklore. This genial spinning of apocryphal yarns is, at its best, an amiably inefficient formulation of experiences and observations in terms of something like a life-history of the phenomena observed. It has, on the one hand, little value, and little purpose, in the way of pragmatic expediency, and so it is not closely akin to the pragmatic-barbarian scheme of life; while, on the other hand, it is also ineffectual as a systematic knowledge of matter-of-fact. It is a quest of knowledge, perhaps of systematic knowledge, and it is carried on under the incentive of the idle curiosity. In this respect it falls in the same class with the civilized man's science; but it seeks knowledge not in terms of opaque matter-of-fact, but in terms of some sort of spiritual life imputed to the facts. It is romantic and Hegelian rather than realistic and Darwinian. The logical necessities of its scheme of thought are necessities of spiritual consistency rather than of quantitative equivalence. It is like science in that it has no ulterior motive beyond the idle craving for a systematic correlation of data; but it is unlike science in that its standardization and correlation of data run in terms of the free play of imputed personal initiative rather than in terms of the constraint of objective cause and effect.

By force of the protracted selective discipline of this past phase of culture, the human nature of civilized mankind is still substantially the human nature of savage man. The ancient equipment of congenital aptitudes and propensities stands over substantially unchanged, though overlaid with barbarian traditions and conventionalities and readjusted by habituation to the exigencies of civilized life. In a measure, therefore, but by no means altogether, scientific inquiry is native to civilized man with his savage heritage, since scientific inquiry proceeds on the same general motive of idle curiosity as guided the savage myth-makers, though it makes use of concepts and standards in great measure alien to the myth-makers' habit of mind. The ancient human predilection for discovering a dramatic play of passion and intrigue in the phenomena of nature still asserts itself. In the most advanced communities, and even among the adepts of modern science, there comes up persistently the revulsion of the native savage against the inhumanly dispassionate sweep of the scientific quest, as well as against the inhumanly ruthless fabric of technological processes that have come out of this search for matter-of-fact knowledge. Very often the savage need of a spiritual interpretation (dramatization) of phenomena breaks through the crust of acquired materialistic habits of thought, to find such refuge as may be had in articles of faith seized on and held by sheer force of instinctive conviction. Science and its creations are more or less uncanny, more or less alien, to that fashion of craving for knowledge that by ancient inheritance animates mankind. Furtively or by an overt breach of consistency, men still seek comfort in marvellous articles of savage-born lore, which contradict the truths of that modern science whose dominion they dare not question, but whose findings at the same time go beyond the breaking-point of their jungle-fed spiritual sensibilities.

The ancient ruts of savage thought and conviction are smooth and easy; but however sweet and indispensable the archaic ways of thinking may be to the civilized man's peace of mind, yet such is the binding force of matter-of-fact analysis and inference under modern conditions that the findings of science are not questioned on the whole. The name of science is after all a word to conjure with.

So much so that the name and the mannerisms, at least, if nothing more of science, have invaded all fields of learning and have even overrun territory that belongs to the enemy. So there are "sciences" of theology, law, and medicine, as has already been noted above. And there are such things as Christian Science, and "scientific" astrology, palmistry, and the like. But within the field of learning proper there is a similar predilection for an air of scientific acumen and precision where science does not belong. So that even that large range of knowledge that has to do with general information rather than with theory—what is loosely termed scholarship—tends strongly to take on the name and forms of theoretical statement. However decided the contrast between these branches of knowledge on the one hand, and science properly so called on the other hand, yet even the classical learning, and the humanities generally, fall in with this predilection more and more with each succeeding generation of students. The students of literature, for instance, are more and more prone to substitute critical analysis and linguistic speculation, as the end of their endeavours, in the place of that discipline of taste and that cultivated sense of literary form and literary feeling that must always remain the chief end of literary training, as distinct from philology and the social sciences. There is, of course, no intention to question the legitimacy of a science of philology or of the analytical study of literature as a fact in cultural history, but these things do not constitute training in literary taste, nor can they take the place of

it. The effect of this straining after scientific formulations
in a field alien to the scientific spirit is as curious as it is
wasteful. Scientifically speaking, these quasi-scientific inquiries necessarily begin nowhere and end in the same
place; while in point of cultural gain they commonly
come to nothing better than spiritual abnegation. But
these blindfold endeavours to conform to the canons of
science serve to show how wide and unmitigated the
sway of science is in the modern community.

Scholarship—that is to say, an intimate and systematic
familiarity with past cultural achievements—still holds
its place in the scheme of learning, in spite of the unad-
vised efforts of the short-sighted to blend it with the work
of science, for it affords play for the ancient genial propensities that ruled men's quest of knowledge before the
coming of science or of the outspoken pragmatic barbarism. Its place may not be so large in proportion to
the entire field of learning as it was before the scientific
era got fully under way. But there is no intrinsic antagonism between science and scholarship, as there is between pragmatic training and scientific inquiry. Modern
scholarship shares with modern science the quality of
not being pragmatic in its aim. Like science it has no
ulterior end. It may be difficult here and there to draw
the line between science and scholarship, and it may even
more be unnecessary to draw such a line; yet while the
two ranges of discipline belong together in many ways,
and while there are many points of contact and sympathy
between the two; while the two together make up the

modern scheme of learning; yet there is no need of con-
founding the one with the other, nor can the one do the
work of the other. The scheme of learning has changed
in such manner as to give science the more commanding
place, but the scholar's domain has not thereby been invaded, nor has it suffered contraction at the hands of
science, whatever may be said of the weak-kneed abnegation of some whose place, if they have one, is in the field
of scholarship rather than of science.

All that has been said above has of course nothing to
say as to the intrinsic merits of this quest of matter-of-fact
knowledge. In point of fact, science gives its tone to modern culture. One may approve or one may deprecate the
fact that this opaque, materialistic interpretation of things
pervades modern thinking. That is a question of taste,
about which there is no disputing. The prevalence of this
matter-of-fact inquiry is a feature of modern culture, and
the attitude which critics take toward this phenomenon is
chiefly significant as indicating how far their own habit
of mind coincides with the enlightened common-sense of
civilized mankind. It shows in what degree they are
abreast of the advance of culture. Those in whom the
savage predilection of the barbarian tradition is stronger
than their habituation to civilized life will find that this
dominant factor of modern life is perverse, if not calami-
tous; those whose habits of thought have been fully
shaped by the machine process and scientific inquiry are
likely to find it good. The modern western culture, with

its core of matter-of-fact knowledge, may be better or worse than some other cultural scheme, such as the classic Greek, the medieval Christian, the Hindu, or the Pueblo Indian. Seen in certain lights, tested by certain standards, it is doubtless better; by other standards, worse. But the fact remains that the current cultural scheme, in its maturest growth, is of that complexion; its characteristic force lies in this matter-of-fact insight; its highest discipline and its maturest aspirations are these.

In point of fact, the sober common-sense of civilized mankind accepts no other end of endeavour as self-sufficient and ultimate. That such is the case seems to be due chiefly to the ubiquitous presence of the machine technology and its creations in the life of modern communities. And so long as the machine process continues to hold its dominant place as a disciplinary factor in modern culture, so long must the spiritual and intellectual life of this cultural era maintain the character which the machine process gives it.

But while the scientist's spirit and his achievements stir an unqualified admiration in modern men, and while his discoveries carry conviction as nothing else does, it does not follow that the manner of man which this quest of knowledge produces or requires comes near answering to the current ideal of manhood, or that his conclusions are felt to be as good and beautiful as they are true. The ideal man, and the ideal of human life, even in the apprehension of those who most rejoice in the advances of science, is neither the finikin sceptic in the laboratory nor

the animated slide-rule. The quest of science is relatively new. It is a cultural factor not comprised, in anything like its modern force, among those circumstances
whose selective action in the far past has given to the
race the human nature which it now has. The race
reached the human plane with little of this searching
knowledge of facts; and throughout the greater part of
its life-history on the human plane it has been accustomed
to make its higher generalizations and to formulate its
larger principles of life in other terms than those of
passionless matter-of-fact. This manner of knowledge has
occupied an increasing share of men's attention in the
past, since it bears in a decisive way upon the minor affairs of workday life; but it has never until now been put
in the first place, as the dominant note of human culture.
The normal man, such as his inheritance has made him,
has therefore good cause to be restive under its dominion.

# THE PRECONCEPTIONS OF
# ECONOMIC SCIENCE [1]

✿

## I

WHILE economic science in the remoter past of its
history has been mainly of a taxonomic character, later
writers of all schools show something of a divergence
from the taxonomic line and an inclination to make the
science a genetic account of the economic life process,
sometimes even without an ulterior view to the taxonomic value of the results obtained. This divergence from
the ancient canons of theoretical formulation is to be
taken as an episode of the movement that is going forward in latter-day science generally; and the progressive
change which thus affects the ideals and the objective
point of the modern sciences seems in its turn to be an
expression of that matter-of-fact habit of mind which the
prosy but exacting exigencies of life in a modern industrial
community breed in men exposed to their unmitigated
impact.

In speaking of this matter-of-fact character of the mod-

[1] Reprinted from *The Place of Science in Modern Civilisation*,
1919, pp. 83–179; originally published in three instalments in *The
Quarterly Journal of Economics*, vol. XIII, Jan. and July 1899, and
vol. XIV, Feb. 1900.

ern sciences it has been broadly characterized as "evolutionary"; and the evolutionary method and the evolutionary ideals have been placed in antithesis to the taxonomic
methods and ideals of pre-evolutionary days. But the
characteristic attitude, aims, and ideals which are so designated here are by no means peculiar to the group of sciences that are professedly occupied with a process of development, taking that term in its most widely accepted
meaning. The latter-day inorganic sciences are in this respect like the organic. They occupy themselves with "dynamic" relations and sequences. The question which they
ask is always, What takes place next, and why? Given
a situation wrought out by the forces under inquiry, what
follows as the consequence of the situation so wrought
out? or, What follows upon the accession of a further
element of force? Even in so non-evolutionary a science
as inorganic chemistry the inquiry consistently runs on
a process, an active sequence, and the value of the resulting situation as a point of departure for the next step
in an interminable cumulative sequence. The last step in
the chemist's experimental inquiry into any substance is,
What comes of the substance determined? What will
it do? What will it lead to when it is made the point of
departure in further chemical action? There is no ultimate
term, and no definitive solution except in terms of further
action. The theory worked out is always a theory of a
genetic succession of phenomena, and the relations determined and elaborated into a body of doctrine are always genetic relations. In modern chemistry no cog-

nizance is taken of the honorific bearing of reactions or molecular formulæ. The modern chemist, as contrasted with his ancient congener, knows nothing of the worth, elegance, or cogency of the relations that may subsist between the particles of matter with which he busies himself, for any other than the genetic purpose. The spiritual element and the elements of worth and propensity no longer count. Alchemic symbolism and the hierarchical glamour and virtue that once hedged about the nobler and more potent elements and reagents are almost altogether a departed glory of the science. Even the modest imputation of propensity involved in the construction of a scheme of coercive normality, for the putative guidance of reactions, finds little countenance with the later adepts of chemical science. The science has outlived that phase of its development at which the taxonomic feature was the dominant one.

In the modern sciences, of which chemistry is one, there has been a gradual shifting of the point of view from which the phenomena which the science treats of are apprehended and passed upon; and to the historian of chemical science this shifting of the point of view must be a factor of great weight in the development of chemical knowledge. Something of a like nature is true for economic science; and it is the aim here to present, in outline, some of the successive phases that have passed over the spiritual attitude of the adepts of the science, and to point out the manner in which the transition from one point of view to the next has been made.

. . . The characteristic spiritual attitude or point of view of a given generation or group of economists is shown not so much in their detail work as in their higher syntheses—the terms of their definitive formulations— the grounds of their final valuation of the facts handled for purpose of theory. This line of recondite inquiry into the spiritual past and antecedents of the science has not often been pursued seriously or with singleness of purpose, perhaps because it is, after all, of but slight consequence to the practical efficiency of the present-day science. Still, not a little substantial work has been done towards this end by such writers as Hasbach, Oncken, Bonar, Cannan, and Marshall. And much that is to the purpose is also due to writers outside of economics, for the aims of economic speculation have never been insulated from the work going forward in other lines of inquiry. As would necessarily be the case, the point of view of economists has always been in large part the point of view of the enlightened common-sense of their time. The spiritual attitude of a given generation of economists is therefore in good part a special outgrowth of the ideals and preconceptions current in the world about them.

So, for instance, it is quite the conventional thing to say that the speculations of the Physiocrats were dominated and shaped by the preconception of Natural Rights. Account has been taken of the effect of natural-rights preconceptions upon the Physiocratic schemes of policy and economic reform, as well as upon the details of their doctrines.[2] But little has been said of the significance of these preconceptions for the lower courses of the Physiocrats' theoretical structure. And yet that habit of mind to which the natural-rights view is wholesome and adequate is answerable both for the point of departure and for the objective point of the Physiocratic theories, both for the range of facts to which they turned and for the terms in which they were content to formulate their knowledge of the facts which they handled. The failure of their critics to place themselves at the Physiocratic point of view has led to much destructive criticism of their work; whereas, when seen through Physiocratic eyes, such doctrines as those of the net product and of the barrenness of the artisan class appear to be substantially true.

The speculations of the Physiocrats are commonly accounted the first articulate and comprehensive presentation of economic theory that is in line with later theoretical work. The Physiocratic point of view may, therefore, well be taken as the point of departure in an attempt to trace that shifting of aims and norms of procedure that comes into view in the work of later economists when compared with earlier writers.

Physiocratic economics is a theory of the working-out of the Law of Nature (*loi naturelle*) in its economic bearing, and this Law of Nature is a very simple matter.

---

[2] See, for instance, Hasbach, *Allgemeine philosophische Grundlagen der von François Quesnay und Adam Smith begründeten politischen Oekonomie*.

Les lois naturelles sont ou physiques ou morales.

On entend ici, par loi physique, *le cours réglé de tout évènement physique de l'ordre naturel, évidemment le plus avantageux au genre humain.*

On entend ici, par loi morale, *la règle de toute action humaine de l'ordre morale, conforme à l'ordre physique évidemment le plus avantageux au genre humain.*

Ces lois forment ensemble ce qu'on appelle la *loi naturelle.* Tous les hommes et toutes les puissances humaines doivent être soumis à ces lois souveraines, instituées par l'Être-Suprême: elles sont immuables et irréfragables, et les meilleures lois possible.[3]

The settled course of material facts tending beneficently to the highest welfare of the human race—this is the final term in the Physiocratic speculations. This is the touchstone of substantiality. Conformity to these "immutable and unerring" laws of nature is the test of economic truth. The laws are immutable and unerring, but that does not mean that they rule the course of events with a blind fatality that admits of no exception and no divergence from the direct line. Human nature may, through infirmity or perversity, wilfully break over the beneficent trend of the laws of nature; but to the Physiocrat's sense of the matter the laws are none the less im-

---

[3] Quesnay, *Droit Naturel,* chap. 5 (ed. Daire, *Physiocrates,* pp. 52-3).

mutable and irrefragable on that account. They are not empirical generalizations on the course of phenomena, like the law of falling bodies or of the angle of reflection; although many of the details of their action are to be determined only by observation and experience, helped out, of course, by interpretation of the facts of observation under the light of reason. So, for instance, Turgot, in his *Réflections*, empirically works out a doctrine of the reasonable course of development through which wealth is accumulated and reaches the existing state of unequal distribution; so also his doctrines of interest and of money. The immutable natural laws are rather of the nature of canons of conduct governing nature than generalizations of mechanical sequence, although in a general way the phenomena of mechanical sequence are details of the conduct of nature working according to these canons of conduct. The great law of the order of nature is of the character of a propensity working to an end, to the accomplishment of a purpose. The processes of nature working under the quasi-spiritual stress of this immanent propensity may be characterized as nature's habits of life. Not that nature is conscious of its travail, and knows and desires the worthy end of its endeavours; but for all that there is a quasi-spiritual nexus between antecedent and consequent in the scheme of operation in which nature is engaged. Nature is not uneasy about interruptions of its course or occasional deflections from the direct line through an untoward conjunction of mechanical causes, nor does the validity of the great overruling law suffer through such an episode. The introduction of a mere mechanically effective causal factor cannot thwart the course of Nature from reaching the goal to which she animistically tends. Nothing can thwart this teleological propensity of Nature except counter-activity or divergent activity of a similarly teleological kind. Men can break over the law, and have short-sightedly and wilfully done so; for men are also agents who guide their actions by an end to be achieved. Human conduct is activity of the same kind—on the same plane of spiritual reality or competency—as the course of Nature, and it may therefore traverse the latter. The remedy for this short-sighted traffic of misguided human nature is enlightenment— *"instruction publique et privée des lois de l'ordre naturel."* [4]

The nature in terms of which all knowledge of phenomena—for the present purpose economic phenomena —is to be finally synthesized is, therefore, substantially of a quasi-spiritual or animistic character. The laws of nature are in the last resort teleological: they are of the nature of a propensity. The substantial fact in all the sequences of nature is the end to which the sequence naturally tends, not the brute fact of mechanical compulsion or causally effective forces. Economic theory is accordingly the theory (1) of how the efficient causes of the *ordre naturel* work in an orderly unfolding sequence, guided by the underlying natural laws—the propensity

---

[4] Quesnay, *Droit Naturel,* chap. 5 (ed. Daire, *Physiocrates,* pp. 52–3).

immanent in nature to establish the highest well-being of mankind—and (2) of the conditions imposed upon human conduct by these natural laws in order to reach the ordained goal of supreme human welfare. The conditions so imposed on human conduct are as definitive as the laws and the order by force of which they are imposed; and the theoretical conclusions reached, when these laws and this order are known, are therefore expressions of absolute economic truth. Such conclusions are an expression of reality, but not necessarily of fact.

Now, the objective end of this propensity that determines the course of nature is human well-being. But economic speculation has to do with the workings of nature only so far as regards the *ordre physique*. And the laws of nature in the *ordre physique,* working through mechanical sequence, can only work out the physical well-being of man, not necessarily the spiritual. This propensity to the physical well-being of man is therefore the law of nature to which economic science must bring its generalizations, and this law of physical beneficence is the substantial ground of economic truth. Wanting this, all our speculations are vain; but having its authentication, they are definitive. The great, typical function, to which all the other functioning of nature is incidental if not subsidiary, is accordingly that of the alimentation, nutrition, of mankind. In so far, and only in so far, as the physical processes contribute to human sustenance and fullness of life, can they, therefore, further the great work of nature. Whatever processes contribute to human sustenance by adding to the material available for human assimilation and nutrition, by increasing the substance disposable for human comfort, therefore count towards the substantial end. All other processes, however serviceable in other than this physiological respect, lack the substance of economic reality. Accordingly, human industry is productive, economically speaking, if it heightens the effectiveness of the natural processes out of which the material of human sustenance emerges; otherwise not. The test of productivity, of economic reality in material facts, is the increase of nutritive material. Whatever employment of time or effort does not afford an increase of such material is unproductive, however profitable it may be to the person employed, and however useful or indispensable it may be to the community. The type of such productive industry is the husbandman's employment, which yields a substantial (nutritive) gain. The artisan's work may be useful to the community and profitable to himself, but its economic effect does not extend beyond an alteration of the form in which the material afforded by nature already lies at hand. It is formally productive only, not really productive. It bears no part in the creative or generative work of nature; and therefore it lacks the character of economic substantiality. It does not enhance nature's output of vital force. The artisan's labours, therefore, yield no net product, whereas the husbandman's labours do.

Whatever constitutes a material increment of this output of vital force is wealth, and nothing else is. The theory of value contained in this position has not to do with value according to men's appraisement of the valuable article. Given items of wealth may have assigned to them certain relative values at which they exchange, and these conventional values may differ more or less widely from the natural or intrinsic value of the goods in question; but all that is beside the substantial point. The point in question is not the degree of predilection shown by certain individuals or bodies of men for certain goods. That is a matter of caprice and convention, and it does not directly touch the substantial ground of the economic life. The question of value is a question of the extent to which the given item of wealth forwards the end of Nature's unfolding process. It is valuable, intrinsically and really, in so far as it avails the great work which Nature has in hand.

Nature, then, is the final term in the Physiocratic speculations. Nature works by impulse and in an unfolding process, under the stress of a propensity to the accomplishment of a given end. This propensity, taken as the final cause that is operative in any situation, furnishes the basis on which to co-ordinate all our knowledge of those efficient causes through which Nature works to her ends. For the purpose of economic theory proper, this is the ultimate ground of reality to which our quest of economic truth must penetrate. But back of Nature and her works there is, in the Physiocratic scheme of the universe, the Creator, by whose all-wise and benevolent power the order of nature has been established in all the strength and beauty of its inviolate and immutable perfection. But the Physiocratic conception of the Creator is essentially a deistic one: he stands apart from the course of nature which he has established, and keeps his hands off. In the last resort, of course, *"Dieu seul est producteur. Les hommes travaillent, receuillent, économisent, conservent; mais* économiser *n'est pas* produire."[5] But this last resort does not bring the Creator into economic theory as a fact to be counted with in formulating economic laws. He serves a homiletical purpose in the Physiocratic speculations rather than fills an office essential to the theory. He comes within the purview of the theory by way of authentication rather than as a subject of inquiry or a term in the formulation of economic knowledge. The Physiocratic God can scarcely be said to be an economic fact, but it is otherwise with that Nature whose ways and means constitute the subject-matter of the Physiocratic inquiry.

When this natural system of the Physiocratic speculation is looked at from the side of the psychology of the investigators, or from that of the logical premises employed, it is immediately recognized as essentially animistic. It runs consistently on animistic ground; but it is animism of a high grade—highly integrated and enlightened, but, after all, retaining very much of that primitive force and naïveté which characterize the animistic explanations of phenomena in vogue among the untroubled barbarians. It is not the disjected animism of the vulgar,

---

[5] Dupont de Nemours, *Correspondance avec J.-B. Say* (ed. Daire, *Physiocrates*, première partie, p. 399).

who see a wilful propensity—often a wilful perversity —in given objects or situations to work towards a given outcome, good or bad. It is not the gambler's haphazard sense of fortuitous necessity or the housewife's belief in lucky days, numbers, or phases of the moon. The Physiocrat's animism rests on a broader outlook, and does not proceed by such an immediately impulsive imputation of propensity. The teleological element—the element of propensity—is conceived in a large way, unified and harmonized, as a comprehensive order of nature as a whole. But it vindicates its standing as a true animism by never becoming fatalistic and never being confused or confounded with the sequence of cause and effect. It has reached the last stage of integration and definition, beyond which the way lies downward from the high, quasi-spiritual ground of animism to the tamer levels of normality and causal uniformities.

There is already discernible a tone of dispassionate and colourless "tendency" about the Physiocratic animism, such as to suggest a wavering towards the side of normality. This is especially visible in such writers as the half-protestant Turgot. In his discussion of the development of farming, for instance, Turgot speaks almost entirely of human motives and the material conditions under which the growth takes place. There is little metaphysics in it, and that little does not express the law of nature in an adequate form. But, after all has been said, it remains true that the Physiocrat's sense of substantiality is not satisfied until he reaches the animistic ground; and it remains true also that the arguments of their opponents made little impression on the Physiocrats so long as they were directed to other than this animistic ground of their doctrine. This is true in great measure even of Turgot, as witness his controversy with Hume. Whatever criticism is directed against them on other grounds is met with impatience, as being inconsequential, if not disingenuous.[6]

To an historian of economic theory the source and the line of derivation whereby this precise form of the order-of-nature preconception reached the Physiocrats are of first-rate importance; but it is scarcely a question to be taken up here—in part because it is too large a question to be handled here, in part because it has met with adequate treatment at more competent hands,[7] and in part because it is somewhat beside the immediate point under discussion. This point is the logical, or perhaps better the psychological, value of the Physiocrats' preconception, as a factor in shaping their point of view and the terms of their definitive formulation of economic knowledge. For this purpose it may be sufficient to point out that the preconception in question belongs to the generation in which the Physiocrats lived, and that it is the guiding norm of all serious thought that found ready assimilation into the common-sense views of that time. It is the characteristic and controlling feature of what may be called the

---

[6] See, for instance, the concluding chapters of La Rivière's *Ordre Naturel des Sociétés Politiques.*

[7] E.g., Hasbach, *loc. cit.*; Bonar, *Philosophy and Political Economy*, Book II; Ritchie, *Natural Rights.*

common-sense metaphysics of the eighteenth century, especially so far as concerns the enlightened French community.

It is to be noted as a point bearing more immediately
on the question in hand that this imputation of final causes
to the course of phenomena expresses a spiritual attitude
which has prevailed, one might almost say, always and
everywhere, but which reached its finest, most effective
development, and found its most finished expression, in
the eighteenth-century metaphysics. It is nothing recondite; for it meets us at every turn, as a matter of course,
in the vulgar thinking of today—in the pulpit and in
the market-place—although it is not so ingenuous, nor
does it so unquestionedly hold the primacy in the thinking
of any class today as it once did. It meets us likewise,
with but little change of features, at all past stages of culture, late or early. Indeed, it is the most generic feature
of human thinking, so far as regards a theoretical or
speculative formulation of knowledge. Accordingly, it
seems scarcely necessary to trace the lineage of this characteristic preconception of the era of enlightenment,
through specific channels, back to the ancient philosophers
or jurists of the empire. Some of the specific forms of
its expression—as, for instance, the doctrine of Natural
Rights—are no doubt traceable through medieval channels to the teachings of the ancients; but there is no need
of going over the brook for water, and tracing back to
specific teachings the main features of that habit of mind
or spiritual attitude of which the doctrines of Natural

Rights and the Order of Nature are specific elaborations only. This dominant habit of mind came to the generation of the Physiocrats on the broad ground of group inheritance, not by lineal devolution from any one of the great thinkers of past ages who had thrown its deliverances into a similarly competent form for the use of his own generation.

In leaving the Physiocratic discipline and the immediate sphere of Physiocratic influence for British ground, we are met by the figure of Hume. Here, also, it will be impracticable to go into details as to the remoter line of derivation of the specific point of view that we come upon on making the transition, for reasons similar to those already given as excuse for passing over the similar question with regard to the Physiocratic point of view. Hume is, of course, not primarily an economist; but that placid unbeliever is none the less a large item in any inventory of eighteenth-century economic thought. Hume was not gifted with a facile acceptance of the group inheritance that made the habit of mind of his generation. Indeed, he was gifted with an alert, though somewhat histrionic, scepticism touching everything that was well received. It is his office to prove all things, though not necessarily to hold fast that which is good.

Aside from the strain of affectation discernible in Hume's scepticism, he may be taken as an accentuated expression of that characteristic bent which distinguishes British thinking in his time from the thinking of the Continent, and more particularly of the French. There is in Hume, and in the British community, an insistence on the prosy, not to say the seamy, side of human affairs. He is not content with formulating his knowledge of things in terms of what ought to be or in terms of the objective point of the course of things. He is not even content with adding to the teleological account of phenomena a chain of empirical, narrative generalizations as to the usual course of things. He insists, in season and out of season, on an exhibition of the efficient causes engaged in any sequence of phenomena; and he is sceptical—irreverently sceptical—as to the need or the use of any formulation of knowledge that outruns the reach of his own matter-of-fact, step-by-step argument from cause to effect.

In short, he is too modern to be wholly intelligible to those of his contemporaries who are most neatly abreast of their time. He out-Britishes the British; and, in his footsore quest for a perfectly tame explanation of things, he finds little comfort, and indeed scant courtesy, at the hands of his own generation. He is not in sufficiently naïve accord with the range of preconceptions then in vogue.

But, while Hume may be an accentuated expression of a national characteristic, he is not therefore an untrue expression of this phase of British eighteenth-century thinking. The peculiarity of point of view and of method for which he stands has sometimes been called the critical attitude, sometimes the inductive method, sometimes the materialistic or mechanical, and again, though less aptly, the historical method. Its characteristic is an insistence on matter of fact.

This matter-of-fact animus that meets any historian of economic doctrine on his introduction to British economics is a large, but not the largest, feature of the British scheme of early economic thought. It strikes the attention because it stands in contrast with the relative absence of this feature in the contemporary speculations of the Continent. The most potent, most formative habit of thought concerned in the early development of economic teaching on British ground is best seen in the broader generalizations of Adam Smith, and this more potent factor in Smith is a bent that is substantially identical with that which gives consistency to the speculations of the Physiocrats. In Adam Smith the two are happily combined, not to say blended; but the animistic habit still holds the primacy, with the matter-of-fact as a subsidiary though powerful factor. He is said to have combined deduction with induction. The relatively great prominence given the latter marks the line of divergence of British from French economics, not the line of coincidence; and on this account it may not be out of place to look more narrowly into the circumstances to which the emergence of this relatively greater penchant for a matter-of-fact explanation of things in the British community is due.

To explain the characteristic animus for which Hume stands, on grounds that might appeal to Hume, we should have to inquire into the peculiar circumstances---ultimately material circumstances—that have gone to shape the habitual view of things within the British community, and that so have acted to differentiate the British preconceptions from the French, or from the general range of preconceptions prevalent on the Continent. These peculiar formative circumstances are no doubt to some extent racial peculiarities; but the racial complexion of the British community is not widely different from the French, and especially not widely different from certain other Continental communities which are for the present purpose roughly classed with the French. Race difference can therefore not wholly, nor indeed for the greater part, account for the cultural difference of which this difference in preconceptions is an outcome. Through its cumulative effect on institutions the race difference must be held to have had a considerable effect on the habit of mind of the community; but, if the race difference is in this way taken as the remoter ground of an institutional peculiarity, which in its turn has shaped prevalent habits of thought, then the attention may be directed to the proximate causes, the concrete circumstances, through which this race difference has acted, in conjunction with other ulterior circumstances, to work out the psychological phenomena observed. Race differences, it may be remarked, do not so nearly coincide with national lines of demarcation as differences in the point of view from which things are habitually apprehended or differences in the standards according to which facts are rated.

If the element of race difference be not allowed defini-

tive weight in discussing national peculiarities that underlie the deliverances of common-sense, neither can these
national peculiarities be ·confidently traced to a national
difference in the transmitted learning that enters into the
common-sense view of things. So far as concerns the concrete facts embodied in the learning of the various nations
within the European culture, these nations make up but
a single community. What divergence is visible does not
touch the character of the positive information with which
the learning of the various nations is occupied. Divergence
is visible in the higher syntheses, the methods of handling
the material of knowledge, the basis of valuation of the
facts taken up, rather than in the material of knowledge.
But this divergence must be set down to a cultural difference, a difference of point of view, not to a difference
in inherited information. When a given body of information passes the national frontiers it acquires a new complexion, a new national, cultural physiognomy. It is this
cultural physiognomy of learning that is here under inquiry, and a comparison of early French economics (the
Physiocrats) with early British economics (Adam Smith)
is here entered upon merely with a view to making out
what significance this cultural physiognomy of the science has for the past progress of economic speculation.

The broad features of economic speculation, as it stood
at the period under consideration, may be briefly summed
up, disregarding the element of policy, or expediency,
which is common to both groups of economists, and at-

tending to their theoretical work alone. With the Physiocrats, as with Adam Smith, there are two main points of view from which economic phenomena are treated: (*a*) the matter-of-fact point of view or preconception, which yields a discussion of causal sequences and correlations; and (*b*) what, for want of a more expressive word, is here called the animistic point of view or preconception, which yields a discussion of teleological sequences and correlations—a discussion of the function of this and that "organ," of the legitimacy of this or the other range of facts. The former preconception is allowed a larger scope in the British than in the French economics: there is more of "induction" in the British. The latter preconception is present in both, and is the definitive element in both; but the animistic element is more colourless in the British, it is less constantly in evidence, and less able to stand alone without the support of arguments from cause to effect. Still, the animistic element is the controlling factor in the higher syntheses of both; and for both alike it affords the definitive ground on which the argument finally comes to rest. In neither group of thinkers is the sense of substantiality appeased until this quasi-spiritual ground, given by the natural propensity of the course of events, is reached. But the propensity in events, the natural or normal course of things, as appealed to by the British speculators, suggests less of an imputation of will-power, or personal force, to the propensity in question. It may be added, as has already been said in another place,

that the tacit imputation of will-power or spiritual consistency to the natural or normal course of events has
progressively weakened in the later course of economic
speculation, so that in this respect, the British economists
of the eighteenth century may be said to represent a later
phase of economic inquiry than the Physiocrats.

Unfortunately, but unavoidably, if this question as to
the cultural shifting of the point of view in economic science is taken up from the side of the causes to which the
shifting is traceable, it will take the discussion back to
ground on which an economist must at best feel himself
to be but a raw layman, with all a layman's limitations
and ineptitude, and with the certainty of doing badly
what might be done well by more competent hands. But,
with a reliance on charity where charity is most needed, it
is necessary to recite summarily what seems to be the psychological bearing of certain cultural facts.

A cursory acquaintance with any of the more archaic
phases of human culture enforces the recognition of this
fact—that the habit of construing the phenomena of the
inanimate world in animistic terms prevails pretty much
universally on these lower levels. Inanimate phenomena
are apprehended to work out a propensity to an end; the
movements of the elements are construed in terms of
quasi-personal force. So much is well authenticated by
the observations on which anthropologists and ethnologists draw for their materials. This animistic habit, it may
be said, seems to be more effectual and far-reaching

among those primitive communities that lead a predatory life.

But along with this feature of archaic methods of thought or of knowledge, the picturesqueness of which has drawn the attention of all observers, there goes a second feature, no less important for the purpose in hand, though less obtrusive. The latter is of less interest to the men who have to do with the theory of cultural development, because it is a matter of course. This second feature of archaic thought is the habit of also apprehending facts in non-animistic, or impersonal, terms. The imputation of propensity in no case extends to all the mechanical facts in the case. There is always a substratum of matter of fact, which is the outcome of an habitual imputation of causal sequence, or, perhaps better, an imputation of mechanical continuity, if a new term be permitted. The agent, thing, fact, event, or phenomenon, to which propensity, will-power, or purpose is imputed, is always apprehended to act in an environment which is accepted as spiritually inert. There are always opaque facts as well as self-directing agents. Any agent acts through means which lend themselves to his use on other grounds than that of spiritual compulsion, although spiritual compulsion may be a large feature in any given case.

The same features of human thinking, the same two complementary methods of correlating facts and handling them for the purposes of knowledge, are similarly in constant evidence in the daily life of men in our own community. The question is, in great part, which of the two bears the greater part in shaping human knowledge at any given time and within any given range of knowledge or of facts.

Other features of the growth of knowledge, which are remoter from the point under inquiry, may be of no less consequence to a comprehensive theory of the development of culture and of thought; but it is of course out of the question here to go farther afield. The present inquiry will have enough to do with these two. No other features are correlative with these, and these merit discussion on account of their intimate bearing on the point of view of economics. The point of interest with respect to these two correlative and complementary habits of thought is the question of how they have fared under the changing exigencies of human culture; in what manner they come, under given cultural circumstances, to share the field of knowledge between them; what is the relative part of each in the composite point of view in which the two habits of thought express themselves at any given cultural stage.

The animistic preconception enforces the apprehension of phenomena in terms generically identical with the terms of personality or individuality. As a certain modern group of psychologists would say, it imputes to objects and sequences an element of habit and attention similar in kind, though not necessarily in degree, to the like spiritual attitude present in the activities of a personal agent. The matter-of-fact preconception, on the other hand, enforces a handling of facts without imputation of personal force or attention, but with an imputation of mechanical continuity, substantially the preconception which has reached a formulation at the hands of scientists under the name of conservation of energy or persistence of quantity. Some appreciable resort to the latter method of knowledge is unavoidable at any cultural stage, for it is indispensable to all industrial efficiency. All technological processes and all mechanical contrivances rest, psychologically speaking, on this ground. This habit of thought is a selectively necessary consequence of industrial life, and, indeed, of all human experience in making use of the material means of life. It should therefore follow that, in a general way, the higher the culture, the greater the share of the mechanical preconception in shaping human thought and knowledge, since, in a general way, the stage of culture attained depends on the efficiency of industry. The rule, while it does not hold with anything like extreme generality, must be admitted to hold to a good extent; and to that extent it should hold also that, by a selective adaptation of men's habits of thought to the exigencies of those cultural phases that have actually supervened, the mechanical method of knowledge should have gained in scope and range. Something of the sort is borne out by observation.

A further consideration enforces the like view. As the community increases in size, the range of observation of the individuals in the community also increases; and continually wider and more far-reaching sequences of a mechanical kind have to be taken account of. Men have to

adapt their own motives to industrial processes that are
not safely to be construed in terms of propensity, predilection, or passion. Life in an advanced industrial community does not tolerate a neglect of mechancial fact; for
the mechanical sequences through which men, at an appreciable degree of culture, work out their livelihood are
no respecters of persons or of will-power. Still, on all but
the higher industrial stages, the coercive discipline of industrial life, and of the scheme of life that inculcates regard for the mechanical facts of industry, is greatly mitigated by the largely haphazard character of industry, and
by the great extent to which man continues to be the
prime mover in industry. So long as industrial efficiency is
chiefly a matter of the handicraftsman's skill, dexterity,
and diligence, the attention of men in looking to the industrial process is met by the figure of the workman, as
the chief and characteristic factor; and thereby it comes
to run on the personal element in industry.

But, with or without mitigation, the scheme of life
which men perforce adopt under exigencies of an advanced industrial situation shapes their habits of thought
on the side of their behaviour, and thereby shapes their
habits of thought to some extent for all purposes. Each
individual is but a single complex of habits of thought,
and the same psychical mechanism that expresses itself in
one direction as conduct expresses itself in another direction as knowledge. The habits of thought formed in the
one connexion, in response to stimuli that call for a response in terms of conduct, must, therefore, have their

effect when the same individual comes to respond to stimuli that call for a response in terms of knowledge. The
scheme of thought or of knowledge is in good part a re-
verberation of the scheme of life. So that, after all has
been said, it remains true that with the growth of industrial organization and efficiency there must, by selection
and by adaptation, supervene a greater resort to the mechanical or dispassionate method of apprehending facts.

But the industrial side of life is not the whole of it, nor
does the scheme of life in vogue in any community or at
any cultural stage comprise industrial conduct alone.
The social, civic, military, and religious interests come in
for their share of attention, and between them they commonly take up by far the larger share of it. Especially is
this true so far as concerns those classes among whom we
commonly look for a cultivation of knowledge for knowledge's sake. The discipline which these several interests
exert does not commonly coincide with the training given
by industry. So the religious interest, with its canons of
truth and of right living, runs exclusively on personal relations and the adaptation of conduct to the predilections
of a superior personal agent. The weight of its discipline,
therefore, falls wholly on the animistic side. It acts to
heighten our appreciation of the spiritual bearing of
phenomena and to discountenance a matter-of-fact apprehension of things. The sceptic of the type of Hume
has never been in good repute with those who stand
closest to the accepted religious truths. The bearing of
this side of our culture upon the development of econom-

ics is shown by what the medieval scholars had to say on economic topics.

The disciplinary effects of other phases of life, outside of the industrial and the religious, is not so simple a matter; but the discussion here approaches nearer to the point of immediate inquiry—namely, the cultural situation in the eighteenth century, and its relation to economic speculation—and this ground of interest in the question may help to relieve the topic of the tedium that of right belongs to it.

In the remoter past of which we have records, and even in the more recent past, occidental man, as well as man elsewhere, has eminently been a respecter of persons. Wherever the warlike activity has been a large feature of the community's life, much of human conduct in society has proceeded on a regard for personal force. The scheme of life has been a scheme of personal aggression and subservience, partly in the naïve form, partly conventionalized in a system of status. The discipline of social life for the present purpose, in so far as its canons of conduct rest on this element of personal force in the unconventionalized form, plainly tends to the formation of a habit of apprehending and co-ordinating facts from the animistic point of view. So far as we have to do with life under a system of status, the like remains true, but with a difference. The regime of status inculcates an unremitting and very nice discrimination and observance of distinctions of personal superiority and inferiority. To the criterion of personal force, or will-power, taken in its immediate bearing on conduct, is added the criterion of personal excellence-in-general, regardless of the first-hand potency of the given person as an agent. This criterion of conduct requires a constant and painstaking imputation of personal value, regardless of fact. The discrimination enjoined by the canons of status proceeds on an invidious comparison of persons in respect of worth, value, potency, virtue, which must, for the present purpose, be taken as putative. The greater or less personal value assigned a given individual or a given class under the canons of status is not assigned on the ground of visible efficiency, but on the ground of a dogmatic allegation accepted on the strength of an uncontradicted categorical affirmation simply. The canons of status hold their ground by force of pre-emption. Where distinctions of status are based on a putative worth transmitted by descent from honourable antecedents, the sequence of transmission to which appeal is taken as the arbiter of honour is of a putative and animistic character rather than a visible mechanical continuity. The habit of accepting as final what is prescriptively right in the affairs of life has as its reflex in the affairs of knowledge the formula, *Quid ab omnibus, quid ubique creditur credendum est.*

Even this meagre account of the scheme of life that characterizes a regime of status should serve to indicate what is its disciplinary effect in shaping habits of thought, and therefore in shaping the habitual criteria of knowledge and of reality. A culture whose institutions are a framework of invidious comparisons implies, or rather

involves and comprises, a scheme of knowledge whose
definitive standards of truth and substantiality are of an
animistic character; and, the more undividedly the canons
of status and ceremonial honour govern the conduct of
the community, the greater the facility with which the sequence of cause and effect is made to yield before the
higher claims of a spiritual sequence or guidance in the
course of events. Men consistently trained to an unremitting discrimination of honour, worth, and personal
force in their daily conduct, and to whom these criteria afford the definitive ground of sufficiency in co-ordinating
facts for the purposes of life, will not be satisfied to fall
short of the like definitive ground of sufficiency when they
come to co-ordinate facts for the purposes of knowledge
simply. The habits formed in unfolding his activity in
one direction, under the impulse of a given interest, assert
themselves when the individual comes to unfold his activity in any other direction, under the impulse of any other
interest. If his last resort and highest criterion of truth in
conduct is afforded by the element of personal force and
invidious comparison, his sense of substantiality or truth
in the quest of knowledge will be satisfied only when a
like definitive ground of animistic force and invidious
comparison is reached. But when such ground is reached,
he rests content and pushes the inquiry no farther. In his
practical life he has acquired the habit of resting his case
on an authentic deliverance as to what is absolutely right.
This absolutely right and good final term in conduct has
the character of finality only when conduct is construed

in a ceremonial sense; that is to say, only when life is conceived as a scheme of conformity to a purpose outside and beyond the process of living. Under the regime of status this ceremonial finality is found in the concept of worth or honour. In the religious domain it is the concept of virtue, sanctity, or taboo. Merit lies in what one is, not in what one does. The habit of appeal to ceremonial finality, formed in the school of status, goes with the individual in his quest of knowledge, as a dependence upon a similarly authentic norm of absolute truth—a similar seeking of a final term outside and beyond the range of knowledge.

The discipline of social and civic life under a regime of status, then, reinforces the discipline of the religious life; and the outcome of the resulting habituation is that the canons of knowledge are cast in the animistic mould and converge to a ground of absolute truth, and this absolute truth is of a ceremonial nature. Its subject-matter is a reality regardless of fact.

The outcome, for science, of the religious and social life of the civilization of status, in occidental culture, was a structure of quasi-spiritual appreciations and explanations, of which astrology, alchemy, and medieval theology and metaphysics are competent, though somewhat one-sided, exponents. Throughout the range of this early learning the ground of correlation of phenomena is in part the supposed relative potency of the facts correlated; but it is also in part a scheme of status, in which facts are scheduled according to a hierarchical gradation of worth or merit, having only a ceremonial relation to the observed phenomena. Some elements (some metals, for instance) are noble, others base; some planets, on grounds of ceremonial efficacy, have a sinister influence, others a beneficent one; and it is a matter of serious consequence whether they are in the ascendant, and so on.

The body of learning through which the discipline of animism and invidious comparison transmitted its effects to the science of economics was what is known as natural theology, natural rights, moral philosophy, and natural law. These several disciplines or bodies of knowledge had wandered far from the naïve animistic standpoint at the time when economic science emerged, and much the same is true as regards the time of the emergence of other modern sciences. But the discipline which makes for an animistic formulation of knowledge continued to hold the primacy in modern culture, although its dominion was never altogether undivided or unmitigated. Occidental culture has long been largely an industrial culture; and, as already pointed out, the discipline of industry, and of life in an industrial community, does not favour the animistic preconception. This is especially true as regards industry which makes large use of mechanical contrivances. The difference in these respects between occidental industry and science, on the one hand, and the industry and science of other cultural regions, on the other hand, is worth noting in this connexion. The result has been that the sciences, as that word is understood in later usage, have come forward gradually, and in a certain rough parallelism with the development of industrial processes and industrial organization. It is possible to hold that both modern industry (of the mechanical sort) and modern science centre about the region of the North Sea. It is still more palpably true that within this general area the sciences, in the recent past, show a family likeness to the civil and social institutions of the communities in which they have been cultivated, this being true to the greatest extent of the higher or speculative sciences; that is, in that range of knowledge in which the animistic preconception can chiefly and most effectively find application. There is, for instance, in the eighteenth century a perceptible parallelism between the divergent character of British and Continental culture and institutions, on the one hand, and the dissimilar aims of British and Continental speculation, on the other hand.

Something has already been said of the difference in preconceptions between the French and the British economists of the eighteenth century. It remains to point out the correlative cultural difference between the two communities, to which it is conceived that the difference in scientific animus is in great measure due. It is, of course, only the general features, the general attitude of the speculators, that can be credited to the difference in culture. Differences of detail in the specific doctrines held could be explained only on a much more detailed analysis than can be entered on here, and after taking account of facts which cannot here be even allowed for in detail.

Aside from the greater resort to mechanical contriv·

ances and the larger scale of organization in British industry, the further cultural peculiarities of the British community run in the same general direction. British religious life and beliefs had less of the element of fealty—personal or discretionary mastery and subservience—and more of a tone of fatalism. The civil institutions of the British had not the same rich personal content as those of the French. The British subject owed allegiance to an impersonal law rather than to the person of a superior. Relatively, it may be said that the sense of status, as a coercive factor, was in abeyance in the British community. Even in the warlike enterprise of the British community a similar characteristic is traceable. Warfare is, of course, a matter of personal assertion. Warlike communities and classes are necessarily given to construing facts in terms of personal force and personal ends. They are always superstitious. They are great sticklers for rank and precedent, and zealously cultivate those distinctions and ceremonial observances in which a system of status expresses itself. But, while warlike enterprise has by no means been absent from the British scheme of life, the geographical and strategic isolation of the British community has given a characteristic turn to their military relations. In recent times British warlike operations have been conducted abroad. The military class has consequently in great measure been segregated out from the body of the community, and the ideals and prejudices of the class have not been transfused through the general body with the same facility and effect that they might otherwise have had. The British community at home has seen the campaign in great part from the standpoint of the "sinews of war."

The outcome of all these national peculiarities of circumstance and culture has been that a different scheme of life has been current in the British community from what has prevailed on the Continent. There has resulted the formation of a different body of habits of thought and a different animus in their handling of facts. The preconception of causal sequence has been allowed larger scope in the correlation of facts for purposes of knowledge; and, where the animistic preconception has been resorted to, as it always has in the profounder reaches of learning, it has commonly been an animism of a tamer kind.

Taking Adam Smith as an exponent of this British attitude in theoretical knowledge, it is to be noted that, while he formulates his knowledge in terms of a propensity (natural laws) working teleologically to an end, the end or objective point which controls the formulation has not the same rich content of vital human interest or advantage as is met with in the Physiocratic speculations. There is perceptibly less of an imperious tone in Adam Smith's natural laws than in those of the contemporary French economists. It is true, he sums up the institutions with which he deals in terms of the ends which they should subserve, rather than in terms of the exigencies and habits of life out of which they have arisen; but he does not with the same tone of finality appeal to the end subserved as a final cause through whose coercive guidance the complex of phenomena is kept to its appointed task. Under his hands the restraining, compelling agency retires farther into the background, and appeal is taken to it neither so directly nor on so slight provocation.

But Adam Smith is too large a figure to be disposed of in a couple of concluding paragraphs. At the same time his work and the bent which he gave to economic speculation are so intimately bound up with the aims and bias that characterize economics in its next stage of development that he is best dealt with as the point of departure for the Classical School rather than merely as a British counterpart of Physiocracy. Adam Smith will accordingly be considered in immediate connexion with the bias of the Classical School and the incursion of Utilitarianism into economics.

## II

Adam Smith's animistic bent asserts itself more plainly and more effectually in the general trend and aim of his discussion than in the details of theory. "Adam Smith's *Wealth of Nations* is, in fact, so far as it has one single purpose, a vindication of the unconscious law present in the separate actions of men when these actions are directed by a certain strong personal motive." [8] Both in the *Theory of the Moral Sentiments* and in the *Wealth of Nations* there are many passages that testify to his abiding conviction that there is a wholesome trend in the

[8] Bonar, *Philosophy and Political Economy*, pp. 177-8.

natural course of things, and the characteristically optimistic tone in which he speaks for natural liberty is but an expression of this conviction. An extreme resort to this animistic ground occurs in his plea for freedom of investment.[9]

In the proposition that men are "led by an invisible hand," Smith does not fall back on a meddling Providence who is to set human affairs straight when they are in danger of going askew. He conceives the Creator to be very continent in the matter of interference with the natural course of things. The Creator has established the natural order to serve the ends of human welfare; and he has very nicely adjusted the efficient causes comprised in the natural order, including human aims and motives, to this work that they are to accomplish. The guidance of the invisible hand takes place not by way of interposition, but through a comprehensive scheme of contrivances established from the beginning. For the purpose of economic theory, man is conceived to be consistently self-

---

[9] "Every individual is continually exerting himself to find out the most advantageous employment for whatever capital he can command. It is his own advantage, and not that of the society, which he has in view. But the study of his own advantage naturally, or rather necessarily, leads him to prefer that employment which is most advantageous to the society. . . . By directing that industry in such a manner as its produce may be of the greatest value, he intends only his own gain; and he is in this, as in many other cases, led by an invisible hand to promote an end which was no part of his intention. Nor is it always the worse for society that it was no part of it. By pursuing his own interest he frequently promotes that of the society more effectually than when he really intends to promote it."—*Inquiry into the Nature and Causes of the Wealth of Nations*, Book IV, chap. 2.

seeking; but this economic man is a part of the mechanism of nature, and his self-seeking traffic is but a means whereby, in the natural course of things, the general welfare is worked out. The scheme as a whole is guided by the end to be reached, but the sequence of events through which the end is reached is a causal sequence which is not broken into episodically. The benevolent work of guidance was performed in first establishing an ingenious mechanism of forces and motives capable of accomplishing an ordained result, and nothing beyond the enduring constraint of an established trend remains to enforce the divine purpose in the resulting natural course of things.

The sequence of events, including human motives and human conduct, is a causal sequence; but it is also something more, or, rather, there is also another element of continuity besides that of brute cause and effect, present even in the step-by-step process whereby the natural course of things reaches its final term. The presence of such a quasi-spiritual or non-causal element is evident from two (alleged) facts. (1) The course of things may be deflected from the direct line of approach to that consummate human welfare which is its legitimate end. The natural trend of things may be overborne by an untoward conjuncture of causes. There is a distinction, often distressingly actual and persistent, between the legitimate and the observed course of things. If "natural," in Adam Smith's use, meant necessary, in the sense of causally determined, no divergence of events from the natural or legitimate course of things would be possible. If the

mechanism of nature, including man, were a mechanically competent contrivance for achieving the great artificer's design, there could be no such episodes of blunder-
ing and perverse departure from the direct path as
Adam Smith finds in nearly all existing arrangements.
Institutional facts would then be "natural." [10] (2) When
things have gone wrong, they will right themselves if
interference with the natural course ceases; whereas, in
the case of a causal sequence simply, the mere cessation of
interference will not leave the outcome the same as if no
interference had taken place. This recuperative power of
nature is of an extra-mechanical character. The continuity
of sequence by force of which the natural course of things
prevails is, therefore, not of the nature of cause and effect, since it bridges intervals and interruptions in the
causal sequence.[11] Adam Smith's use of the term "real"
in statements of theory—as, for example, "real value,"
"real price" [12]—is evidence to this effect. "Natural" com-

---

[10] The discrepancy between the actual, causally determined situation and the divinely intended consummation is the metaphysical
ground of all that inculcation of morality and enlightened policy that
makes up so large a part of Adam Smith's work. The like, of course,
holds true for all moralists and reformers who proceed on the assumption of a providential order.

[11] "In the political body, however, the wisdom of nature has fortunately made ample provision for remedying many of the bad effects
of the folly and injustice of man; in the same manner as it has done
in the natural body, for remedying those of his sloth and intemperance."—*Wealth of Nations*, Book IV, chap. 9.

[12] E.g., "the real measure of the exchangeable value of all commodities."—*Wealth of Nations*, Book I, chap. 5, and repeatedly in
the like connexion.

monly has the same meaning as "real" in this connexion.[13] Both "natural" and "real" are placed in contrast with the actual; and, in Adam Smith's apprehension, both have a substantiality different from and superior to facts. The view involves a distinction between reality and fact, which survives in a weakened form in the theories of "normal" prices, wages, profits, costs, in Adam Smith's successors.

This animistic prepossession seems to pervade the earlier of his two monumental works in a greater degree than the later. In the *Moral Sentiments* recourse is had to the teleological ground of the natural order more freely and with perceptibly greater insistence. There seems to be reason for holding that the animistic preconception weakened or, at any rate, fell more into the background as his later work of speculation and investigation proceeded. The change shows itself also in some details of his economic theory, as first set forth in the *Lectures*, and afterwards more fully developed in the *Wealth of Nations*. So, for instance, in the earlier presentation of the matter, "the division of labour is the immediate cause of opulence"; and this division of labour, which is the chief

---

[13] E.g., Book I, chap 7: "When the price of any commodity is neither more nor less than what is sufficient to pay the rent of the land, the wages of the labour, and the profits of the stock employed in raising, preparing, and bringing it to market, according to their *natural* rates, the commodity is then sold for what may be called its *natural* price." "The actual price at which any commodity is commonly sold is called its market price. It may be either above or below or exactly the same with its natural price."

condition of economic well-being, "flows from a direct propensity in human nature for one man to barter with another." [14] The "propensity" in question is here appealed to as a natural endowment immediately given to man with a view to the welfare of human society, and without any attempt at further explanation of how man has come by it. No causal explanation of its presence or character is offered. But the corresponding passage of the *Wealth of Nations* handles the question more cautiously. [15] Other parallel passages might be compared, with much the same effect. The guiding hand has withdrawn farther from the range of human vision.

However, these and other like filial expressions of a devout optimism need, perhaps, not be taken as integral features of Adam Smith's economic theory, or as seriously affecting the character of his work as an economist. They are the expression of his general philosophical and theological views, and are significant for the present purpose chiefly as evidences of an animistic and optimistic bent. They go to show what is Adam Smith's accepted

[14] *Lectures of Adam Smith* (ed. Cannan, 1896), p. 169.
[15] "This division of labour, from which so many advantages are derived, is not originally the effect of any human wisdom, which foresees and intends that general opulence to which it gives occasion. It is the necessary though very slow and gradual consequence of a certain propensity in human nature which has in view no such extensive utility—the propensity to truck, barter, and exchange one thing for another. Whether this propensity be one of those original principles in human nature of which no further account can be given, or whether, as seems more probable, it be the necessary consequence of the faculties of reason and speech, it belongs not to our present subject to inquire."—*Wealth of Nations*, Book I, chap. 2.

ground of finality—the ground to which all his speculations on human affairs converge—but they do not in any
great degree show the teleological bias guiding his formulation of economic theory in detail.

The effective working of the teleological bias is best
seen in Smith's more detailed handling of economic phenomena—in his discussion of what may loosely be called
economic institutions—and in the criteria and principles
of procedure by which he is guided in incorporating these
features of economic life into the general structure of his
theory. A fair instance, though perhaps not the most
telling one, is the discussion of the "real and nominal
price," and of the "natural and market price" of commodities, already referred to above.[16] The "real" price
of commodities is their value in terms of human life.
At this point Smith differs from the Physiocrats, with
whom the ultimate terms of value are afforded by human
sustenance taken as a product of the functioning of brute
nature; the cause of the difference being that the Physiocrats conceived the natural order which works towards
the material well-being of man to comprise the non-
human environment only, whereas Adam Smith includes
man in this concept of the natural order, and, indeed,
makes him the central figure in the process of production.
With the Physiocrats, production is the work of nature;
with Adam Smith, it is the work of man and nature, with
man in the foreground. In Adam Smith, therefore, la-

---

[16] *Wealth of Nations*, Book I, chaps. 5–7.

bour is the final term in valuation. This "real" value of
commodities is the value imputed to them by the economist under the stress of his teleological preconception. It
has little, if any, place in the course of economic events,
and no bearing on human affairs, apart from the sentimental influence which such a preconception in favour of
a "real value" in things may exert upon men's notions of
what is the good and equitable course to pursue in their
transactions. It is impossible to gauge this real value of
goods; it cannot be measured or expressed in concrete
terms. Still, if labour exchanges for a varying quantity of
goods, "it is their value which varies, not that of the
labour which purchases them." [17] The values which practically attach to goods in men's handling of them are conceived to be determined without regard to the real value
which Adam Smith imputes to the goods; but, for all that,
the substantial fact with respect to these market values is
their presumed approximation to the real values teleologically imputed to the goods under the guidance of inviolate
natural laws. The real, or natural, value of articles has
no causal relation to the value at which they exchange.
The discussion of how values are determined in practice
runs on the motives of the buyers and sellers, and the relative advantage enjoyed by the parties to the transaction.[18]
It is a discussion of a process of valuation, quite unrelated to the "real," or "natural," price of things, and

[17] Ibid., Book I, chap. 5.
[18] As, e.g., the entire discussion of the determination of Wages,
Profits, and Rent, in Book I, chaps 8–11.

quite unrelated to the grounds on which things are held
to come by their real, or natural, price; and yet, when the
complex process of valuation has been traced out in terms
of human motives and the exigencies of the market, Adam
Smith feels that he has only cleared the ground. He
then turns to the serious business of accounting for value
and price theoretically, and making the ascertained facts
articulate with his teleological theory of economic life.[19]

The occurrence of the words "ordinary" and "average" in this connexion need not be taken too seriously.
The context makes it plain that the equality which commonly subsists between the ordinary or average rates, and
the natural rates, is a matter of coincidence, not of identity. Not only are there temporary deviations, but there
may be a permanent divergence between the ordinary and
the natural price of a commodity; as in case of a monopoly or of produce grown under peculiar circumstances of
soil or climate.[20]

---

[19] "There is in every society or neighbourhood an ordinary or
average rate both of wages and profit in every different employment
of labour and stock. This rate is naturally regulated . . . partly
by the general circumstances of the society. . . . There is, likewise,
in every society or neighbourhood an ordinary or average rate of
rent, which is regulated, too. . . . These ordinary or average rates
may be called the natural rates of wages, profit, and rent, at the
time and place in which they commonly prevail. When the price of
any commodity is neither more nor less than what is sufficient to pay
the rent of the land, the wages of the labour, and the profits of the
stock employed in raising, preparing, and bringing it to market,
according to their natural rates, the commodity is then sold for what
may be called its natural price."—*Wealth of Nations*, Book I, chap. 7.
[20] "Such commodities may continue for whole centuries together

The natural price coincides with the price fixed by competition, because competition means the unimpeded play of those efficient forces through which the nicely adjusted mechanism of nature works out the design to accomplish which it was contrived. The natural price is reached through the free interplay of the factors of production, and it is itself an outcome of production. Nature, including the human factor, works to turn out the goods; and the natural value of the goods is their appraisement from the standpoint of this productive process of nature. Natural value is a category of production; whereas, notoriously, exchange value or market price is a category of distribution. And Adam Smith's theoretical handling of market price aims to show how the factors of human predilection and human wants at work in the higgling of the market bring about a result in passable consonance with the natural laws that are conceived to govern production.

The natural price is a composite result of the blending of the three "component parts of the price of commodities"—the natural wages of labour, the natural profits of stock, and the natural rent of land; and each of these three components is in its turn the measure of the productive effect of the factor to which it pertains. The further discussion of these shares in distribution aims to account for the facts of distribution on the ground of the productivity of the factors which are held to share the

---

to be sold at this high price; and that part of it which resolves itself into the rent of land is, in this case, the part which is generally paid above its natural rate."—Ibid.

product between them. That is to say, Adam Smith's preconception of a productive natural process as the basis of his economic theory dominates his aims and procedure when he comes to deal with phenomena that cannot be stated in terms of production. The causal sequence in the process of distribution is, by Adam Smith's own showing, unrelated to the causal sequence in the process of production; but, since the latter is the substantial fact, as viewed from the standpoint of a teleological natural order, the former must be stated in terms of the latter before Adam Smith's sense of substantiality, or "reality," is satisfied. Something of the same kind is, of course, visible in the Physiocrats and in Cantillon. It amounts to an extension of the natural-rights preconception to economic theory. Adam Smith's discussion of distribution as a function of productivity might be traced in detail through his handling of Wages, Profits, and Rent; but, since the aim here is a brief characterization only, and not an exposition, no farther pursuit of this point seems feasible.

It may, however, be worth while to point out another line of influence along which the dominance of the teleological preconception shows itself in Adam Smith. This is the normalization of data, in order to bring them into consonance with an orderly course of approach to the putative natural end of economic life and development. The result of this normalization of data is, on the one hand, the use of what James Steuart calls "conjectural history" in dealing with past phases of economic life, and, on the other hand, a statement of present-day phenomena in terms of what legitimately ought to be according to the God-given end of life rather than in terms of unconstrued observation. Account is taken of the facts (supposed or observed) ostensibly in terms of causal sequence, but the imputed causal sequence is construed to run on lines of teleological legitimacy.

A familiar instance of this "conjectural history," in a highly and effectively normalized form, is the account of "that early and rude state of society which precedes both the accumulation of stock and the appropriation of land." [21] It is needless at this day to point out that this "early and rude state," in which "the whole produce of labour belongs to the labourer," is altogether a figment. The whole narrative, from the putative origin down, is not only supposititious, but it is merely a schematic presentation of what should have been the course of past development, in order to lead up to that ideal economic situation which would satisfy Adam Smith's preconception.[22] As the narrative comes nearer the region of known latter-day facts, the normalization of the data becomes more difficult and receives more detailed attention; but the change in method is a change of degree rather than of kind. In the "early and rude state" the coincidence of the "natural" and the actual course of events is immediate and undisturbed, there being no refractory data at hand;

---

[21] *Wealth of Nations*, Book I, chap. 6; also chap. 8.
[22] For an instance of how these early phases of industrial development appear, when not seen in the light of Adam Smith's preconception, see, among others, Bücher, *Entstehung der Volkswirtschaft*.

but in the later stages and in the present situation, where refractory facts abound, the co-ordination is difficult, and the coincidence can be shown only by a free abstraction from phenomena that are irrelevant to the teleological trend and by a laborious interpretation of the rest. The facts of modern life are intricate, and lend themselves to statement in the terms of the theory only after they have been subjected to a "higher criticism."

The chapter "Of the Origin and Use of Money" [23] is an elegantly normalized account of the origin and nature of an economic institution, and Adam Smith's further discussion of money runs on the same lines. The origin of money is stated in terms of the purpose which money should legitimately serve in such a community as Adam Smith considered right and good, not in terms of the motives and exigencies which have resulted in the use of money and in the gradual rise of the existing method of payment and accounts. Money is "the great wheel of circulation," which effects the transfer of goods in process of production and the distribution of the finished goods to the consumers. It is an organ of the economic commonwealth rather than an expedient of accounting and a conventional repository of wealth.

It is perhaps superfluous to remark that to the "plain man," who is not concerned with the "natural course of things," in a consummate *Geldwirtschaft*, the money that passes his hand is not a "great wheel of circulation." To

[23] Book I, chap. 4.

the Samoyed, for instance, the reindeer which serves him as unit of value is wealth in the most concrete and tangible form. Much the same is true of coin, or even of bank-notes, in the apprehension of unsophisticated people among ourselves today. And yet it is in terms of the habits and conditions of life of these "plain people" that the development of money will have to be accounted for if it is to be stated in terms of cause and effect.

The few scattered passages already cited may serve to illustrate how Adam Smith's animistic or teleological bent shapes the general structure of his theory and gives it consistency. The principle of definitive formulation in Adam Smith's economic knowledge is afforded by a putative purpose that does not at any point enter causally into the economic life process which he seeks to know. This formative or normative purpose or end is not freely conceived to enter as an efficient agent in the events discussed, or to be in any way consciously present in the process. It can scarcely be taken as an animistic agency engaged in the process. It sanctions the course of things, and gives legitimacy and substance to the sequence of events, so far as this sequence may be made to square with the requirements of the imputed end. It has therefore a ceremonial or symbolical force only, and lends the discussion a ceremonial competency; although with economists who have been in passable agreement with Adam Smith as regards the legitimate end of economic life this ceremonial consistency, or consistency *de jure*, has for many purposes been accepted as the formulation of a causal continuity in the phenomena that have been interpreted in its terms. Elucidations of what normally ought to happen, as a matter of ceremonial necessity, have in this way come to pass for an account of matters of fact.

But, as has already been pointed out, there is much more to Adam Smith's exposition of theory than a formulation of what ought to be. Much of the advance he achieved over his predecessors consists in a larger and more painstaking scrutiny of facts, and a more consistent tracing out of causal continuity in the facts handled. No doubt, his superiority over the Physiocrats, that characteristic of his work by virtue of which it superseded theirs in the farther growth of economic science, lies to some extent in his recourse to a different, more modern ground of normality—a ground more in consonance with the body of preconceptions that have had the vogue in later generations. It is a shifting of the point of view from which the facts are handled; but it comes in great part to a substitution of a new body of preconceptions for the old, or a new adaptation of the old ground of finality, rather than an elimination of all metaphysical or animistic norms of valuation. With Adam Smith, as with the Physiocrats, the fundamental question, the answer to which affords the point of departure and the norm of procedure, is a question of substantiality or economic "reality." With both, the answer to this question is given naïvely, as a deliverance of common-sense. Neither is disturbed by doubts as to this deliverance of common-sense or by any need of scrutinizing it. To the Physiocrats this substantial ground of economic reality is the nutritive process of Nature. To Adam Smith it is Labour. His reality has the advantage of being the deliverance of the common-sense of a more modern community, and one that has maintained itself in force more widely and in better consonance with the facts of latter-day industry. The Physiocrats owe their preconception of the productiveness of nature to the habits of thoughts of a community in whose economic life the dominant phenomenon was the owner of agricultural land. Adam Smith owes his preconception in favour of labour to a community in which the obtrusive economic feature of the immediate past was handicraft and agriculture, with commerce as a scarcely secondary phenomenon.

So far as Adam Smith's economic theories are a tracing out of the causal sequence in economic phenomena, they are worked out in terms given by these two main directions of activity—human effort directed to the shaping of the material means of life, and human effort and discretion directed to a pecuniary gain. The former is the great, substantial productive force; the latter is not immediately, or proximately, productive.[24] Adam Smith still has too lively a sense of the nutritive purpose of the order of nature freely to extend the concept of productiveness to any activity that does not yield a material increase of the creature comforts. His instinctive appreciation of the

---

[24] See Book II, chap. 5, "Of the Different Employment of Capitals."

substantial virtue of whatever effectually furthers nutrition even leads him into the concession that "in agriculture nature labours along with man," although the general tenor of his argument is that the productive force with which the economist always has to count is human labour. This recognized substantiality of labour as productive is, as has already been remarked, accountable for his effort to reduce to terms of productive labour such a category of distribution as exchange value.

With but slight qualification, it will hold that, in the causal sequence which Adam Smith traces out in his economic theories proper (contained in the first three books of the *Wealth of Nations*), the causally efficient factor is conceived to be human nature in these two relations—of productive efficiency and pecuniary gain through exchange. Pecuniary gain—gain in the material means of life through barter—furnishes the motive force to the economic activity of the individual; although productive efficiency is the legitimate, normal end of the community's economic life. To such an extent does this concept of man's seeking his ends through "truck, barter, and exchange" pervade Adam Smith's treatment of economic processes that he even states production in its terms, and says that "labour was the first price, the original purchase-money, that was paid for all things." [25] The

[25] Ibid., Book I, chap. 5. See also the plea for free trade, Book IV, chap. 2: "But the annual revenue of every society is always precisely equal to the exchangeable value of the whole annual produce of its industry, or, rather, is precisely the same thing with that exchangeable value."

human nature engaged in this pecuniary traffic is conceived in somewhat hedonistic terms, and the motives and movements of men are normalized to fit the requirements of a hedonistically conceived order of nature. Men are very much alike in their native aptitudes and propensities; [26] and, so far as economic theory need take account of these aptitudes and propensities, they are aptitudes for the production of the "necessaries and conveniences of life," and propensities to secure as great a share of these creature comforts as may be.

Adam Smith's conception of normal human nature—that is to say, the human factor which enters causally in the process which economic theory discusses—comes, on the whole, to this: Men exert their force and skill in a mechanical process of production, and their pecuniary sagacity in a competitive process of distribution, with a view to individual gain in the material means of life. These material means are sought in order to the satisfaction of men's natural wants through their consumption. It is true, much else enters into men's endeavours in the struggle for wealth, as Adam Smith points out; but this consumption comprises the legitimate range of incentives, and a theory which concerns itself with the natural course of things need take but incidental account of what does not come legitimately in the natural course. In point of fact, there are appreciable "actual," though scarcely "real," departures from this rule. They are spurious and

---

[26] "The difference of natural talents in different men is in reality much less than we are aware of."—Ibid., Book I, chap. 2.

insubstantial departures, and do not properly come within the purview of the stricter theory. And, since human nature is strikingly uniform, in Adam Smith's apprehension, both the efforts put forth and the consumptive effect accomplished may be put in quantitative terms and treated algebraically, with the result that the entire range of phenomena comprised under the head of consumption need be but incidentally considered; and the theory of production and distribution is complete when the goods or the values have been traced to their disappearance in the hands of their ultimate owners. The reflex effect of consumption upon production and distribution is, on the whole, quantitative only.

Adam Smith's preconception of a normal teleological order of procedure in the natural course, therefore, affects not only those features of theory where he is avowedly concerned with building up a normal scheme of the economic process; through his normalizing the chief causal factor engaged in the process, it affects also his arguments from cause to effect.[27] What makes this latter feature worth particular attention is the fact that his successors

---

[27] "Mit diesen philosophischen Ueberzeugungen tritt nun Adam Smith an die Welt der Erfahrung heran, und es ergiebt sich ihm die Richtigkeit der Principien. Der Reiz der Smith'schen Schriften beruht zum grossen Teile darauf, dass Smith die Principien in so innige Verbindung mit dem Thatsächlichen gebracht. Hie und da werden dann auch die Principien, was durch diese Verbindung veranlasst wird, an ihren Spitzen etwas abgeschliffen, ihre allzuscharfe Ausprägung dadurch vermieden. Nichtsdestoweniger aber bleiben sie stets die leitenden Grundgedanken."—Richard Zeyss, *Adam Smith und der Eigennutz* (Tübingen, 1889), p. 110.

carried this normalization farther, and employed it with less frequent reference to the mitigating exceptions which Adam Smith notices by the way.

The reason for that farther and more consistent normalization of human nature which gives us the "economic man" at the hands of Adam Smith's successors lies, in great part, in the utilitarian philosophy that entered in force and in consummate form at about the turning of the century. Some credit in the work of normalization is due also to the farther supersession of handicraft by the "capitalistic" industry that came in at the same time and in pretty close relation with the utilitarian views.

After Adam Smith's day, economics fell into profane hands. Apart from Malthus, who, of all the greater economists, stands nearest to Adam Smith on such metaphysical heads as have an immediate bearing upon the premises of economic science, the next generation do not approach their subject from the point of view of a divinely instituted order; nor do they discuss human interests with that gently optimistic spirit of submission that belongs to the economist who goes to his work with the fear of God before his eyes. Even with Malthus the recourse to the divinely sanctioned order of nature is somewhat sparing and temperate. But it is significant for the later course of economic theory that, while Malthus may well be accounted the truest continuer of Adam Smith, it was the undevout utilitarians that became the spokesmen of the science after Adam Smith's time.

There is no wide breach between Adam Smith and the utilitarians, either in details of doctrine or in the concrete conclusions arrived at as regards questions of policy. On these heads Adam Smith might well be classed as a moderate utilitarian, particularly so far as regards his economic work. Malthus has still more of a utilitarian air— so much so, indeed, that he is not infrequently spoken of as a utilitarian. This view, convincingly set forth by Mr. Bonar,[28] is no doubt well borne out by a detailed scrutiny of Malthus's economic doctrines. His humanitarian bias is evident throughout, and his weakness for considerations of expediency is the great blemish of his scientific work. But, for all that, in order to an appreciation of the change that came over classical economics with the rise of Benthamism, it is necessary to note that the agreement in this matter between Adam Smith and the disciples of Bentham, and less decidedly that between Malthus and the latter, is a coincidence of conclusions rather than an identity of preconceptions.[29]

With Adam Smith the ultimate ground of economic reality is the design of God, the teleological order; and

[28] See, e.g., *Malthus and his Work*, especially Book III, as also the chapter on Malthus in *Philosophy and Political Economy*, Book III, "Modern Philosophy: Utilitarian Economics," chap. 1, "Malthus."

[29] Ricardo is here taken as a utilitarian of the Benthamite colour, although he cannot be classed as a disciple of Bentham. His hedonism is but the uncritically accepted metaphysics comprised in the common-sense of his time, and his substantial coincidence with Bentham goes to show how well diffused the hedonist preconception was at the time.

his utilitarian generalizations, as well as the hedonistic character of his economic man, are but methods of the working out of this natural order, not the substantial and self-legitimating ground. Shifty as Malthus's metaphysics are, much the same is to be said for him.[30] Of the utilitarians proper the converse is true, although here, again, there is by no means utter consistency. The substantial economic ground is pleasure and pain; the teleological order (even the design of God, where that is admitted) is the method of its working-out.

It may be unnecessary here to go into the farther implications, psychological and ethical, which this preconception of the utilitarians involves. And even this much may seem a taking of excessive pains with a distinction that marks no tangible difference. But a reading of the classical doctrines, with something of this metaphysics of political economy in mind, will show how, and in great part why, the later economists of the classical line diverged from Adam Smith's tenets in the early years of the century, until it has been necessary to interpret Adam Smith somewhat shrewdly in order to save him from heresy.

The post-Bentham economics is substantially a theory of value. This is altogether the dominant feature of the body of doctrines; the rest follows from, or is adapted to, this central discipline. The doctrine of value is of very great importance also in Adam Smith; but Adam

---

[30] Cf. Bonar, *Malthus and his Work*, pp. 323–36.

Smith's economics is a theory of the production and apportionment of the material means of life.[31] With Adam Smith, value is discussed from the point of view of production. With the utilitarians, production is discussed from the point of view of value. The former makes value an outcome of the process of production; the latter make production the outcome of a valuation process.

The point of departure with Adam Smith is the "productive power of labour."[32] With Ricardo it is a pecuniary problem concerned in the distribution of ownership;[33] but the classical writers are followers of Adam Smith, and improve upon and correct the results arrived at by him, and the difference of point of view, therefore, becomes evident in their divergence from him, and the different distribution of emphasis, rather than in a new and antagonistic departure.

The reason for this shifting of the centre of gravity from production to valuation lies, proximately, in Bentham's revision of the "principles" of morals. Ben-

---

[31] His work is an "Inquiry into the Nature and Causes of the Wealth of Nations."

[32] "The annual labour of every nation is the fund which originally supplies it with all the necessaries and conveniences of life which it annually consumes, and which consists always either in the immediate produce of that labour or in what is purchased with that produce from other nations."—*Wealth of Nations*, "Introduction and Plan," opening paragraph.

[33] "The produce of the earth—all that is derived from its surface by the united application of labour, machinery, and capital—is divided among three classes of the community. . . . To determine the laws which regulate this distribution, is the principal problem of political economy."—*Political Economy*, Preface.

tham's philosophical position is, of course, not a self-explanatory phenomenon, nor does the effect of Benthamism extend only to those who are avowed followers of Bentham; for Bentham is the exponent of a cultural change that affects the habits of thought of the entire community. The immediate point of Bentham's work, as affecting the habits of thought of the educated community, is the substitution of hedonism (utility) in place of achievement of purpose, as a ground of legitimacy and a guide in the normalization of knowledge. Its effect is most patent in speculations on morals, where it inculcates determinism. Its close connexion with determinism in ethics points the way to what may be expected of its working in economics. In both cases the result is that human action is construed in terms of the causal forces of the environment, the human agent being, at the best, taken as a mechanism of commutation, through the workings of which the sensuous effects wrought by the impinging forces of the environment are, by an enforced process of valuation, transmuted without quantitative discrepancy into moral or economic conduct, as the case may be. In ethics and economics alike the subject-matter of the theory is this valuation process that expresses itself in conduct, resulting, in the case of economic conduct, in the pursuit of the greatest gain or least sacrifice.

Metaphysically or cosmologically considered, the human nature into the emotions of which hedonistic ethics and economics inquire is an intermediate term in a causal sequence, of which the initial and the terminal members are sensuous impressions and the details of conduct. This intermediate term conveys the sensuous impulse without loss of force to its eventuation in conduct. For the purpose of the valuation process through which the impulse is so conveyed, human nature may, therefore, be accepted as uniform; and the theory of the valuation process may be formulated quantitatively, in terms of the material forces affecting the human sensory and of their equivalents in the resulting activity. In the language of economics, the theory of value may be stated in terms of the consumable goods that afford the incentive to effort and the expenditure undergone in order to procure them. Between these two there subsists a necessary equality; but the magnitudes between which the equality subsists are hedonistic magnitudes, not magnitudes of kinetic energy nor of vital force, for the terms handled are sensuous terms. It is true, since human nature is substantially uniform, passive, and unalterable in respect of men's capacity for sensuous affection, there may also be presumed to subsist a substantial equality between the psychological effect to be wrought by the consumption of goods, on the one side, and the resulting expenditure of kinetic or vital force, on the other side; but such an equality is, after all, of the nature of a coincidence, although there should be a strong presumption in favour of its prevailing on an average and in the common run of cases. Hedonism, however, does not postulate uniformity between men except in the respect of sensuous cause and effect.

The theory of value which hedonism gives is, therefore, a theory of cost in terms of discomfort. By virtue of the hedonistic equilibrium reached through the valuation process, the sacrifice or expenditure of sensuous reality involved in acquisition is the equivalent of the sensuous gain secured. An alternative statement might perhaps be made, to the effect that the measure of the value of goods is not the sacrifice or discomfort undergone, but the sensuous gain that accrues from the acquisition of the goods; but this is plainly only an alternative statement, and there are special reasons in the economic life of the time why the statement in terms of cost, rather than in terms of "utility," should commend itself to the earlier classical economists.

On comparing the utilitarian doctrine of value with earlier theories, then, the case stands somewhat as follows. The Physiocrats and Adam Smith contemplate value as a measure of the productive force that realizes itself in the valuable article. With the Physiocrats this productive force is the "anabolism" of Nature (to resort to a physiological term); with Adam Smith it is chiefly human labour directed to heightening the serviceability of the materials with which it is occupied. Production causes value in either case. The post-Bentham economics contemplates value as a measure of, or as measured by, the irksomeness of the effort involved in procuring the valuable goods. As Mr. E. C. K. Gonner has admirably pointed out,[34] Ricardo—and the like holds true of classi-

[34] In the introductory essay to his edition of Ricardo's *Political Economy*. See, e.g., paragraphs 9 and 24.

cal economics generally—makes cost the foundation of value, not its cause. This resting of value on cost takes place through a valuation. Anyone who will read Adam Smith's theoretical exposition to as good purpose as Mr. Gonner has read Ricardo will scarcely fail to find that the converse is true in Adam Smith's case. But the causal relation of cost to value holds only as regards "natural" or "real" value in Adam Smith's doctrine. As regards market price, Adam Smith's theory does not differ greatly from that of Ricardo on this head. He does not overlook the valuation process by which market price is adjusted and the course of investment is guided, and his discussion of this process runs in terms that should be acceptable to any hedonist.

The shifting of the point of view that comes into economics with the acceptance of utilitarian ethics and its correlate, the associationist psychology, is in great part a shifting to the ground of causal sequence as contrasted with that of serviceability to a preconceived end. This is indicated even by the main fact already cited—that the utilitarian economists make exchange value the central feature of their theories, rather than the conduciveness of industry to the community's material welfare. Hedonistic exchange value is the outcome of a valuation process enforced by the apprehended pleasure-giving capacities of the items valued. And in the utilitarian theories of production, arrived at from the standpoint so

given by exchange value, the conduciveness to welfare is
not the objective point of the argument. This objective
point is rather the bearing of productive enterprise upon
the individual fortunes of the agents engaged, or upon
the fortunes of the several distinguishable classes of
beneficiaries comprised in the industrial community; for
the great immediate bearing of exchange values upon the
life of the collectivity is their bearing upon the distribution of wealth. Value is a category of distribution. The
result is that, as is well shown by Mr. Cannan's discussion,[35] the theories of production offered by the classical
economists have been sensibly scant, and have been carried out with a constant view to the doctrines on distribution. An incidental but telling demonstration of
the same facts is given by Professor Bücher; [36] and in
illustration may be cited Torrens's *Essay on the Production of Wealth*, which is to a good extent occupied with
discussions of value and distribution. The classical theories
of production have been theories of the production of
"wealth"; and "wealth," in classical usage, consists of
material things having exchange value. During the vogue
of the classical economics the accepted characteristic by
which "wealth" has been defined has been its amenability
to ownership. Neither in Adam Smith nor in the Physiocrats is this amenability to ownership made so much of,

---

[35] *Theories of Production and Distribution*, 1776–1848.
[36] *Entstehung der Volkswirtschaft* (second edition). Cf. especially
chaps. 2, 3, 6, and 7.

nor is it in a similar degree accepted as a definite mark of the subject-matter of the science.

As their hedonistic preconception would require, then, it is to the pecuniary side of life that the classical economists give their most serious attention, and it is the pecuniary bearing of any given phenomenon or of any institution that commonly shapes the issue of the argument. The causal sequence about which the discussion centres is a process of pecuniary valuation. It runs on distribution, ownership, acquisition, gain, investment, exchange.[37] In this way the doctrines on production come to take a pecuniary colouring; as is seen in a less degree also in Adam Smith, and even in the Physiocrats, although these earlier economists very rarely, if ever, lose touch with the concept of generic serviceability as the characteristic feature of production. The tradition derived from Adam Smith, which made productivity and serviceability the substantial features of economic life, was not abruptly put aside by his successors, though the emphasis was differently distributed by them in following out the line of investigation to which the tradition pointed the way. In the classical economics the ideas of production and of acquisition are not commonly held apart, and

---

[37] "Even if we put aside all questions which involve a consideration of the effects of industrial institutions in modifying the habits and character of the classes of the community . . . that enough still remains to constitute a separate science, the mere enumeration of the chief terms of economics—wealth, value, exchange, credit, money, capital, and commodity—will suffice to show."—Shirres, *Analysis of the Ideas of Economics* (London, 1893), pp. 8 and 9.

very much of what passes for a theory of production is occupied with phenomena of investment and acquisition. Torrens's *Essay* is a case in point, though by no means an extreme case.

This is as it should be; for to the consistent hedonist the sole motive force concerned in the industrial process is the self-regarding motive of pecuniary gain, and industrial activity is but an intermediate term between the expenditure or discomfort undergone and the pecuniary gain sought. Whether the end and outcome is an invidious gain for the individual (in contrast with or at the cost of his neighbours), or an enhancement of the facility of human life on the whole, is altogether a by-question in any discussion of the range of incentives by which men are prompted to their work or the direction which their efforts take. The serviceability of the given line of activity, for the life purposes of the community or for one's neighbours, "is not of the essence of this contract." These features of serviceability come into the account chiefly as affecting the vendibility of what the given individual has to offer in seeking gain through a bargain.[38]

In hedonistic theory the substantial end of economic life is individual gain; and for this purpose production and acquisition may be taken as fairly coincident, if not identical. Moreover, society, in the utilitarian philosophy,

---

[38] "If a commodity were in no way useful . . . it would be destitute of exchangeable value . . . (but), possessing utility, commodities derive their exchangeable value from two sources," etc.— Ricardo, *Political Economy*, chap. i, sect. i.

is the algebraic sum of the individuals; and the interest of the society is the sum of the interests of the individuals. It follows by easy consequence, whether strictly true or not, that the sum of individual gains is the gain of the society, and that, in serving his own interest in the way of acquisition, the individual serves the collective interest of the community. Productivity or serviceability is, therefore, to be presumed of any occupation or enterprise that looks to a pecuniary gain; and so, by a roundabout path, we get back to the ancient conclusion of Adam Smith, that the remuneration of classes or persons engaged in industry coincides with their productive contribution to the output of services and consumable goods.

A felicitous illustration of the working of this hedonistic norm in classical economic doctrine is afforded by the theory of the wages of superintendence—an element in distribution which is not much more than suggested in Adam Smith, but which receives ampler and more painstaking attention as the classical body of doctrines reaches a fuller development. The "wages of superintendence" are the gains due to pecuniary management. They are the gains that come to the director of the "business"— not those that go to the director of the mechanical process or to the foreman of the shop. The latter are wages simply. This distinction is not altogether clear in the earlier writers, but it is clearly enough contained in the fuller development of the theory.

The undertaker's work is the management of investment. It is altogether of a pecuniary character, and its proximate aim is "the main chance." If it leads, indirectly, to an enhancement of serviceability or a heightened aggregate output of consumable goods, that is a fortuitous circumstance incident to that heightened vendibility on which the investor's gain depends. Yet the classical doctrine says frankly that the wages of superintendence are the remuneration of superior productivity,[39] and the classical theory of production is in good part a doctrine of investment in which the identity of production and pecuniary gain is taken for granted.

The substitution of investment in the place of industry as the central and substantial fact in the process of production is due not to the acceptance of hedonism simply, but rather to the conjunction of hedonism with an economic situation of which the investment of capital and its management for gain was the most obvious feature. The situation which shaped the common-sense apprehension of economic facts at the time was what has since been called a capitalistic system, in which pecuniary enterprise and the phenomena of the market were the dominant and tone-giving facts. But this economic situation was also

[39] Cf., for instance, Senior, *Political Economy* (London, 1872), particularly pp. 88–9 and 130–5, where the wages of superintendence are, somewhat reluctantly, classed under profits; and the work of superintendence is thereupon conceived as being, immediately or remotely, an exercise of "abstinence" and a productive work. The illustration of the bill-broker is particularly apt. The like view of the wages of superintendence is an article of theory with more than one of the later descendants of the classical line.

the chief ground for the vogue of hedonism in economics; so that hedonistic economics may be taken as an interpretation of human nature in terms of the market-place. The market and the "business world," to which the business man in his pursuit of gain was required to adapt his motives, had by this time grown so large that the course of business events was beyond the control of any one person; and at the same time those far-reaching organizations of invested wealth which have latterly come to prevail and to coerce the market were not then in the foreground. The course of market events took its passionless way without traceable relation or deference to any man's convenience and without traceable guidance towards an ulterior end. Man's part in this pecuniary world was to respond with alacrity to the situation, and so adapt his vendible effects to the shifting demand as to realize something in the outcome. What he gained in his traffic was gained without loss to those with whom he dealt, for they paid no more than the goods were worth to them. One man's gain need not be another's loss; and, if it is not, then it is net gain to the community.

Among the striking remoter effects of the hedonistic preconception, and its working out in terms of pecuniary gain, is the classical failure to discriminate between capital as investment and capital as industrial appliances. This is, of course, closely related to the point already spoken of. The appliances of industry further the production of goods, therefore capital (invested wealth) is productive; and the rate of its average remuneration marks the de-

gree of its productiveness.[40] The most obvious fact limiting the pecuniary gain secured by means of invested
wealth is the sum invested. Therefore, capital limits the
productiveness of industry; and the chief and indispensable condition to an advance in material well-being is
the accumulation of invested wealth. In discussing the
conditions of industrial improvement, it is usual to assume
that "the state of the arts remains unchanged," which is,
for all purposes but that of a doctrine of profits per cent,
an exclusion of the main fact. Investments may, further,
be transferred from one enterprise to another. Therefore, and in that degree, the means of production are
"mobile."

Under the hands of the great utilitarian writers, therefore, political economy is developed into a science of
wealth, taking that term in the pecuniary sense, as things
amenable to ownership. The course of things in economic life is treated as a sequence of pecuniary events,
and economic theory becomes a theory of what should
happen in that consummate situation where the permutation of pecuniary magnitudes takes place without disturbance and without retardation. In this consummate
situation the pecuniary motive has its perfect work, and
guides all the acts of economic man in a guileless, colour-

---

[40] Cf. Böhm-Bawerk, *Capital and Interest*, Books II and IV, as
well as the Introduction and chaps. 4 and 5 of Book I. Böhm-
Bawerk's discussion bears less immediately on the present point than
the similarity of the terms employed would suggest.

less, unswerving quest of the greatest gain at the least
sacrifice. Of course, this perfect competitive system, with
its untainted "economic man," is a feat of the scientific
imagination, and is not intended as a competent expression of fact. It is an expedient of abstract reasoning; and
its avowed competency extends only to the abstract principles, the fundamental laws of the science, which hold
only so far as the abstraction holds. But, as happens in
such cases, having once been accepted and assimilated
as real, though perhaps not as actual, it becomes an effective constituent in the inquirer's habits of thought, and
goes to shape his knowledge of facts. It comes to serve
as a norm of substantiality or legitimacy; and facts in
some degree fall under its constraint, as is exemplified by
many allegations regarding the "tendency" of things.

   To this consummation, which Senior speaks of as "the
natural state of man," [41] human development tends by
force of the hedonistic character of human nature; and in
terms of its approximation to this natural state, therefore,
the immature actual situation had best be stated. The
pure theory, the "hypothetical science" of Cairnes, "traces
the phenomena of the production and distribution of
wealth up to their causes, in the principles of human
nature and the laws and events—physical, political, and
social—of the external world." [42] But since the principles

[41] *Political Economy*, p. 87.
[42] *Character and Logical Method of Political Economy* (New
York, 1875), p. 71. Cairnes may not be altogether representative of
the high tide of classicism, but his characterization of the science is
none the less to the point.

of human nature that give the outcome in men's economic conduct, so far as it touches the production and
distribution of wealth, are but the simple and constant
sequence of hedonistic cause and effect, the element of
human nature may fairly be eliminated from the problem,
with great gain in simplicity and expedition. Human
nature being eliminated, as being a constant intermediate
term, and all institutional features of the situation being
also eliminated (as being similar constants under that
natural or consummate pecuniary regime with which the
pure theory is concerned), the laws of the phenomena of
wealth may be formulated in terms of the remaining factors. These factors are the vendible items that men handle
in these processes of production and distribution; and
economic laws come, therefore, to be expressions of the
algebraic relations subsisting between the various elements of wealth and investment—capital, labour, land,
supply and demand of one and the other, profits, interest,
wages. Even such items as credit and population become
dissociated from the personal factor, and figure in the
computation as elemental factors acting and reacting
through a permutation of values over the heads of the
good people whose welfare they are working out.

To sum up: the classical economics, having primarily
to do with the pecuniary side of life, is a theory of a
process of valuation. But since the human nature at
whose hands and for whose behoof the valuation takes
place is simple and constant in its reaction to pecuniary

stimulus, and since no other feature of human nature is legitimately present in economic phenomena than this re-action to pecuniary stimulus, the valuer concerned in the matter is to be overlooked or eliminated; and the theory of the valuation process then becomes a theory of the pecuniary interaction of the facts valued. It is a theory of valuation with the element of valuation left out—a theory of life stated in terms of the normal paraphernalia of life.

In the preconceptions with which classical economics set out were comprised the remnants of natural rights and of the order of nature, infused with that peculiarly mechanical natural theology that made its way into popular vogue on British ground during the eighteenth century and was reduced to a neutral tone by the British penchant for the commonplace—stronger at this time than at any earlier period. The reason for this growing penchant for the commonplace, for the explanation of things in causal terms, lies partly in the growing resort to mechanical processes and mechanical prime movers in industry, partly in the (consequent) continued decline of the aristocracy and the priesthood, and partly in the growing density of population and the consequent greater specialization and wider organization of trade and business. The spread of the discipline of the natural sciences, largely incident to the mechanical industry, counts in the same direction; and obscurer factors in modern culture may have had their share.

The animistic preconception was not lost, but it lost

tone; and it partly fell into abeyance, particularly so far as regards its avowal. It is visible chiefly in the unavowed readiness of the classical writers to accept as imminent and definitive any possible outcome which the writer's habit or temperament inclined him to accept as right and good. Hence the visible inclination of classical economists to a doctrine of the harmony of interests, and their somewhat uncircumspect readiness to state their generalizations in terms of what ought to happen according to the ideal requirements of that consummate *Geldwirtschaft* to which men "are impelled by the provisions of nature." [43] By virtue of their hedonistic preconceptions, their habituation to the ways of a pecuniary culture, and their unavowed animistic faith that nature is in the right, the classical economists knew that the consummation to which, in the nature of things, all things tend, is the frictionless and beneficent competitive system. This competitive ideal, therefore, affords the normal, and conformity to its requirements affords the test of absolute economic truth. The standpoint so gained selectively guides the attention of the classical writers in their observation and apprehension of facts, and they come to see evidence of conformity or approach to the normal in the most unlikely places. Their observation is, in great part, interpretative, as observation commonly is. What is peculiar to the classical economists in this respect is their particular norm of procedure in the work of interpreta-

---

[43] Senior, *Political Economy*, p. 87.

tion. And, by virtue of having achieved a standpoint of absolute economic normality, they became a "deductive" school, so called, in spite of the patent fact that they were pretty consistently employed with an inquiry into the causal sequence of economic phenomena.

The generalization of observed facts becomes a normalization of them, a statement of the phenomena in terms of their coincidence with, or divergence from, that normal tendency that makes for the actualization of the absolute economic reality. This absolute or definitive ground of economic legitimacy lies beyond the causal sequence in which the observed phenomena are conceived to be interlinked. It is related to the concrete facts neither as cause nor as effect in any such way that the causal relation may be traced in a concrete instance. It has little causally to do either with the "mental" or with the "physical" data with which the classical economist is avowedly employed. Its relation to the process under discussion is that of an extraneous—that is to say, a ceremonial—legitimation. The body of knowledge gained by its help and under its guidance is, therefore, a taxonomic science.

So, by way of a concluding illustration, it may be pointed out that money, for instance, is normalized in terms of the legitimate economic tendency. It becomes a measure of value and a medium of exchange. It has become primarily an instrument of pecuniary commutation, instead of being, as under the earlier normalization of Adam Smith, primarily a great wheel of circulation for the diffusion of consumable goods. The terms in which the laws of money, as of the other phenomena of pecuniary life, are formulated, are terms which connote its normal function in the life-history of objective values as they live and move and have their being in the consummate pecuniary situation of the "natural" state. To a similar work of normalization we owe those creatures of the myth-maker, the quantity theory and the wages-fund.

## III

In what has already been said, it has appeared that the changes which have supervened in the preconceptions of the earlier economists constitute a somewhat orderly succession. The feature of chief interest in this development has been a gradual change in the received grounds of finality to which the successive generations of economists have brought their theoretical output, on which they have been content to rest their conclusions, and beyond which they have not been moved to push their analysis of events or their scrutiny of phenomena. There has been a fairly unbroken sequence of development in what may be called the canons of economic reality; or, to put it in other words, there has been a precession of the point of view from which facts have been handled and valued for the purpose of economic science.

The notion which has in its time prevailed so widely, that there is in the sequence of events a consistent trend which it is the office of the science to ascertain and turn to account—this notion may be well founded or not. But that there is something of such a consistent trend in the sequence of the canons of knowledge under whose guidance the scientist works is not only a generalization from the past course of things, but lies in the nature of the case; for the canons of knowledge are of the nature of habits of thought, and habit does not break with the past, nor do the hereditary aptitudes that find expression in habit vary gratuitously with the mere lapse of time. What is true in this respect, for instance, in the domain of law and institutions is true, likewise, in the domain of science. What men have learned to accept as good and definitive for the guidance of conduct and of human relations remains true and definitive and unimpeachable until the exigencies of a later, altered situation enforce a variation from the norms and canons of the past, and so give rise to a modification of the habits of thought that decide what is, for the time, right in human conduct. So in science the ancient ground of finality remains a good and valid test of scientific truth until the altered exigencies of later life enforce habits of thought that are not wholly in consonance with the received notions as to what constitutes the ultimate, self-legitimating term—the substantial reality—to which knowledge in any given case must penetrate.

This ultimate term or ground of knowledge is always of a metaphysical character. It is something in the way of a preconception, accepted uncritically, but applied in criticism and demonstration of all else with which the science is concerned. So soon as it comes to be criticized, it is in a way to be superseded by a new, more or less altered formulation; for criticism of it means that it is no longer fit to survive unaltered in the altered complex of habits of thought to which it is called upon to serve as fundamental principle. It is subject to natural selection and selective adaptation, as are other conventions. The underlying metaphysics of scientific research and purpose, therefore, changes gradually and, of course, incompletely, much as is the case with the metaphysics underlying the common law and the schedule of civil rights. As in the legal framework the now avowedly useless and meaningless preconceptions of status and caste and precedent are even yet at the most metamorphosed and obsolescent rather than overpassed—witness the facts of inheritance, vested interests, the outlawry of debts through lapse of time, the competence of the State to coerce individuals into support of a given policy—so in the science the living generation has not seen an abrupt and traceless disappearance of the metaphysics that fixed the point of view of the early classical political economy. This is true even for those groups of economists who have most incontinently protested against the absurdity of the classical doctrines and methods. In Professor Marshall's words, "There has been no real breach of continuity in the development of the science."

But, while there has been no breach, there has none the less been change—more far-reaching change than some of us are glad to recognize; for who would not be glad to read his own modern views into the convincing words of the great masters?

Seen through modern eyes and without effort to turn past gains to modern account, the metaphysical or preconceptional furniture of political economy as it stood about the middle of this century may come to look quite curious. The two main canons of truth on which the science proceeded, and with which the inquiry is here concerned, were: (*a*) a hedonistic-associational psychology, and (*b*) an uncritical conviction that there is a meliorative trend in the course of events, apart from the conscious ends of the individual members of the community. This axiom of a meliorative developmental trend fell into shape as a belief in an organic or quasi-organic (physiological) [44] life process on the part of the economic community or of the nation; and this belief carried with it something of a constraining sense of self-realizing cycles of growth, maturity, and decay in the life-history of nations or communities.

Neglecting what may for the immediate purpose be negligible in this outline of fundamental tenets, it will bear the following construction: (*a*) On the ground of the hedonistic or associational psychology, all spiritual continuity and any consequent teleological trend is tacitly denied so far as regards individual conduct, where the later psychology, and the sciences which build on this

---

[44] So, e.g., Roscher, Comte, the early socialists, J. S. Mill, and later Spencer, Schaeffle, Wagner.

later psychology, insist upon and find such a teleological trend at every turn. (*b*) Such a spiritual or quasi-spiritual continuity and teleological trend is uncritically affirmed as regards the non-human sequence or the sequence of events in the affairs of collective life, where the modern sciences diligently assert that nothing of the kind is discernible, or that, if it is discernible, its recognition is beside the point, so far as concerns the purposes of the science.

This position, here outlined with as little qualification as may be admissible, embodies the general metaphysical ground of that classical political economy that affords the point of departure for Mill and Cairnes, and also for Jevons. And what is to be said of Mill and Cairnes in this connexion will apply to the later course of the science, though with a gradually lessening force.

By the middle of the century the psychological premises of the science are no longer so neat and succinct as they were in the days of Bentham and James Mill. At J. S. Mill's hands, for instance, the naïvely quantitative hedonism of Bentham is being supplanted by a sophisticated hedonism, which makes much of an assumed qualitative divergence between the different kinds of pleasures that afford the motives of conduct. This revision of hedonistic dogma, of course, means a departure from the strict hedonistic ground. Correlated with this advance, more closely in the substance of the change than in the assignable dates, is a concomitant improvement—at least, set forth as an improvement—upon the received associational psychology, whereby "similarity" is brought in to supplement "contiguity" as a ground of connexion between ideas. This change is well shown in the work of J. S. Mill and Bain. In spite of all the ingenuity spent in maintaining the associational legitimacy of this new article of theory, it remains a patent innovation and a departure from the ancient standpoint. As is true of the improved hedonism, so it is true of the new theory of association that it is no longer able to construe the process which it discusses as a purely mechanical process, a concatenation of items simply. Similarity of impressions implies a comparison of impressions by the mind in which the association takes place, and thereby it implies some degree of constructive work on the part of the perceiving subject. The perceiver is thereby construed to be an agent in the work of perception; therefore, he must be possessed of a point of view and an end dominating the perceptive process. To perceive the similarity, he must be guided by an interest in the outcome, and must "attend." The like applies to the introduction of qualitative distinctions into the hedonistic theory of conduct. Apperception in the one case and discretion in the other cease to be the mere registration of a simple and personally uncoloured sequence of permutations enforced by the factors of the external world. There is implied a spiritual—that is to say, active—"teleological" continuity of process on the part of the perceiving or of the discretionary agent, as the case may be.

It is on the ground of their departure from the stricter hedonistic premises that Mill and, after him, Cairnes are able, for instance, to offer their improvement upon the earlier doctrine of cost of production as determining value. Since it is conceived that the motives which guide men in their choice of employments and of domicile differ from man to man and from class to class, not only in degree, but in kind, and since varying antecedents, of heredity and of habit, variously influence men in their choice of a manner of life, therefore the mere quantitative pecuniary stimulus cannot be depended on to decide the outcome without recourse. There are determinable variations in the alacrity with which different classes or communities respond to the pecuniary stimulus; and in so far as this condition prevails, the classes or communities in question are non-competing. Between such non-competing groups the norm that determines values is not the unmitigated norm of cost of production taken absolutely, but only taken relatively. The formula of cost of production is therefore modified into a formula of reciprocal demand. This revision of the cost-of-production doctrine is extended only sparingly, and the emphasis is thrown on the pecuniary circumstances on which depend the formation and maintenance of non-competing groups. Consistency with the earlier teaching is carefully maintained, so far as may be; but extra-pecuniary factors are, after all, even if reluctantly, admitted into the body of the theory. So also, since there are higher and lower motives, higher and lower pleasures—as well as motives differing in degree—it follows that an unguided response even to the mere quantitative pecuniary stimuli may take different directions, and so may result in activities of widely differing outcome. Since activities set up in this way through appeal to higher and lower motives are no longer conceived to represent simply a mechanically adequate effect of the stimuli, working under the control of natural laws that tend to one beneficent consummation, therefore the outcome of activity set up even by the normal pecuniary stimuli may take a form that may or may not be serviceable to the community. Hence *laissez-faire* ceases to be a sure remedy for the ills of society. Human interests are still conceived normally to be at one; but the detail of individual conduct need not, therefore, necessarily serve these generic human interests.[45] Therefore, other inducements than the unmitigated impact of pecuniary exigencies may be necessary to bring about a coincidence of class or individual endeavour with the interests of the community. It becomes incumbent on the advocate of *laissez-faire* to "prove his minor premise." It is no longer self-evident that: "Interests left to themselves tend to harmonious combinations, and to the progressive preponderance of the general good." [46]

[45] "Let us not confound the statement that *human* interests are at one with the statement that *class* interests are at one. The latter I believe to be as false as the former is true. . . . But accepting the major premises of the syllogism, that the interests of human beings are fundamentally the same, how as to the minor?—how as to the assumption that people know their interests in the sense in which they are identical with the interests of others, and that they spontaneously follow them *in this sense?*"—Cairnes, *Essays in Political Economy* (London, 1873), p. 245. This question cannot consistently be asked by an adherent of the stricter hedonism.

[46] Bastiat, quoted by Cairnes, *Essays*, p. 319.

The natural-rights preconception begins to fall away as soon as the hedonistic mechanics have been seriously tampered with. Fact and right cease to coincide, because the individual in whom the rights are conceived to inhere has come to be something more than the field of intersection of natural forces that work out in human conduct. The mechanics of natural liberty—that assumed constitution of things by force of which the free hedonistic play of the laws of nature across the open field of individual choice is sure to reach the right outcome—is the hedonistic psychology; and the passing of the doctrine of natural rights and natural liberty, whether as a premise or as a dogma, therefore coincides with the passing of that mechanics of conduct on the validity of which the theoretical acceptance of the dogma depends. It is, therefore, something more than a coincidence that the half-century which has seen the disintegration of the hedonistic faith and of the associational psychology has also seen the dissipation, in scientific speculations, of the concomitant faith in natural rights and in that benign order of nature of which the natural-rights dogma is a corollary.

It is, of course, not hereby intended to say that the later psychological views and premises imply a less close dependence of conduct on environment than do the earlier ones. Indeed, the reverse may well be held to be true. The pervading characteristic of later thinking is the constant recourse to a detailed analysis of phenomena in causal terms. The modern catchword, in the present connexion, is "response to stimulus"; but the manner in which this response is conceived has changed. The fact, and ultimately the amplitude, at least in great part, of the reaction to stimulus, is conditioned by the forces in impact; but the constitution of the organism, as well as its attitude at the moment of impact, in great part decides what will serve as a stimulus, as well as what the manner and direction of the response will be.

The later psychology is biological, as contrasted with the metaphysical psychology of hedonism. It does not conceive the organism as a causal hiatus. The causal sequence in the "reflex arc" is, no doubt, continuous; but the continuity is not, as formerly, conceived in terms of spiritual substance transmitting a shock: it is conceived in terms of the life activity of the organism. Human conduct, taken as the reaction of such an organism under stimulus, may be stated in terms of tropism, involving, of course, a very close-knit causal sequence between the impact and the response, but at the same time imputing to the organism a habit of life and a self-directing and selective attention in meeting the complex of forces that make up its environment. The selective play of his tropismatic complex that constitutes the organism's habit of life under the impact of the forces of the environment counts as discretion.

So far, therefore, as it is to be placed in contrast with the hedonistic phase of the older psychological doctrines, the characteristic feature of the newer conception is the recognition of a selectively self-directing life process in the agent. While hedonism seeks the causal determinant of conduct in the (probable) outcome of action, the later conception seeks this determinant in the complex of propensities that constitutes man a functioning agent, that is to say, a personality. Instead of pleasure ultimately determining what human conduct shall be, the tropismatic propensities that eventuate in conduct ultimately determine what shall be pleasurable. For the purpose in hand, the consequence of the transition to the altered conception of human nature and its relation to the environment is that the newer view formulates conduct in terms of personality, whereas the earlier view was content to formulate it in terms of its provocation and its by-product. Therefore, for the sake of brevity, the older preconceptions of the science are here spoken of as construing human nature in inert terms, as contrasted with the newer, which construes it in terms of functioning.

It has already appeared above that the second great article of the metaphysics of classical political economy—the belief in a meliorative trend or a benign order of nature—is closely connected with the hedonistic conception of human nature; but this connexion is more intimate and organic than appears from what has been said above. The two are so related as to stand or fall together, for the latter is but the obverse of the former. The doctrine of a trend in events imputes purpose to the sequence of events; that is, it invests this sequence with a discretionary, teleological character, which asserts itself in a constraint over all the steps in the sequence by which the supposed objective point is reached. But discretion touching a given end must be single, and must alone cover all the acts by which the end is to be reached. Therefore, no discretion resides in the intermediate terms through which the end is worked out. Therefore, man being such an intermediate term, discretion cannot be imputed to him without violating the supposition. Therefore, given an indefeasible meliorative trend in events, man is but a mechanical intermediary in the sequence. It is as such a mechanical intermediate term that the stricter hedonism construes human nature.[47] Accordingly, when more of teleological activity came to be imputed to man, less was thereby allowed to the complex of events. Or it may be put in the converse form: When less of a teleological continuity came to be imputed to the course of events, more was thereby imputed to man's life process. The latter form of statement probably suggests the direction in which the causal relation runs, more nearly than the former. The change whereby the two metaphysical premises in question have lost their earlier force and symmetry, therefore, amounts to a (partial) shifting of the seat of putative personality from inanimate phenomena to man.

It may be mentioned in passing, as a detail lying perhaps afield, yet not devoid of significance for latter-day economic speculation, that this elimination of personality, and so of teleological content, from the sequence of

[47] It may be remarked, by the way, that the use of the differential calculus and similar mathematical expedients in the discussion of marginal utility and the like, proceeds on this psychological ground, and that the theoretical results so arrived at are valid to the full extent only if this hedonistic psychology is accepted.

events, and its increasing imputation to the conduct of the human agent, is incident to a growing resort to an apprehension of phenomena in terms of process rather than in terms of outcome, as was the habit in earlier schemes of knowledge. On this account the categories employed are, in a gradually increasing degree, categories of process —"dynamic" categories. But categories of process applied to conduct, to discretionary action, are teleological categories: whereas categories of process applied in the case of a sequence where the members of the sequence are not conceived to be charged with discretion, are, by the force of this conception itself, non-teleological, quantitative categories. The continuity comprised in the concept of process as applied to conduct is consequently a spiritual, teleological continuity; whereas the concept of process under the second head, the non-teleological sequence, comprises a continuity of a quantitative, causal kind, substantially the conservation of energy. In its turn the growing resort to categories of process in the formulation of knowledge is probably due to the epistemological discipline of modern mechanical industry, the technological exigencies of which enforce a constant recourse to the apprehension of phenomena in terms of process, differing therein from the earlier forms of industry, which neither obtruded visible mechanical process so constantly upon the apprehension nor so imperatively demanded an articulate recognition of continuity in the processes actually involved. The contrast in this respect is still more pronounced between the discipline of modern life in an industrial community and the discipline of life under the conventions of status and exploit that formerly prevailed.

To return to the benign order of nature, or the meliorative trend—its passing, as an article of economic faith, was not due to criticism levelled against it by the later classical economists on grounds of its epistemological incongruity. It was tried on its merits, as an alleged account of facts; and the weight of evidence went against it. The belief in a self-realizing trend had no sooner reached a competent and exhaustive statement—e.g., at Bastiat's hands, as a dogma of the harmony of interests specifically applicable to the details of economic life— than it began to lose ground. With his usual concision and incisiveness, Cairnes completed the destruction of Bastiat's special dogma, and put it for ever beyond a rehearing. But Cairnes is not a destructive critic of the classical political economy, at least not in intention; he is an interpreter and continuer—perhaps altogether the clearest and truest continuer—of the classical teaching. While he confuted Bastiat and discredited Bastiat's peculiar dogma, he did not thereby put the order of nature bodily out of the science. He qualified and improved it, very much as Mill qualified and improved the tenets of the hedonistic psychology. As Mill and the ethical speculation of his generation threw more of personality into the hedonistic psychology, so Cairnes and the speculators on scientific method (such as Mill and Jevons) attenuated the imputation of personality or teleological content to the process of material cause and effect. The work is, of course, by no means an achievement of Cairnes alone; but he is, perhaps, the best exponent of this advance in economic theory. In Cairnes's redaction this foundation of the science became the concept of a colourless normality.

It was in Cairnes's time the fashion for speculators in other fields than the physical sciences to look to those sciences for guidance in method and for legitimation of the ideals of scientific theory which they were at work to realize. More than that, the large and fruitful achievements of the physical sciences had so far taken men's attention captive as to give an almost instinctive predilection for the methods that had approved themselves in that field. The ways of thinking which had on this ground become familiar to all scholars occupied with any scientific inquiry, had permeated their thinking on any subject whatever. This is eminently true of British thinking.

It had come to be a commonplace of the physical sciences that "natural laws" are of the nature of empirical generalizations simply, or even of the nature of arithmetical averages. Even the underlying preconception of the modern physical sciences—the law of the conservation of energy, or persistence of quantity—was claimed to be an empirical generalization, arrived at inductively and verified by experiment. It is true, the alleged proof of the law took the whole conclusion for granted at the start, and used it constantly as a tacit axiom at every step in the argument which was to establish its truth; but that fact serves rather to emphasize than to call in question the abiding faith which these empiricists had in the sole effi-

cacy of empirical generalization. Had they been able
overtly to admit any other than an associational origin of
knowledge, they would have seen the impossibility of accounting on the mechanical grounds of association for the
premise on which all experience of mechanical fact rests.
That any other than a mechanical origin should be assigned to experience, or that any other than a so-conceived
empirical ground was to be admitted for any general principle, was incompatible with the prejudices of men trained
in the school of the associational psychology, however
widely they perforce departed from this ideal in practice.
Nothing of the nature of a personal element was to be
admitted into these fundamental empirical generalizations; and nothing, therefore, of the nature of a discretionary or teleological movement was to be comprised in
the generalizations to be accepted as "natural laws." Natural laws must in no degree be imbued with personality,
must say nothing of an ulterior end; but for all that they
remained "laws" of the sequences subsumed under them.
So far is the reduction to colourless terms carried by Mill,
for instance, that he formulates the natural laws as empirically ascertained sequences simply, even excluding or
avoiding all imputation of causal continuity, as that term
is commonly understood by the unsophisticated. In Mill's
ideal no more of organic connexion or continuity between the members of a sequence is implied in subsuming
them under a law of causal relationship than is given by
the ampersand. He is busied with dynamic sequences, but
he persistently confines himself to static terms.

Under the guidance of the associational psychology, therefore, the extreme of discontinuity in the deliverances of inductive research is aimed at by those economists— Mill and Cairnes being taken as typical—whose names have been associated with deductive methods in modern science. With a fine sense of truth they saw that the notion of causal continuity, as a premise of scientific generalization, is an essentially metaphysical postulate; and they avoided its treacherous ground by denying it, and construing causal sequence to mean a uniformity of co-existences and successions simply. But, since a strict uniformity is nowhere to be observed at first hand in the phenomena with which the investigator is occupied, it has to be found by a laborious interpretation of the phenomena and a diligent abstraction and allowance for disturbing circumstances, whatever may be the meaning of a disturbing circumstance where causal continuity is denied. In this work of interpretation and expurgation the investigator proceeds on a conviction of the orderliness of the natural sequence. *Natura non facit saltum:* a maxim which has no meaning within the stricter limits of the associational theory of knowledge.

Before anything can be said as to the orderliness of the sequence, a point of view must be chosen by the speculator, with respect to which the sequence in question does or does not fulfil this condition of orderliness; that is to say, with respect to which it is a sequence. The endeavour to avoid all metaphysical premises fails here as everywhere. The associationists, to whom economics owes its transition from the older classical phase to the modern or quasi-classical, chose as their guiding point of view the metaphysical postulate of congruity—in substance, the "similarity" of the associationist theory of knowledge. This must be called their *proton pseudos*, if associationism pure and simple is to be accepted. The notion of congruity works out in laws of resemblance and equivalence, in both of which it is plain to the modern psychologist that a metaphysical ground of truth, antecedent to and controlling empirical data, is assumed. But the use of the postulate of congruence as a test of scientific truth has the merit of avoiding all open dealing with an imputed substantiality of the data handled, such as would be involved in the overt use of the concept of causation. The data are congruous among themselves, as items of knowledge; and they may therefore be handled in a logical synthesis and concatenation on the basis of this congruence alone, without committing the scientist to an imputation of a kinetic or motor relation between them. The metaphysics of process is thereby avoided, in appearance. The sequences are uniform or consistent with one another, taken as articles of theoretical synthesis simply; and so they become elements of a system or discipline of knowledge in which the test of theoretical truth is the congruence of the system with its premises.

In all this there is a high-wrought appearance of matter-of-fact, and all metaphysical subreption of a non-empirical or non-mechanical standard of reality or substantiality is avoided in appearance. The generalizations which make

up such a system of knowledge are, in this way, stated in
terms of the system itself; and when a competent formulation of the alleged uniformities has been so made in
terms of their congruity or equivalence with the prime
postulates of the system, the work of theoretical inquiry
is done.

The concrete premises from which proceeds the systematic knowledge of this generation of economists are
certain very concise assumptions concerning human nature, and certain slightly less concise generalizations of
physical fact,[48] presumed to be mechanically empirical
generalizations. These postulates afford the standard of
normality. Whatever situation or course of events can be
shown to express these postulates without mitigation is
normal; and wherever a departure from this normal
course of things occurs, it is due to disturbing causes—
that is to say, to causes not comprised in the main premises of the science—and such departures are to be taken
account of by way of qualification. Such departures and
such qualification are constantly present in the facts to be
handled by the science; but, being not congruous with the
underlying postulates, they have no place in the body of
the science. The laws of the science, that which makes
up the economist's theoretical knowledge, are laws of
the normal case. The normal case does not occur in concrete fact. These laws are, therefore, in Cairnes's terminology, "hypothetical" truths; and the science is a "hypo-

[48] See, e.g., Cairnes, *Character and Logical Method* (New York),
p. 71.

thetical" science. They apply to concrete facts only as the facts are interpreted and abstracted from, in the light of the underlying postulates. The science is, therefore, a theory of the normal case, a discussion of the concrete facts of life in respect of their degree of approximation to the normal case. That is to say, it is a taxonomic science.

Of course, in the work actually done by these economists this standpoint of rigorous normality is not consistently maintained; nor is the unsophisticated imputation of causality to the facts under discussion consistently avoided. The associationist postulate, that causal sequence means empirical uniformity simply, is in great measure forgotten when the subject-matter of the science is handled in detail. Especially is it true that in Mill the dry light of normality is greatly relieved by a strong common-sense. But the great truths or laws of the science remain hypothetical laws; and the test of scientific reality is congruence with the hypothetical laws, not coincidence with matter-of-fact events.

The earlier, more archaic metaphysics of the science, which saw in the orderly correlation and sequence of events a constraining guidance of an extra-causal, teleological kind, in this way becomes a metaphysics of normality which asserts no extra-causal constraint over events, but contents itself with establishing correlations, equivalencies, homologies, and theories concerning the conditions of an economic equilibrium. The movement, the process of economic life, is not overlooked, and it may even be said that it is not neglected; but the pure theory, in its final deliverances, deals not with the dynamics, but with the statics of the case. The concrete subject-matter of the science is, of course, the process of economic life—that is unavoidably the case—and in so far the discussion must be accepted as work bearing on the dynamics of the phenomena discussed; but even then it remains true that the aim of this work in dynamics is a determination and taxis of the outcome of the process under discussion rather than a theory of the process as such. The process is rated in terms of the equilibrium to which it tends or should tend, not conversely. The outcome of the process, taken in its relation of equivalence within the system, is the point at which the inquiry comes to rest. It is not primarily the point of departure for an inquiry into what may follow. The science treats of a balanced system rather than of a proliferation. In this lies its characteristic difference from the later evolutionary sciences. It is this characteristic bent of the science that leads its spokesman, Cairnes, to turn so kindly to chemistry rather than to the organic sciences, when he seeks an analogy to economics among the physical sciences.[49] What Cairnes has in mind in his appeal to chemistry, is, of course, the received, extremely taxonomic (systematic) chemistry of his own time, not the tentatively genetic theories of a slightly later day.

It may seem that in the characterization just offered of

---

[49] *Character and Logical Method,* p. 62.

the standpoint of normality in economics there is too
strong an implication of colourlessness and impartiality.
The objection holds as regards much of the work of the
modern economists of the classical line. It will hold true
even as to much of Cairnes's work; but it cannot be admitted as regards Cairnes's ideal of scientific aim and
methods. The economists whose theories Cairnes received
and developed assuredly did not pursue the discussion
of the normal case with an utterly dispassionate animus.
They had still enough of the older teleological metaphysics left to give colour to the accusation brought
against them that they were advocates of *laissez-faire*.
The preconception of the utilitarians—in substance the
natural-rights preconception—that unrestrained human
conduct will result in the greatest human happiness, retains so much of its force in Cairnes's time as is implied
in the then current assumption that what is normal is also
right. The economists, and Cairnes among them, not only
are concerned to find out what is normal and to determine what consummation answers to the normal, but they
also are at pains to approve that consummation. It is
this somewhat uncritical and often unavowed identification of the normal with the right that gives colourable
ground for the widespread vulgar prejudice, to which
Cairnes draws attention,[50] that political economy "sanctions" one social arrangement and "condemns" another.
And it is against this uncritical identification of two essen-

---

[50] *Essays in Political Economy*, pp. 260–4.

tially unrelated principles or categories that Cairnes's
essay on "Political Economy and Laissez-Faire," and in
good part also that on Bastiat, are directed. But, while
this is one of the many points at which Cairnes has substantially advanced the ideals of the science, his own concluding argument shows him to have been but half-way
emancipated from the prejudice, even while most effectively combating it.[51] It is needless to point out that the
like prejudice is still present in good vigour in many later
economists who have had the full benefit of Cairnes's
teachings on this head.[52] Considerable as Cairnes's
achievement in this matter undoubtedly was, it effected
a mitigation rather than an elimination of the untenable
metaphysics against which he contended.

The advance in the general point of view from animistic teleology to taxonomy is shown in a curiously succinct
manner in a parenthetical clause of Cairnes's in a chapter
on Normal Value.[53] With his acceptance of the later
point of view involved in the use of the new term, Cairnes
becomes the interpreter of the received theoretical results.
The received positions are not subjected to a destructive
criticism. The aim is to complete them where they fall

[51] See especially *Essays*, pp. 263-4.
[52] It may be interesting to point out that the like identification of
the categories of normality and right gives the dominant note of
Mr. Spencer's ethical and social philosophy, and that later economists
of the classical line are prone to be Spencerians.
[53] "Normal value (called by Adam Smith and Ricardo 'natural
value,' and by Mill 'necessary value,' but best expressed, it seems to
me, by the term which I have used)."—*Leading Principles* (New
York), p. 45.

short and to cut off what may be needless or what may run beyond the safe ground of scientific generalization. In his work of redaction, Cairnes does not avow—probably he is not sensible of—any substantial shifting of the point of view or any change in the accepted ground of theoretic reality. But his advance to an unteleological taxonomy none the less changes the scope and aim of his theoretical discussion. The discussion of Normal Value may be taken in illustration.

Cairnes is not content to find (with Adam Smith) that value will "naturally" coincide with or be measured by cost of production, or even (with Mill) that cost of production must, in the long run, "necessarily" determine value. "This . . . is to take a much too limited view of the range of this phenomenon." [54] He is concerned to determine not only this general tendency of values to a normal, but all those characteristic circumstances as well which condition this tendency and which determine the normal to which values tend. His inquiry pursues the phenomena of value in a normal economic system rather than the manner and rate of approach of value relations to a teleologically or hedonistically defensible consummation. It therefore becomes an exhaustive but very discriminating analysis of the circumstances that bear upon market values, with a view to determine what circumstances are normally present; that is to say, what circumstances conditioning value are commonly effective and

---

[54] *Leading Principles*, p. 45.

at the same time in consonance with the premises of economic theory. These effective conditions, in so far as they are not counted anomalous and, therefore, to be set aside in the theoretical discussion, are the circumstances under which a hedonistic valuation process in any modern industrial community is held perforce to take place—the circumstances which are held to enforce a recognition and rating of the pleasure-bearing capacity of facts. They are not, as under the earlier cost-of-production doctrines, the circumstances which determine the magnitude of the forces spent in the production of the valuable article. Therefore, the normal (natural) value is no longer (as with Adam Smith, and even to some extent with his classical successors) the primary or initial fact in value theory, the substantial fact of which the market value is an approximate expression and by which the latter is controlled. The argument does not, as formerly, set out from that expenditure of personal force which was once conceived to constitute the substantial value of goods, and then construe market value to be an approximate and uncertain expression of this substantial fact. The direction in which the argument runs is rather the reverse of this. The point of departure is taken from the range of market values and the process of bargaining by which these values are determined. This latter is taken to be a process of discrimination between various kinds and degrees of discomfort, and the average or consistent outcome of such a process of bargaining constitutes normal value. It is only by virtue of a presumed equivalence between the discomfort undergone and the concomitant expenditure, whether of labour or of wealth, that the normal value so determined is conceived to be an expression of the productive force that goes into the creation of the valuable goods. Cost being only in uncertain equivalence with sacrifice or discomfort, as between different persons, the factor of cost falls into the background; and the process of bargaining, which is in the foreground, being a process of valuation, a balancing of individual demand and supply, it follows that a law of reciprocal demand comes in to supplant the law of cost. In all this the proximate causes at work in the determination of values are plainly taken account of more adequately than in earlier cost-of-production doctrines; but they are taken account of with a view to explaining the mutual adjustment and interrelation of elements in a system rather than to explain either a developmental sequence or the working out of a foreordained end.

This revision of the cost-of-production doctrine, whereby it takes the form of a law of reciprocal demand, is in good part effected by a consistent reduction of cost to terms of sacrifice—a reduction more consistently carried through by Cairnes than it had been by earlier hedonists, and extended by Cairnes's successors with even more far-reaching results. By this step the doctrine of cost is not only brought into closer accord with the neo-hedonistic premises, in that it in a greater degree throws the stress upon the factor of personal discrimination, but it also gives the doctrine a more general bearing upon economic conduct and increases its serviceability as a comprehensive principle for the classification of economic phenomena. In the further elaboration of the hedonistic theory of value at the hands of Jevons and the Austrians the same principle of sacrifice comes to serve as the chief ground of procedure.

Of the foundations of later theory, in so far as the postulates of later economists differ characteristically from those of Mill and Cairnes, little can be said in this place. Nothing but the very general features of the later development can be taken up; and even these general features of the existing theoretic situation cannot be handled with the same confidence as the corresponding features of a past phase of speculation. With respect to writers of the present or the more recent past the work of natural selection, as between variants of scientific aim and animus and between more or less divergent points of view, has not yet taken effect; and it would be over-hazardous to attempt an anticipation of the results of the selection that lies in great part yet in the future. As regards the directions of theoretical work suggested by the names of Professor Marshall, Mr. Cannan, Professor Clark, Mr. Pierson, Professor Loria, Professor Schmoller, the Austrian group—no off-hand decision is admissible as between these candidates for the honor, or, better, for the work, of continuing the main current of economic speculation and inquiry. No attempt will here be made even to pass a verdict on the relative claims of the recognized two or three main "schools" of theory, beyond the somewhat obvious finding that, for the purpose in hand, the so-called Austrian school is scarcely distinguishable from the neo-classical, unless it be in the different distribution of emphasis. The divergence between the modernized classical views, on the one hand, and the historical and Marxist schools, on the other hand, is wider—so much so, indeed, as to bar out a consideration of the postulates of the latter under the same head of inquiry with the former. The inquiry, therefore, confines itself to the one line standing most obviously in unbroken continuity with that body of classical economics whose life-history has been traced in outline above. And, even for this phase of modernized classical economics, it seems necessary to limit discussion, for the present, to a single strain, selected as standing peculiarly close to the classical source, at the same time that it shows unmistakable adaptation to the later habits of thought and methods of knowledge.

For this later development in the classical line of political economy, Mr. Keynes's book may fairly be taken as the maturest exposition of the aims and ideals of the science; while Professor Marshall excellently exemplifies the best work that is being done under the guidance of the classical antecedents. As, after a lapse of a dozen or fifteen years from Cairnes's days of full conviction, Mr. Keynes interprets the aims of modern economic science, it has less of the "hypothetical" character assigned it by Cairnes; that is to say, it confines its inquiry less closely

to the ascertainment of the normal case and the interpretative subsumption of facts under the normal. It takes
fuller account of the genesis and developmental continuity of all features of modern economic life, gives
more and closer attention to institutions and their history.
This is, no doubt, due, in part at least, to impulse received
from German economists; and in so far it also reflects the
peculiarly vague and bewildered attitude of protest that
characterizes the earlier expositions of the historical
school. To the same essentially extraneous source is traceable the theoretic blur embodied in Mr. Keynes's attitude of tolerance towards the conception of economics as
a "normative" science having to do with "economic
ideals," or an "applied economics" having to do with
"economic precepts." [55] An inchoate departure from the
consistent taxonomic ideals shows itself in the tentative
resort to historical and genetic formulations, as well as in
Mr. Keynes's pervading inclination to define the scope of
the science, not by exclusion of what are conceived to be
non-economic phenomena, but by disclosing a point of
view from which all phenomena are seen to be economic
facts. The science comes to be characterized not by the
delimitation of a range of facts, as in Cairnes,[56] but as an
inquiry into the bearing which all facts have upon men's
economic activity. It is no longer that certain phenomena

[55] *Scope and Method of Political Economy* (London, 1891),
chaps. 1 and 2.
[56] *Character and Logical Method*; e.g., Lecture II, especially
pp. 53-4 and 71.

belong within the science, but rather that the science is concerned with any and all phenomena as seen from the point of view of the economic interest. Mr. Keynes does not go fully to the length which this last proposition indicates. He finds that political economy "treats of the phenomena arising out of the economic activities of mankind in society"; [57] but, while the discussion by which he leads up to this definition might be construed to say that all the activities of mankind in society have an economic bearing, and should therefore come within the view of the science, Mr. Keynes does not carry out his elucidation of the matter to that broad conclusion. Neither can it be said that modern political economy has, in practice, taken on the scope and character which this extreme position would assign it.

The passage from which the above citation is taken is highly significant also in another and related bearing, and it is at the same time highly characteristic of the most effective modernized classical economics. The subject-matter of the science has come to be the "economic activities" of mankind, and the phenomena in which these activities manifest themselves. So Professor Marshall's work, for instance, is, in aim, even if not always in achievement, a theoretical handling of human activity in its economic bearing—an inquiry into the multiform phases and ramifications of that process of valuation of the material means of life by virtue of which man is an

---

[57] *Scope and Method of Political Economy*, chap. 3, particularly p. 97.

economic agent. And still it remains an inquiry directed
to the determination of the conditions of an equilibrium
of activities and a quiescent normal situation. It is not
in any eminent degree an inquiry into cultural or institutional development as affected by economic exigencies or
by the economic interest of the men whose activities are
analysed and portrayed. Any sympathetic reader of Professor Marshall's great work—and that must mean every
reader—comes away with a sense of swift and smooth
movement and interaction of parts; but it is the movement of a consummately conceived and self-balanced
mechanism, not that of a cumulatively unfolding process
or an institutional adaptation to cumulatively unfolding
exigencies. The taxonomic bearing is, after all, the dominant feature. It is significant of the same point that even
in his discussion of such vitally dynamic features of the
economic process as the differential effectiveness of different labourers or of different industrial plants, as well
as of the differential advantages of consumers, Professor
Marshall resorts to an adaptation of so essentially taxonomic a category as the received concept of rent. Rent is
a pecuniary category, a category of income, which is essentially a final term, not a category of the motor term,
work or interest.[58] It is not a factor or a feature of the
process of industrial life, but a phenomenon of the pecuniary situation which emerges from this process under
given conventional circumstances. However far-reaching

---

[58] "Interest" is, of course, here used in the sense which it has in
modern psychological discussion.

and various the employment of the rent concept in economic theory has been, it has through all permutations remained, what it was to begin with, a rubric in the classification of incomes. It is a pecuniary, not an industrial category. In so far as resort is had to the rent concept in the formulation of a theory of the industrial process— as in Professor Marshall's work—it comes to a statement of the process in terms of its residue. Let it not seem presumptuous to say that, great and permanent as is the value of Professor Marshall's exposition of quasi-rents and the like, the endeavour which it involves to present in terms of a concluded system what is of the nature of a fluent process has made the exposition unduly bulky, unwieldy, and inconsequent.

There is a curious reminiscence of the perfect taxonomic day in Mr. Keynes's characterization of political economy as a "positive science," "the sole province of which is to establish economic uniformities"; [59] and, in this resort to the associationist expedient of defining a natural law as a "uniformity," Mr. Keynes is also borne out by Professor Marshall.[60] But this and other survivals of the taxonomic terminology, or even of the taxonomic canons of procedure, do not hinder the economists of the modern school from doing effective work of a character that must be rated as genetic rather than taxonomic. Professor Marshall's work in economics is not unlike that

---

[59] *Scope and Method of Political Economy*, p. 46.
[60] *Principles of Economics*, vol. I, Book I, chap. 6, sect. 6, especially p. 105 (3d edition).

of Asa Gray in botany, who, while working in great part
within the lines of "systematic botany" and adhering to
its terminology, and on the whole also to its point of
view, very materially furthered the advance of the science
outside the scope of taxonomy.

Professor Marshall shows an aspiration to treat economic life as a development; and, at least superficially,
much of his work bears the appearance of being a discussion of this kind. In this endeavour his work is typical of
what is aimed at by many of the later economists. The
aim shows itself with a persistent recurrence in his *Principles*. His chosen maxim is, *Natura non facit saltum*
—a maxim that might well serve to designate the prevailing attitude of modern economists towards questions of
economic development as well as towards questions of
classification or of economic policy. His insistence on the
continuity of development and of the economic structure
of communities is a characteristic of the best work along
the later line of classical political economy. All this gives
an air of evolutionism to the work. Indeed, the work of
the neo-classical economics might be compared, probably
without offending any of its adepts, with that of the early
generation of Darwinians, though such a comparison
might somewhat shrewdly have to avoid any but superficial features. Economists of the present day are commonly evolutionists, in a general way. They commonly
accept, as other men do, the general results of the evolutionary speculation in those directions in which the evolutionary method has made its way. But the habit of

handling by evolutionist methods the facts with which
their own science is concerned has made its way among
the economists to but a very uncertain degree.

The prime postulate of evolutionary science, the preconception constantly underlying the inquiry, is the notion of a cumulative causal sequence; and writers on economics are in the habit of recognizing that the phenomena
with which they are occupied are subject to such a law of
development. Expressions of assent to this proposition
abound. But the economists have not worked out or hit
upon a method by which the inquiry in economics may
consistently be conducted under the guidance of this postulate. Taking Professor Marshall as exponent, it appears that, while the formulations of economic theory are
not conceived to be arrived at by way of an inquiry into
the developmental variation of economic institutions and
the like, the theorems arrived at are held, and no doubt
legitimately, to apply to the past,[61] and with due reserve
also to the future, phases of the development. But these
theorems apply to the various phases of the development
not as accounting for the developmental sequence, but as
limiting the range of variation. They say little, if anything, as to the order of succession, as to the derivation
and the outcome of any given phase, or as to the causal
relation of one phase of any given economic convention or
scheme of relations to any other. They indicate the conditions of survival to which any innovation is subject, sup-

---

[61] See, e.g., Professor Marshall's "Reply" to Professor Cunningham
in the *Economic Journal* for 1892, pp. 508–13.

posing the innovation to have taken place, not the conditions of variational growth. The economic laws, the "statements of uniformity," are therefore, when construed in an evolutionary bearing, theorems concerning the superior or the inferior limit of persistent innovations, as the case may be.[62] It is only in this negative, selective bearing that the current economic laws are held to be laws of developmental continuity; and it should be added that they have hitherto found but relatively scant application at the hands of the economists, even for this purpose.

Again, as applied to economic activities under a given situation, as laws governing activities in equilibrium, the economic laws are, in the main, laws of the limits within which economic action of a given purpose runs. They are theorems as to the limits which the economic (commonly the pecuniary) interest imposes upon the range of activities to which the other life interests of men incite, rather than theorems as to the manner and degree in which the economic interest creatively shapes the general scheme of life. In great part they formulate the normal inhibitory effect of economic exigencies rather than the cumulative modification and diversification of human activities through the economic interest, by initiating and guiding habits of life and of thought. This, of course, does not go to say that economists are at all slow to credit the economic exigencies with a large share in the

---

[62] This is well illustrated by what Professor Marshall says of the Ricardian law of rent in his "Reply," cited above.

growth of culture; but, while claims of this kind are large and recurrent, it remains true that the laws which make up the framework of economic doctrine are, when construed as generalizations of causal relation, laws of conservation and selection, not of genesis and proliferation. The truth of this, which is but a commonplace generalization, might be shown in detail with respect to such fundamental theorems as the laws of rent, of profits, of wages, of the increasing or diminishing returns of industry, of population, of competitive prices, of cost of production.

In consonance with this quasi-evolutionary tone of the neo-classical political economy, or as an expression of it, comes the further clarified sense that nowadays attaches to the terms "normal" and economic "laws." The laws have gained in colourlessness, until it can no longer be said that the concept of normality implies approval of the phenomena to which it is applied.[63] They are in an increasing degree laws of conduct, though they still continue to formulate conduct in hedonistic terms; that is to say, conduct is construed in terms of its sensuous effect, not in terms of its teleological content. The light of the science is a drier light than it was, but it continues to be shed upon the accessories of human action rather than upon the process itself. The categories employed for the purpose of knowing this economic conduct with which the

---

[63] See, e.g., Marshall, *Principles*, Book I, chap. 6, sect. 6, pp. 105–8. The like dispassionateness is visible in most other modern writers on theory; as, e.g., Clark, Cannan, and the Austrians.

scientists occupy themselves are not the categories under which the men at whose hands the action takes place themselves apprehend their own action at the instant of acting. Therefore, economic conduct still continues to be somewhat mysterious to the economists; and they are forced to content themselves with adumbrations whenever the discussion touches this central, substantial fact.

All this, of course, is intended to convey no dispraise of the work done, nor in any way to disparage the theories which the passing generation of economists have elaborated, or the really great and admirable body of knowledge which they have brought under the hand of the science; but only to indicate the direction in which the inquiry in its later phases—not always with full consciousness—is shifting as regards its categories and its point of view. The discipline of life in a modern community, particularly the industrial life, strongly reinforced by the modern sciences, has divested our knowledge of non-human phenomena of that fullness of self-directing life that was once imputed to them, and has reduced this knowledge to terms of opaque causal sequence. It has thereby narrowed the range of discretionary, teleological action to the human agent alone; and so it is compelling our knowledge of human conduct, in so far as it is distinguished from the non-human, to fall into teleological terms. Foot-pounds, calories, geometrically progressive procreation, and doses of capital, have not been supplanted by the equally uncouth denominations of habits, propensities, aptitudes, and conventions, nor does there seem to be any probability that they will be; but the discussion which continues to run in terms of the former class of concepts is in an increasing degree seeking support in concepts of the latter class.

# THE LIMITATIONS OF

# MARGINAL UTILITY [1]

✿

THE limitations of the marginal-utility economics are
sharp and characteristic. It is from first to last a doctrine of value, and in point of form and method it is a
theory of valuation. The whole system, therefore, lies
within the theoretical field of distribution, and it has but
a secondary bearing on any other economic phenomena
than those of distribution—the term being taken in its
accepted sense of pecuniary distribution, or distribution
in point of ownership. Now and again an attempt is
made to extend the use of the principle of marginal utility beyond this range, so as to apply it to questions of
production, but hitherto without sensible effect, and
necessarily so. The most ingenious and the most promis-
ing of such attempts have been those of Mr. Clark,
whose work marks the extreme range of endeavour, and
the extreme degree of success in so seeking to turn a
postulate of distribution to account for a theory of production. But the outcome has been a doctrine of the production of values, and value, in Mr. Clark's as in other
utility systems, is a matter of valuation; which throws
the whole excursion back into the field of distribution.

[1] Reprinted from *The Place of Science in Modern Civilisation*,
1919, pp. 231–51; originally published in *The Journal of Political
Economy*, vol. XVII, Nov. 1909.

Similarly, as regards attempts to make use of this principle in an analysis of the phenomena of consumption, the best results arrived at are some formulation of the pecuniary distribution of consumption goods.

Within this limit range marginal-utility theory is of a wholly statical character. It offers no theory of a movement of any kind, being occupied with the adjustment of values to a given situation. Of this, again, no more convincing illustration need be had than is afforded by the work of Mr. Clark, which is not excelled in point of earnestness, perseverance, or insight. For all their use of the term "dynamic," neither Mr. Clark nor any of his associates in this line of research have yet contributed anything at all appreciable to a theory of genesis, growth, sequence, change, process, or the like, in economic life. They have had something to say as to the bearing which given economic changes, accepted as premises, may have on valuation, and so on distribution; but as to the causes of change or the unfolding sequence of the phenomena of economic life they have had nothing to say hitherto; nor can they, since their theory is not drawn in causal terms but in terms of teleology.

In all this the marginal-utility school is substantially at one with the classical economics of the nineteenth century, the difference between the two being that the former is confined within narrower limits and sticks more consistently to its teleological premises. Both are teleological, and neither can consistently admit arguments from cause to effect in the formulation of their main articles of theory. Neither can deal theoretically with phenomena of change, but at the most only with rational adjustment to change which may be supposed to have supervened.

To the modern scientist the phenomena of growth and change are the most obtrusive and most consequential facts observable in economic life. For an understanding of modern economic life the technological advance of the past two centuries—e.g., the growth of the industrial arts—is of the first importance; but marginal-utility theory does not bear on this matter, nor does this matter bear on marginal-utility theory. As a means of theoretically accounting for this technological movement in the past or in the present, or even as a means of formally, technically stating it as an element in the current economic situation, that doctrine and all its works are altogether idle. The like is true for the sequence of change that is going forward in the pecuniary relations of modern life; the hedonistic postulate and its propositions of differential utility neither have served nor can serve an inquiry into these phenomena of growth, although the whole body of marginal-utility economics lies within the range of these pecuniary phenomena. It has nothing to say to the growth of business usages and expedients or to the concomitant changes in the principles of conduct which govern the pecuniary relations of men, which condition and are conditioned by these altered relations of business life or which bring them to pass.

It is characteristic of the school that wherever an element of the cultural fabric, an institution or any institutional phenomenon, is involved in the facts with which the theory is occupied, such institutional facts are taken for granted, denied, or explained away. If it is a question of price, there is offered an explanation of how exchanges may take place with such effect as to leave money and price out of the account. If it is a question of credit, the effect of credit extension on business traffic is left on one side and there is an explanation of how the borrower and lender co-operate to smooth out their respective income streams of consumable goods or sensations of consumption. The failure of the school in this respect is consistent and comprehensive. And yet these economists are lacking neither in intelligence nor in information. They are, indeed, to be credited, commonly, with a wide range of information and an exact control of materials, as well as with a very alert interest in what is going on; and apart from their theoretical pronouncements the members of the school habitually profess the sanest and most intelligent views of current practical questions, even when these questions touch matters of institutional growth and decay.

The infirmity of this theoretical scheme lies in its postulates, which confine the inquiry to generalizations of the teleological or "deductive" order. These postulates, together with the point of view and logical method that follow from them, the marginal-utility school shares with other economists of the classical line—for

this school is but a branch or derivative of the English
classical economists of the nineteenth century. The
substantial difference between this school and the generality of classical economists lies mainly in the fact
that in the marginal-utility economics the common postulates are more consistently adhered to at the same time
that they are more neatly defined and their limitations
are more adequately realized. Both the classical school
in general and its specialized variant, the marginal-
utility school, in particular, take as their common point
of departure the traditional psychology of the early
nineteenth-century hedonists, which is accepted as a
matter of course or of common notoriety and is held
quite uncritically. The central and well-defined tenet so
held is that of the hedonistic calculus. Under the guidance of this tenet and of the other psychological conceptions associated and consonant with it, human conduct is conceived of and interpreted as a rational response to the exigencies of the situation in which
mankind is placed; as regards economic conduct it is
such a rational and unprejudiced response to the stimulus of anticipated pleasure and pain—being, typically
and in the main, a response to the promptings of anticipated pleasure, for the hedonists of the nineteenth
century and of the marginal-utility school are in the
main of an optimistic temper.[2] Mankind is, on the whole

---

[2] The conduct of mankind differs from that of the brutes in being
determined by anticipated sensations of pleasure and pain, instead
of actual sensations. Hereby, in so far, human conduct is taken out

and normally, (conceived to be) clear-sighted and far-sighted in its appreciation of future sensuous gains and losses, although there may be some (inconsiderable) difference between men in this respect. Men's activities differ, therefore, (inconsiderably) in respect of the alertness of the response and the nicety of adjustment of irksome pain-cost to apprehended future sensuous gain; but, on the whole, no other ground or line or guidance of conduct than this rationalistic calculus falls properly within the cognizance of the economic hedonists. Such a theory can take account of conduct only in so far as it is rational conduct, guided by deliberate and exhaustively intelligent choice—wise adaptation to the demands of the main chance.

The external circumstances which condition conduct are variable, of course, and so they will have a varying effect upon conduct; but their variation is, in effect, construed to be of such a character only as to vary the degree of strain to which the human agent is subject by contact with these external circumstances. The cultural elements involved in the theoretical scheme, elements that are of the nature of institutions, human rela-

---

of the sequence of cause and effect and falls instead under the rule of sufficient reason. By virtue of this rational faculty in man the connexion between stimulus and response is teleological instead of causal.

The reason for assigning the first and decisive place to pleasure, rather than to pain, in the determination of human conduct, appears to be the (tacit) acceptance of that optimistic doctrine of a beneficent order of nature which the nineteenth century inherited from the eighteenth.

tions governed by use and wont in whatever kind and
connexion, 'are not subject to inquiry but are taken for
granted as pre-existing in a finished, typical form and
as making up a normal and definitive economic situation, under which and in terms of which human intercourse is necessarily carried on. This cultural situation
comprises a few large and simple articles of institutional
furniture, together with their logical implications or
corollaries; but it includes nothing of the consequences
or effects caused by these institutional elements. The
cultural elements so tacitly postulated as immutable
conditions precedent to economic life are ownership and
free contract, together with such other features of the
scheme of natural rights as are implied in the exercise
of these. These cultural products are, for the purpose
of the theory, conceived to be given *a priori* in unmitigated force. They are part of the nature of things; so
that there is no need of accounting for them or in-
quiring into them, as to how they have come to be such
as they are, or how and why they have changed and
are changing, or what effect all this may have on the
relations of men who live by or under this cultural
situation.

Evidently the acceptance of these immutable premises,
tacitly, because uncritically and as a matter of course, by
hedonistic economics gives the science a distinctive character and places it in contrast with other sciences whose
premises are of a different order. As has already been
indicated, the premises in question, so far as they are

peculiar to the hedonistic economics, are (*a*) a certain institutional situation, the substantial feature of which is the natural right of ownership, and (*b*) the hedonistic calculus. The distinctive character given to this system of theory by these postulates and by the point of view resulting from their acceptance may be summed up broadly and concisely in saying that the theory is confined to the ground of sufficient reason instead of proceeding on the ground of efficient cause. The contrary is true of modern science, generally (except mathematics), particularly of such sciences as have to do with the phenomena of life and growth. The difference may seem trivial. It is serious only in its consequences. The two methods of inference—from sufficient reason and from efficient cause—are out of touch with one another and there is no transition from one to the other, no method of converting the procedure or the results of the one into those of the other. The immediate consequence is that the resulting economic theory is of a teleological character—"deductive" or "*a priori*" as it is often called —instead of being drawn in terms of cause and effect. The relation sought by this theory among the facts with which it is occupied is the control exercised by future (apprehended) events over present conduct. Current phenomena are dealt with as conditioned by their future consequences; and in strict marginal-utility theory they can be dealt with only in respect of their control of the present by consideration of the future. Such a (logical) relation of control or guidance between the future and the present of course involves an exercise of intelligence, a taking thought, and hence an intelligent agent through whose discriminating forethought the apprehended future may affect the current course of events; unless, indeed, one were to admit something in the way of a providential order of nature or some occult line of stress of the nature of sympathetic magic. Barring magical and providential elements, the relation of sufficient reason runs by way of the interested discrimination, the forethought, of an agent who takes thought of the future and guides his present activity by regard for this future. The relation of sufficient reason runs only from the (apprehended) future in the present, and it is solely of an intellectual, subjective, personal, teleological character and force; while the relation of cause and effect runs only in the contrary direction, and it is solely of an objective, impersonal, materialistic character and force. The modern scheme of knowledge, on the whole, rests, for its definitive ground, on the relation of cause and effect; the relation of sufficient reason being admitted only provisionally and as a proximate factor in the analysis, always with the unambiguous reservation that the analysis must ultimately come to rest in terms of cause and effect. The merits of this scientific animus, of course, do not concern the present argument.

Now, it happens that the relation of sufficient reason enters very substantially into human conduct. It is this element of discriminating forethought that distinguishes human conduct from brute behaviour. And since the economist's subject of inquiry is this human conduct, that relation necessarily comes in for a large share of his attention in any theoretical formulation of economic phenomena, whether hedonistic or otherwise. But while modern science at large has made the causal relation the sole ultimate ground of theoretical formulation; and while the other sciences that deal with human life admit the relation of sufficient reason as a proximate, supplementary, or intermediate ground, subsidiary, and subservient to the argument from cause to effect; economics has had the misfortune—as seen from the scientific point of view—to let the former supplant the latter. It is, of course, true that human conduct is distinguished from other natural phenomena by the human faculty for taking thought, and any science that has to do with human conduct must face the patent fact that the details of such conduct consequently fall into the teleological form; but it is the peculiarity of the hedonistic economics that by force of its postulates its attention is confined to this teleological bearing of conduct alone. It deals with this conduct only in so far as it may be construed in rationalistic, teleological terms of calculation and choice. But it is at the same time no less true that human conduct, economic or otherwise, is subject to the sequence of cause and effect, by force of such elements as habituation and conventional requirements. But facts of this order, which are to modern science of graver interest than the teleological details

of conduct, necessarily fall outside the attention of the
hedonistic economist, because they cannot be construed
in terms of sufficient reason, such as his postulates demand, or be fitted into a scheme of teleological doctrines.

There is, therefore, no call to impugn these premises
of the marginal-utility economics within their field.
They commend themselves to all serious and uncritical
persons at the first glance. They are principles of action
which underlie the current, business-like scheme of economic life, and as such, as practical grounds of conduct,
they are not to be called in question without questioning the existing law and order. As a matter of course,
men order their lives by these principles and, practically,
entertain no question of their stability and finality. That
is what is meant by calling them institutions; they are
settled habits of thought common to the generality of
men. But it would be mere absent-mindedness in any
student of civilization therefore to admit that these or
any other human institutions have this stability which is
currently imputed to them or that they are in this way
intrinsic to the nature of things. The acceptance by the
economists of these or other institutional elements as
given and immutable limits their inquiry in a particular
and decisive way. It shuts off the inquiry at the point
where the modern scientific interest sets in. The institutions in question are no doubt good for their purpose
as institutions, but they are not good as premises for a
scientific inquiry into the nature, origin, growth, and
effects of these institutions and of the mutations which

they undergo and which they bring to pass in the community's scheme of life.

To any modern scientist interested in economic phenomena, the chain of cause and effect in which any given phase of human culture is involved, as well as the cumulative changes wrought in the fabric of human conduct itself by the habitual activity of mankind, are matters of more engrossing and more abiding interest than the method of inference by which an individual is presumed invariably to balance pleasure and pain under given conditions that are presumed to be normal and invariable. The former are questions of the life-history of the race or the community, questions of cultural growth and of the fortunes of generations; while the latter is a question of individual casuistry in the face of a given situation that may arise in the course of this cultural growth. The former bear on the continuity and mutations of that scheme of conduct whereby mankind deals with its material means of life; the latter, if it is conceived in hedonistic terms, concerns a disconnected episode in the sensuous experience of an individual member of such a community.

In so far as modern science inquires into the phenomena of life, whether inanimate, brute, or human, it is occupied about questions of genesis and cumulative change, and it converges upon a theoretical formulation in the shape of a life-history drawn in causal terms. In so far as it is a science in the current sense of the term, any science, such as economics, which has to do with human conduct, becomes a genetic inquiry into the human scheme of life; and where, as in economics, the subject of inquiry is the conduct of man in his dealings with the material means of life, the science is necessarily an inquiry into the life-history of material civilization, on a more or less extended or restricted plan. Not that the economist's inquiry isolates material civilization from all other phases and bearings of human culture, and so studies the motions of an abstractly conceived "economic man." On the contrary, no theoretical inquiry into this material civilization that shall be at all adequate to any scientific purpose can be carried out without taking this material civilization in its causal, that is to say, its genetic, relations to other phases and bearings of the cultural complex; without studying it as it is wrought upon by other lines of cultural growth and as working its effects in these other lines. But in so far as the inquiry is economic science, specifically, the attention will converge upon the scheme of material life and will take in other phases of civilization only in their correlation with the scheme of material civilization.

Like all human culture, this material civilization is a scheme of institutions—institutional fabric and institutional growth. But institutions are an outgrowth of habit. The growth of culture is a cumulative sequence of habituation, and the ways and means of it are the habitual response of human nature to exigencies that vary incontinently, cumulatively, but with something of a con-

sistent sequence in the cumulative variations that so go
forward—incontinently, because each new move creates
a new situation which induces a further new variation
in the habitual manner of response; cumulatively, because each new situation is a variation of what has gone
before it and embodies as causal factors all that has
been effected by what went before; consistently, because
the underlying traits of human nature (propensities, aptitudes, and what not) by force of which the response
takes place, and on the ground of which the habituation takes effect, remain substantially unchanged.

Evidently an economic inquiry which occupies itself
exclusively with the movements of this consistent, elemental human nature under given, stable institutional
conditions—such as is the case with the current hedonistic economics—can reach statical results alone; since
it makes abstraction from those elements that make for
anything but a statical result. On the other hand an
adequate theory of economic conduct, even for statical
purposes, cannot be drawn in terms of the individual
simply—as is the case in the marginal-utility economics
—because it cannot be drawn in terms of the underlying
traits of human nature simply; since the response that
goes to make up human conduct takes place under institutional norms and only under stimuli that have an
institutional bearing; for the situation that provokes
and inhibits action in any given case is itself in great
part of institutional, cultural derivation. Then, too, the
phenomena of human life occur only as phenomena of

the life of a group or community: only under stimuli due
to contact with the group and only under the (habitual)
control exercised by canons of conduct imposed by the
group's scheme of life. Not only is the individual's conduct hedged about and directed by his habitual relations
to his fellows in the group, but these relations, being
of an institutional character, vary as the institutional
scheme varies. The wants and desires, the end and
aim, the ways and means, the amplitude and drift of
the individual's conduct are functions of an institutional
variable that is of a highly complex and wholly unstable character.

The growth and mutations of the institutional fabric
are an outcome of the conduct of the individual members of the group, since it is out of the experience of
the individuals, through the habituation of individuals,
that institutions arise; and it is in this same experience
that these institutions act to direct and define the aims
and end of conduct. It is, of course, on individuals that
the system of institutions imposes those conventional
standards, ideals, and canons of conduct that make up
the community's scheme of life. Scientific inquiry in this
field, therefore, must deal with individual conduct and
must formulate its theoretical results in terms of individual conduct. But such an inquiry can serve the
purposes of a genetic theory only if and in so far as this
individual conduct is attended to in those respects in
which it counts toward habituation, and so toward
change (or stability) of the institutional fabric, on the

one hand, and in those respects in which it is prompted
and guided by the received institutional conceptions and
ideals on the other hand. The postulates of marginal
utility, and the hedonistic preconceptions generally, fail
at this point in that they confine the attention to such
bearings of economic conduct as are conceived not to be
conditioned by habitual standards and ideals and to have
no effect in the way of habituation. They disregard or
abstract from the causal sequence of propensity and
habituation in economic life and exclude from theoretical
inquiry all such interest in the facts of cultural growth,
in order to attend to those features of the case that are
conceived to be idle in this respect. All such facts of institutional force and growth are put on one side as not
being germane to pure theory; they are to be taken
account of, if at all, by afterthought, by a more or less
vague and general allowance for inconsequential disturbances due to occasional human infirmity. Certain institutional phenomena, it is true, are comprised among
the premises of the hedonists, as has been noted above;
but they are included as postulates *a priori*. So the institution of ownership is taken into the inquiry not as a
factor of growth or an element subject to change, but
as one of the primordial and immutable facts of the
order of nature, underlying the hedonistic calculus.
Property, ownership, is presumed as the basis of hedonistic discrimination and it is conceived to be given in
its finished (nineteenth-century) scope and force. There
is no thought either of a conceivable growth of this

definitive nineteenth-century institution out of a cruder
past or of any conceivable cumulative change in the
scope and force of ownership in the present or future.
Nor is it conceived that the presence of this institutional
element in men's economic relations in any degree affects
or disguises the hedonistic calculus, or that its pecuniary
conceptions and standards in any degree standardize,
colour, mitigate, or divert the hedonistic calculator
from the direct and unhampered quest of the net sensuous gain. While the institution of property is included
in this way among the postulates of the theory, and is
even presumed to be ever-present in the economic situation, it is allowed to have no force in shaping economic
conduct, which is conceived to run its course to its hedonistic outcome as if no such institutional factor intervened
between the impulse and its realization. The institution
of property, together with all the range of pecuniary
conceptions that belong under it and that cluster about
it, are presumed to give rise to no habitual or conventional canons of conduct or standards of valuation, no
proximate ends, ideals, or aspirations. All pecuniary notions arising from ownership are treated simply as expedients of computation which mediate between the pain-
cost and the pleasure-gain of hedonistic choice, without
lag, leak, or friction; they are conceived simply as the
immutably correct, God-given notation of the hedonistic
calculus.

The modern economic situation is a business situation,
in that economic activity of all kinds is commonly con-

trolled by business considerations. The exigencies of modern life are commonly pecuniary exigencies. That is to say, they are exigencies of the ownership of property. Productive efficiency and distributive gain are both rated in terms of price. Business considerations are considerations of price, and pecuniary exigencies of whatever kind in the modern communities are exigencies of price. The current economic situation is a price system. Economic institutions in the modern civilized scheme of life are (prevailingly) institutions of the price system. The accountancy to which all phenomena of modern economic life are amenable is an accountancy in terms of price; and by the current convention there is no other recognized scheme of accountancy, no other rating, either in law or in fact, to which the facts of modern life are held amenable. Indeed, so great and pervading a force has this habit (institution) of pecuniary accountancy become that it extends, often as a matter of course, to many facts which properly have no pecuniary bearing and no pecuniary magnitude, as, e.g., works of art, science, scholarship, and religion. More or less freely and fully, the price system dominates the current common-sense in its appreciation and rating of these non-pecuniary ramifications of modern culture; and this in spite of the fact that, on reflection, all men of normal intelligence will freely admit that these matters lie outside the scope of pecuniary valuation.

Current popular taste and the popular sense of merit and demerit are notoriously affected in some degree by pecuniary considerations. It is a matter of common notoriety, not to be denied or explained away, that pecuniary ("commercial") tests and standards are habitually made use of outside of commercial interests proper. Precious stones, it is admitted, even by hedonistic economists, are more esteemed than they would be if they were more plentiful and cheaper. A wealthy person meets with more consideration and enjoys a larger measure of good repute than would fall to the share of the same person with the same habit of mind and body and the same record of good and evil deeds if he were poorer. It may well be that this current "commercialization" of taste and appreciation has been overstated by superficial and hasty critics of contemporary life, but it will not be denied that there is a modicum of truth in the allegation. Whatever substance it has, much or little, is due to carrying over into other fields of interest the habitual conceptions induced by dealing with and thinking of pecuniary matters. These "commercial" conceptions of merit and demerit are derived from business experience. The pecuniary tests and standards so applied outside of business transactions and relations are not reducible to sensuous terms of pleasure and pain. Indeed, it may, e.g., be true, as is commonly believed, that the contemplation of a wealthy neighbour's pecuniary superiority yields painful rather than pleasurable sensations as an immediate result; but it is equally true that such a wealthy neighbour is, on the whole, more highly regarded and more consider-

ately treated than another neighbour who differs from
the former only in being less enviable in respect of
wealth.

It is the institution of property that gives rise to these
habitual grounds of discrimination, and in modern
times, when wealth is counted in terms of money, it is
in terms of money value that these tests and standards
of pecuniary excellence are applied. This much will be
admitted. Pecuniary institutions induce pecuniary habits
of thought which affect men's discrimination outside of
pecuniary matters; but the hedonistic interpretation
alleges that such pecuniary habits of thought do not affect
men's discrimination in pecuniary matters. Although
the institutional scheme of the price system visibly dominates the modern community's thinking in matters
that lie outside the economic interest, the hedonistic economists insist, in effect, that this institutional scheme
must be accounted of no effect within that range of
activity to which it owes its genesis, growth, and persistence. The phenomena of business, which are peculiarly and uniformly phenomena of price, are in the
scheme of the hedonistic theory reduced to non-pecuniary
hedonistic terms and the theoretical formulation is carried out as if pecuniary conceptions had no force within
the traffic in which such conceptions originate. It is admitted that preoccupation with commercial interests
has "commercialized" the rest of modern life, but the
"commercialization" of commerce is not admitted. Business transactions and computations in pecuniary terms,

such as loans, discounts, and capitalization, are without hesitation or abatement converted into terms of hedonistic utility, and conversely.

It may be needless to take exception to such conversion from pecuniary into sensuous terms, for the theoretical purpose for which it is habitually made; although, if need were, it might not be excessively difficult to show that the whole hedonistic basis of such a conversion is a psychological misconception. But it is to the remoter theoretical consequences of such a conversion that exception is to be taken. In making the conversion, abstraction is made from whatever elements do not lend themselves to its terms; which amounts to abstracting from precisely those elements of business that have an institutional force and that therefore would lend themselves to scientific inquiry of the modern kind—those (institutional) elements whose analysis might contribute to an understanding of modern business and of the life of the modern business community as contrasted with the assumed primordial hedonistic calculus.

The point may perhaps be made clearer. Money and the habitual resort to its use are conceived to be simply the ways and means by which consumable goods are acquired, and therefore simply a convenient method by which to procure the pleasurable sensations of consumption; these latter being in hedonistic theory the sole and overt end of all economic endeavour. Money values have therefore no other significance than that of purchasing power over consumable goods, and money is simply an expedient of computation. Investment, credit extensions, loans of all kinds and degrees, with payment of interest and the rest, are likewise taken simply as intermediate steps between the pleasurable sensations of consumption and the efforts induced by the anticipation of these sensations, other bearings of the case being disregarded. The balance being kept in terms of the hedonistic consumption, no disturbance arises in this pecuniary traffic so long as the extreme terms of this extended hedonistic equation—pain-cost and pleasure-gain—are not altered, what lies between these extreme terms by being merely algebraic notation employed for convenience of accountancy. But such is not the run of the facts in modern business. Variations of capitalization, e.g., occur without its being practicable to refer them to visibly equivalent variations either in the state of the industrial arts or in the sensations of consumption. Credit extensions tend to inflation of credit, rising prices, overstocking of markets, etc., likewise without a visible or securely traceable correlation in the state of the industrial arts or in the pleasures of consumption; that is to say, without a visible basis in those material elements to which the hedonistic theory reduces all economic phenomena. Hence the run of the facts, in so far, must be thrown out of the theoretical formulation. The hedonistically presumed final purchase of consumable goods is habitually not contemplated in the pursuit of business enterprise. Business men habitually aspire to accumulate wealth in excess of the limits of practicable consumption, and the wealth so accumulated is not intended to be converted by a final transaction of purchase into consumable goods or sensations of consumption. Such commonplace facts as these, together with the endless web of business detail of a like pecuniary character, do not in hedonistic theory raise a question as to how these conventional aims, ideals, aspirations, and standards have come into force or how they affect the scheme of life in business or outside of it; they do not raise those questions because such questions cannot be answered in the terms which the hedonistic economists are content to use, or, indeed, which their premises permit them to use. The question which arises is how to explain the facts away: how theoretically to neutralize them so that they will not have to appear in the theory, which can then be drawn in direct and unambiguous terms of rational hedonistic calculation. They are explained away as being aberrations due to oversight or lapse of memory on the part of business men, or to some failure of logic or insight. Or they are construed and interpreted into the rationalistic terms of the hedonistic calculus by resort to an ambiguous use of the hedonistic concepts. So that the whole "money economy," with all the machinery of credit and the rest, disappears in a tissue of metaphors to reappear theoretically expurgated, sterilized, and simplified into a "refined system of barter," culminating in a net aggregate maximum of pleasurable sensations of consumption.

But since it is in just this unhedonistic, unrationalistic

pecuniary traffic that the tissue of business life consists;
since it is this peculiar conventionalism of aims and standards that differentiates the life of the modern business
community from any conceivable earlier or cruder phase
of economic life; since it is in this tissue of pecuniary intercourse and pecuniary concepts, ideals, expedients, and
aspirations that the conjunctures of business life arise and
run their course of felicity and devastation; since it is
here that those institutional changes take place which
distinguish one phase or era of the business community's
life from any other; since the growth and change of
these habitual, conventional elements make the growth
and character of any business era or business community;
any theory of business which sets these elements aside
or explains them away misses the main facts which it
has gone out to seek. Life and its conjunctures and institutions being of this complexion, however much that
state of the case may be deprecated, a theoretical account of the phenomena of this life must be drawn in
these terms in which the phenomena occur. It is not
simply that the hedonistic interpretation of modern economic phenomena is inadequate or misleading; if the
phenomena are subjected to the hedonistic interpretation
in the theoretical analysis they disappear from the
theory; and if they would bear the interpretation in
fact they would disappear in fact. If, in fact, all the
conventional relations and principles of pecuniary intercourse were subject to such a perpetual rationalized, cal-
culating revision, so that each article of usage, appre-

ciation, or procedure must approve itself *de novo* on hedonistic grounds of sensuous expediency to all concerned at every move, it is not conceivable that the institutional fabric would last over night.

# THE SAVAGE STATE OF THE
# INDUSTRIAL ARTS [1]

☼

TECHNOLOGICAL knowledge is of the nature of a common stock, held and carried forward collectively by the community, which is in this relation to be conceived as a going concern. The state of the industrial arts is a fact of group life, not of individual or private initiative or innovation. It is an affair of the collectivity, not a creative achievement of individuals working self-sufficiently in severalty or in isolation. In the main, the state of the industrial arts is always a heritage out of the past; it is always in process of change, perhaps, but the substantial body of it is knowledge that has come down from earlier generations. New elements of insight and proficiency are continually being added and worked into this common stock by the experience and initiative of the current generation, but such novel elements are always and everywhere slight and inconsequential in comparison with the body of technology that has been carried over from the past.

Each successive move in advance, every new wrinkle of novelty, improvement, invention, adaptation, every further detail of workmanlike innovation, is of course

[1] Reprinted from *The Instinct of Workmanship and the State of the Industrial Arts*, 1914, pp. 103–37.

made by individuals and comes out of individual experience and initiative, since the generations of mankind live only in individuals. But each move so made is necessarily made by individuals immersed in the community and exposed to the discipline of group life as it runs in the community, since all life is necessarily group life. The phenomena of human life occur only in this form. It is only as an outcome of this discipline that comes with the routine of group life, and by help of the commonplace knowledge diffused through the community, that any of its members are enabled to make any new move that may in this way be traceable to their individual initiative. Any new technological departure necessarily takes its rise in the workmanlike endeavours of given individuals, but it can do so only by force of their familiarity with the body of knowledge which the group already has in hand. A new departure is always and necessarily an improvement on or alteration in that state of the industrial arts that is already in the keeping of the group at large; and every expedient or innovation, great or small, that so is hit upon goes into effect by going into the common stock of technological resources carried by the group. It can take effect only in this way. Such group solidarity is a necessity of the case, both for the acquirement and use of this immaterial equipment that is spoken of as the state of the industrial arts and for its custody and transmission from generation to generation.

Within this common stock of technology some special

branch or line of proficiency, bearing on some special craft or trade, may be held in a degree of isolation by some caste-like group within the community, limited by consanguinity, initiation, and the like, and so it may be held somewhat out of the common stock and transmitted in some degree of segregation. In the lower cultures the elements of technology that are so engrossed by a fraction of the community and held out of the common stock are most commonly of a magical or ceremonial nature, rather than effective elements of workmanship; since any such matters of ritual observance lend themselves with greater facility to exclusive use and transmission within lines of class limitation than do the matter-of-fact devices of actual workmanship. In the lower cultures the exclusive training and information so held and transmitted in segregation by various secret organizations appear in the main to be of this magical or ceremonial character [2]; although there is no reason to doubt that this technological make-believe is taken quite seriously and counts as a substantial asset in the apprehension of its possessors. In a more advanced state of the industrial arts, where ownership and the specialization of industry have had their effect, trade secrets, patent, and copyrights are often of substantial value, and these are held in segregation from the common stock of technology. But it is evident without argu-

[2] Cf. e.g., Hutton Webster, *Primitive Secret Societies,* especially chaps. 3, 4, 5; Spencer and Gillen, *Native Tribes of Central Australia,* chaps. 7, 8, 9, 16.

ment that facts of this class are after all of no grave or enduring consequence in comparison with the great commonplace body of knowledge and skill current in the community. At the same time, any such segregated line of technological gain and transmission, if it has any appreciable significance for the state of the industrial arts and is not wholly made up of ritual observances, leans so greatly on the technological equipment at large that its isolation is at the most partial and one-sided; it takes effect only by the free use of the general body of knowledge which is not so engrossed, and it has also in all cases been acquired and elaborated only by the free use of that commonplace knowledge that is held in no man's exclusive possession. Such is more particularly the case in all but those latest phases of the industrial development in which the volume of the technology and the consequent specialization of occupations have been carried very far.

In the earlier, or rather in all but the late phases of culture and technology, this immaterial equipment at large is accessible to all members of the community as a matter of course through the unavoidable discipline that comes with the workday routine of getting along. Few, if any, can avoid acquiring the essential elements of the industrial scheme by use of which the community lives, although they need not each gain any degree of proficiency in all the manual operations or industrial processes in which this technological scheme goes into effect, and few can avoid being so trained into the logic of the current scheme that their habitual thinking will in all these bearings run within the bounds of experience embodied in this general scheme.

All have free access to this common stock of immaterial equipment, but in all known cultures there is also found some degree of special training and some appreciable specialization of knowledge and occupations; which is carried forward by expert workmen whose peculiar and exceptional proficiency is confined to some one or a few distinct lines of craft. And in all, or at least in all but the lowest known cultures, the available evidence goes to say that this joint stock of technological mastery can be maintained and carried forward only by way of some such specialization of training and differentiation of employments. No one is competent to acquire such mastery of all the lines of industry included in the general scheme as would enable him (or her) to transmit the state of the industrial arts to succeeding generations unimpaired at all points.

Some degree of specialization there always is, even where there appears to be no urgent technological need of it. The circumstances of their life differ sufficiently for different individuals, so that a certain individuation in workmanship will result from commonplace experience, even apart from any deliberate specialization of occupations. And with any considerable increase in the size of the group a more or less deliberate specialization of occupations will also set in. Individuals who are in this way occupied wholly or mainly with some one par-

ticular line of work will carry proficiency in this line to
a higher pitch than the generality of workmen and will
bring out details of technological procedure that may
never fully become the common possession of the group
at large, that may not in all details become part of the
commonplace technological information current in the
community. There seems, in fact, never to have been a
time when the industrial scheme was so slight and narrow that all members of the community could master it
in the greatest feasible degree of proficiency at every
point. But at the same time it holds true for all the more
archaic phases of the development that all members of
the community appear always to have had a comprehensive and passably exhaustive acquaintance with
the technique of all industries practised in their time.

This necessary specialization and detail training has
large consequences for the growth of technology as well
as for its custody and transmission. It follows that a
large and widely diversified industrial scheme is impossible except in a community of some size—large enough
to support a number and variety of special occupations.
In effect, substantial gains in industrial insight and
proficiency can apparently be worked out only through
such close and sustained attention to a given line of
work as can be given only within the lines of a specialized occupation. At the same time the industrial community must comprise a full complement of such specialized occupations, and must also be bound together in
a system of communication sufficiently close and facile

to allow the technological contents of all these occupations to be readily assimilated into a systematic whole. The industrial system so worked out need not be of the same extent as any one local group of the people who get their living by its use; but it seems to be required that if several local groups are effectively to be comprised in a single industrial system conditions of peace must prevail among them. Community of language seems also to be nearly necessary to the maintenance of such a system. Where the various local groups are on hostile terms, each will tend to have an industrial system of its own, with a technological character somewhat distinct from its neighbours.[3] If the degree of isolation is pronounced, so that traffic and communication do not run freely between groups, the size of the local group will limit the state of the industrial arts somewhat rigidly; and on the other hand a marked advance in the industrial arts, such as the domestication of crop plants or animals or the introduction of metals, is likely to bring about such a redistribution of population and industry as to increase the effective size of the community.[4]

---

[3] Cf. for instance, Codrington, *The Melanesians;* Seligmann, *The Melanesians of British New Guinea.*

[4] These considerations may of course imply nothing, directly, as to the size of the political organization or of the national territory or population; though national boundaries are likely both to affect and to be affected by such changes in the industrial system. A community may be small, relatively to the industrial system in and by which it lives, and may yet, if conditions of peace permit it, stand in such a relation of complement or supplement to a larger complex

Among the peoples on the lower levels of culture there prevails commonly a considerable degree of isolation, or even of estrangement. In a great degree each community is thrown on its own resources, and under these circumstances the size of the community may become a matter of decisive importance for the industrial arts. Where a serious decline in the numbers of any of these savage or barbarous peoples is recorded, it is also commonly noted that they have suffered a concomitant decay in their technological knowledge and workmanship.[5] In view of these considerations it is probably safe to say that under settled conditions any community is, commonly, no larger than is required to keep up and

of industrial groups as to make it in effect an integral part of a larger community, so far as regards its technology. So, for instance, Switzerland and Denmark are an integral part of the cultural and industrial community of the western civilization as effectually as they might be with an area and population equal to those of the United Kingdom or the German Empire, and they are doubtless each a more essential part in this community than Russia. At the same time, as things go within this western culture, national boundaries have a very considerable obstructive effect in industrial affairs and in the growth of technology. It will probably be conceded on the one hand that any appreciable decline in the aggregate population of Christendom would result in some curtailment or retardation of the technological advance in which these peoples are jointly and severally engaged; and it is likewise to be conceded on the other hand that the like effect would follow on any marked degree of success from the efforts of those patriotic and dynastic statesmen who are endeavouring to set these peoples asunder in an armed estrangement and neutrality.

[5] Cf., as an extreme case, Matilda C. Stevenson, "The Sia," *Report Bur. Eth.*, XI (1889–90).

The like decline is known to have occurred in many parts of Europe consequent on the decline of population due to the Black Death and the Plague.

carry forward the state of the industrial arts as it runs. The known evidence appears to warrant the generalization that the state of the industrial arts is limited by the size of the industrial community, and that whenever a given community is broken up or suffers a serious diminution of numbers its technological heritage will deteriorate and dwindle even though it may apparently have been meagre enough before.

The considerations recited above are matters of commonplace observation and might fairly be taken for granted without argument. But so much of current and recent theoretical speculation proceeds on tacit assumptions at variance with these commonplaces that it seems pertinent to recall them, particularly since they will come in as premises in later passages of the inquiry.

Given the material environment, the rate and character of the technological gains made in any community will depend on the initiative and application of its members, in so far as the growth of institutions has not seriously diverted the genius of the race from its natural bent; it will depend immediately and obviously on individual talent for workmanship—on the workmanlike bent and capacity of the individual members of the community. Therefore any difference of native endowment in this respect between the several races will show itself in the character of their technological achievements as well as in the rate of gain. Races differ among themselves in this matter, both as to the kind and as to the degree of technological proficiency of which they are capable.[6] It is perhaps as needless to insist on this spiritual difference between the various racial stocks as it would be difficult to determine the specific differences that are known to exist, or to exhibit them convincingly in detail. To some such ground much of the distinctive character of different peoples is no doubt to be assigned, though much also may as well be traceable to local peculiarities of environment and of institutional circumstances. Something of the kind, a specific difference in the genius of the people, is by common consent assigned, for instance, in explanation of the pervasive difference in technology and workmanship between the western culture and the Far East. The like difference in "genius" is still more convincingly shown where different races have long been living near one another under settled cultural conditions.[7]

It should be noted in the same connexion that hybrid peoples, such as those of Europe or of Japan, where somewhat widely distinct racial stocks are mingled, should afford a great variety and wide individual variation of native gifts, in workmanship as in other respects. Hybrid stocks, indeed, have a wider range of usual variability than the combined extreme limits of the

---

[6] On such native differences between the leading races of Europe, cf., e.g., G. V. de Lapouge, *Les Sélections Sociales* and *L'Aryen*; O. Ammon, *Die Gesellschaftsordnung*; G. Sergi, *Arii e Italici*.

[7] For instance, the Japanese and the Ainu, the Polynesians and the Melanesians, the Cingalese and the Veddas. On the last named, cf. Seligmann, *The Veddas.*

racial types that enter into the composition of the hybrid. So that a great variety, even aberration and eccentricity, of native gifts is to be looked for in such cases, and this wide range of variation in workmanlike initiative should show itself in the technology of any such peoples. Yet there may still prevail a strikingly determinate difference between any two such hybrid populations, both in the characteristic features of their technology and in their routine workmanship; as is illustrated in the contrast between Japan and the western nations. These racial differences in point of endowment may be slight in the first instance, but as they work cumulatively their ulterior effect may still be very marked; and they may result in marked differences not only in respect of the character of the technological situation at a given point of time but also in the rate of advance and the direction taken by the technological advance. So in the case of the Far East, as contrasted with the occidental peoples, the genius of the races engaged has prevailingly taken the direction of proficiency in handicraft, rather than that somewhat crude but efficient recourse to mechanical expedients which chiefly distinguishes the technology of the West.

The stability of racial types makes it possible to study the innate characters of the existing population under less complex and confusing circumstances than those of the cultural situation in which this population is now found. By going back into the earlier phases of the western culture the scrutiny of the living population of Europe and its colonies can, in effect, be pushed back in a fragmentary way over an interval of some thousands of years. Such acquaintance as may in this way be gained with the spiritual make-up of the peoples of the western culture at any point in its past history and prehistory should bear immediately and without serious abatement on the native character of the generation in whose hands the fortunes of that culture now rest; provided only that the inquiry assures itself of the racial continuity, racial identity, of these peoples through this period of time. This question of race identity is no longer a matter of serious debate so far as concerns the peoples of northern and western Europe, within the effective bounds of the occidental civilization and as far back as the beginning of the neolithic period. Assuredly there is debate and uncertainty as to local details of racial mixture in nearly all parts of this cultural area at some point in past time, but these uncertainties of detail are not of such a nature or such magnitude as to vitiate the data for an inquiry into the general characteristics of the races concerned. By and large, the mixture of races in north Europe has apparently not varied greatly since early neolithic times, and the changes that have taken place are known with some confidence, in the main. Much the same holds true for the Mediterranean seaboard, although the changes in that region appear to have been more considerable and are perhaps less readily traceable. For northern and western Europe taken together, in spite of considerable local fluctuations, the variations in the general racial composition of the peoples has, on the whole, not been extensive or extremely serious since the latter part of the stone age. The three great racial stocks [8] of western civilization have apparently shared their joint dominance in this culture among themselves since about the time when the use of bronze first came into Europe, which should be before the close of the stone age. And these three stocks are not greatly alien to one another; two of them, the Mediterranean and the blond, being apparently somewhat closely related in point of descent and therefore presumably in point of spiritual make-up.

It is with less confidence that any student of these modern cultures can test his case by evidence drawn from existing or historical communities living on the savage or lower barbarian plane and not closely related, racially, to the peoples of western Europe. The discrepancies in such a case are of two kinds: (a) The racial type, and therefore the spiritual (instinctive) make-up of these alien savages or barbarians, is not the same as that of the modern Europeans; hence the culture worked out under the control of their somewhat different endowment of instincts should come to a different result, particularly since any such racial discrepancy in the mat-

---

[8] Cf. W. Z. Ripley, *The Races of Europe*; G. Sergi, *The Mediterranean Race*; G. V. de Lapouge, *L'Aryen*; cf. also, J. Deniker, *Les races européennes*, and "Les six races composant la population de l'Europe," *Journal Anthropological Institute*, vol. XXXIV.

ter of instincts should be expected to work cumulatively
to a different cultural outcome. These alien communities of the lower cultures can therefore not be accepted
off-hand as representing an earlier phase of occidental
civilization. This infirmity attaches to any recourse to
an existing savage or barbarian community for object-
lessons to illustrate the working of European human nature in similarly primitive circumstances, in the degree
in which the community in question may be remote from
the Europeans in point of racial type; which reduces
itself to a difficult question as to the point in the family-
tree of the races of man from which the two contrasted
races have diverged, and of the number, character, and
magnitude of the racial mutations that may have intervened between the presumed point of divergence and
the existing racial types so contrasted. (*b*) It is commonly said, and it is presumably true enough, that all
known communities on the lower levels of culture are
far from a state of primitive savagery; that they are not
to be taken as genuinely archaic, but are the result either
of a comparatively late reversion, under special circumstances, from a past higher stage, or they are peoples
which have undergone so protracted an experience in
savagery that their present state is one of extreme sophis-
tication in all "the beastly devices of the heathen,"
rather than substantially an early or archaic type of
culture, such as would have marked a transient stage
in the development of those peoples that have attained
civilized life.

No doubt there is some substance to these objections, but they contain rather a modicum of truth than an inclusive presentation of the facts relevant to the case. As to (*a*), the races of man are, after all, more alike than unlike, and the evidence drawn from the experience of any one racial stock or mixture is not to be disregarded as having no significance for the probable course of things experienced by any other racial stock during a corresponding interval in its life-history. Yet there is doubtless a wide and debatable margin of error to be allowed for in the use of all evidence of this class. As to (*b*), by virtue of the stability of racial types the populations of existing communities of the lower cultures should be today what they were at the outset, in respect of the most substantial factor in their present situation, their spiritual (instinctive) make-up; and this unaltered complement of instincts should, under similar circumstances and with a moderate allowance of time, work out substantially the same general run of cultural results whether the resulting phase of culture were reached by approach from a near and untroubled beginning or by regression from a "higher plane." So that the existing communities of savages or lower barbarians should present a passably competent object-lesson in archaic savagery and barbarism whether their past has been higher, lower, or simply more of the same.

All this, of course, assumes the stability of racial types. But since, tacitly, that assumption is habitually made by ethnologists, all that calls for apology or explanation here is the avowal of it. The greater proportion of ethnological generalizations on this range of questions would be quite impotent without that assumption as their major premise. What has not commonly been assumed or admitted, except by subconscious implication, is the necessary corollary that these stable types with which ethnologists and anthropologists busy themselves must have arisen by mutation from previously existing types, rather than by a long continued and divergent accumulation of insensible variations. A result of avowing such a view of the genesis of races will be that the various races cannot be regarded as being all of the same date and racial maturity, or of the same significance for any discussion bearing on the higher cultures. The races engaged in the western culture will presumably be found to be of relatively late date, as having arisen out of relatively late mutational departures, as rated in terms of the aggregate life-history of mankind. Presumably also many of the other races will be found to be somewhat widely out of touch with the members of this occidental aggregation of racial stocks; some more, others less remotely related to them, according as their mutational pedigree may be found to indicate.

An advantage derivable from such an avowal of the stability of types, as against its covert assumption and overt disavowal, is that it enables the student to look

for the beginning, in time and space, of any given racial
stock with which his inquiry is concerned, and to handle
it as a unit throughout its life-history.

In all probability each of the leading racial stocks of
Europe began its life-history on what would currently
be accounted a low level of savagery. And yet this phase
of savagery, whatever it may have been like, will have
been removed from the first beginnings of human culture by a long series of thousands of years. That such
was the case, for instance, with the European blond is
scarcely to be questioned [9]; and it is at least highly probable that the other stocks now associated with the blond,
though probably older, must also have come into being relatively late in the life-history of the species.

Vague as this dating may be, it signifies that the initial
phase in the life-history of at least one, and presumably
of all, of the leading races of Europe falls in a savage
culture of a relatively advanced kind as compared with
the rudest human beginnings. Therefore when these

---

[9] The available evidence indicates that the dolicho-blond race of
northern Europe probably originated in a mutation (from the Mediterranean as its parent stock?) during the early neolithic period, that
is to say about at the beginning of the neolithic in western Europe.
There is less secure ground for conjecture as to the date and circumstances under which any one of the other European races originated,
but the date and place of their origin seems to lie outside of Europe
and earlier than the European neolithic period. Unfortunately there
has been little direct or succinct discussion of this matter among anthropologists hitherto.—Cf. "The Mutation Theory and the Blond
Race," *Journal of Race Development*, April 1913 [republished in
*The Place of Science in Modern Civilization*, 1919, pp. 457–76].

stocks began life, and so were required to make good their survival, the selective conditions imposed on them, and to which they were required to conform on pain of extinction, were the conditions of a savage culture which had already made some appreciable advance in the arts of life. They had not to meet brute nature in the helpless nakedness of those remote ancestors in whom humanity first began. Mutationally speaking, the stock was born to the use of tools and to the facile mastery of a relatively advanced technology. And conversely it is a fair inference that these stocks that have peopled Europe would have been unfit to survive if they had come into the world before some appreciable advance in technology had been made. That is to say, these stocks could not by native gift have been fit for a wild life, in the unqualified sense of the term; nor have they ever lived a life of nature in any such sense. They came into the savage world after the race had lived through many thousand years of technological experience and (presumably) many successive mutational alterations of racial type, and they were fitted to the exigencies of the savage world into which they came rather than those of any earlier phase of savagery. The youngest of them, the latest mutant, emerged in early neolithic times, and since he eminently made good his fitness to survive under those conditions he presumably emerged with such an endowment of traits, physical and spiritual, as those conditions called for; and also presumably with no appreciable burden of aptitudes, propensities, instincts, capacities that would be disserviceable, or perhaps even that would be wholly unserviceable, in the circumstances in which he was placed. And since the other racial elements of the European population, at least the two main ones, do not differ at all radically from the blond in their native capacities, it is likewise to be presumed that they also emerged from a mutation under circumstances of culture, and especially of technology, not radically different in degree from those that first surrounded the blond.

The difference between these three racial stocks is much more evident in their physical traits than in their instinctive gifts or their intellectual capacity; and yet the similarity of the three is so great and distinctive even on the physical side that anthropologists are inclined to class the three together as all and several distinctively typical of a "white" or "caucasic" race, to which they are held collectively to belong. Something to the like effect seems to hold true for the distinctive groups of racial stocks that have made the characteristic civilizations of the Far East on the one hand and of southern Asia on the other hand; and something similar might, again, be said for the group of stocks that were concerned in the ancient civilizations of America.

It may be pertinent to add that, except for a long antecedent growth of technology, that is to say a long continued cumulative experience in workmanship, with the resultant accumulated knowledge of the ways and means of life, none of the characteristic races of Europe could have survived. In the absence of these antecedent technological gains, together with the associated growth of institutions, such mutants, with their characteristic gifts and limitations, must have perished.

On that level of savagery on which these European stocks began, and to which the several European racial types with their typical endowment of instincts are presumably adapted, men appear to have lived a fairly peaceable, though by no means an indolent life; in relatively small groups or communities; without any of the more useful domestic animals, though probably with some domestic plants; and busied with getting their living by daily work. Since they survived under the conditions offered them it is to be presumed that these men and women, say of the early neolithic time, took instinctively and kindly to those activities and mutual relations that would further the life of the group; and that, on the whole, they took less kindly and instinctively to such activities as would bring damage and discomfort on their neighbours and themselves.[10] Any

10 The Melanesians may be contrasted with the Baltic peoples in this respect, though the comparison is perhaps rather suggestive than convincing. The Melanesians are apparently endowed with a very respectable capacity for workmanship, as regards both insight and application, and with a relatively high sense of economic expediency. They are also possessed of an alert and enduring group solidarity. But they apparently lack that reasonable degree of "humanity" and congenital tolerance that has on the whole kept the peoples of the Baltic region from fatal extravagances of cruelty and sustained hatred between groups. Not that any excess of humanity has marked the course of culture in North Europe. But it seems at least admissible to say

racial type of which this had not been true, under the conditions known then to have prevailed in their habitat, must have presently disappeared from the face of the land, and the later advance of the western culture would not have known their breed. Some other racial type, temperamentally so constituted as better to meet these requirements of survival under neolithic conditions, would have taken their place and would have left their own offspring to populate the region.[11]

What is known of the conditions of life in early neolithic times [12] indicates that the first requisite of competitive survival was a more or less close attention to the business in hand, the providing of subsistence for the

that mutual hatred, distrust, and disparagement falls more readily into abeyance among these peoples than among the Melanesians; particularly when and in so far as the material interest of the several groups visibly suffers from a continued free run of extravagant animosity. The difference in point of native propensity may not be very marked, but such degree of it as there is has apparently thrown the balance in such a way that the Baltic peoples have, technologically, had the advantage of a wide and relatively easy contact and communication; whereas the Melanesians have during an equally protracted experience spent themselves largely on interstitial animosities. —Cf. Codrington, *The Melanesians*; Seligmann, *The Melanesians of British New Guinea*.

[11] These considerations apparently apply with peculiar force to the blond race, in that the evidence of early times goes to argue that this stock never lived in isolation from other, rival stocks. It began presumably as a small minority in a community made up chiefly of a different racial type, its parent stock, and in an environment at large in which at least one rival stock was present in force from near the outset; so that race competition, that is to say competition in terms of births and deaths, was instant and unremitting. And this competition the given conditions enforced in terms of group subsistence.

[12] Cf., e.g., Sophus Müller, *Vor Oldtid*, "Stenalderen."

group and the rearing of offspring—a closer attention, for instance, than was given to this business by those other rival stocks whom the successful ones displaced; all of which throws into the foreground as indispensable native traits of the successful race the parental bent and the sense of workmanship, rather than those instinctive traits that make for disturbance of the peace.[13]

But through it all the suggestion insinuates itself that the latest, or youngest, of the three main European stocks, the blond, has more rather than less of the pugnacious and predatory temper than the other two, and that this stock made its way to the front in spite of, if not by force of these traits. The advantage of the blond as a fighter seems to have been due in part to an adventurous and pugnacious temper, but also in part to a superior physique—superior for the purpose of fighting hand to hand or with the implements chiefly used in warfare and piracy down to a date within the nineteenth century. The same physical traits of mass, stature, and katabolism will likewise have been of great advantage in the quest of a livelihood under the conditions that prevailed in the North Sea region, the habitat of the dolicho-blond, in the stone age. Something to the same effect is true of the spiritual traits which are said to characterize the blond—a certain canny temerity

---

[13] It has not commonly been noted, though it will scarcely be questioned, that fighting capacity and the propensity to fight have rarely, if ever, been successful in the struggle between races and peoples when brought into competition with a diligent growing of crops and children, if success be counted in terms of race survival.

and unrest.[14] So that the point is left somewhat in doubt; the traits which presently made the northern blond the most formidable disturber of the peace of Europe and kept him so for many centuries may at the outset have been chiefly conducive to the survival of the type by their serviceability for industrial purposes under the peculiar circumstances of climate and topography in which the race first came up and made good its survival.

In modern speculations on the origins of culture and the early history of mankind it has until recently been usual to assume, uncritically, that human communities have from the outset of the race been entangled in an inextricable web of mutual hostilities and beset with an all-pervading sentiment of fear; that the "state of nature" was a state of blood and wounds, expressing itself in universal malevolence and suspicion. Latterly, students of primitive culture, and more especially those engaged at first hand in field work, who come in contact with peoples of the lower culture, have been coming to realize that the facts do not greatly support such a presumption, and that a community which has to make its own living by the help of a rudimentary technological

---

[14] It is apparently an open question whether these spiritual traits are properly to be ascribed to the dolicho-blond as traits of that type taken by itself, rather than traits characteristic of the hybrid offspring of the blond stock crossed on one or other of the racial stocks associated with it in the populations of Europe. The evidence at large seems rather to bear out the view that any hybrid population is likely to be endowed with an exceptional degree of that restlessness and discontent that go to make up what is spoken of as a "spirit of enterprise" in the race.

equipment cannot afford to be habitually occupied with annoying its neighbours, particularly so long as its neighbours have not accumulated a store of portable wealth which will make raiding worth while. No doubt, many savage and barbarian peoples live in a state of conventional feud or habitual, even if intermittent, war and predation, without substantial inducement in the way of booty. But such communities commonly are either so placed that an easy livelihood affords them a material basis for following after these higher things out of mere fancy [15]; or they are peoples living precariously hand to mouth and fighting for their lives, in great part from a fancied impossibility of coming to terms with their alien and unnaturally cruel neighbours.[16] Communities of the latter class are often living in a state of squalor and discomfort, with a population far short of what their environment would best support even with their inefficient industrial organization and equipment, and their technology is usually ill suited to a settled life and unpromising for any possible advance to a higher culture. There is no urgent reason for assuming that the races which have made their way to a greater technological efficiency, with settled life and a large population, must have come up from this particular phase of civilization as their starting-point, or that such a culture

---

[15] As, e.g., the inhabitants of many Polynesian islands at the time of their discovery. See, also, Codrington, *The Melanesians*.

[16] Not an unusual state of things among the Melanesians and Micronesians, and in a degree among the Australians.

should have been favourable to the survival and increase of the leading racial stocks of Europe, since it does not appear to be especially favourable to the success of the communities known to be now living after that fashion.[17]

The preconception that early culture must have been warlike has not yet disappeared even among students of these phenomena, though it is losing their respect; but a derivative of it still has much currency, to the effect that all savage peoples, as also the peoples of the lower barbarism, live in a state of universal and unremitting fear, particularly fear of the unknown. This chronic fear is presumed to show itself chiefly in religion and other superstitious practices, where it is held to explain many things that are otherwise obscure. There is not a little evidence from extant savage communities looking in this direction, and more from the lower barbarian cultures that are characteristically warlike.[18] Wherever this animus is found its effect is to waste effort and divert it to religious and magical practices and so to hinder the free unfolding of workmanship by enjoining a cumbersome routine of ritual and by warning the technologist off forbidden ground. But it is doubtless a hasty generalization to carry all this over uncritically and make it apply to all peoples of the lower culture, past and present. It is known not to be true of many existing

[17] See note, p. 195.
[18] E.g., some Australian natives and some of the lower Malay cultures.

communities,[19] and the evidence of it in some ancient cultures is very dubious. Such a characterization of the neolithic culture of Europe, whether north-European or Aegean, finds no appreciable support in the archæological evidence. These two regions are the most significant for the neolithic period in Europe, and the material from both is relatively very poor in weapons, as contrasted with tools, on the one hand, and there is at the same time little or nothing to indicate the prevalence of superstitious practices based on fear. Indeed, the material is surprisingly poor in elements of any kind that can safely be set down to the account of religion or magic, whether as inspired by fear or by more genial sentiments. It is one of the puzzles that beset any student who insists on finding everywhere a certain normal course of cultural sequence, which should in the early times include, among other things, a fearsome religion, a wide fabric of magical practices, and an irrepressible craving for manslaughter. And when, presently, something of a symbolism and apparatus of superstition comes into view, in the late neolithic and bronze ages, the common run of it is by no means suggestive of superstitious fear and religious atrocities. The most common and characteristic objects of this class are certain figurines and certain symbolical elements suggestive of fecundity, such as might be looked for in a peaceable, sedentary, agricultural culture on a small

[19] E.g., the Pueblo and the Eskimo.

scale.[20] A culture virtually without weapons, whose gods are mothers and whose religious observances are a ritual of fecundity, can scarcely be a culture of dread and of derring-do. With the fighting barbarians, on the other hand, male deities commonly take the first rank, and their ritual symbolizes the mastery of the god and the servitude of the worshipper.

It is true, of course, that both of weapons and of cult objects far the greater number that were once in use will have disappeared, since most of the implements and utensils of stone-age cultures are, notoriously, made of wood or similar perishable materials.[21] So that the finds give no complete series of the appliances in use in their time; whole series of objects that were of first-rate importance in that culture having probably disappeared without leaving a trace But what is true in this respect of weapons and cult objects should be equally true of tools, or nearly so. So that the inference to be drawn

---

[20] Indeed, such as very suggestively to recall the ritual objects and observances of the Pueblo Indians.

[21] For an extreme case of this among living communities, see Skeat and Blagden, *Pagan Races of the Malay Peninsula*, vol. I, pp. 242–50, where the generalization is set down (p. 248) that "the rudimentary stage of culture through which these tribes have passed, and in some cases are still passing, may perhaps be more accurately described as a wood and bone age than as an age of stone," in as much as the evidence goes to show that before they began to get metals from the Malays their only implements of a more durable material were "the anvil and hammer (unwrought) . . . the whetstone, chips or flakes used as knives, and cooking stones." From the different character of their environment this recourse to wood and bone could scarcely have been carried to such an extreme by the savages of the Baltic region.

from the available material would be that the early
neolithic culture of north Europe, the Aegean, and other
explored localities presumed to belong in the same racial
and cultural complex, must have been of a prevailingly
peaceable complexion. With the advance in technology
and in the elaboration and abundance of objects that
comes into sight progressively through the later neolithic
period, down to its close, this disproportion between
tools and weapons (and cult objects) grows more impressive and more surprising. Hitherto this disproportion has been more in evidence in the Scandinavian finds
than in the other related fields of stone-age culture, unless an exception should be made in favour of the late
neolithic sites explored at Anau.[22] But this archæological
outcome, setting off the Baltic stone age as peculiarly
scant of weapons and peculiarly rich in tools, may be
provisional only, and may be due to the more exhaustive
exploration of the Scandinavian countries and the un-
commonly abundant material from that region. In the
later (mainly Scandinavian) neolithic material, where
the weapons are to be counted by dozens the tools are
to be counted by hundreds, according to a scheme of
classification in which everything that can be construed
as a weapon is so classed, and there are many more
hundreds of the one class than there are dozens of the
other.[23] As near as can be made out, cult objects are

---

[22] Cf. Pumpelly, *Explorations in Turkestan.*
[23] A casual visit to the Scandinavian museums will scarcely convey
this impression. To meet the prepossessions of the public, and perhaps

similarly infrequent among these materials even after some appreciable work in pottery comes in evidence.

What has just been said is after all of a negative character. It says that nothing like a warlike, predatory, or fearsome origin can be proven from the archæological material for the neolithic culture of those racial stocks that have counted for most in the early periods of Europe. The presumption raised by this evidence, however, is fairly strong. And considerations of the material circumstances in which this early culture was placed, as well as of the spiritual traits characteristically required by these circumstances and shown by the races in question, point to a similar conclusion. The proclivity to unreasoning fear that is visible in the superstitious practices of so many savage communities and counts for so much in the routine of their daily life,[24] is to all appearance not so considerable an element in the make-up of the chief European stocks. Perhaps it enters in a less degree in the spiritual nature of the European blond than in that of any other race; that race—or its hybrid offspring —has at any rate proved less amenable to religious control than any other, and has also shown less hesitation in the face of unknown contingencies. And the circumstances of the presumed initial phase of the life-history

of the experts, the weapons are made much of in the showcases, as is to be expected; but they are relatively scarce in the store-rooms, where the tools on the other hand are rather to be estimated by the cubic yard than counted by the piece.

[24] Seen, e.g., in the observance and sanction of taboo in many of the lower cultures.

of this race would appear not to have favoured a spiritual (instinctive) type largely biased by an alert and powerful sentiment of unreasoning fear. So also an aggressive humanitarian sentiment is as well at home in the habits of thought of the north-European peoples as in any other, such as sorts ill with a native predatory animus. If it be assumed, as seems probable, that the situation which selectively tested the fitness of this stock to survive was that of the early post-glacial time, when its habitat in Europe was slowly being cleared of the ice-sheet, it would appear antecedently probable that the new (mutant) type, which made good its survival in following up the retreating fringe of the ice-sheet and populating the land so made available, will not have been a people peculiarly given to fear or to predation. A great facility of this kind, with its concomitants of caution, conservatism, suspicion, and cruelty, would not be serviceable for a race so placed.[25]

---

[25] The Eskimo are placed in circumstances that are in some respects similar to those presumed to have conditioned the life of the blond race and its hybrids during the early phases of its life-history, and among the traits that have made for the survival of the Eskimo is undoubtedly to be counted the somewhat genial good-fellowship of that race, coupled as it is with a notable disinclination to hostilities. So also the Indians of the North-West Coast, whose situation perhaps parallels that of the neolithic Baltic culture more closely even than the Eskimo, are not among the notably warlike peoples of the earth, although they undoubtedly show more of a predatory animus than their northern neighbours. In this case it is probably safe to say that their technological achievements have in no degree been furthered by such warlike enterprise as they have shown, and that their comfort and success as a race would have been even more marked if they had been gifted

Even if it were a possible undertaking it would not be much to the present purpose to trace out in detail the many slow and fumbling moves by which any given race or people, in Europe or elsewhere, have worked out the technological particulars that have led from the beginnings down through the primitive and later growth of culture. Such a work belongs to the ethnologists and archæologists; and it is summed up in the proposition that men have applied common-sense, more or less hesitatingly and with more or less refractory limitations, to the facts with which they have had to deal; that they have accumulated a knowledge of technological expedients and processes from generation to generation, always going on what had already been achieved in ways and means, and gradually discarding or losing such elements of the growing technological scheme as seemed no longer to be worth while,[26] and carrying along a good

with less of the warlike spirit and had kept the peace more consistently throughout their habitat than they have done.—Cf. Franz Boas, "The Central Eskimo," Bureau of American Ethnology *Report*, 1884–5; the same, "The Secret Societies and Social Organization of the Kwakiutl Indians," *Report*, National Museum, 1895; A. P. Niblack, "Coast Indians of Southern Alaska and Northern British Columbia," ibid., 1888.

[26] Such loss by neglect of technological elements that have been superseded may have serious consequences in case a people of somewhat advanced attainments suffers a material set-back either in its industrial circumstances or in its cultural situation more at large—as happened, e.g., in the Dark Ages of Europe. In such case it is likely to result that the community will be unable to fall back on a state of the industrial arts suited to the reduced circumstances into which it finds itself thrown, having lost the use of many of the technological elements familiar to earlier generations that lived under similar cir-

many elements that were of no material effect but were imposed by the logic of the scheme or of its underlying principles (habits of thought).

Of the early technological development in Europe, so far as it is genetically connected with the later western civilization, the culture of the Baltic region affords as good and illustrative an object-lesson as may be had; its course is relatively well known, simple, and unbroken. Palæolithic times do not count in this development, as the neolithic culture begins with a new break in Europe.

It is known, then, that by early neolithic times on the narrow Scandinavian waters men had learned to make and use certain rude stone and bone implements found in the kitchen-middens (refuse heaps, shell-mounds of Denmark), that they had ways and appliances (the nature of which is not known) for collecting certain shellfish and for catching such game and fish as their habitat afforded, and that they presently, if not from the outset, had acquired the use of certain crop plants and had learned to make pottery of a crude kind. From this as a point of departure in the period of the kitchen-middens the stone implements were presently improved and multiplied, the methods of working the material

cumstances, and so the industrial community finds itself in many respects driven to make a virtually new beginning, from a more rudimentary starting-point than the situation might otherwise call for. This in turn acts to throw the people back to a more archaic phase of technology and of institutions than the initial cultural loss sustained by the community would of itself appear to warrant.

(flint) and of using the products of the flint industry were gradually improved and extended, until in the long course of time the utmost that has anywhere been achieved in that class of industry was reached. Domestic animals began to be added to the equipment relatively early,[27] though at a long interval from the neolithic beginnings as counted in absolute time. Improvement and extension in all lines of stoneworking and woodworking industry went forward; except that stone-dressing and masonry are typically absent, owing, no doubt, to the extensive use of woodwork instead.[28] Along with this advance in the mechanic arts goes a growing density of population and a wide extension of tillage; until, at the coming of bronze, the evidence shows that these communities were populous, prosperous, and highly skilled in those industrial arts that lay within their technological range.

Apart from the pottery, which may have some merit as an art product, there is very little left to show what may have been their proficiency in the decorative arts, or what was their social organization or their religious life. The evidences of warlike enterprise and religious practices are surprisingly scanty, being chiefly the doubt-

---

[27] Sophus Müller, *Vor Oldtid*, "Stenalderen," sec. 3, "Tidsforhold i den ældre Stenalder"; O. Montelius, *Les temps préhistoriques en Suède*, chap. 1, p. 20.

[28] Compare the case of the Indians of the North-West Coast, who have occupied a region comparable to the neolithic Baltic area in the distribution of land and water as well as in the abundance of good timber.

ful evidence of many and somewhat elaborate tombs. From the tombs (mounds and barrows) and their distribution something may be inferred as to the social organization; and the evidence on this head seems to indicate a widespread agricultural population, living (probably) in small communities, without much centralized or authoritative control, but with some appreciable class differences in the distribution of wealth in the later phases of the period.

With interruptions, more or less serious, from time to time, and with increasing evidence of a penchant for warlike or predatory enterprise on the one hand and of class distinctions on the other hand, much the same story runs on through the ages of bronze and early iron. Evidences of borrowing from outside, mainly the borrowing of decorative technique and technological elements, are scattered through the course of this development from very early times, showing that there was always some intercourse, perhaps constant intercourse, with other peoples more or less distant. So that in time, by the beginning of the bronze age, there is evidence of settled trade relations with peoples as remote as the Mediterranean seaboard.

In many of its details this prehistoric culture shows something of the same facility in the use of mechanical expedients as has come so notably forward again in the late development of the industrial arts of western Europe. It is in its mechanical efficiency that the technology of the latter-day western culture stands out pre-eminent, and it is similarly its easy command of the mechanical factors with which it deals that chiefly distinguishes the prehistoric technology of north Europe. In other respects the prehistoric material from this region does not argue a high level of civilization. There are no ornate or stupendous structures; what there is of the kind is mounds and barrows of moderately great size and using only undressed stone where any is used, but making a mechanically effective use of this. There is, indeed, nothing from the stone age in the way of edifices, fabrics, or decorative work that is to be classed, in point of excellence in design or execution, with the polished-flint woodworking axe or chisel of that time. From the bronze age at its best there is much excellent bronze-work of great merit both in workmanship and in decorative effect; but the artistic merit of this work (from the middle and early half of the bronze age) lies almost wholly in its workmanlike execution and in the freedom and adequacy with which very simple mechanical elements of decoration are employed. It is an art which appeals to the sense of beauty chiefly through the sense of workmanship, shown both in the choice of materials and decorative elements and in the use made of them. When this art aspires to more ambitious decorative effects or to representation of life forms, or indeed to any representation that has not been conventionalized almost past recognition, as it does in the later periods of the bronze age, the result is that it can be commended for its workmanship alone, and so far as regards artistic effect it is mainly misspent workmanship.[29]

The same workmanlike insight and facility comes in evidence in the matter of borrowing, already spoken of. Borrowing goes on throughout this prehistoric culture, and the borrowed elements are assimilated with such dispatch and effect as to make them seem home-bred almost from the start. It is a borrowing of technological elements, which are rarely employed except in full and competent adaptation to the uses to which they are turned; so much so that the archæologists find it exceptionally difficult to trace the borrowed elements to specific sources, in spite of the great volume and frequency of this borrowing.

There is a further and obscurer aspect to this facile borrowing. In the cultures where the technological and decorative elements are first invented, or acquired at first-hand by slow habituation, there will in the nature of the case come in with them into the scheme of technology or of art more or less, but presumably a good deal, of extraneous or extrinsic by-products of their acquirement, in the way of magical or symbolic efficacy imputed and adhering to them in the habits of thought of their makers and users. Something of this kind has already been set out in some detail as regards the domestication and early use of the crop plants and ani-

[29] Sophus Müller, *Vor Oldtid*, "Bronzealderen," secs. 13, 14; Montelius, *Les temps préhistoriques en Suède*, chap. 2.

mals; [30] and the like is currently held to be true, perhaps in a higher degree, for the beginnings of art, both representative and decorative, by the latter-day students of that subject; the beginnings of art being held to have been magical and symbolic in the main, so far as regards the prime motives to its inception and its initial principles. [31]

In the origination and indigenous working-out of any given technological factor, e.g., such as the use of the crop plants or the domestic animals, elements of imputed anthropomorphism are likely to be comprised in the habitual apprehension of the nature of these factors, and so find lodgment in the technological routine that has to do with them; the result being, chiefly, a limitation on their uses and on the ways and means by which they are utilized, together with a margin of lost motion in the way of magical and religious observances presumed to be intrinsic to the due working of such factors. The ritual connected with tillage and cattle-breeding shows this magical side of a home-bred technology perhaps as felicitously as anything; but similar phenomena are by no means infrequent in the mechanic arts, and in the fine arts these principles of symbolism and the like are commonly present in such force as to afford

---

[30] *The Instinct of Workmanship and the State of the Industrial Arts*, chap. 2, on "Contamination of Instincts in Primitive Technology."

[31] Cf., e.g., C. A. Haddon, *Evolution in Art*, section on "Magic and Religion."

ground for distinguishing one school or epoch of art from another.

Now, when any given technological or decorative element crosses the frontier between one culture and another, in the course of borrowing, it is likely to happen that it will come into the new culture stripped of most or all of its anthropomorphic or spiritual virtues and limitations, more particularly, of course, if the cultural frontier in question is at the same time a linguistic frontier; since the borrowing is likely to be made from motives of workmanlike expediency, and the putative spiritual attributes of the facts involved are not obvious to men who have not been trained to impute them. The chief exception to such a rule would be any borrowing that takes effect on religious grounds, in which case, of course, the magical or symbolic efficacy of the borrowed elements are the substance that is sought in the borrowing. Herein, presumably, lies much of the distinctive character of the north-European prehistoric culture, which was in an eminent degree built up out of borrowed elements, so far as concerns both its technology and its art. And to this free and voluminous borrowing may likewise be due the apparent poverty of this early culture in religious or magical elements.

A further effect follows. The borrowing being (relatively) unencumbered with ritual restrictions and magical exactions attached to their employment, they would fall into the scheme of things as mere matter-of-fact, to

be handled with the same freedom and unhindered sagacity with which a workman makes use of his own
hands, and could, without reservation, be turned to any
use for which they were mechanically suited. Something of symbolism and superstition might, of course,
be carried over in the borrowing, and something more
would unavoidably be bred into the borrowed elements
in the course of their use; but the free start would
always count for something in the outcome, both as
regards the rate of progress made in the exploitation
of the expedients acquired by borrowing and in the
character of the technological system at large into which
they had been introduced. Both the relative freedom
from magical restraint and the growth of home-made
anthropomorphic imputations may easily be detected
in the course of this northern culture and in its outcome in modern times. Cattle, for instance, are a borrowed technological fact in the Baltic and North Sea
region, but superstitious practices seem never to have
attached to cattle-breeding in that region in such volume and rigorous exaction as may be found nearer the
original home of the domesticated species; and yet the
volume of folklore, mostly of a genial and relatively
unobstructive character, that has in later times grown
up about the care of cattle in the Scandinavian countries
is by no means inconsiderable.

# THE THEORY OF THE

# LEISURE CLASS¹

✿

## PECUNIARY EMULATION

IN the sequence of cultural evolution the emergence
of a leisure class coincides with the beginning of ownership. This is necessarily the case, for these two institutions result from the same set of economic forces. In
the inchoate phase of their development they are but
different aspects of the same general facts of social
structure.

It is as elements of social structure—conventional
facts—that leisure and ownership are matters of interest for the purpose in hand. An habitual neglect of work
does not constitute a leisure class; neither does the
mechanical fact of use and consumption constitute ownership. The present inquiry, therefore, is not concerned
with the beginning of indolence, nor with the beginning
of the appropriation of useful articles to individual consumption. The point in question is the origin and nature
of a conventional leisure class on the one hand and the

---

¹ Reprinted from *The Theory of the Leisure Class*, 1899, pp. 22-
67, 363-400.

beginnings of individual ownership as a conventional right or equitable claim on the other hand.

The early differentiation out of which the distinction between a leisure and a working class arises is a division maintained between men's and women's work in the lower stages of barbarism. Likewise the earliest form of ownership is an ownership of the women by the able-bodied men of the community. The facts may be expressed in more general terms, and truer to the import of the barbarian theory of life, by saying that it is an ownership of the woman by the man.

There was undoubtedly some appropriation of useful articles before the custom of appropriating women arose. The usages of existing archaic communities in which there is no ownership of women is warrant for such a view. In all communities the members, both male and female, habitually appropriate to their individual use a variety of useful things; but these useful things are not thought of as owned by the person who appropriates and consumes them. The habitual appropriation and consumption of certain slight personal effects goes on without raising the question of ownership; that is to say, the question of a conventional, equitable claim to extraneous things.

The ownership of women begins in the lower barbarian stages of culture, apparently with the seizure of female captives. The original reason for the seizure and appropriation of women seems to have been their usefulness as trophies. The practice of seizing women from the enemy as trophies gave rise to a form of ownership-marriage, resulting in a household with a male head. This was followed by an extension of slavery to other captives and inferiors, besides women, and by an extension of ownership-marriage to other women than those seized from the enemy. The outcome of emulation under the circumstances of a predatory life, therefore, has been on the one hand a form of marriage resting on coercion, and on the other hand the custom of ownership. The two institutions are not distinguishable in the initial phase of their development; both arise from the desire of the successful men to put their prowess in evidence by exhibiting some durable result of their exploits. Both also minister to that propensity for mastery which pervades all predatory communities. From the ownership of women the concept of ownership extends itself to include the products of their industry, and so there arises the ownership of things as well as of persons.

In this way a consistent system of property in goods is gradually installed. And although in the latest stages of the development, the serviceability of goods for consumption has come to be the most obtrusive element of their value, still, wealth has by no means yet lost its utility as a honorific evidence of the owner's prepotence.

Wherever the institution of private property is found, even in a slightly developed form, the economic process bears the character of a struggle between men for the possession of goods. It has been customary in economic theory, and especially among those economists who adhere with least faltering to the body of modernized classical doctrines, to construe this struggle for wealth as being substantially a struggle for subsistence. Such is, no doubt, its character in large part during the earlier and less efficient phases of industry. Such is also its character in all cases where the "niggardliness of nature" is so strict as to afford but a scanty livelihood to the community in return for strenuous and unremitting application to the business of getting the means of subsistence. But in all progressing communities an advance is presently made beyond this early stage of technological development. Industrial efficiency is presently carried to such a pitch as to afford something appreciably more than a bare livelihood to those engaged in the industrial process. It has not been unusual for economic theory to speak of the further struggle for wealth on this new industrial basis as a competition for an increase of the comforts of life,—primarily for an increase of the physical comforts which the consumption of goods affords.

The end of acquisition and accumulation is conventionally held to be the consumption of the goods accumulated—whether it is consumption directly by the owner of the goods or by the household attached to him and for this purpose identified with him in theory. This is at least felt to be the economically legitimate end of acquisition, which alone it is incumbent on the theory to take account of. Such consumption may of course be conceived to serve the consumer's physical wants—his physical comfort—or his so-called higher wants—spiritual, æsthetic, intellectual, or what not; the latter class of wants being served indirectly by an expenditure of goods, after the fashion familiar to all economic readers.

But it is only when taken in a sense far removed from its naïve meaning that consumption of goods can be said to afford the incentive from which accumulation invariably proceeds. The motive that lies at the root of ownership is emulation; and the same motive of emulation continues active in the further development of the institution to which it has given rise and in the development of all those features of the social structure which this institution of ownership touches. The possession of wealth confers honour; it is an invidious distinction. Nothing equally cogent can be said for the consumption of goods, nor for any other conceivable incentive to acquisition, and especially not for any incentive to the accumulation of wealth.

It is of course not to be overlooked that in a community where nearly all goods are private property the necessity of earning a livelihood is a powerful and ever-present incentive for the poorer members of the community. The need of subsistence and of an increase of physical comfort may for a time be the dominant motive of acquisition for those classes who are habitually employed at manual labour, whose subsistence is on a precarious footing, who possess little and ordinarily accumulate little; but it will appear in the course of the discussion that even in the case of these impecunious classes the predominance of the motive of physical want is not so decided as has sometimes been assumed. On the other hand, so far as regards those members and classes of the community who are chiefly concerned in the accumulation of wealth, the incentive of subsistence or of physical comfort never plays a considerable part. Ownership began and grew into a human institution on grounds unrelated to the subsistence minimum. The dominant incentive was from the outset the invidious distinction attaching to wealth, and, save temporarily and by exception, no other motive has usurped the primacy at any later stage of the development.

Property set out with being booty held as trophies of the successful raid. So long as the group had departed but little from the primitive communal organization, and so long as it still stood in close contact with other hostile groups, the utility of things or persons owned lay chiefly in an invidious comparison between their possessor and the enemy from whom they were taken. The habit of distinguishing between the interests of the individual and those of the group to which he belongs is apparently a later growth. Invidious comparison between the possessor of the honorific booty and his less successful neighbours within the group was no doubt present early as an element of the utility of the things possessed, though this was not at the outset the chief element of their value. The man's prowess was still primarily the group's prowess, and the possessor of the booty felt himself to be primarily the keeper of the honour of his group. This appreciation of exploit from the communal point of view is met with also at later stages of social growth, especially as regards the laurels of war.

But so soon as the custom of individual ownership begins to gain consistency, the point of view taken in making the invidious comparison on which private property rests will begin to change. Indeed, the one change is but the reflex of the other. The initial phase of ownership, the phase of acquisition by naïve seizure and conversion, begins to pass into the subsequent stage of an incipient organization of industry on the basis of private property (in slaves); the horde develops into a more or less self-sufficing industrial community; possessions then come to be valued not so much as evidence of successful foray, but rather as evidence of the prepotence of the possessor of these goods over other individuals within the community. The invidious comparison now becomes primarily a comparison of the owner with the other members of the group. Property is still of the nature of trophy, but, with the cultural advance, it becomes more and more a trophy of successes scored in the game of ownership carried on between the members of the group under the quasi-peaceable methods of nomadic life.

Gradually, as industrial activity further displaces predatory activity in the community's everyday life and

in men's habits of thought, accumulated property more
and more replaces trophies of predatory exploit as the
conventional exponent of prepotence and success. With
the growth of settled industry, therefore, the possession
of wealth gains in relative importance and effectiveness
as a customary basis of repute and esteem. Not that
esteem ceases to be awarded on the basis of other, more
direct evidence of prowess; not that successful predatory aggression or warlike exploit ceases to call out the
approval and admiration of the crowd, or to stir the
envy of the less successful competitors; but the opportunities for gaining distinction by means of this direct
manifestation of superior force grow less available both
in scope and frequency. At the same time opportunities
for industrial aggression, and for the accumulation of
property by the quasi-peaceable methods of nomadic industry, increase in scope and availability. And it is even
more to the point that property now becomes the most
easily recognized evidence of a reputable degree of success as distinguished from heroic or signal achievement.
It therefore becomes the conventional basis of esteem.
Its possession in some amount becomes necessary in
order to any reputable standing in the community. It
becomes indispensable to accumulate, to acquire property, in order to retain one's good name. When accumulated goods have in this way once become the accepted badge of efficiency, the possession of wealth
presently assumes the character of an independent and
definitive basis of esteem. The possession of goods,

whether acquired aggressively by one's own exertion or passively by transmission through inheritance from others, becomes a conventional basis of reputability. The possession of wealth, which was at the outset valued simply as an evidence of efficiency, becomes, in popular apprehension, itself a meritorious act. Wealth is now itself intrinsically honourable and confers honour on its possessor. By a further refinement, wealth acquired passively by transmission from ancestors or other antecedents presently becomes even more honorific than wealth acquired by the possessor's own effort; but this distinction belongs at a later stage in the evolution of the pecuniary culture and will be spoken of in its place.

Prowess and exploit may still remain the basis of award of the highest popular esteem, although the possession of wealth has become the basis of commonplace reputability and of a blameless social standing. The predatory instinct and the consequent approbation of predatory efficiency are deeply ingrained in the habits of thought of those peoples who have passed under the discipline of a protracted predatory culture. According to popular award, the highest honours within human reach may, even yet, be those gained by an unfolding of extraordinary predatory efficiency in war, or by a quasi-predatory efficiency in statecraft; but for the purposes of a commonplace decent standing in the community these means of repute have been replaced by the acquisition and accumulation of goods. In order to stand well in the eyes of the community, it is necessary to come up to a certain, somewhat indefinite, conventional standard of wealth; just as in the earlier predatory stage it is necessary for the barbarian man to come up to the tribe's standard of physical endurance, cunning, and skill at arms. A certain standard of wealth in the one case, and of prowess in the other, is a necessary condition of reputability, and anything in excess of this normal amount is meritorious.

Those members of the community who fall short of this, somewhat indefinite, normal degree of prowess or of property suffer in the esteem of their fellow-men; and consequently they suffer also in their own esteem, since the usual basis of self-respect is the respect accorded by one's neighbours. Only individuals with an aberrant temperament can in the long run retain their self-esteem in the face of the disesteem of their fellows. Apparent exceptions to the rule are met with, especially among people with strong religious convictions. But these apparent exceptions are scarcely real exceptions, since such persons commonly fall back on the putative approbation of some supernatural witness of their deeds.

So soon as the possession of property becomes the basis of popular esteem, therefore, it becomes also a requisite to that complacency which we call self-respect. In any community where goods are held in severalty it is necessary, in order to his own peace of mind, that an individual should possess as large a portion of goods as others with whom he is accustomed to class himself; and it is extremely gratifying to possess something more

than others. But as fast as a person makes new acquisi-
tions, and becomes accustomed to the resulting new
standard of wealth, the new standard forthwith ceases
to afford appreciably greater satisfaction than the earlier
standard did. The tendency in any case is constantly to
make the present pecuniary standard the point of departure for a fresh increase of wealth; and this in turn
gives rise to a new standard of sufficiency and a new
pecuniary classification of one's self as compared with
one's neighbours. So far as concerns the present question, the end sought by accumulation is to rank high in
comparison with the rest of the community in point of
pecuniary strength. So long as the comparison is dis-
tinctly unfavourable to himself, the normal, average
individual will live in chronic dissatisfaction with his
present lot; and when he has reached what may be
called the normal pecuniary standard of the community,
or of his class in the community, this chronic dissatisfaction will give place to a restless straining to place a
wider and ever-widening pecuniary interval between
himself and this average standard. The invidious comparison can never become so favourable to the individual
making it that he would not gladly rate himself still
higher relatively to his competitors in the struggle for
pecuniary reputability.

In the nature of the case, the desire for wealth can
scarcely be satiated in any individual instance, and evidently a satiation of the average or general desire for
wealth is out of the question. However widely, or

equally, or "fairly," it may be distributed, no general increase of the community's wealth can make any approach to satiating this need, the ground of which is the desire of everyone to excel everyone else in the accumulation of goods. If, as is sometimes assumed, the incentive to accumulation were the want of subsistence or of physical comfort, then the aggregate economic wants of a community might conceivably be satisfied at some point in the advance of industrial efficiency; but since the struggle is substantially a race for reputability on the basis of an invidious comparison, no approach to a definitive attainment is possible.

What has just been said must not be taken to mean that there are no other incentives to acquisition and accumulation than this desire to excel in pecuniary standing and so gain the esteem and envy of one's fellow-men. The desire for added comfort and security from want is present as a motive at every stage of the process of accumulation in a modern industrial community; although the standard of sufficiency in these respects is in turn greatly affected by the habit of pecuniary emulation. To a great extent this emulation shapes the methods and selects the objects of expenditure for personal comfort and decent livelihood.

Besides this, the power conferred by wealth also affords a motive to accumulation. That propensity for purposeful activity and that repugnance to all futility of effort which belong to man by virtue of his character as an agent do not desert him when he emerges from the naïve communal culture where the dominant note of life is the unanalysed and undifferentiated solidarity of the individual with the group with which his life is bound up. When he enters upon the predatory stage, where self-seeking in the narrower sense becomes the dominant note, this propensity goes with him still, as the pervasive trait that shapes his scheme of life. The propensity for achievement and the repugnance to futility remain the underlying economic motive. The propensity changes only in the form of its expression and in the proximate objects to which it directs the man's activity. Under the regime of individual ownership the most available means of visibly achieving a purpose is that afforded by the acquisition and accumulation of goods; and as the self-regarding antithesis between man and man reaches fuller consciousness, the propensity for achievement—the instinct of workmanship—tends more and more to shape itself into a straining to excel others in pecuniary achievement. Relative success, tested by an invidious pecuniary comparison with other men, becomes the conventional end of action. The currently accepted legitimate end of effort becomes the achievement of a favourable comparison with other men; and therefore the repugnance to futility to a good extent coalesces with the incentive of emulation. It acts to accentuate the struggle for pecuniary reputability by visiting with a sharper disapproval all shortcoming and all evidence of shortcoming in point of pecuniary success. Purposeful effort comes to mean, primarily, effort directed to or resulting in a more creditable showing of accumulated wealth. Among the motives which lead men to accumulate wealth, the primacy, both in scope and intensity, therefore, continues to belong to this motive of pecuniary emulation.

In making use of the term "invidious," it may perhaps be unnecessary to remark, there is no intention to extol or depreciate, or to commend or deplore any of the phenomena which the word is used to characterize. The term is used in a technical sense as describing a comparison of persons with a view to rating and grading them in respect of relative worth or value—in an æsthetic or moral sense—and so awarding and defining the relative degrees of complacency with which they may legitimately be contemplated by themselves and by others. An invidious comparison is a process of valuation of persons in respect of worth.

## CONSPICUOUS LEISURE

If its working were not disturbed by other economic forces or other features of the emulative process, the immediate effect of such a pecuniary struggle as has just been described in outline would be to make men industrious and frugal. This result actually follows, in some measure, so far as regards the lower classes, whose ordinary means of acquiring goods is productive labour. This is more especially true of the labouring classes in a sedentary community which is at an agricultural stage of industry, in which there is a considerable subdivision of property, and whose laws and customs secure to these classes a more or less definite share of the product of their industry. These lower classes can in any case not avoid labour, and the imputation of labour is therefore not greatly derogatory to them, at least not within their class. Rather, since labour is their recognized and accepted mode of life, they take some emulative pride in a reputation for efficiency in their work, this being often the only line of emulation that is open to them. For those for whom acquisition and emulation is possible only within the field of productive efficiency and thrift, the struggle for pecuniary reputability will in some measure work out in an increase of diligence and parsimony. But certain secondary features of the emulative process, yet to be spoken of, come in to very materially circumscribe and modify emulation in these directions among the pecuniarily inferior classes as well as among the superior class.

But it is otherwise with the superior pecuniary class, with which we are here immediately concerned. For this class also the incentive to diligence and thrift is not absent; but its action is so greatly qualified by the secondary demands of pecuniary emulation, that any inclination in this direction is practically overborne and any incentive to diligence tends to be of no effect. The most imperative of these secondary demands of emulation, as well as the one of widest scope, is the requirement of abstention from productive work. This is true in an especial degree for the barbarian stage of culture. During the predatory culture labour comes to be associated in men's habits of thought with weakness and subjection to a master. It is therefore a mark of inferiority, and therefore comes to be accounted unworthy of man in his best estate. By virtue of this tradition labour is felt to be debasing, and this tradition has never died out. On the contrary, with the advance of social differentiation it has acquired the axiomatic force due to ancient and unquestioned prescription.

In order to gain and to hold the esteem of men it is not sufficient merely to possess wealth or power. The wealth or power must be put in evidence, for esteem is awarded only on evidence. And not only does the evidence of wealth serve to impress one's importance on others and to keep their sense of his importance alive and alert, but it is of scarcely less use in building up and preserving one's self-complacency. In all but the lowest stages of culture the normally constituted man is comforted and upheld in his self-respect by "decent surroundings" and by exemption from "menial offices." Enforced departure from his habitual standard of decency, either in the paraphernalia of life or in the kind and amount of his everyday activity, is felt to be a slight upon his human dignity, even apart from all conscious consideration of the approval or disapproval of his fellows.

The archaic theoretical distinction between the base and the honourable in the manner of a man's life retains very much of its ancient force even today. So much so

that there are few of the better class who are not possessed of an instinctive repugnance for the vulgar forms
of labour. We have a realizing sense of ceremonial uncleanness attaching in an especial degree to the occupations which are associated in our habits of thought with
menial service. It is felt by all persons of refined taste
that a spiritual contamination is inseparable from certain
offices that are conveniently required of servants. Vulgar
surroundings, mean (that is to say, inexpensive) habita-
tions, and vulgarly productive occupations are unhesitat-
ingly condemned and avoided. They are incompatible
with life on a satisfactory spiritual plane—with "high
thinking." From the days of the Greek philosophers to
the present, a degree of leisure and of exemption from
contact with such industrial processes as serve the immediate everyday purposes of human life has ever been
recognized by thoughtful men as a prerequisite to a
worthy or beautiful, or even a blameless, human life. In
itself and in its consequences the life of leisure is beautiful and ennobling in all civilized men's eyes.

This direct, subjective value of leisure and of other
evidences of wealth is no doubt in great part secondary
and derivative. It is in part a reflex of the utility of leisure as a means of gaining the respect of others, and in
part it is the result of a mental substitution. The performance of labour has been accepted as a conventional
evidence of inferior force; therefore it comes itself, by a
mental short-cut, to be regarded as intrinsically base.

During the predatory stage proper, and especially

during the earlier stages of the quasi-peaceable development of industry that follows the predatory stage, a life of leisure is the readiest and most conclusive evidence of pecuniary strength, and therefore of superior force; provided always that the gentleman of leisure can live in manifest ease and comfort. At this stage wealth consists chiefly of slaves, and the benefits accruing from the possession of riches and power take the form chiefly of personal service and the immediate products of personal service. Conspicuous abstention from labour therefore becomes the conventional mark of superior pecuniary achievement and the conventional index of reputability; and conversely, since application to productive labour is a mark of poverty and subjection, it becomes inconsistent with a reputable standing in the community. Habits of industry and thrift, therefore, are not uniformly furthered by a prevailing pecuniary emulation. On the contrary, this kind of emulation indirectly discountenances participation in productive labour. Labour would unavoidably become dishonourable, as being an evidence of poverty, even if it were not already accounted indecorous under the ancient tradition handed down from an earlier cultural stage. The ancient tradition of the predatory culture is that productive effort is to be shunned as being unworthy of able-bodied men, and this tradition is reinforced rather than set aside in the passage from the predatory to the quasi-peaceable manner of life.

Even if the institution of a leisure class had not come

in with the first emergence of individual ownership, by force of the dishonour attaching to productive employment, it would in any case have come in as one of the early consequences of ownership. And it is to be remarked that, while the leisure class existed in theory from the beginning of predatory culture, the institution takes on a new and fuller meaning with the transition from the predatory to the next succeeding pecuniary stage of culture. It is from this time forth a "leisure class" in fact as well as in theory. From this point dates the institution of the leisure class in its consummate form.

During the predatory stage proper the distinction between the leisure and the labouring class is in some degree a ceremonial distinction only. The able-bodied men jealously stand aloof from whatever is, in their apprehension, menial drudgery; but their activity in fact contributes appreciably to the sustenance of the group. The subsequent stage of quasi-peaceable industry is usually characterized by an established chattel slavery, herds of cattle, and a servile class of herdsmen and shepherds; industry has advanced so far that the community is no longer dependent for its livelihood on the chase or on any other form of activity that can fairly be classed as exploit. From this point on, the characteristic feature of leisure-class life is a conspicuous exemption from all useful employment.

The normal and characteristic occupations of the class in this mature phase of its life-history are in form very much the same as in its earlier days. These occupations are government, war, sports, and devout observances. Persons unduly given to difficult theoretical niceties may hold that these occupations are still incidentally and indirectly "productive"; but it is to be noted as decisive of the question in hand that the ordinary and ostensible motive of the leisure class in engaging in these occupations is assuredly not an increase of wealth by productive effort. At this as at any other cultural stage, government and war are, at least in part, carried on for the pecuniary gain of those who engage in them; but it is gain obtained by the honourable method of seizure and conversion. These occupations are of the nature of predatory, not of productive, employment. Something similar may be said of the chase, but with a difference. As the community passes out of the hunting stage proper, hunting gradually becomes differentiated into two distinct employments. On the one hand it is a trade, carried on chiefly for gain; and from this the element of exploit is virtually absent, or it is at any rate not present in a sufficient degree to clear the pursuit of the imputation of gainful industry. On the other hand, the chase is also a sport— an exercise of the predatory impulse simply. As such it does not afford any appreciable pecuniary incentive, but it contains a more or less obvious element of exploit. It is this latter development of the chase—purged of all imputation of handicraft—that alone is meritorious and fairly belongs in the scheme of life of the developed leisure class.

Abstention from labour is not only a honorific or meritorious act, but it presently comes to be a requisite of
decency. The insistence on property as the basis of reputability is very naïve and very imperious during the
early stages of the accumulation of wealth. Abstention
from labour is the conventional evidence of wealth and
is therefore the conventional mark of social standing;
and this insistence on the meritoriousness of wealth leads
to a more strenuous insistence on leisure. *Nota notæ est
nota rei ipsius.* According to well-established laws of human nature, prescription presently seizes upon this conventional evidence of wealth and fixes it in men's habits
of thought as something that is in itself substantially
meritorious and ennobling; while productive labour at
the same time and by a like process becomes in a double
sense intrinsically unworthy. Prescription ends by making labour not only disreputable in the eyes of the community, but morally impossible to the noble, freeborn
man, and incompatible with a worthy life.

This taboo on labour has a further consequence in the
industrial differentiation of classes. As the population
increases in density and the predatory group grows into
a settled industrial community, the constituted authorities and the customs governing ownership gain in scope
and consistency. It then presently becomes impracticable
to accumulate wealth by simple seizure, and, in logical
consistency, acquisition by industry is equally impossible
for high-minded and impecunious men. The alternative
open to them is beggary or privation. Wherever the

canon of conspicuous leisure has a chance undisturbed to work out its tendency, there will therefore emerge a secondary, and in a sense spurious, leisure class—abjectly poor and living a precarious life of want and discomfort, but morally unable to stoop to gainful pursuits. The decayed gentleman and the lady who has seen better days are by no means unfamiliar phenomena even now. This pervading sense of the indignity of the slightest manual labour is familiar to all civilized peoples, as well as to peoples of a less advanced pecuniary culture. In persons of delicate sensibility, who have long been habituated to gentle manners, the sense of the shamefulness of manual labour may become so strong that, at a critical juncture, it will even set aside the instinct of self-preservation. So, for instance, we are told of certain Polynesian chiefs, who, under the stress of good form, preferred to starve rather than carry their food to their mouths with their own hands. It is true, this conduct may have been due, at least in part, to an excessive sanctity or taboo attaching to the chief's person. The taboo would have been communicated by the contact of his hands, and so would have made anything touched by him unfit for human food. But the taboo is itself a derivative of the unworthiness or moral incompatibility of labour; so that even when construed in this sense the conduct of the Polynesian chiefs is truer to the canon of honorific leisure than would at first appear. A better illustration, or at least a more unmistakable one, is afforded by a certain king of France, who is said to have lost his life through an excess of moral stamina in the observance of good form. In the absence of the functionary whose office it was to shift his master's seat, the king sat uncomplaining before the fire and suffered his royal person to be toasted beyond recovery. But in so doing he saved his Most Christian Majesty from menial contamination.

> Summum crede nefas animam præferre pudori,
> Et propter vitam vivendi perdere causas.

It has already been remarked that the term "leisure," as here used, does not connote indolence or quiescence. What it connotes is non-productive consumption of time. Time is consumed non-productively (1) from a sense of the unworthiness of productive work, and (2) as an evidence of pecuniary ability to afford a life of idleness. But the whole of the life of the gentleman of leisure is not spent before the eyes of the spectators who are to be impressed with that spectacle of honorific leisure which in the ideal scheme makes up his life. For some part of the time his life is perforce withdrawn from the public eye, and of this portion which is spent in private the gentleman of leisure should, for the sake of his good name, be able to give a convincing account. He should find some means of putting in evidence the leisure that is not spent in the sight of the spectators. This can be done only indirectly, through the exhibition of some tangible, lasting results of the leisure so spent—in a manner analogous to the familiar exhibition of tangible, lasting products of the labour performed for the gentleman of leisure by handicraftsmen and servants in his employ.

The lasting evidence of productive labour is its material product—commonly some article of consumption. In the case of exploit it is similarly possible and usual to procure some tangible result that may serve for exhibition in the way of trophy or booty. At a later phase of the development it is customary to assume some badge or insignia of honour that will serve as a conventionally accepted mark of exploit, and which at the same time indicates the quantity or degree of exploit of which it is the symbol. As the population increases in density, and as human relations grow more complex and numerous, all the details of life undergo a process of elaboration and selection; and in this process of elaboration the use of trophies develops into a system of rank, titles, degrees, and insignia, typical examples of which are heraldic devices, medals, and honorary decorations.

As seen from the economic point of view, leisure, considered as an employment, is closely allied in kind with the life of exploit; and the achievements which characterize a life of leisure, and which remain as its decorous criteria, have much in common with the trophies of exploit. But leisure in the narrower sense, as distinct from exploit and from any ostensibly productive employment of effort on objects which are of no intrinsic use, does not commonly leave a material product. The criteria of a past performance of leisure therefore commonly take the form of "immaterial" goods. Such immaterial evidences of past leisure are quasi-scholarly or quasi-artistic accomplishments and a knowledge of processes and incidents which do not conduce directly to the furtherance of human life. So, for instance, in our time there is the knowledge of the dead languages and the occult sciences; of correct spelling; of syntax and prosody; of the various forms of domestic music and other household art; of the latest proprieties of dress, furniture, and equipage; of games, sports, and fancy-bred animals, such as dogs and race-horses. In all these branches of knowledge the initial motive from which their acquisition proceeded at the outset, and through which they first came into vogue, may have been something quite different from the wish to show that one's time had not been spent in industrial employment; but unless these accomplishments had approved themselves as serviceable evidence of an unproductive expenditure of time, they would not have survived and held their place as conventional accomplishments of the leisure class.

These accomplishments may, in some sense, be classed as branches of learning. Beside and beyond these there is a further range of social facts which shade off from the region of learning into that of physical habit and dexterity. Such are what is known as manners and breeding, polite usage, decorum, and formal and ceremonial observances generally. This class of facts are even more immediately and obtrusively presented to the observation, and they are therefore more widely and more imperatively insisted on as required evidences of a reputable degree of leisure. It is worth while to remark that all that class of ceremonial observances which are classed under the general head of manners hold a more important place in the esteem of men during the stage of culture at which conspicuous leisure has the greatest vogue as a mark of reputability, than at later stages of the cultural development. The barbarian of the quasi-peaceable stage of industry is notoriously a more high-bred gentleman, in all that concerns decorum, than any but the very exquisite among the men of a later age. Indeed, it is well known, or at least it is currently believed, that manners have progressively deteriorated as society has receded from the patriarchal stage. Many a gentleman of the old school has been provoked to remark regretfully upon the under-bred manners and bearing of even the better classes in the modern industrial communities; and the decay of the ceremonial code— or, as it is otherwise called, the vulgarization of life —among the industrial classes proper has become one of the chief enormities of latter-day civilization in the eyes of all persons of delicate sensibilities. The decay which the code has suffered at the hands of a busy people testifies—all deprecation apart—to the fact that decorum is a product and an exponent of leisure-class life and thrives in full measure only under a regime of status.

The origin, or better the derivation, of manners is, no doubt, to be sought elsewhere than in a conscious effort on the part of the well-mannered to show that much time has been spent in acquiring them. The proximate end of innovation and elaboration has been the higher effectiveness of the new departure in point of beauty or of expressiveness. In great part the ceremonial code of decorous usages owes its beginning and its growth to the desire to conciliate or to show good-will, as anthropologists and sociologists are in the habit of assuming, and this initial motive is rarely if ever absent from the conduct of well-mannered persons at any stage of the later development. Manners, we are told, are in part an elaboration of gesture, and in part they are symbolical and conventionalized survivals representing former acts of dominance or of personal service or of personal contact. In large part they are an expression of the relation of status—a symbolic pantomime of mastery on the one hand and of subservience on the other. Wherever at the present time the predatory habit of mind, and the consequent attitude of mastery and of subservience, gives its character to the accredited scheme of life, there the importance of all punctilios of conduct is extreme, and the assiduity with which the ceremonial observance of rank and titles is attended to approaches closely to the ideal set by the barbarian of the quasi-peaceable nomadic culture. Some of the Continental countries afford good illustrations of this spiritual survival. In these communities the archaic ideal is similarly approached as regards the esteem accorded to manners as a fact of intrinsic worth.

Decorum set out with being symbol and pantomime and with having utility only as an exponent of the facts and qualities symbolized; but it presently suffered the transmutation which commonly passes over symbolical facts in human intercourse. Manners presently came, in popular apprehension, to be possessed of a substantial utility in themselves; they acquired a sacramental character, in great measure independent of the facts which they originally prefigured. Deviations from the code of decorum have become intrinsically odious to all men, and good breeding is, in everyday apprehension, not simply an adventitious mark of human excellence, but an integral feature of the worthy human soul. There are few things that so touch us with instinctive revulsion as a breach of decorum; and so far have we progressed in the direction of imputing intrinsic utility to the ceremonial observances of etiquette that few of us, if any, can dissociate an offence against etiquette from a sense of the substantial unworthiness of the offender. A breach of faith may be condoned, but a breach of decorum can not. "Manners maketh man."

None the less, while manners have this intrinsic utility, in the apprehension of the performer and the beholder alike, this sense of the intrinsic rightness of decorum is only the proximate ground of the vogue of manners and breeding. Their ulterior, economic ground is to be sought in the honorific character of that leisure or non-productive employment of time and effort without which good manners are not acquired. The knowledge

and habit of good form come only by long-continued
use. Refined tastes, manners, and habits of life are a
useful evidence of gentility, because good breeding requires time, application, and expense, and can therefore
not be compassed by those whose time and energy are
taken up with work. A knowledge of good form is *prima
facie* evidence that that portion of the well-bred person's life which is not spent under the observation of
the spectator has been worthily spent in acquiring accomplishments that are of no lucrative effect. In the last
analysis the value of manners lies in the fact that they
are the voucher of a life of leisure. Therefore, conversely, since leisure is the conventional means of pecuniary repute, the acquisition of some proficiency in
decorum is incumbent on all who aspire to a modicum
of pecuniary decency.

So much of the honourable life of leisure as is not
spent in the sight of spectators can serve the purposes
of reputability only in so far as it leaves a tangible,
visible result that can be put in evidence and can be
measured and compared with products of the same class
exhibited by competing aspirants for repute. Some such
effect, in the way of leisurely manners and carriage, etc.,
follows from simple persistent abstention from work,
even where the subject does not take thought of the
matter and studiously acquire an air of leisurely opulence and mastery. Especially does it seem to be true
that a life of leisure in this way persisted in through
several generations will leave a persistent, ascertainable

effect in the conformation of the person, and still more in his habitual bearing and demeanour. But all the suggestions of a cumulative life of leisure, and all the proficiency in decorum that comes by the way of passive habituation, may be further improved upon by taking thought and assiduously acquiring the marks of honourable leisure, and then carrying the exhibition of these adventitious marks of exemption from employment out in a strenuous and systematic discipline. Plainly, this is a point at which a diligent application of effort and expenditure may materially further the attainment of a decent proficiency in the leisure-class proprieties. Conversely, the greater the degree of proficiency and the more patent the evidence of a high degree of habituation to observances which serve no lucrative or other directly useful purpose, the greater the consumption of time and substance impliedly involved in their acquisition, and the greater the resultant good repute. Hence, under the competitive struggle for proficiency in good manners, it comes about that much pains is taken with the cultivation of habits of decorum; and hence the details of decorum develop into a comprehensive discipline, conformity to which is required of all who would be held blameless in point of repute. And hence, on the other hand, this conspicuous leisure of which decorum is a ramification grows gradually into a laborious drill in deportment and an education in taste and discrimination as to what articles of consumption are decorous and what are the decorous methods of consuming them.

In this connexion it is worthy of notice that the pos-
sibility of producing pathological and other idiosyncrasies of person and manner by shrewd mimicry and a
systematic drill have been turned to account in the deliberate production of a cultured class—often with a
very happy effect. In this way, by the process vulgarly
known as snobbery, a syncopated evolution of gentle
birth and breeding is achieved in the case of a goodly
number of families and lines of descent. This syncopated
gentle birth gives results which, in point of serviceability
as a leisure-class factor in the population, are in no wise
substantially inferior to others who may have had a
longer but less arduous training in the pecuniary proprieties.

There are, moreover, measurable degrees of conformity to the latest accredited code of the punctilios as regards decorous means and methods of consumption. Differences between one person and another in the degree
of conformity to the ideal in these respects can be compared, and persons may be graded and scheduled with
some accuracy and effect according to a progressive scale
of manners and breeding. The award of reputability in
this regard is commonly made in good faith, on the
ground of conformity to accepted canons of taste in the
matters concerned, and without conscious regard to the
pecuniary standing or the degree of leisure practised by
any given candidate for reputability; but the canons of
taste according to which the award is made are constantly
under the surveillance of the law of conspicuous leisure,

and are indeed constantly undergoing change and revision to bring them into closer conformity with its requirements. So that while the proximate ground of discrimination may be of another kind, still the pervading principle and abiding test of good breeding is the requirement of a substantial and patent waste of time. There may be some considerable range of variation in detail within the scope of this principle, but they are variations of form and expression, not of substance.

Much of the courtesy of everyday intercourse is of course a direct expression of consideration and kindly good-will, and this element of conduct has for the most part no need of being traced back to any underlying ground of reputability to explain either its presence or the approval with which it is regarded; but the same is not true of the code of proprieties. These latter are expressions of status. It is of course sufficiently plain, to anyone who cares to see, that our bearing towards menials and other pecuniarily dependent inferiors is the bearing of the superior member in a relation of status, though its manifestation is often greatly modified and softened from the original expression of crude dominance. Similarly, our bearing towards superiors, and in great measure towards equals, expresses a more or less conventionalized attitude of subservience. Witness the masterful presence of the high-minded gentleman or lady, which testifies to so much of dominance and independence of economic circumstances, and which at the same time appeals with such convincing force to our sense of what is right and gracious. It is among this highest leisure class, who have no superiors and few peers, that decorum finds its fullest and maturest expression; and it is this highest class also that gives decorum that definitive formulation which serves as a canon of conduct for the classes beneath. And here also the code is most obviously a code of status and shows most plainly its incompatibility with all vulgarly productive work. A divine assurance and an imperious complaisance, as of one habituated to require subservience and to take no thought for the morrow, is the birthright and the criterion of the gentleman at his best; and it is in popular apprehension even more than that, for this demeanour is accepted as an intrinsic attribute of superior worth, before which the base-born commoner delights to stoop and yield.

As has been indicated . . . there is reason to believe that the institution of ownership has begun with the ownership of persons, primarily women. The incentives to acquiring such property have apparently been: (1) a propensity for dominance and coercion; (2) the utility of these persons as evidence of the prowess of their owner; (3) the utility of their services.

Personal service holds a peculiar place in the economic development. During the stage of quasi-peaceable industry, and especially during the earlier development of industry within the limits of this general stage, the utility of their services seems commonly to be the dominant motive to the acquisition of property in persons. Servants are valued for their services. But the dominance of this motive is not due to a decline in the absolute importance of the other two utilities possessed by servants. It is rather that the altered circumstances of life accentuate the utility of servants for this last-named purpose. Women and other slaves are highly valued, both as an evidence of wealth and as a means of accumulating wealth. Together with cattle, if the tribe is a pastoral one, they are the usual form of investment for a profit. To such an extent may female slavery give its character to the economic life under the quasi-peaceable culture that the woman even comes to serve as a unit of value among peoples occupying this cultural stage—as for instance in Homeric times. Where this is the case there need be little question but that the basis of the industrial system is chattel slavery and that the women are commonly slaves. The great, pervading human relation in such a system is that of master and servant. The accepted evidence of wealth is the possession of many women, and presently also of other slaves engaged in attendance on their master's person and in producing goods for him.

A division of labour presently sets in, whereby personal service and attendance on the master becomes the special office of a portion of the servants, while those who are wholly employed in industrial occupations proper are removed more and more from all immediate relation to the person of their owner. At the same time those servants whose office is personal service, including domestic duties, come gradually to be exempted from productive industry carried on for gain.

This process of progressive exemption from the common run of industrial employment will commonly begin with the exemption of the wife, or the chief wife. After the community has advanced to settled habits of life, wife-capture from hostile tribes becomes impracticable as a customary source of supply. Where this cultural advance has been achieved, the chief wife is ordinarily of gentle blood, and the fact of her being so will hasten her exemption from vulgar employment. The manner in which the concept of gentle blood originates, as well as the place which it occupies in the development of marriage, cannot be discussed in this place. For the purpose in hand it will be sufficient to say that gentle blood is blood which has been ennobled by protracted contact with accumulated wealth or unbroken prerogative. The woman with these antecedents is preferred in marriage, both for the sake of a resulting alliance with her powerful relatives and because a superior worth is felt to inhere in blood which has been associated with many goods and great power. She will still be her husband's chattel, as she was her father's chattel before her purchase, but she is at the same time of her father's gentle blood; and hence there is a moral incongruity in her occupying herself with the debasing employments of her fellow-servants. However completely she may be subject to her master, and however inferior to the male members of the social stratum in which her birth has

placed her, the principle that gentility is transmissible
will act to place her above the common slave; and so
soon as this principle has acquired a prescriptive authority it will act to invest her in some measure with that
prerogative of leisure which is the chief mark of gentility. Furthered by this principle of transmissible gentility
the wife's exemption gains in scope, if the wealth of her
owner permits it, until it includes exemption from debasing menial service as well as from handicraft. As the
industrial development goes on and property becomes
massed in relatively fewer hands, the conventional standard of wealth of the upper class rises. The same tendency to exemption from handicraft, and in the course of
time from menial domestic employments, will then assert itself as regards the other wives, if such there are,
and also as regards other servants in immediate attendance upon the person of their master. The exemption
comes more tardily the remoter the relation in which
the servant stands to the person of the master.

If the pecuniary situation of the master permits it,
the development of a special class of personal or body
servants is also furthered by the very grave importance
which comes to attach to this personal service. The master's person, being the embodiment of worth and honour, is of the most serious consequence. Both for his
reputable standing in the community and for his self-
respect, it is a matter of moment that he should have at
his call efficient specialized servants, whose attendance
upon his person is not diverted from this their chief of-

# The Leisure Class 251

fice by any by-occupation. These specialized servants are useful more for show than for service actually performed. In so far as they are not kept for exhibition simply, they afford gratification to their master chiefly in allowing scope to his propensity for dominance. It is true, the care of the continually increasing household apparatus may require added labour; but since the apparatus is commonly increased in order to serve as a means of good repute rather than as a means of comfort, this qualification is not of great weight. All these lines of utility are better served by a larger number of more highly specialized servants. There results, therefore, a constantly increasing differentiation and multiplication of domestic and body servants, along with a concomitant progressive exemption of such servants from productive labour. By virtue of their serving as evidence of ability to pay, the office of such domestics regularly tends to include continually fewer duties, and their service tends in the end to become nominal only. This is especially true of those servants who are in most immediate and obvious attendance upon their master. So that the utility of these comes to consist, in great part, in their conspicuous exemption from productive labour and in the evidence which this exemption affords of their master's wealth and power.

After some considerable advance has been made in the practice of employing a special corps of servants for the performance of a conspicuous leisure in this manner, men begin to be preferred above women for services that bring them obtrusively into view. Men, especially lusty, personable fellows, such as footmen and other menials should be, are obviously more powerful and more expensive than women. They are better fitted for this work, as showing a larger waste of time and of human energy. Hence it comes about that in the economy of the leisure class the busy housewife of the early patriarchal days, with her retinue of hard-working handmaidens, presently gives place to the lady and the lackey.

In all grades and walks of life, and at any stage of the economic development, the leisure of the lady and of the lackey differs from the leisure of the gentleman in his own right in that it is an occupation of an ostensibly laborious kind. It takes the form, in large measure, of a painstaking attention to the service of the master, or to the maintenance and elaboration of the household paraphernalia; so that it is leisure only in the sense that little or no productive work is performed by this class, not in the sense that all appearance of labour is avoided by them. The duties performed by the lady, or by the household or domestic servants, are frequently arduous enough, and they are also frequently directed to ends which are considered extremely necessary to the comfort of the entire household. So far as these services conduce to the physical efficiency or comfort of the master or the rest of the household, they are to be accounted productive work. Only the residue of employment left after deduction of this effective work is to be classed as a performance of leisure.

But much of the services classed as household cares in modern everyday life, and many of the "utilities" required for a comfortable existence by civilized man, are of a ceremonial character. They are, therefore, properly to be classed as a performance of leisure in the sense in which the term is here used. They may be none the less imperatively necessary from the point of view of decent existence; they may be none the less requisite for personal comfort even, although they may be chiefly or wholly of a ceremonial character. But in so far as they partake of this character they are imperative and requisite because we have been taught to require them under pain of ceremonial uncleanness or unworthiness. We feel discomfort in their absence, but not because their absence results directly in physical discomfort; nor would a taste not trained to discriminate between the conventionally good and the conventionally bad take offence at their omission. In so far as this is true the labour spent in these services is to be classed as leisure; and when performed by others than the economically free and self-directing head of the establishment, they are to be classed as vicarious leisure.

The vicarious leisure performed by housewives and menials, under the head of household cares, may frequently develop into drudgery, especially where the competition for reputability is close and strenuous. This is frequently the case in modern life. Where this happens, the domestic service which comprises the duties of this servant class might aptly be designated as wasted effort, rather than as vicarious leisure. But the latter term has the advantage of indicating the line of derivation of these domestic offices, as well as of neatly suggesting the substantial economic ground of their utility; for these occupations are chiefly useful as a method of imputing pecuniary reputability to the master or to the household on the ground that a given amount of time and effort is conspicuously wasted in that behalf.

In this way, then, there arises a subsidiary or derivative leisure class, whose office is the performance of a vicarious leisure for the behoof of the reputability of the primary or legitimate leisure class. This vicarious leisure class is distinguished from the leisure class proper by a characteristic feature of its habitual mode of life. The leisure of the master class is, at least ostensibly, an indulgence of a proclivity for the avoidance of labour and is presumed to enhance the master's own well-being and fullness of life; but the leisure of the servant class exempt from productive labour is in some sort a performance exacted from them, and is not normally or primarily directed to their own comfort. The leisure of the servant is not his own leisure. So far as he is a servant in the full sense, and not at the same time a member of a lower order of the leisure class proper, his leisure normally passes under the guise of specialized service directed to the furtherance of his master's' fullness of life. Evidence of this relation of subservience is obviously present in the servant's carriage and manner of life. The like is often true of the wife throughout the protracted

economic stage during which she is still primarily a servant—that is to say, so long as the household with a male
head remains in force. In order to satisfy the requirements of the leisure-class scheme of life, the servant
should show not only an attitude of subservience, but
also the effects of special training and practice in subservience. The servant or wife should not only perform
certain offices and show a servile disposition, but it is
quite as imperative that they should show an acquired
facility in the tactics of subservience—a trained conformity to the canons of effectual and conspicuous subservience. Even today it is this aptitude and acquired skill in
the formal manifestation of the servile relation that constitutes the chief element of utility in our highly paid
servants, as well as one of the chief ornaments of the
well-bred housewife.

The first requisite of a good servant is that he should
conspicuously know his place. It is not enough that he
knows how to effect certain desired mechanical results;
he must, above all, know how to effect these results in
due form. Domestic service might be said to be a spiritual rather than a mechanical function. Gradually there
grows up an elaborate system of good form, specifically
regulating the manner in which this vicarious leisure of
the servant class is to be performed. Any departure from
these canons of form is to be deprecated, not so much
because it evinces a shortcoming in mechanical efficiency,
or even that it shows an absence of the servile attitude
and temperament, but because, in the last analysis, it

shows the absence of special training. Special training in personal service costs time and effort, and where it is obviously present in a high degree, it argues that the servant who possesses it neither is nor has been habitually engaged in any productive occupation. It is *prima facie* evidence of a vicarious leisure extending far back in the past. So that trained service has utility, not only as gratifying the master's instinctive liking for good and skilful workmanship and his propensity for conspicuous dominance over those whose lives are subservient to his own, but it has utility also as putting in evidence a much larger consumption of human service than would be shown by the mere present conspicuous leisure performed by an untrained person. It is a serious grievance if a gentleman's butler or footman performs his duties about his master's table or carriage in such unformed style as to suggest that his habitual occupation may be ploughing or sheep-herding. Such bungling work would imply inability on the master's part to procure the service of specially trained servants; that is to say, it would imply inability to pay for the consumption of time, effort, and instruction required to fit a trained servant for special service under an exacting code of forms. If the performance of the servant argues lack of means on the part of his master, it defeats its chief substantial end; for the chief use of servants is the evidence they afford of the master's ability to pay.

What has just been said might be taken to imply that the offence of an under-trained servant lies in a direct suggestion of inexpensiveness or of usefulness. Such, of course, is not the case. The connexion is much less immediate. What happens here is what happens generally. Whatever approves itself to us on any ground at the outset, presently comes to appeal to us as a gratifying thing in itself; it comes to rest in our habits of thought as substantially right. But in order that any specific canon of deportment shall maintain itself in favour, it must continue to have the support of, or at least not be incompatible with, the habit or aptitude which constitutes the norm of its development. The need of vicarious leisure, or conspicuous consumption of service, is a dominant incentive to the keeping of servants. So long as this remains true it may be set down without much discussion that any such departure from accepted usage as would suggest an abridged apprenticeship in service would presently be found insufferable. The requirement of an expensive vicarious leisure acts indirectly, selectively, by guiding the formation of our taste—of our sense of what is right in these matters—and so weeds out unconformable departures by withholding approval of them.

As the standard of wealth recognized by common consent advances, the possession and exploitation of servants as a means of showing superfluity undergoes a refinement. The possession and maintenance of slaves employed in the production of goods argues wealth and prowess, but the maintenance of servants who produce nothing argues still higher wealth and position. Under this principle there arises a class of servants, the more numerous the better, whose sole office is fatuously to wait upon the person of their owner, and so to put in evidence his ability unproductively to consume a large amount of service. There supervenes a division of labour among the servants or dependents whose life is spent in maintaining the honour of the gentleman of leisure. So that, while one group produces goods for him, another group, usually headed by the wife, or chief wife, consumes for him in conspicuous leisure; thereby putting in evidence his ability to sustain large pecuniary damage without impairing his superior opulence.

This somewhat idealized and diagrammatic outline of the development and nature of domestic service comes nearest being true for that cultural stage which has here been named the "quasi-peaceable" stage of industry. At this stage personal service first rises to the position of an economic institution, and it is at this stage that it occupies the largest place in the community's scheme of life. In the cultural sequence, the quasi-peaceable stage follows the predatory stage proper, the two being successive phases of barbarian life. Its characteristic feature is a formal observance of peace and order, at the same time that life at this stage still has too much of coercion and class antagonism to be called peaceable in the full sense of the word. For many purposes, and from another point of view than the economic one, it might as well be named the stage of status. The method of human relation during this stage, and the spiritual attitude of men at this level of culture, is well summed up under that term.

But as a descriptive term to characterize the prevailing methods of industry, as well as to indicate the trend of industrial development at this point in economic evolution, the term "quasi-peaceable" seems preferable. So far as concerns the communities of the western culture, this phase of economic development probably lies in the past, except for a numerically small though very conspicuous fraction of the community in whom the habits of thought peculiar to the barbarian culture have suffered but a relatively slight disintegration.

Personal service is still an element of great economic importance, especially as regards the distribution and consumption of goods; but its relative importance even in this direction is no doubt less than it once was. The best development of this vicarious leisure lies in the past rather than in the present; and its best expression in the present is to be found in the scheme of life of the upper leisure class. To this class the modern culture owes much in the way of the conservation of traditions, usages, and habits of thought which belong on a more archaic cultural plane, so far as regards their widest acceptance and their most effective development.

In the modern industrial communities the mechanical contrivances available for the comfort and convenience of everyday life are highly developed. So much so that body servants, or, indeed, domestic servants of any kind, would now scarcely be employed by anybody except on the ground of a canon of reputability carried over by tradition from earlier usage. The only exception would

be servants employed to attend on the persons of the
infirm and the feeble-minded. But such servants properly come under the head of trained nurses rather than
under that of domestic servants, and they are, therefore,
an apparent rather than a real exception to the rule.

The proximate reason for keeping domestic servants,
for instance, in the moderately well-to-do household of
today, is (ostensibly) that the members of the household are unable without discomfort to compass the work
required by such a modern establishment. And the reason
for their being unable to accomplish it is (1) that they
have too many "social duties," and (2) that the work
to be done is too severe and that there is too much of it.
These two reasons may be restated as follows: (1) Under a mandatory code of decency, the time and effort
of the members of such a household are required to be
ostensibly all spent in a performance of conspicuous leisure, in the way of calls, drives, clubs, sewing-circles,
sports, charity organizations, and other like social functions. Those persons whose time and energy are employed in these matters privately avow that all these observances, as well as the incidental attention to dress and
other conspicuous consumption, are very irksome but
altogether unavoidable. (2) Under the requirement of
conspicuous consumption of goods, the apparatus of living has grown so elaborate and cumbrous, in the way
of dwellings, furniture, bric-à-brac, wardrobe, and meals,
that the consumers of these things cannot make way
with them in the required manner without help. Per-

sonal contact with the hired persons whose aid is called
in to fulfil the routine of decency is commonly distasteful to the occupants of the house, but their presence is
endured and paid for, in order to delegate to them a
share in this onerous consumption of household goods.
The presence of domestic servants, and of the special
class of body servants in an eminent degree, is a concession of physical comfort to the moral need of pecuniary
decency.

The largest manifestation of vicarious leisure in modern life is made up of what are called domestic duties.
These duties are fast becoming a species of services performed, not so much for the individual behoof of the
head of the household as for the reputability of the
household taken as a corporate unit—a group of which
the housewife is a member on a footing of ostensible
equality. As fast as the household for which they are
performed departs from its archaic basis of ownership-
marriage, these household duties of course tend to fall
out of the category of vicarious leisure in the original
sense, except so far as they are performed by hired servants. That is to say, since vicarious leisure is possible only
on a basis of status or of hired service, the disappearance
of the relation of status from human intercourse at any
point carries with it the disappearance of vicarious leisure
so far as regards that much of life. But it is to be added,
in qualification of this qualification, that so long as the
household subsists, even with a divided head, this class
of non-productive labour performed for the sake of

household reputability must still be classed as vicarious leisure, although in a slightly altered sense. It is now leisure performed for the quasi-personal corporate household, instead of, as formerly, for the proprietary head of the household.

## THE HIGHER LEARNING AS AN EXPRESSION OF THE PECUNIARY CULTURE

To the end that suitable habits of thought on certain heads may be conserved in the incoming generation, a scholastic discipline is sanctioned by the common-sense of the community and incorporated into the accredited scheme of life. The habits of thought which are so formed under the guidance of teachers and scholastic traditions have an economic value—a value as affecting the serviceability of the individual—no less real than the similar economic value of the habits of thought formed without such guidance under the discipline of everyday life. Whatever characteristics of the accredited scholastic scheme and discipline are traceable to the predilections of the leisure class or to the guidance of the canons of pecuniary merit are to be set down to the account of that institution, and whatever economic value these features of the educational scheme possess are the expression in detail of the value of that institution. It will be in place, therefore, to point out any peculiar features of the educational system which are traceable to the leisure-class scheme of life, whether as regards the aim and method of the discipline, or as regards the compass and character of the body of knowledge inculcated. It is in learning proper, and more particularly in the higher learning, that the influence of leisure-class ideals is most patent; and since the purpose here is not to make an exhaustive collation of data showing the effect of the pecuniary culture upon education, but rather to illustrate the method and trend of leisure-class influence in education, a survey of certain salient features of the higher learning, such as may serve this purpose, is all that will be attempted.

In point of derivation and early development, learning is somewhat closely related to the devotional function of the community, particularly to the body of observances in which the service rendered the supernatural leisure class expresses itself. The service by which it is sought to conciliate supernatural agencies in the primitive cults is not an industrially profitable employment of the community's time and effort. It is, therefore, in great part, to be classed as a vicarious leisure performed for the supernatural powers with whom negotiations are carried on and whose good-will the service and the professions of subservience are conceived to procure. In great part, the early learning consisted in an acquisition of knowledge and facility in the service of a supernatural agent. It was therefore closely analogous in character to the training required for the domestic service of a temporal master. To a great extent, the knowledge acquired

under the priestly teachers of the primitive community
was a knowledge of ritual and ceremonial; that is to say,
a knowledge of the most proper, most effective, or most
acceptable manner of approaching and of serving the
preternatural agents. What was learned was how to
make oneself indispensable to these powers, and so to
put oneself in a position to ask, or even to require, their
intercession in the course of events or their abstention
from interference in any given enterprise. Propitiation
was the end, and this end was sought, in great part, by
acquiring facility in subservience. It appears to have been
only gradually that other elements than those of efficient
service of the master found their way into the stock of
priestly or shamanistic instruction.

The priestly servitor of the inscrutable powers that
move in the external world came to stand in the position
of a mediator between these powers and the common
run of uninstructed humanity; for he was possessed of a
knowledge of the supernatural etiquette which would
admit him into the presence. And as commonly happens
with mediators between the vulgar and their masters,
whether the masters be natural or preternatural, he
found it expedient to have the means at hand tangibly to
impress upon the vulgar the fact that these inscrutable
powers would do what he might ask of them. Hence,
presently, a knowledge of certain natural processes which
could be turned to account for spectacular effect, together with some sleight of hand, came to be an integral
part of priestly lore. Knowledge of this kind passes for

knowledge of the "unknowable," and it owes its service-ability for the sacerdotal purpose to its recondite character. It appears to have been from this source that learning, as an institution, arose, and its differentiation from this its parent stock of magic ritual and shamanistic fraud has been slow and tedious, and is scarcely yet complete even in the most advanced of the higher seminaries of learning.

The recondite element in learning is still, as it has been in all ages, a very attractive and effective element for the purpose of impressing, or even imposing upon, the unlearned; and the standing of the savant in the mind of the altogether unlettered is in great measure rated in terms of intimacy with the occult forces. So, for instance, as a typical case, even so late as the middle of this century, the Norwegian peasants have instinctively formulated their sense of the superior erudition of such doctors of divinity as Luther, Melanchthon, Peder Dass, and even so late a scholar in divinity as Grundtvig, in terms of the Black Art. These, together with a very comprehensive list of minor celebrities, both living and dead, have been reputed masters in all magical arts; and a high position in the ecclesiastical personnel has carried with it, in the apprehension of these good people, an implication of profound familiarity with magical practice and the occult sciences. There is a parallel fact nearer home, similarly going to show the close relationship, in popular apprehension, between erudition and the unknowable; and it will at the same time serve to illustrate, in somewhat coarse outline, the bent which leisure-class life gives to the cognitive interest. While the belief is by no means confined to the leisure class, that class today comprises a disproportionately large number of believers in occult sciences of all kinds and shades. By those whose habits of thought are not shaped by contact with modern industry, the knowledge of the unknowable is still felt to be the ultimate if not the only true knowledge.

Learning, then, set out with being in some sense a by-product of the priestly vicarious leisure class; and, at least until a recent date, the higher learning has since remained in some sense a by-product or by-occupation of the priestly classes. As the body of systematized knowledge increased, there presently arose a distinction, traceable very far back in the history of education, between esoteric and exoteric knowledge; the former—so far as there is a substantial difference between the two—comprising such knowledge as is primarily of no economic or industrial effect, and the latter comprising chiefly knowledge of industrial processes and of natural phenomena which were habitually turned to account for the material purposes of life. This line of demarcation has in time become, at least in popular apprehension, the normal line between the higher learning and the lower.

It is significant, not only as an evidence of their close affiliation with the priestly craft, but also as indicating that their activity to a good extent falls under that category of conspicuous leisure known as manners and breeding, that the learned class in all primitive communities are great sticklers for form, precedent, gradations of rank, ritual, ceremonial vestments, and learned paraphernalia generally. This is of course to be expected, and it goes to say that the higher learning, in its incipient phase, is a leisure-class occupation—more specifically an occupation of the vicarious leisure class employed in the service of the supernatural leisure class. But this predilection for the paraphernalia of learning goes also to indicate a further point of contact or of continuity between the priestly office and the office of the savant. In point of derivation, learning, as well as the priestly office, is largely an outgrowth of sympathetic magic; and this magical apparatus of form and ritual therefore finds its place with the learned class of the primitive community as a matter of course. The ritual and paraphernalia have an occult efficacy for the magical purpose; so that their presence as an integral factor in the earlier phases of the development of magic and science is a matter of expediency, quite as much as of affectionate regard for symbolism simply.

This sense of the efficacy of symbolic ritual, and of sympathetic effect to be wrought through dexterous rehearsal of the traditional accessories of the act or end to be compassed, is of course present more obviously and in larger measure in magical practice than in the discipline of the sciences, even of the occult sciences. But there are, I apprehend, few persons with a cultivated sense of scholastic merit to whom the ritualistic accessories of science are altogether an idle matter. The very great tenacity with which these ritualistic paraphernalia persist through the later course of the development is evident to anyone who will reflect on what has been the history of learning in our civilization. Even today there are such things in the usage of the learned community as the cap and gown, matriculation, initiation, and graduation ceremonies, and the conferring of scholastic degrees, dignities, and prerogatives in a way which suggests some sort of a scholarly apostolic succession. The usage of the priestly orders is no doubt the proximate source of all these features of learned ritual, vestments, sacramental initiation, the transmission of peculiar dignities and virtues by the imposition of hands, and the like; but their derivation is traceable back of this point, to the source from which the specialized priestly class proper received them in the course of differentiation by which the priest came to be distinguished from the sorcerer on the one hand and from the menial servant of a temporal master on the other hand. So far as regards both their derivation and their psychological content, these usages and the conceptions on which they rest belong to a stage in cultural development no later than that of the angekok and the rain-maker. Their place in the later phases of devout observance, as well as in the higher educational system, is that of a survival from a very early animistic phase of the development of human nature.

These ritualistic features of the educational system

of the present and of the recent past, it is quite safe to
say, have their place primarily in the higher, liberal,
and classic institutions and grades of learning, rather
than in the lower, technological, or practical grades and
branches of the system. So far as they possess them, the
lower and less reputable branches of the educational
scheme have evidently borrowed these things from the
higher grades; and their continued persistence among
the practical schools, without the sanction of the continued example of the higher and classic grades, would
be highly improbable, to say the least. With the lower
and practical schools and scholars, the adoption and cultivation of these usages is a case of mimicry—due to a
desire to conform as far as may be to the standards of
scholastic reputability maintained by the upper grades
and classes, who have come by these accessory features
legitimately, by the right of lineal devolution.

The analysis may even be safely carried a step farther.
Ritualistic survivals and reversions come out in fullest
vigour and with the freest air of spontaneity among
those seminaries of learning which have to do primarily
with the education of the priestly and leisure classes. Accordingly it should appear, and it does pretty plainly
appear, on a survey of recent developments in college
and university life, that wherever schools founded for
the instruction of the lower classes in the immediately
useful branches of knowledge grow into institutions of
the higher learning, the growth of ritualistic ceremonial
and paraphernalia and of elaborate scholastic "functions"

goes hand in hand with the transition of the schools in question from the field of homely practicality into the higher, classical sphere. The initial purpose of these schools, and the work with which they have chiefly had to do at the earlier of these two stages of their evolution, has been that of fitting the young of the industrious classes for work. On the higher, classical plane of learning to which they commonly tend, their dominant aim becomes the preparation of the youth of the priestly and the leisure classes—or of an incipient leisure class—for the consumption of goods, material and immaterial, according to a conventionally accepted, reputable scope and method. This happy issue has commonly been the fate of schools founded by "friends of the people" for the aid of struggling young men, and where this transition is made in good form there is commonly, if not invariably, a coincident change to a more ritualistic life in the schools.

In the school life of today, learned ritual is in a general way best at home in schools whose chief end is the cultivation of the "humanities." This correlation is shown, perhaps more neatly than anywhere else, in the life-history of the American colleges and universities of recent growth. There may be many exceptions from the rule, especially among those schools which have been founded by the typically reputable and ritualistic churches, and which, therefore, started on the conservative and classical plane or reached the classical position by a short-cut; but the general rule as regards the col-

leges founded in the newer American communities during the present century has been that, so long as the
community has remained poor, and so long as the constituency from which the colleges have drawn their pupils
has been dominated by habits of industry and thrift, so
long the reminiscences of the medicine-man have found
but a scant and precarious acceptance in the scheme of
college life. But so soon as wealth begins appreciably to
accumulate in the community, and so soon as a given
school begins to lean on a leisure-class constituency, there
comes also a perceptibly increased insistence on scholastic
ritual and on conformity to the ancient forms as regards
vestments and social and scholastic solemnities. So, for
instance, there has been an approximate coincidence between the growth of wealth among the constituency
which supports any given college of the Middle West
and the date of acceptance—first into tolerance and then
into imperative vogue—of evening dress for men and
of the decolleté for women, as the scholarly vestments
proper to occasions of learned solemnity or to the seasons
of social amenity within the college circle. Apart from
the mechanical difficulty of so large a task, it would
scarcely be a difficult matter to trace this correlation. The
like is true of the vogue of the cap and gown.

Cap and gown have been adopted as learned insignia
by many colleges of this section within the last few
years; and it is safe to say that this could scarcely have
occurred at a much earlier date, or until there had grown
up a leisure-class sentiment of sufficient volume in the

community to support a strong movement of reversion towards an archaic view as to the legitimate end of education. This particular item of learned ritual, it may be noted, would not only commend itself to the leisure-class sense of the fitness of things, as appealing to the archaic propensity for spectacular effect and the predilection for antique symbolism; but it at the same time fits into the leisure-class scheme of life as involving a notable element of conspicuous waste. The precise date at which the reversion to cap and gown took place, as well as the fact that it affected so large a number of schools at about the same time, seems to have been due in some measure to a wave of atavistic sense of conformity and reputability that passed over the community at that period.

It may not be entirely beside the point to note that in point of time this curious reversion seems to coincide with the culmination of a certain vogue of atavistic sentiment and tradition in other directions also. The wave of reversion seems to have received its initial impulse in the psychologically disintegrating effects of the Civil War. Habituation to war entails a body of predatory habits of thought, whereby clannishness in some measure replaces the sense of solidarity, and a sense of invidious distinction supplants the impulse to equitable, everyday serviceability. As an outcome of the cumulative action of these factors, the generation which follows a season of war is apt to witness a rehabilitation of the element of status, both in its social life and in its scheme of devout observances and other symbolic or ceremonial forms. Throughout the eighties, and less plainly traceable through the seventies also, there was perceptible a gradually advancing wave of sentiment favouring quasi-predatory business habits, insistence on status, anthropomorphism, and conservatism generally. The more direct and unmediated of these expressions of the barbarian temperament, such as the recrudescence of outlawry and the spectacular quasi-predatory careers of fraud run by certain "captains of industry," came to a head earlier and were appreciably on the decline by the close of the seventies. The recrudescence of anthropomorphic sentiment also seems to have passed its most acute stage before the close of the eighties. But the learned ritual and paraphernalia here spoken of are a still remoter and more recondite expression of the barbarian animistic sense; and these, therefore, gained vogue and elaboration more slowly and reached their most effective development at a still later date. There is reason to believe that the culmination is now already past. Except for the new impetus given by a new war experience, and except for the support which the growth of a wealthy class affords to all ritual, and especially to whatever ceremonial is wasteful and pointedly suggests gradations of status, it is probable that the late improvements and augmentation of scholastic insignia and ceremonial would gradually decline. But while it may be true that the cap and gown, and the more strenuous observance of scholastic proprieties which came with them, were floated in on this postbellum tidal wave of reversion to barbarism, it is also no doubt true that such a ritualistic reversion could not have been effected in the college scheme of life until the accumulation of wealth in the hands of a propertied class had gone far enough to afford the requisite pecuniary ground for a movement which should bring the colleges of the country up to the leisure-class requirements in the higher learning. The adoption of the cap and gown is one of the striking atavistic features of modern college life, and at the same time it marks the fact that these colleges have definitively become leisure-class establishments, either in actual achievement or in aspiration.

As further evidence of the close relation between the educational system and the cultural standards of the community, it may be remarked that there is some tendency latterly to substitute the captain of industry in place of the priest as the head of seminaries of the higher learning. The substitution is by no means complete or unequivocal. Those heads of institutions are best accepted who combine the sacerdotal office with a high degree of pecuniary efficiency. There is a similar but less pronounced tendency to entrust the work of instruction in the higher learning to men of some pecuniary qualification. Administrative ability and skill in advertising the enterprise count for rather more than they once did, as qualifications for the work of teaching. This applies especially in those agencies that have most to do with the everyday facts of life, and it is particularly true of schools in the economically single-minded communities.

This partial substitution of pecuniary for sacerdotal efficiency is a concomitant of the modern transition from conspicuous leisure to conspicuous consumption, as the chief means of reputability. The correlation of the two facts is probably clear without further elaboration.

The attitude of the schools and of the learned class towards the education of women serves to show in what manner and to what extent learning has departed from its ancient station of priestly and leisure-class prerogative, and it indicates also what approach has been made by the truly learned to the modern, economic or industrial, matter-of-fact standpoint. The higher schools and the learned professions were until recently taboo to the women. These establishments were from the outset, and have in great measure continued to be, devoted to the education of the priestly and leisure classes.

The women, as has been shown elsewhere, were the original subservient class, and to some extent, especially so far as regards their nominal or ceremonial position, they have remained in that relation down to the present. There has prevailed a strong sense that the admission of women to the privileges of the higher learning (as to the Eleusinian mysteries) would be derogatory to the dignity of the learned craft. It is therefore only very recently, and almost solely in the industrially most advanced communities, that the higher grades of schools have been freely opened to women. And even under the urgent circumstances prevailing in the modern industrial communities, the highest and most reputable universities show an extreme reluctance in making the move. The sense of class worthiness, that is to say of status, of a honorific differentiation of the sexes according to a distinction between superior and inferior intellectual dignity, survives in a vigorous form in these corporations of the aristocracy of learning. It is felt that the women should, in all propriety, acquire only such knowledge as may be classed under one or the other of two heads: (1) such knowledge as conduces immediately to a better performance of domestic service—the domestic sphere; (2) such accomplishments and dexterity, quasi-scholarly and quasi-artistic, as plainly come in under the head of a performance of vicarious leisure. Knowledge is felt to be unfeminine if it is knowledge which expresses the unfolding of the learner's own life, the acquisition of which proceeds on the learner's own cognitive interest, without prompting from the canons of propriety, and without reference back to a master whose comfort or good repute is to be enhanced by the employment or the exhibition of it. So, also, all knowledge which is useful as evidence of leisure, other than vicarious leisure, is scarcely feminine.

For an appreciation of the relation which these higher seminaries of learning bear to the economic life of the community, the phenomena which have been reviewed are of importance rather as indications of a general attitude than as being in themselves facts of first-rate economic consequence. They go to show what is the instinctive attitude and animus of the learned class towards the life process of an industrial community. They serve as an exponent of the stage of development, for the industrial purpose, attained by the higher learning and by the learned class, and so they afford an indication as to what may fairly be looked for from this class at points where the learning and the life of the class bear more immediately upon the economic life and efficiency of the community, and upon the adjustment of its scheme of life to the requirements of the time. What these ritualistic survivals go to indicate is a prevalence of conservatism, if not of reactionary sentiment, especially among the higher schools where the conventional learning is cultivated.

To these indications of a conservative attitude is to be added another characteristic which goes in the same direction, but which is a symptom of graver consequence than this playful inclination to trivialities of form and ritual. By far the greater number of American colleges and universities, for instance, are affiliated to some religious denomination and are somewhat given to devout observances. Their putative familiarity with scientific methods and the scientific point of view should presumably exempt the faculties of these schools from animistic habits of thought; but there is still a considerable proportion of them who profess an attachment to the anthropomorphic beliefs and observances of an earlier culture. These professions of devotional zeal are, no doubt, to a good extent expedient and perfunctory, both on the part of the schools in their corporate capacity, and on the part of the individual members of the corps of instructors; but it cannot be doubted that there is after all a very appreciable element of anthropomorphic sentiment present in the higher schools. So far as this is the case it must be set down as the expression of an archaic, animistic habit of mind. This habit of mind must necessarily assert itself to some extent in the instruction offered, and to this extent its influence in shaping the habits of thought of the student makes for conservatism and reversion; it acts to hinder his development in the direction of matter-of-fact knowledge, such as best serves the ends of industry.

The college sports, which have so great a vogue in the reputable seminaries of learning today, tend in a similar direction; and, indeed, sports have much in common with the devout attitude of the colleges, both as regards their psychological basis and as regards their disciplinary effect. But this expression of the barbarian temperament is to be credited primarily to the body of students, rather than to the temper of the schools as such; except in so far as the colleges or the college officials—as sometimes happens—actively countenance and foster the growth of sports. The like is true of college fraternities as of college sports, but with a difference. The latter are chiefly an expression of the predatory impulse simply; the former are more specifically an expression of that heritage of clannishness which is so large a feature in the temperament of the predatory barbarian. It is also noticeable that a close relation subsists between the fraternities and the sporting activity of the schools. . . . It is scarcely necessary further to discuss the economic value of this training in sports and in factional organization and activity.

But all these features of the scheme of life of the learned class, and of the establishments dedicated to the conservation of the higher learning, are in a great measure incidental only. They are scarcely to be accounted organic elements of the professed work of research and instruction for the ostensible pursuit of which the schools exist. But these symptomatic indications go to establish a presumption as to the character of the work performed —as seen from the economic point of view—and as to the bent which the serious work carried on under their auspices gives to the youth who resort to the schools. The presumption raised by the considerations already offered is that in their work also, as well as in their ceremonial, the higher schools may be expected to take a conservative position; but this presumption must be checked by a comparison of the economic character of the work actually performed, and by something of a survey of the learning whose conservation is entrusted to the higher schools. On this head, it is well known that the accredited seminaries of learning have, until a recent date, held a conservative position. They have taken an attitude of deprecation towards all innovations. As a general rule a new point of view or a new formulation of knowledge has been countenanced and taken up within the schools only after these new things have made their way outside of the schools. As exceptions from this rule are chiefly to be mentioned innovations of an inconspicuous kind and departures which do not bear in any tangible way upon the conventional point of view or upon the conventional scheme of life; as, for instance, details of fact in the mathematico-physical sciences, and new readings and interpretations of the classics, especially such as have a philological or literary bearing only. Except within the domain of the "humanities," in the narrow sense, and except so far as the traditional point of view of the humanities has been left intact by the innovators, it has generally held true that the accredited learned class and the seminaries of the higher learning have looked askance at all innovation. New views, new departures in scientific theory, especially new departures which touch the theory of human relations at any point, have found a place in the scheme of the university tardily and by a reluctant tolerance, rather than by a cordial welcome; and the men who have occupied themselves with such efforts to widen the scope of human knowledge have not commonly been well received by their learned contemporaries. The higher schools have not commonly given their countenance to a serious advance in the methods or the content of knowledge until the innovations have outlived their youth and much of their usefulness—after they have become commonplaces of the intellectual furniture of a new generation which has grown up under, and has had its habits of thought shaped by, the new, extra-scholastic body of knowledge and the new standpoint. This is true of the recent past. How far it may be true of the immediate present it would be hazardous to say, for it is impossible to see present-day facts in such perspective as to get a fair conception of their relative proportions.

So far, nothing has been said of the Mæcenas function of the well-to-do, which is habitually dwelt on at some length by writers and speakers who treat of the development of culture and of social structure. This leisure-class function is not without an important bearing on the higher learning and on the spread of knowledge and culture. The manner and the degree in which the class furthers learning through patronage of this kind is sufficiently familiar. It has been frequently presented in affectionate and effective terms by spokesmen whose familiarity with the topic fits them to bring home to their hearers the profound significance of this cultural factor. These spokesmen, however, have presented the matter from the point of view of the cultural interest, or of the interest of reputability, rather than from that of the economic interest. As apprehended from the economic point of view, and valued for the purpose of industrial serviceability, this function of the well-to-do, as well as the intellectual attitude of members of the well-to-do class, merits some attention and will bear illustration.

By way of characterization of the Mæcenas relation, it is to be noted that, considered externally, as an economic or industrial relation simply, it is a relation of status. The scholar under patronage performs the duties of a learned life vicariously for his patron, to whom a certain repute inures after the manner of the good repute imputed to a master for whom any form of vicarious leisure is performed. It is also to be noted that, in point of historical fact, the furtherance of learning or the maintenance of scholarly activity through the Mæcenas relation has most commonly been a furtherance of proficiency in classical lore or in the humanities. This knowledge tends to lower rather than to heighten the industrial efficiency of the community.

Further, as regards the direct participation of the members of the leisure class in the furtherance of knowledge. The canons of reputable living act to throw such intellectual interest as seeks expression among the class on the side of classical and formal erudition, rather than on the side of the sciences that bear some relation to the community's industrial life. The most frequent excursions into other than classical fields of knowledge on the part of members of the leisure class are made into the discipline of law and of the political, and more especially the administrative, sciences. These so-called sciences are substantially bodies of maxims of expediency for guidance in the leisure-class office of government, as conducted on a proprietary basis. The interest with which this discipline is approached is therefore not commonly the intellectual or cognitive interest simply. It is largely the practical interest of the exigencies of that relation of mastery in which the members of the class are placed. In point of derivation, the office of government is a predatory function, pertaining integrally to the archaic leisure-class scheme of life. It is an exercise of control and coercion over the population from which the class draws its sustenance. This discipline, as well as incidents of practice which give it its content, therefore has some attraction for the class apart from all questions of cognition. All this holds true wherever and so long as the governmental office continues, in form or in substance, to be a proprietary office; and it holds true beyond that limit, in so far as the tradition of the more archaic phase of governmental evolution has lasted on into the later life of those modern communities for whom proprietary government by a leisure class is now beginning to pass away.

For that field of learning within which the cognitive or intellectual interest is dominant—the sciences properly so called—the case is somewhat different, not only as regards the attitude of the leisure class, but as regards the whole drift of the pecuniary culture. Knowledge for its own sake, the exercise of the faculty of comprehension without ulterior purpose, should, it might be expected, be sought by men whom no urgent material interest diverts from such a quest. The sheltered industrial position of the leisure class should give free play to the cognitive interest in members of this class, and we should consequently have, as many writers confidently find that we do have, a very large proportion of scholars, scientists, savants, derived from this class and deriving their incentive to scientific investigation and speculation from the discipline of a life of leisure. Some such result is to be looked for, but there are features of the leisure-class scheme of life, already sufficiently dwelt upon, which go to divert the intellectual interest of this class to other subjects than that causal sequence in phenomena which makes the content of the sciences. The habits of thought which characterize the life of the class run on the personal relation of dominance, and on the derivative, invidious concepts of honour, worth, merit, character, and the like. The causal sequence which makes up the subject-matter of science is not visible from this point of view. Neither does good repute attach to knowledge of facts that are vulgarly useful. Hence it should appear probable that the interest of the invidious comparison with respect to pecuniary or other honorific merit should occupy the attention of the leisure class, to the neglect of the cognitive interest. Where this latter interest asserts itself it should commonly be diverted to fields of speculation or investigation which are reputable and futile, rather than to the quest of scientific knowledge. Such indeed has been the history of priestly and leisure-class learning so long as no considerable body of systematized knowledge had been intruded into the scholastic discipline from an extra-scholastic source. But since the relation of mastery and subservience is ceasing to be the dominant and formative factor in the community's life process, other features of the life process and other points of view are forcing themselves upon the scholars.

The true-bred gentleman of leisure should, and does, see the world from the point of view of the personal relation; and the cognitive interest, so far as it asserts itself in him, should seek to systematize phenomena on this basis. Such indeed is the case with the gentleman of the old school, in whom the leisure-class ideals have suffered no disintegration; and such is the attitude of his latter-day descendant, in so far as he has fallen heir to the full complement of upper-class virtues. But the ways of heredity are devious, and not every gentleman's son is to the manor born. Especially is the transmission of the habits of thought which characterize the predatory master somewhat precarious in the case of a line of descent in which but one or two of the latest steps have lain within the leisure-class discipline. The chances of occurrence of a strong congenital or acquired bent towards the exercise of the cognitive aptitudes are apparently best in those members of the leisure class who are of lower-class or middle-class antecedents—that is to say, those who have inherited the complement of aptitudes proper to the industrious classes, and who owe their place in the leisure class to the possession of qualities which count for more today than they did in the times when the leisure-class scheme of life took shape. But even outside the range of these later accessions to the leisure class there are an appreciable number of individuals in whom the invidious interest is not sufficiently dominant to shape their theoretical views, and in whom the proclivity to theory is sufficiently strong to lead them into the scientific quest.

The higher learning owes the intrusion of the sciences in part to these aberrant scions of the leisure class, who have come under the dominant influence of the latter-day tradition of impersonal relation and who have inherited a complement of human aptitudes differing in certain salient features from the temperament which is characteristic of the regime of status. But it owes the presence of this alien body of scientific knowledge also in part, and in a higher degree, to members of the industrious classes who have been in sufficiently easy circumstances to turn their attention to other interests than that of finding daily sustenance, and whose inherited aptitudes run back of the regime of status in the respect that the invidious and anthropomorphic point of view does not dominate their intellectual processes. As between these two groups which approximately comprise the effective force of scientific progress, it is the latter that has contributed the most. And with respect to both it seems to be true that they are not so much the source as the vehicle, or at the most they are the instrument of commutation, by which the habits of thought enforced upon the community, through contact with its environment under the exigencies of modern associated life and the mechanical industries, are turned to account for theoretical knowledge.

Science, in the sense of an articulate recognition of causal sequence in phenomena, whether physical or social, has been a feature of the western culture only since the industrial process in the western communities has come to be substantially a process of mechanical contrivances in which man's office is that of discrimination and valuation of material forces. Science has flourished somewhat in the same degree as the industrial life of the community has conformed to this pattern, and somewhat in the same degree as the industrial interest has dominated the community's life. And science, and scientific theory especially, has made headway in the several departments of human life and knowledge in proportion as each of these several departments has successively come into closer contact with the industrial process and the economic interest; or perhaps it is truer to say, in proportion as each of them has successively escaped from the dominance of the conceptions of personal relation or status, and of the derivative canons of anthropomorphic fitness and honorific worth.

It is only as the exigencies of modern industrial life have enforced the recognition of causal sequence in the practical contact of mankind with their environment, that men have come to systematize the phenomena of this environment, and the facts of their own contact with it, in terms of causal sequence. So that while the higher learning in its best development, as the perfect flower of scholasticism and classicism, was a by-product of the priestly office and the life of leisure, so modern science may be said to be a by-product of the industrial process. Through these groups of men, then—investigators, savants, scientists, inventors, speculators—most of whom have done their most telling work outside the shelter of the schools, the habits of thought enforced by the modern industrial life have found coherent expression and elaboration as a body of theoretical science having to do with the causal sequence of phenomena. And from this extra-scholastic field of scientific speculation, changes of method and purpose have from time to time been intruded into the scholastic discipline.

In this connexion it is to be remarked that there is a very perceptible difference of substance and purpose between the instruction offered in the primary and secondary schools, on the one hand, and in the higher seminaries of learning, on the other hand. The difference in point of immediate practicality of the information imparted and of the proficiency acquired may be of some consequence and may merit the attention which it has from time to time received; but there is a more substantial difference in the mental and spiritual bent which is favoured by the one and the other discipline. This divergent trend in discipline between the higher and the lower learning is especially noticeable as regards the primary education in its latest development in the advanced industrial communities. Here the instruction is directed chiefly to proficiency or dexterity, intellectual and manual, in the apprehension and employment of impersonal facts, in their causal rather than in their honorific incidence. It is true, under the traditions of the earlier days, when the primary education was also predominantly a leisure-class commodity, a free use is still made of emulation as a spur to diligence in the common run of primary schools; but even this use of emulation as an expedient is visibly declining in the primary grades of instruction in communities where the lower education is not under the guidance of the ecclesiastical or military tradition. All this holds true in a peculiar degree, and more especially on the spiritual side, of such portions of the educational system as have been immediately affected by kindergarten methods and ideals.

The peculiarly non-invidious trend of the kindergarten discipline, and the similar character of the kindergarten influence in primary education beyond the limits of the kindergarten proper, should be taken in connexion with what has already been said of the peculiar spiritual attitude of leisure-class womankind under the circumstances of the modern economic situation. The kindergarten discipline is at its best—or at its farthest remove from ancient patriarchal and pedagogical ideals —in the advanced industrial communities, where there is a considerable body of intelligent and idle woman, and where the system of status has somewhat abated in rigour under the disintegrating influence of industrial life and in the absence of a consistent body of military and ecclesiastical traditions. It is from these women in easy circumstances that it gets its moral support. The aims and methods of the kindergarten commend themselves with especial effect to this class of women who are ill at ease under the pecuniary code of reputable life. The kindergarten, and whatever the kindergarten spirit counts for in modern education, therefore, is to be set down, along with the "new-woman movement," to the account of that revulsion against futility and invidious comparison which the leisure-class life under modern circumstances induces in the women most immediately exposed to its discipline. In this way it appears that, by indirection, the institution of a leisure class here again favours the growth of a non-invidious attitude, which may, in the long run, prove a menace to the stability of the institution itself, and even to the institution of individual ownership on which it rests.

During the recent past some tangible changes have taken place in the scope of college and university teaching. These changes have in the main consisted in a partial displacement of the humanities—those branches of learning which are conceived to make for the traditional "culture," character, tastes, and ideals—by those more matter-of-fact branches which make for civic and industrial efficiency. To put the same thing in other words, those branches of knowledge which make for efficiency (ultimately productive efficiency) have gradually been gaining ground against those branches which make for a heightened consumption or a lowered industrial efficiency and for a type of character suited to the

regime of status. In this adaptation of the scheme of
instruction the higher schools have commonly been
found on the conservative side; each step which they
have taken in advance has been to some extent of the
nature of a concession. The sciences have been intruded
into the scholar's discipline from without, not to say
from below. It is noticeable that the humanities which
have so reluctantly yielded ground to the sciences are
pretty uniformly adapted to shape the character of the
student in accordance with a traditional self-centred
scheme of consumption; a scheme of contemplation and
enjoyment of the true, the beautiful, and the good, according to a conventional standard of propriety and excellence, the salient feature of which is leisure—*otium
cum dignitate*. In language veiled by their own habituation to the archaic, decorous point of view, the spokesmen of the humanities have insisted upon the ideal
embodied in the maxim, *fruges consumere nati*. This
attitude should occasion no surprise in the case of schools
which are shaped by and rest upon a leisure-class culture.

The professed grounds on which it has been sought,
as far as might be, to maintain the received standards
and methods of culture intact are likewise characteristic
of the archaic temperament and of the leisure-class theory of life. The enjoyment and the bent derived from
habitual contemplation of the life, ideals, speculations,
and methods of consuming time and goods in vogue
among the leisure class of classical antiquity, for instance, is felt to be "higher," "nobler," "worthier,"

than what results in these respects from a like familiarity with the everyday life and the knowledge and aspirations of commonplace humanity in a modern community. That learning the content of which is an unmitigated knowledge of latter-day men and things is by comparison "lower," "base," "ignoble"—one even hears the epithet "sub-human" applied to this matter-of-fact knowledge of mankind and of everyday life.

This contention of the leisure-class spokesmen of the humanities seems to be substantially sound. In point of substantial fact, the gratification and the culture, or the spiritual attitude or habit of mind, resulting from an habitual contemplation of the anthropomorphism, clannishness, and leisurely self-complacency of the gentleman of an early day, or from a familiarity with the animistic superstitions and the exuberant truculence of the Homeric heroes, for instance, is, æsthetically considered, more legitimate than the corresponding results derived from a matter-of-fact knowledge of things and a contemplation of latter-day civic or workmanlike efficiency. There can be but little question that the first-named habits have the advantage in respect of æsthetic or honorific value, and therefore in respect of the "worth" which is made the basis of award in the comparison. The content of the canons of taste, and more particularly of the canons of honour, is in the nature of things a resultant of the past life and circumstances of the race, transmitted to the later generation by in-

heritance or by tradition; and the fact that the protracted
dominance of a predatory, leisure-class scheme of life
has profoundly shaped the habit of mind and the point
of view of the race in the past, is a sufficient basis for an
æsthetically legitimate dominance of such a scheme of
life in very much of what concerns matters of taste in
the present. For the purpose in hand, canons of taste
are race habits, acquired through a more or less protracted habituation to the approval or disapproval of the
kind of things upon which a favourable or unfavourable
judgment of taste is passed. Other things being equal,
the longer and more unbroken the habituation, the more
legitimate is the canon of taste in question. All this
seems to be even truer of judgments regarding worth
or honour than of judgments of taste generally.

But whatever may be the æsthetic legitimacy of the
derogatory judgment passed on the newer learning by
the spokesmen of the humanities, and however substantial may be the merits of the contention that the classic
lore is worthier and results in a more truly human culture and character, it does not concern the question in
hand. The question in hand is as to how far these
branches of learning, and the point of view for which
they stand in the educational system, help or hinder an
efficient collective life under modern industrial circumstances—how far they further a more facile adaptation
to the economic situation of today. The question is an
economic, not an æsthetic one; and the leisure-class

standards of learning which find expression in the deprecatory attitude of the higher schools towards matter-of-fact knowledge are, for the present purpose, to be valued from this point of view only. For this purpose the use of such epithets as "noble," "base," "higher," "lower," etc., is significant only as showing the animus and the point of view of the disputants; whether they contend for the worthiness of the new or of the old. All these epithets are honorific or humilific terms; that is to say, they are terms of invidious comparison, which in the last analysis fall under the category of the reputable or the disreputable; that is, they belong within the range of ideas that characterizes the scheme of life of the regime of status; that is, they are in substance an expression of sportsmanship—of the predatory and animistic habit of mind; that is, they indicate an archaic point of view and theory of life, which may fit the predatory stage of culture and of economic organization from which they have sprung, but which are, from the point of view of economic efficiency in the broader sense, disserviceable anachronisms.

The classics, and their position of prerogative in the scheme of education to which the higher seminaries of learning cling with such a fond predilection, serve to shape the intellectual attitude and lower the economic efficiency of the new learned generation. They do this not only by holding up an archaic ideal of manhood, but also by the discrimination which they inculcate with respect to the reputable and the disreputable in knowledge. This result is accomplished in two ways: (1) by inspiring an habitual aversion to what is merely useful, as contrasted with what is merely honorific in learning, and so shaping the tastes of the novice that he comes in good faith to find gratification of his tastes solely, or almost solely, in such exercise of the intellect as normally results in no industrial or social gain; and (2) by consuming the learner's time and effort in acquiring knowledge which is of no use, except in so far as this learning has by convention become incorporated into the sum of learning required of the scholar, and has thereby affected the terminology and diction employed in the useful branches of knowledge. Except for this terminological difficulty—which is itself a consequence of the vogue of the classics in the past—a knowledge of the ancient languages, for instance, would have no practical bearing for any scientist or any scholar not engaged on work primarily of a linguistic character. Of course all this has nothing to say as to the cultural value of the classics, nor is there any intention to disparage the discipline of the classics or the bent which their study gives to the student. That bent seems to be of an economically disserviceable kind, but this fact— somewhat notorious indeed—need disturb no one who has the good fortune to find comfort and strength in the classical lore. The fact that classical learning acts to derange the learner's workmanlike aptitudes should fall lightly upon the apprehension of those who hold work-manship of small account in comparison with the culti-vation of decorous ideals:

> Iam fides et pax et honos pudorque
> Priscus et neglecta redire virtus
> Audet.

Owing to the circumstance that this knowledge has become part of the elementary requirements in our system of education, the ability to use and to under-stand certain of the dead languages of southern Europe is not only gratifying to the person who finds occasion to parade his accomplishments in this respect, but the evi-dence of such knowledge serves at the same time to recommend any savant to his audience, both lay and learned. It is currently expected that a certain number of years shall have been spent in acquiring this sub-stantially useless information, and its absence creates a presumption of hasty and precarious learning, as well as of a vulgar practicality that is equally obnoxious to the conventional standards of sound scholarship and in-tellectual force.

The case is analogous to what happens in the purchase of any article of consumption by a purchaser who is not an expert judge of materials or of workmanship. He makes his estimate of the value of the article chiefly on the ground of the apparent expensiveness of the finish of those decorative parts and features which have no immediate relation to the intrinsic usefulness of the article; the presumption being that some sort of ill-defined proportion subsists between the substantial value of the article and the expense of adornment added in order to sell it. The presumption that there can ordinarily be no sound scholarship where a knowledge of the classics and humanities is wanting leads to a conspicuous waste of time and labour on the part of the general body of students in acquiring such knowledge. The conventional insistence on a modicum of conspicuous waste as an incident of all reputable scholarship has affected our canons of taste and of serviceability in matters of scholarship in much the same way as the same principle has influenced our judgment of the serviceability of manufactured goods.

It is true, since conspicuous consumption has gained more and more on conspicuous leisure as a means of repute, the acquisition of the dead languages is no longer so imperative a requirement as it once was, and its talismanic virtue as a voucher of scholarship has suffered a concomitant impairment. But while this is true, it is also true that the classics have scarcely lost in absolute value as a voucher of scholastic respectability, since for this purpose it is only necessary that the scholar should be able to put in evidence some learning which is conventionally recognized as evidence of wasted time; and the classics lend themselves with great facility to this use. Indeed, there can be little doubt that it is their utility as evidence of wasted time and effort, and hence of the pecuniary strength necessary in order to afford this waste, that has secured to the classics their position of prerogative in the scheme of the higher learning, and has led to their being esteemed the most honorific of all learning. They serve the decorative ends of leisure-class learning better than any other body of knowledge, and hence they are an effective means of reputability.

In this respect the classics have until lately had scarcely a rival. They still have no dangerous rival on the continent of Europe, but lately, since college athletics have won their way into a recognized standing as an accredited field of scholarly accomplishment, this latter branch of learning—if athletics may be freely classed as learning—has become a rival of the classics for the primacy in leisure-class education in American and English schools. Athletics have an obvious advantage over the classics for the purpose of leisure-class learning, since success as an athlete presumes, not only a waste of time, but also a waste of money, as well as the possession of certain highly unindustrial archaic traits of character and temperament. In the German universities the place of athletics and Greek-letter fraternities, as a leisure-class scholarly occupation, has in some measure been supplied by a skilled and graded inebriety and a perfunctory duelling.

The leisure class and its standards of virtue—archaism and waste—can scarcely have been concerned in the introduction of the classics into the scheme of the higher learning; but the tenacious retention of the classics by the higher schools, and the high degree of reputability which still attaches to them, are no doubt due to their conforming so closely to the requirements of archaism and waste.

"Classic" always carries this connotation of wasteful and archaic, whether it is used to denote the dead languages or the obsolete or obsolescent forms of thought and diction in the living language, or to denote other items of scholarly activity or apparatus to which it is applied with less aptness. So the archaic idiom of the English language is spoken of as "classic" English. Its use is imperative in all speaking and writing upon serious topics, and a facile use of it lends dignity to even the most commonplace and trivial string of talk. The newest form of English diction is of course never written; the sense of that leisure-class propriety which requires archaism in speech is present even in the most illiterate or sensational writers in sufficient force to prevent such a lapse. On the other hand, the highest and most conventionalized style of archaic diction is—quite characteristically—properly employed only in communications between an anthropomorphic divinity and his subjects. Midway between these extremes lies the everyday speech of leisure-class conversation and literature.

Elegant diction, whether in writing or speaking, is an effective means of reputability. It is of moment to know with some precision what is the degree of archaism conventionally required in speaking on any given topic. Usage differs appreciably from the pulpit to the marketplace; the latter, as might be expected, admits the use of relatively new and effective words and turns of expression, even by fastidious persons. A discriminate avoidance of neologisms is honorific, not only because it argues that time has been wasted in acquiring the obsolescent habit of speech, but also as showing that the speaker has from infancy habitually associated with persons who have been familiar with the obsolescent idiom. It thereby goes to show his leisure-class antecedents. Great purity of speech is presumptive evidence of several successive lives spent in other than vulgarly useful occupations; although its evidence is by no means entirely conclusive to this point.

As felicitous an instance of futile classicism as can well be found, outside of the Far East, is the conventional spelling of the English language. A breach of the proprieties in spelling is extremely annoying and will discredit any writer in the eyes of all persons who are possessed of a developed sense of the true and beautiful. English orthography satisfies all the requirements of the canons of reputability under the law of conspicuous waste. It is archaic, cumbrous, and ineffective; its acquisition consumes much time and effort; failure to acquire it is easy of detection. Therefore it is the first and readiest test of reputability in learning, and conformity to its ritual is indispensable to a blameless scholastic life.

On this head of purity of speech, as at other points where a conventional usage rests on the canons of archaism'and waste, the spokesmen for the usage instinctively take an apologetic attitude. It is contended, in substance, that a punctilious use of ancient and accredited locutions will serve to convey thought more adequately and more precisely than would the straightforward use of the latest form of spoken English; whereas it is notorious that the ideas of today are effectively expressed in the slang of today. Classic speech has the honorific virtue of dignity; it commands attention and respect as being the accredited method of communication under the leisure-class scheme of life, because it carries a pointed sugges-tion of the industrial exemption of the speaker. The advantage of the accredited locutions lies in their reputa-bility; they are reputable because they are cumbrous and out of date, and therefore argue waste of time and ex-emption from the use and the need of direct and forcible speech.

# THE CULTURAL INCIDENCE OF
# THE MACHINE PROCESS [1]

✿

SO far as regards the non-mechanical factors of culture, such as religion, politics, and even business enterprise, the present is in a very large degree comparable
with the scheme of things that prevailed on the Continent of Europe in the seventeenth century. And so far
as the working of these cultural factors is undisturbed
by forces that were not present in the older days, they
should logically again work out in such a situation as
came to prevail in central Europe in the course of the
eighteenth century. The modern situation, of course, is
drawn on a larger scale; but that is due to the intrusion
of a new technology, a different "state of the industrial
arts," and not to a substantially altered range of religious, political, or business conceptions. The pitch of
squalor that characterized vulgar life in the busier Continental countries at the close of the great era of politics
could probably not be reached again, but that again is
due, not to these spiritual factors of cultural growth, but
to the altered state of the industrial arts. The factor in
the modern situation that is alien to the ancient regime

[1] Reprinted by permission of Charles Scribner's Sons, New York,
from *The Theory of Business Enterprise*, 1904, pp. 302–73.

is the machine technology, with its many and wide ramifications.

Business conceptions and business methods were present in vigorous growth in central Europe in the sixteenth and seventeenth centuries, as they had been in south Europe from a slightly earlier date; although the large sweep of business enterprise is not had until a later date, being conditioned by the machine technology. Business methods and the apparatus of business traffic develop very promptly whenever and wherever the situation calls for them; such is the teaching of economic history.[2] There is nothing recondite about them, little that has to be acquired by a protracted, cumulative experience running over many generations, such as is involved in technological development. This business development in earlier modern times, together with the accumulations of funded wealth that came of this business enterprise, ran their course to a finish in Continental Europe, leaving no basis for a new start. The new start from which the current situation takes its rise, in Europe and elsewhere, was given to the Continental peoples by the English, ready-made, in the so-called Industrial Revolution. The natural-rights metaphysics, to which

---

[2] The perfected system of business principles rests on the historical basis of free institutions, and so presumes a protracted historical growth of these institutions; but a highly efficient, though less perfect, business system was worked out in a relatively short time by the south and central European peoples in early modern times on the basis of a less consummate system of rights.—Cf. Ehrenberg, *Zeitalter der Fugger;* Sombart, *Kapitalismus,* vol. II, chaps. 8, 14, 15.

the eventual breakdown of the old Continental system owed its specific character, came also from the English.

In point of blood and cultural descent the population of Great Britain did not differ materially from their neighbours across the Channel or across the North Sea.[3] But from the beginning of the modern cultural era Great Britain stood outside of the general European situation, by force of its physical isolation. So that during the modern era, down to the close of the eighteenth century, the British community was in the position of an interested third party rather than a participant in the political concert of Europe. The era of "state-making," so called, is an era in which England interferes, but is, on the whole, not greatly interfered with, so far as her own home affairs are concerned. England, and presently Great Britain, being reduced to law and order under one crown and living in a condition of isolation and (relatively) of internal peace, the cultural growth of that country took a relatively peaceable direction. The dominant note of everyday life was industry and trade, not dynastic politics and war. This national experience gave as its outcome constitutional government and the modern industrial technology, together with the animus and the point of view of the modern materialistic science. The point of departure for the more recent, current situation, therefore, is a twofold one: (1) the British

[3] Cf. Keane, *Man, Past and Present*, chap. 14; W. Z. Ripley, *Races of Europe*; Lapouge, *L'Aryen*; Montelius, *Les temps préhistoriques en Suède*, etc.; Andreas Hansen, *Menneskeslægtens Ælde*.

peaceable variant of the western culture has contributed
constitutional methods and natural rights, together with
the machine technology brought in under the head of
the "industrial revolution"; and (2) there are the patriotic ideals and animosities left as a residue of the
warlike political traffic in Continental Europe.

Since the new departure, made on the basis of natural
rights and modern industrial and scientific methods, the
complex of nations and of international relations is a
single, not a twofold one. The stage over which affairs,
political, industrial, and cultural, run their course is no
longer Continental or British, but cosmopolitan, comprising all civilized communities and all civilized interests. So
that there is not now, as there was in the sixteenth and
seventeenth centuries, an isolation hospital for technology, science, and civil rights, set apart from the general
current of cultural development. Whatever the forces at
work in the modern situation may eventually bring to
pass, therefore, the outcome must touch all communities
in the same way and in approximately the same degree.
If the outcome is dynastic politics and armament again
played to a finish in popular squalor, aristocratic virtues,
and universal bankruptcy, there will be no peaceable
community of matter-of-fact mechanics and shopkeepers
left in reserve from which to make a new cultural and
industrial start. The modern technology has, in a manner, cut away the ground out of which it first grew and
from which it gathered force to reshape the course of
history. It has made it impossible for any community to

stand peaceably outside of the great complex of nations.

But within the comprehensive situation of today there is this new factor, the machine process. . . . The machine process pervades the modern life and dominates it in a mechanical sense. Its dominance is seen in the enforcement of precise mechanical measurements and adjustment and the reduction of all manner of things, purposes and acts, necessities, conveniences, and amenities of life, to standard units. . . . The point of immediate interest here is the further bearing of the machine process upon the growth of culture—the disciplinary effect which this movement for standardization and mechanical equivalence has upon the human material.

This discipline falls more immediately on the workmen engaged in the mechanical industries, and only less immediately on the rest of the community which lives in contact with this sweeping machine process. Wherever the machine process extends, it sets the pace for the workmen, great and small. The pace is set, not wholly by the particular processes in the details of which the given workman is immediately engaged, but in some degree by the more comprehensive process at large into which the given detail process fits. It is no longer simply that the individual workman makes use of one or more mechanical contrivances for effecting certain results. Such used to be his office in the earlier phases of the use of machines, and the work which he now has in hand still has much of that character. But such a characterization of the workman's part in industry misses the peculiarly modern feature of the case. He now does this work as a factor involved in a mechanical process whose movement controls his motions. It remains true, of course, as it always has been true, that he is the intelligent agent concerned in the process, while the machine, furnace, roadway, or retort are inanimate structures devised by man and subject to the workman's supervision. But the process comprises him and his intelligent motions, and it is by virtue of his necessarily taking an intelligent part in what is going forward that the mechanical process has its chief effect upon him. The process standardizes his supervision and guidance of the machine. Mechanically speaking, the machine is not his to do with it as his fancy may suggest. His place is to take thought of the machine and its work in terms given him by the process that is going forward. His thinking in the premises is reduced to standard units of gauge and grade. If he fails of the precise measure, by more or less, the exigencies of the process check the aberration and drive home the absolute need of conformity.

There results a standardization of the workman's intellectual life in terms of mechanical process, which is more unmitigated and precise the more comprehensive and consummate the industrial process in which he plays a part. This must not be taken to mean that such work need lower the degree of intelligence of the workman. No doubt the contrary is nearer the truth. He is a more efficient workman the more intelligent he is, and the discipline of the machine process ordinarily increases his efficiency even for work in a different line from that by which the discipline is given. But the intelligence required and inculcated in the machine industry is of a peculiar character. The machine process is a severe and insistent disciplinarian in point of intelligence. It requires close and unremitting thought, but it is thought which runs in standard terms of quantitative precision. Broadly, other intelligence on the part of the workman is useless; or it is even worse than useless, for a habit of thinking in other than quantitative terms blurs the workman's quantitative apprehension of the facts with which he has to do.[4]

In so far as he is a rightly gifted and fully disciplined workman, the final term of his *habitual* thinking is mechanical efficiency, understanding "mechanical" in the sense in which it is used above. But mechanical efficiency is a matter of precisely adjusted cause and effect. What the discipline of the machine industry inculcates, therefore, in the habits of life and of thought of the workman, is regularity of sequence and mechanical precision; and the intellectual outcome is an habitual resort to terms of measurable cause and effect, together with a relative neglect and disparagement of such exercise of the intellectual faculties as does not run on these lines.

---

[4] If, e.g., he takes to myth-making and personifies the machine or the process and imputes purpose and benevolence to the mechanical appliances, after the manner of current nursery tales and pulpit oratory, he is sure to go wrong.

Of course, in no case and with no class does the discipline of the machine process mould the habits of life and of thought fully into its own image. There is present in the human nature of all classes too large a residue of the propensities and aptitudes carried over from the past and working to a different result. The machine's regime has been of too short duration, strict as its discipline may be, and the body of inherited traits and traditions is too comprehensive and consistent to admit of anything more than a remote approach to such a consummation.

The machine process compels a more or less unremitting attention to phenomena of an impersonal character and to sequences and correlations not dependent for their force upon human predilection nor created by habit and custom. The machine throws out anthropomorphic habits of thought. It compels the adaptation of the workman to his work, rather than the adaptation of the work to the workman. The machine technology rests on a knowledge of impersonal, material cause and effect, not on the dexterity, diligence, or personal force of the workman, still less on the habits and propensities of the workman's superiors. Within the range of this machine-guided work, and within the range of modern life so far as it is guided by the machine process, the course of things is given mechanically, impersonally, and the resultant discipline is a discipline in the handling of impersonal facts for mechanical effect. It inculcates thinking in terms of opaque, impersonal cause and effect, to the neglect of those norms of validity that rest on usage and on the conventional standards handed down by usage. Usage counts for little in shaping the processes of work of this kind or in shaping the modes of thought induced by work of this kind.

The machine process gives no insight into questions of good and evil, merit and demerit, except in point of material causation, nor into the foundations or the constraining force of law and order, except such mechanically enforced law and order as may be stated in terms of pressure, temperature, velocity, tensile strength, etc.[5] The machine technology takes no cognizance of conventionally established rules of precedence; it knows neither manners nor breeding and can make no use of any of the attributes of worth. Its scheme of knowledge and of inference is based on the laws of material causation, not on those of immemorial custom, authenticity, or authoritative enactment. Its metaphysical basis is the law of cause and effect, which in the thinking of its adepts has displaced even the law of sufficient reason.[6]

The range of conventional truths, or of institutional

---

[5] Such expressions as "good and ill," "merit and demerit," "law and order," when applied to technological facts or to the outcome of material science, are evidently only metaphorical expressions, borrowed from older usage and serviceable only as figures of speech.

[6] Tarde, *Psychologie Economique*, vol. I, pp. 122–31, offers a characterization of the psychology of modern work, contrasting, among other things, the work of the machine workman with that of the handicraftsman in respect of its psychological requirements and effects. It may be taken as a temperate formulation of the current commonplaces on this topic, and seems to be fairly wide of the mark.

legacies, which it traverses is very comprehensive, being, indeed, all-inclusive. It is but little more in accord with the newer, eighteenth-century conventional truths of natural rights, natural liberty, natural law, or natural religion, than with the older norms of the true, the beautiful, and the good which these displaced. Anthropomorphism, under whatever disguise, is of no use and of no force here.

The discipline exercised by the mechanical occupations, in so far as it is in question here, is a discipline of the habits of thought. It is, therefore, as processes of thought, methods of apperception, and sequences of reasoning, that these occupations are of interest for the present purpose; it is as such that they have whatever cultural value belongs to them. They have such a value, therefore, somewhat in proportion as they tax the mental faculties of those employed; and the largest effects are to be looked for among those industrial classes who are required to comprehend and guide the processes, rather than among those who serve merely as mechanical auxiliaries of the machine process. Not that the latter are exempt from the machine's discipline, but it falls upon them blindly and enforces an uncritical acceptance of opaque results, rather than a theoretical insight into the causal sequences which make up the machine process. The higher degree of training in such matter-of-fact habits of thought is accordingly to be looked for among the higher ranks of skilled mechanics, and perhaps still more decisively among those who stand in an engineering or supervisory relation to the processes. It counts more forcibly and farthest among those who are required to exercise what may be called a mechanical discretion in the guidance of the industrial processes, who, as one might say, are required to administer the laws of causal sequence that run through material phenomena, who therefore must learn to think in the terms in which the machine processes work.[7] The metaphysical ground, the assumptions, on which such thinking proceeds must be such as will hold good for the sequence of material

---

[7] For something more than a hundred years past this change in the habits of thought of the workman has been commonly spoken of as a deterioration or numbing of his intelligence. But that seems too sweeping a characterization of the change brought on by habituation to machine work. It is safe to say that such habituation brings a change in the workman's habits of thought—in the direction, method, and content of his thinking—heightening his intelligence for some purposes and lowering it for certain others. No doubt, on the whole, the machine's discipline lowers the intelligence of the workman for such purposes as were rated high as marks of intelligence before the coming of the machine, but it appears likewise to heighten his intelligence for such purposes as have been brought to the front by the machine. If he is by nature scantily endowed with the aptitudes that would make him think effectively in terms of the machine process, if he has intellectual capacity for other things and not for this, then the training of the machine may fairly be said to lower his intelligence, since it hinders the full development of the only capacities of which he is possessed. The resulting difference in intellectual training is a difference in kind and direction, not necessarily in degree. Cf. Schmoller, *Grundriss der Volkswirtschaftslehre*, vol. I, secs. 85–6, 132; Hobson, *Evolution of Modern Capitalism*, chap. 9, secs. 4 and 5; Cooke Taylor, *Modern Factory System*, pp. 434–5; Sidney and Beatrice Webb, *Industrial Democracy*, e.g. pp. 327 et seq.; K. Th. Reinhold, *Arbeit und Werkzeug*, chap. 10 (particularly pp. 190–8) and chap. 11 (particularly pp. 221–40).

phenomena; that is to say, it is the metaphysical assumptions of modern material science—the law of cause and effect, cumulative causation, conservation of energy, persistence of quantity, or whatever phrase be chosen to cover the concept. The men occupied with the modern material sciences are, accordingly, for the purpose in hand, in somewhat the same case as the higher ranks of those employed in mechanical industry.[8]

Leaving aside the archaic vocations of war, politics, fashion, and religion, the employments in which men are engaged may be distinguished as pecuniary or business employments on the one hand, and industrial or mechanical employments on the other hand.[9] In earlier times, and indeed until an uncertain point in the nineteenth century, such a distinction between employments would not to any great extent have coincided with a difference between occupations. But gradually, as time has passed and production for a market has come to be the rule in industry, there has supervened a differentiation of occupations, or a division of labour, whereby one class of men has taken over the work of purchase and sale and of husbanding a store of accumulated values. Concomitantly, of course, the rest, who may, for lack of

[8] Cf. J. C. Sutherland, "The Engineering Mind," *Popular Science Monthly*, Jan. 1903, pp. 254–6.

[9] Cf. "Industrial and Pecuniary Employments" [especially pp. 287–306 as republished in *The Place of Science in Modern Civilization*, 1919, from the Papers and Proceedings of the Thirteenth Annual Meeting of the American Economic Association, 1901].

means or of pecuniary aptitude, have been less well fitted for pecuniary pursuits, have been relieved of the cares of business and have with increasing specialization given their attention to the mechanical processes involved in this production for a market. In this way the distinction between pecuniary and industrial activities or employments has come to coincide more and more nearly with a difference between occupations. Not that the specialization has even yet gone so far as to exempt any class from all pecuniary care; [10] for even those whose daily occupation is mechanical work still habitually bargain with their employers for their wages and with others for their supplies. So that none of the active classes in modern life is fully exempt from pecuniary work.

But the need of attention to pecuniary matters is less and less exacting, even in the matter of wages and supplies. The scale of wages, for instance, is, for the body of workmen, and also for what may be called the engineering force, becoming more and more a matter of routine, thereby lessening at least the constancy with which occasions for detail bargaining in this respect recur. So also as regards the purchase of consumable

---

[10] As G. F. Steffen has described it: "Those who hire out their labor power or their capital or their land to the entrepreneurs are as a rule not absolutely passive as seen from the point of view of business enterprise. They are not simply inanimate implements in the hands of the entrepreneurs. They are 'enterprising implements' (företagande verktyg) who surrender their undertaking functions only to the extent designated in the contract with the entrepreneur."—*Ekonomisk Tidskrift*, vol. V, p. 256.

goods. In the cities and industrial towns, particularly, the supplying of the means of subsistence has, in great part, become a matter of routine. Retail prices are in an increasing degree fixed by the seller, and in great measure fixed in an impersonal way. This occurs in a particularly evident and instructive way in the practice of the department stores, where the seller fixes the price, and comes in contact with the buyer only through the intervention of a salesman who has no discretion as to the terms of sale. The change that has taken place and that is still going on in this respect is sufficiently striking on comparison with the past in any industrial community, or with the present in any of those communities which we are in the habit of calling "industrially backward."

Conversely, as regards the men in the pecuniary occupations, the business men. Their exemption from taking thought of mechanical facts and processes is likewise only relative. Even those business men whose business is in a peculiar degree remote from the handling of tools or goods, and from the oversight of mechanical processes, as, for example, bankers, lawyers, brokers, and the like, have still, at the best, to take some cognizance of the mechanical apparatus of everyday life; they are at least compelled to take some thought of what may be called the mechanics of consumption. Whereas those business men whose business is more immediately concerned with industry commonly have some knowledge and take some thought of the processes of industry; to some appreciable extent they habitually think in mechanical terms. Their cogitations may habitually run to pecuniary conclusions, and the test to which the force and validity of their reasoning is brought may habitually be the pecuniary outcome; the beginning and end of their more serious thinking is of a pecuniary kind, but it always takes in some general features of the mechanical process along the way. Their exemption from mechanical thinking, from thinking in terms of cause and effect, is, therefore, materially qualified.

But after all qualifications have been made, the fact still is apparent that the everyday life of those classes which are engaged in business differs materially in the respect cited from the life of the classes engaged in industry proper. There is an appreciable and widening difference between the habits of life of the two classes; and this carries with it a widening difference in the discipline to which the two classes are subjected. It induces a difference in the habits of thought and the habitual grounds and methods of reasoning resorted to by each class. There results a difference in the point of view, in the facts dwelt upon, in the methods of argument, in the grounds of validity appealed to; and this difference gains in magnitude and consistency as the differentiation of occupations goes on. So that the two classes come to have an increasing difficulty in understanding one another and appreciating one another's convictions, ideals, capacities, and shortcomings.

The ultimate ground of validity for the thinking of

the business classes is the natural-rights ground of property—a conventional, anthropomorphic fact having an institutional validity, rather than a matter-of-fact validity such as can be formulated in terms of material cause and effect; while the classes engaged in the machine industry are habitually occupied with matters of causal sequence, which do not lend themselves to statement in anthropomorphic terms of natural rights and which afford no guidance in questions of institutional right and wrong, or of conventional reason and consequence. Arguments which proceed on material cause and effect cannot be met with arguments from conventional precedent or dialectically sufficient reason, and conversely.

The thinking required by the pecuniary occupations proceeds on grounds of conventionality, whereas that involved in the industrial occupations runs, in the main, on grounds of mechanical sequence or causation, to the neglect of conventionality. The institution (habit of thought) of ownership or property is a conventional fact; and the logic of pecuniary thinking—that is to say, of thinking on matters of ownership—is a working out of the implications of this postulate, this concept of ownership or property. The characteristic habits of thought given by such work are habits of recourse to conventional grounds of finality or validity, to anthropomorphism, to explanations of phenomena in terms of human relation, discretion, authenticity, and choice. The final ground of certainty in inquiries on this natural-rights plane is always a ground of authenticity, of precedent, or accepted decision. The argument is an argument *de jure*, not *de facto*, and the training given lends facility and certainty in the pursuit of *de jure* distinctions and generalizations, rather than in the pursuit or the assimilation of a *de facto* knowledge of impersonal phenomena. The end of such reasoning is the interpretation of new facts in terms of accredited precedents, rather than a revision of the knowledge drawn from past experience in the matter-of-fact light of new phenomena. The endeavour is to make facts conform to law, not to make the law or general rule conform to facts. The bent so given favours the acceptance of the general, abstract, custom-made rule as something real with a reality superior to the reality of impersonal, non-conventional facts. Such training gives reach and subtlety in metaphysical argument and in what is known as the "practical" management of affairs; it gives executive or administrative efficiency, so-called, as distinguished from mechanical work. "Practical" efficiency means the ability to turn facts to account for the purposes of the accepted conventions, to give a large effect to the situation in terms of the pecuniary conventions in force.[11]

The spiritual attitude given by this training in reasoning *de jure*, from pecuniary premises to pecuniary conclusions, is necessarily conservative. This species of

---

[11] Cf., on the other hand, Reinhold, *Arbeit und Werkzeug*, chaps. 12 and 14, where double-dealing is confused with workmanship, very much after the manner familiar to readers of expositions of the "wages of superintendence," but more broadly and ingeniously than usual.

reasoning assumes the validity of the conventionally established postulates, and is consequently unable to take
a sceptical attitude toward these postulates or toward the
institutions in which these postulates are embodied. It
may lead to scepticism touching other, older, institutions that are at variance with its own (natural-rights)
postulates, but its scepticism cannot touch the natural-
rights ground on which it rests its own case. In the same
manner, of course, the thinking which runs in material
causal sequence cannot take a sceptical attitude toward
its fundamental postulate, the law of cause and effect;
but since reasoning on this materialistic basis does not
visibly go to uphold the received institutions, the attitude given by the discipline of the machine technology
cannot, for the present, be called a conservative attitude.

The business classes are conservative, on the whole,
but such a conservative bent is, of course, not peculiar to
them. These occupations are not the only ones whose
reasoning prevailingly moves on a conventional plane.
Indeed, the intellectual activity of other classes, such as
soldiers, politicians, the clergy, and men of fashion,
moves on a plane of still older conventions; so that if the
training given by business employments is to be characterized as conservative, that given by these other, more
archaic employments should be called reactionary.[12] Ex-

---

[12] Individual exceptions are, of course, to be found in all classes,
but there is, after all, a more or less consistent, prevalent class attitude.
As is well known, clergymen, lawyers, soldiers, civil servants, and
the like are popularly held to be of conservative, if not reactionary

treme conventionalization means extreme conservatism. Conservatism means the maintenance of conventions already in force. On this head, therefore, the discipline of modern business life may be said simply to retain something of the complexion which marks the life of the higher barbarian culture, at the same time that it has not retained the disciplinary force of the barbarian culture in so high a state of preservation as some of the other occupations just named.

The discipline of the modern industrial employments is relatively free from the bias of conventionality, but the difference between the mechanical and the business occupations in this respect is a difference of degree. It is not simply that conventional standards of certainty fall into abeyance for lack of exercise, among the industrial classes. The positive discipline exercised by their work in good part runs counter to the habit of thinking in

---

temper. This vulgar apprehension may be faulty in detail, and especially it may be too sweeping in its generalizations; but there are, after all, few persons not belonging to these classes who will not immediately recognize that this vulgar appraisement of them rests on substantial grounds, even though the appraisement may need qualification. So, also, a conservative animus is seen to pervade all classes more generally in earlier times or on more archaic levels of culture than our own. At the same time, in those early days and in the more archaic cultural regions, the structure of conventionally accepted truths and the body of accredited spiritual or extra-material facts are more comprehensive and rigid, and the thinking on all topics is more consistently held to tests of authenticity as contrasted with tests of sense perception. On the whole, the number and variety of things that are fundamentally and eternally true and good increase as one goes outward from the modern west-European cultural centres into the earlier barbarian past or into the remoter barbarian present.

conventional, anthropomorphic terms, whether the conventionality is that of natural rights or any other. And in respect of this positive training away from conventional norms, there is a large divergence between the several lines of industrial employment. In proportion as a given line of employment has more of the character of a machine process and less of the character of handicraft, the matter-of-fact training which it gives is more pronounced. In a sense more intimate than the inventors of the phrase seem to have appreciated, the machine has become the master of the man who works with it and an arbiter in the cultural fortunes of the community into whose life it has entered.

The intellectual and spiritual training of the machine in modern life, therefore, is very far-reaching. It leaves but a small proportion of the community untouched; but while its constraint is ramified throughout the body of the population, and constrains virtually all classes at some points in their daily life, it falls with the most direct, intimate, and unmitigated impact upon the skilled mechanical classes, for these have no respite from its mastery, whether they are at work or at play.

The ubiquitous presence of the machine, with its spiritual concomitant—workday ideals and scepticism of what is only conventionally valid—is the unequivocal mark of the western culture of today as contrasted with the culture of other times and places. It pervades all classes and strata in a varying degree, but on an average in a greater degree than at any time in the past, and most potently in the advanced industrial communities and in the classes immediately in contact with the mechanical occupations. As the comprehensive mechanical organization of the material side of life has gone on, a heightening of this cultural effect throughout the community has also supervened, and with a farther and faster movement in the same direction a farther accentuation of this "modern" complexion of culture is fairly to be looked for, unless some remedy be found. And as the concomitant differentiation and specialization of occupations goes on, a still more unmitigated discipline falls upon ever-widening classes of the population, resulting in an ever-weakening sense of conviction, allegiance, or piety toward the received institutions.

It is a matter of common notoriety that the modern industrial populations are improvident in a high degree and are apparently incapable of taking care of the pecuniary details of their own life. This applies, not only to factory hands, but also to the general class of highly skilled mechanics, inventors, technological experts. The rule does not hold in any hard and fast way, but it holds with such generality as may fairly be looked for. The present factory population may be compared in this respect with the class of handicraftsmen whom they have displaced, as also with the farming population of the present time, especially the class of small proprietary farmers. The failure of the modern industrial classes on this head is not due to scantier opportunities for saving, whether they are compared with the earlier handicraftsmen or with the modern farmer or peasant; nor is it due to a lack of general intelligence, for a comparison in point of intelligence falls out in favour of the modern industrial workmen. This improvidence is commonly discussed in terms of deprecation, and there is much preaching of thrift and steady habits. But the preaching has no appreciable effect. The trouble seems to be of the nature of habit rather than of reasoned conviction. Other causes may partially explain this improvidence, but the inquiry is at least pertinent how far the absence of property and thrift among them may be traceable to the relative absence of pecuniary training and to the presence of a discipline which is at variance with habits of thrift.

Mere exemption from pecuniary training is not competent alone to explain the patent thriftlessness of modern workmen; the more so since this exemption is but partial and relative. Also, the thriftless classes commonly have an envious appreciation of pecuniary advantages. It is rather the composite effect of exemption from pecuniary training and certain positive requirements of modern life. Among these positive requirements is what has been called the canon of conspicuous waste. Under modern conditions a free expediture in consumable goods is a condition requisite to good repute.[13] This conduces to immediate consumption rather than to saving. What is perhaps still more decisive

---

[13] Cf. *The Theory of the Leisure Class*, especially chaps. 4 and 5.

against thrift on the part of workmen is the fact that the modern large organization of industry requires a high degree of mobility on the part of employees. It requires, in fact, that the labour force and the labour units be mobile, interchangeable, distributable, after the same impersonal fashion as the mechanical contrivances engaged are movable and distributable. The working population is required to be standardized, movable, and interchangeable in much the same impersonal manner as the raw or half-wrought materials of industry. From which it follows that the modern workman cannot advantageously own a home. By force of this latter feature of the case he is discouraged from investing his savings in real property, or, indeed, in any of the impedimenta of living. And the savings-bank account, it may be added, offers no adequate substitute, as an incentive to thrift, in the place of such property as a dwelling-place, which is tangibly and usefully under the owner's hand and persistently requires maintenance and improvement.

The conditions of life imposed upon the working population by the machine industry discourage thrift. But after allowance has been made for this almost physical restraint upon the acquisition of property by the working classes, something is apparently left over, to be ascribed to the moral effect of the machine technology. The industrial classes appear to be losing the instinct of individual ownership. The acquisition of property is ceasing to appeal to them as a natural, self-evident source of comfort and strength. The natural right of property no longer means so much to them as it once did.

A like weakening of the natural-rights animus is visible at another point in the current frame of mind of these classes. The growth of trade-unionism and of what is called the trade-union spirit is a concomitant of industry organized after the manner of a machine process. Historically this growth begins, virtually, with the Industrial Revolution, coming in sporadically, loosely, tentatively, with no precise assignable date, very much as the revolution does. England is the land of its genesis, its "area of characterization," and the place where it has reached its fullest degree of specification and its largest force; just as England is the country in which the modern machine industry took its rise and in which it has had the longest and most consistent life and growth. In this matter other countries are followers of the British lead and apparently borrowers of British precedents and working concepts. Still, the history of the trade-union movement in other countries seems to say that the working classes elsewhere have not advisedly borrowed ideals and methods of organization from their British congeners so much as they have been pushed into the same general attitude and line of conduct by the same general line of exigencies and experiences. Particularly, experience seems to say that it is not feasible to introduce the trade-union spirit or the trade-union rules into any community until the machine industry has had time extensively to standardize the scheme of work and of life for the working classes on mechanical lines. Workmen do not take to full-blown trade-union ideals abruptly on the introduction of those modern business methods which make trade-union action advisable for the working class. A certain interval elapses between the time when business conditions first make trade-union action feasible, as a business proposition, and the time when the body of workmen are ready to act in the spirit of trade-unionism and along the lines which the union animus presently accepts as normal for men in the mechanically organized industries. An interval of discipline in the ways of the mechanically standardized industry, more or less protracted and severe, seems necessary to bring such a proportion of the workmen into line as will give a consensus of sentiment and opinion favourable to trade-union action.

The pervading characteristic of the trade-union animus is the denial of the received natural-rights dogmas wherever the mechanical standardization of modern industry traverses the working of these received natural rights. Recent court decisions in America, as well as decisions in analogous cases in England at that earlier period when the British development was at about the same stage of maturity as the current American situation, testify unequivocally that the common run of trade-union action is at variance with the natural-rights foundation of the common law. Trade-unionism denies individual freedom of contract to the workman, as well as free discretion to the employer to carry on his business as may suit his own ends. Many pious phrases have been invented to disguise this iconoclastic trend of trade-union aims and endeavours; but the courts, standing on a secure and familiar natural-rights footing, have commonly made short work of the shifty sophistications which trade-union advocates have offered for their consideration. They have struck at the root of the matter in declaring trade-union regulations inimical to the natural rights of workman and employer alike, in that they hamper individual liberty and act in restraint of trade. The regulations, therefore, violate that system of law and order which rests on natural rights, although they may be enforced by that *de facto* law and order which is embodied in the mechanical standardization of the industrial processes.

Trade-unionism is an outgrowth of relatively late industrial conditions and has come on gradually as an adaptation of old methods and working arrangements carried over from the days of handicraft and petty trade. It is a movement to adapt, construe, recast, earlier working arrangements with as little lesion to received preconceptions as the new exigencies and the habits of thought bred by them will permit. It is, on its face, an endeavour of compromise between received notions of what "naturally" ought to be in matters of industrial business, on the one hand, and what the new exigencies of industry demand and what the new animus of the workman will tolerate, on the other hand. Trade-unionism is therefore to be taken as a somewhat mitigated expression of what the mechanical standardization of industry inculcates. Hitherto the movement has shown a fairly uninterrupted growth, not only in the numbers of its membership, but in the range and scope of its aims as well; and hitherto it has reached no halting-place in its tentative, shifty, but ever-widening crusade of iconoclasm against the received body of natural rights. The latest, maturest expressions of trade-unionism are, on the whole, the most extreme, in so far as they are directed against the natural rights of property and pecuniary contract.

The nature of the compromise offered by trade-unionism is shown by a schedule of its demands: collective bargaining for wages and employment; arbitration of differences between owners and workmen; standard rates of wages; normal working day, with penalized regulation of hours for men, women, and children; penalized regulation of sanitary and safety appliances; mutual insurance of workmen, to cover accident, disability, and unemployment. In all of this the aim of unionism seldom goes the length of overtly disputing the merits of any given article of natural-rights dogma. It only endeavours to cut into these articles, in point of fact, at points where the dogmas patently traverse the conditions of life imposed on the workmen by the modern industrial system or where they traverse the consensus of sentiment that is coming to prevail among these workmen.

When unionism takes an attitude of overt hostility to the natural-rights institutions of property and free contract, it ceases to be unionism simply and passes over into something else, which may be called socialism for want of a better term. Such an extreme iconoclastic position, which would overtly assert the mechanical standardization of industry as against the common-law standardization of business, seems to be the logical outcome to which the trade-union animus tends, and to which some approach has latterly been made by more than one trade-unionist body, but which is, on the whole, yet in the future, if, indeed, it is to be reached at all. On the whole, the later expressions go farther in this direction than the earlier; and the animus of the leaders, as well as of the more wide-awake body of unionist workmen, appears to go farther than their official utterances.

A detail of trade-union history may be cited in illustration of their attitude toward the natural-rights principles that underlie modern business relations. As is well known, trade-unions have somewhat consistently avoided pecuniary responsibility for the actions of their members or officials. They avoid incorporation. Practically an employer has had no recourse in case he suffers from a failure on the part of his union workmen to live up to the terms of an agreement made with the union. In English practice this exemption from pecuniary responsibility has acquired much of the force of law, and indeed was supposed to have gained the countenance of statutory enactment, until, within the past few months, the so-called Taff Vale decision of the House of Lords reversed the views which had come to prevail on this head. This decision, by the most conservative tribunal of the British nation, is too recent to permit its consequences for trade-unionism to be appreciated. But it seems fair to expect that the question which the decision brings home to the unions will be, How is this court-made pecuniary responsibility to be evaded? not, How is it to be lived up to? Patently,[14] the decision is unexceptionable under common-law rules; but, also patently,[15] it broadly traverses trade-union practice and is wholly alien to the attitude of the trade-unionists.[16]

The animus shown by the trade-unionists in this shirking of pecuniary responsibility is characteristic of their attitude toward common-law rules. The unions and

---

[14] As, e.g., Mr. W. G. S. Adams cogently points out in a recent number of *The Journal of Political Economy* (Dec. 1902).

[15] As Mr. Webb shows (*Industrial Democracy*, 1902, pp. xxiv-xxxvi).

[16] The historical explanation of this House of Lords reversal of trade-union practice is probably to be found in the conservative, or rather reactionary, trend given to British sentiment by the imperialist policy of the last two or three decades, accentuated by the experiences of the Boer War. The Boer War seems to mark a turning-point in the growth of sentiment and institutions. Since the seventies the imperialist interest, that is to say, the dynastic interest, has been coming into the foreground among the interests that engage the attention of the British community. It seems now to have definitively gained the first place, and may be expected in the immediate future to dominate British policy both at home and abroad. Concomitantly, it may be remarked, the British community has been slowing down, if not losing ground, in industrial animus, technological efficiency, and scientific spirit. Cf. Hobson, *Imperialism*, part II, chaps. 1 and 3.

their methods of work are essentially extra-legal. It is only reluctantly, as defendants if at all, that unions are accustomed to appear in court. When they make a move for statutory enactment, as for the enforcement of a normal day or of sanitary and safeguarding regulations, it is prevailingly to criminal law that they turn.

To all this it might, of course, be said that the workmen who make up the trade-union element take the course indicated simply because their selfish interest urges them to this course; that their common necessities and common weakness constrain them to stand together and to act collectively in dealing with their employers; while the fact that their demands have no standing in court constrains them to seek their ends by extra-legal means of coercion. But this objection is little else than another way of saying that the exigencies forced upon the workmen by the mechanically standardized industrial system are extra-legal exigencies—exigencies which do not run in business terms and therefore are not amenable to the natural-rights principles of property and contract that underlie business relations; that they can therefore not be met on common-law ground; and that they therefore compel the workmen to see them from another point of view and seek to dispose of them by an appeal to other principles than those afforded by the common-law standpoint. That is to say, in other words, these exigencies which compel the trade-unionists to take thought of their case in other terms than those afforded by existing legal institutions are the means whereby the discipline of the machine industry is enforced and made effective for recasting the habits of thought of the workmen. The harsh discipline of these exigencies of livelihood drives home the new point of view and holds the workmen consistently to it. But that is not all that the mechanical standardization of industry does in the case; it also furnishes the new terms in which the revised scheme of economic life takes form. The revision of the scheme aimed at by trade-union action runs, not in terms of natural liberty, individual property rights, individual discretion, but in terms of standardized livelihood and mechanical necessity; it is formulated, not in terms of business expediency, but in terms of industrial, technological standard units and standard relations.

The above presentation of the case of trade-unionism is of course somewhat schematic, as such a meagre, incidental discussion necessarily must be. It takes account only of those features of trade-unionism which characteristically mark it off from that business scheme of things with which it comes in conflict. There are, of course, many survivals, pecuniary and others, in the current body of trade-union demands, and much of the trade-union argument is carried on in business terms. The crudities and iniquities of the trade-union campaign are sufficiently many and notorious to require no rehearsal here. These crudities and iniquities commonly bulk large in the eyes of critics who pass an opinion on trade-unionism from the natural-rights point of view;

and, indeed, they may deserve all the disparaging attention that is given them. Trade-unionism does not fit into the natural-rights scheme of right and honest living; but therein, in great part, lies its cultural significance. It is of the essence of the case that the new aims, ideals, and expedients do not fit into the received institutional structure; and that the classes who move in trade-unions are, however crudely and blindly, endeavouring, under the compulsion of the machine process, to construct an institutional scheme on the lines imposed by the new exigencies given by the machine process.

The point primarily had in view in entering on this characterization of trade-unionism was that under the discipline of the mechanically standardized industry certain natural rights, particularly those of property and free contract, are in a degree falling into abeyance among those classes who are most immediately subjected to this discipline. It may be added that other classes also, to an uncertain extent, sympathize with the trade-unionists and are affected with a similar (mild and equivocal) distrust of the principles of natural liberty. When distrust of business principles rises to such a pitch as to become intolerant of all pecuniary institutions, and leads to a demand for the abrogation of property rights rather than a limitation of them, it is spoken of as "socialism" or "anarchism." This socialistic disaffection is widespread among the advanced industrial peoples. No other cultural phenomenon is so threatening to the received economic and political structure; none is so unprecedented or so perplexing for practical men of affairs to deal with. The immediate point of danger in the socialistic disaffection is a growing disloyalty to the natural-rights institution of property, but this is backed by a similar failure of regard for other articles of the institutional furniture handed down from the past. The classes affected with socialistic vagaries protest against the existing economic organization, but they are not necessarily averse to a somewhat rigorous economic organization on new lines of their own choosing. They demand an organization on industrial as contrasted with business lines. Their sense of economic solidarity does not seem to be defective, indeed it seems to many of their critics to be unnecessarily pronounced; but it runs on lines of industrial coherence and mechanical constraint, not on lines given by pecuniary conjunctures and conventional principles of economic right and wrong.

There is little agreement among socialists as to a programme for the future. Their constructive proposals are ill-defined and inconsistent and almost entirely negative. The negative character of the socialistic propaganda has been made a point of disparagement by its critics, perhaps justly. But their predilection for shifty iconoclasm, as well as the vagueness and inconsistency of their constructive proposals, are in the present connexion to be taken as evidence that the attitude of the socialists cannot be expressed in positive terms given by the institutions at present in force. It may also be evidence of the untenability of the socialistic ideals; but the merits of the socialist contentions do not concern the present inquiry. The question here is as to the nature and causes of the socialist disaffection; it does not concern the profounder and more delicate point, as to the validity of the socialist contentions. Current socialism is an animus of dissent from received traditions. The degree and the direction of this dissent varies greatly, but it is, within the socialist scheme of thought, agreed that the institutional forms of the past are unfit for the work of the future.[17]

---

[17] All this applies to anarchism as well as to socialism; similarly to several minor categories of dissentients. In their negative proposals the socialists and anarchists are fairly agreed. It is in the metaphysical postulates of their protest and in their constructive aims that they part company. Of the two, the socialists are more widely out of touch with the established order. They are also more hopelessly negative and destructive in their ideals, as seen from the standpoint of the established order. This applies to the later socialists rather than to the earlier, and it applies, of course, only to the lower-class, "democratic" socialists, not to the so-called state and Christian socialists.

Anarchism proceeds on natural-rights ground, and is accordingly in touch with the postulates of the existing property arrangements to that extent. It is a more unmitigated working out of the same postulates. It is a system of "natural liberty" unqualified to the extent even of not admitting prescriptive ownership. Its basis is a (divinely instituted) order of nature, the keynote of which is an inalienable freedom and equality of the individual, quite in the eighteenth-century spirit. It is in this sense an offshoot of the Romantic school of thought. Anarchism is a *de jure* scheme, which takes no account of mechanical exigencies but rests its case altogether on anthropomorphic postulates of natural rights. It is, from the natural-rights standpoint, substantially sound, though senselessly extreme.

The socialistic disaffection has been set down to envy, class hatred, discontent with their own lot by comparison with that of others, and to a mistaken view of their own interests. This criticism may be well enough as far as it goes, but it does not touch socialism in those respects in which it differs from other movements into which this range of motives enters; that is to say, it touches, not the specific traits of socialism, but the common features of popular discontent. History shows many such movements of discontent, pushed on by real or fancied privation and iniquity; and past experience recorded in history should lead us to expect that, under the guidance of such motives and such reasoning as is currently imputed to the socialists by their conservative critics, the malcontents would demand a redistribution of property, a reorganization of ownership on such new lines

What may be called the normal socialism, socialism of the later, more dangerous, and more perplexing kind, does not build on the received metaphysical basis of the "natural order." It demands a reconstruction of the social fabric, but it does not know on what lines the reconstruction is to be carried out. The natural rights of the individual are not accepted as the standard (except by certain large bodies of neophytes, especially rural American, who are carrying under socialist mottoes the burden of animosities and preconceptions that once made populism), but nothing definite is put in the place of this outworn standard. The socialists of the line, in so far as there is any consensus among them, profess that the mechanical exigencies of the industrial system must decide what the social structure is to be, but beyond this vague generality they have little to offer. And this mechanical standardization can manifestly afford no basis for legislation on civil rights. Indeed, it is difficult to see how any scheme of civil rights, much or little, can find a place in a socialistic reorganization.

as would favour the discontented classes. But such is not the trend of socialistic thinking. It looks to the disappearance of property rights rather than their redistribution. The entire range of doctrines covered by the theory of distribution in the received economics is essentially (and characteristically) neglected by the modern socialist speculations.[18]

The perplexity of those who protest against a supposedly imminent socialistic subversion of property rights is of a twofold kind: (1) The absence of proprietary rights is incomprehensible, and a living together in society without defined ownership of the means of living is held to be impracticable; ownership of goods, in the apprehension of the conservative critics, is involved in the presence of goods. (2) Ownership of the means of living is an inalienable right of man, ethically inevitable; the cancelment of property rights is felt to violate a fundamental principle of morals. All this, of course, proceeds on the assumption that the in-

[18] The "scientific socialism" of Marx and Engels as promulgated during the third quarter of the nineteenth century was not of this negative character. It was a product of Hegelianism blended with the conceptions of natural rights, its chief count being the "claim to the full product of labour." This socialism never made serious inroads among the working classes outside of Germany—the home of Hegelianism. Even in that country the most vigorous growth of socialistic sentiment came after Hegelianism had begun to yield to Darwinian methods of thought, and this later growth has been progressively less Marxian and less positive. Marxism is now little more than a *pro forma* confession of faith. Avowed socialism is practically taking on the character described above, except so far as it has grown opportunist and has sought affiliation with the liberal democratic movement and the reformers.

stitution of ownership cannot be abrogated, as being an elemental function of human nature and an integral factor in the order of things in which human life belongs.

To the modern socialist all this is coming to be less and less convincing. In this respect there is a fairly well-marked progressive change in the attitude of the professed socialists. Their position is progressively less capable of being formulated as a business proposition; their demands are progressively more difficult to state in the form of a pecuniary claim. The claim to the full product of labour, which once filled a large place in socialistic clamours and had a great carrying-force during the earlier three-quarters of the nineteenth century, has gradually fallen into abeyance, both with the agitators and the adherents of the propaganda, during the last generation. Today this claim is an afterthought in the advocate's presentation of socialism, more frequently than it is a point of departure for the argument, and it is made more of by the proselytes, who have carried the metaphysics of it over from the current common-sense of the business community, than by the socialists of confirmed standing. The claim to the full product is an article of natural-rights dogma, and as such it is a reminiscence of the institutional situation from which socialism departs, rather than a feature of the prospective situation to which socialistic sentiment looks.

The like obsolescence of the sense of equity in ownership is visible in the attitude taken by strikers in the large, mechanically organized industries, outside of the ranks of avowed socialism. These strikers are less and less deterred by considerations of vested rights, property rights, owner's interests, and the like. The principle that a man may do what he will with his own is losing its binding force with large classes in the community, apparently because the spiritual ground on which rests the notion of "his own" is being cut away by the latter-day experience of these classes. Abridgment of proprietary discretion, confiscation of proprietary rights, is growing gradually less repugnant to the industrial populace; and the question of indemnity for eventual loss is more and more falling into neglect. With the socialistic element the question is not, What shall be done in the way of readjustment of property claims? but, What is to be done to abolish them? [19]

The question of equity or inequity in the distribution of wealth presumes the validity of ownership rights on some basis or other, or at least it presumes the validity of some basis on which the claims of ownership may be discussed. Ownership is the major premise

[19] Where members of the well-to-do classes avow socialistic sentiments and ideals, it commonly turns out to be a merely humanitarian aspiration for a more "equitable" redistribution of wealth, a readjustment of the scheme of ownership with some improved safeguarding of the "reasonable" property claims of all members of the community. What "socialist" reform commonly means to this contingent of well-to-do irregulars is some scheme of equal rights of ownership for all. Whereas to socialists of the line equal rights of ownership is as idle a proposition as an equal right of citizens to sell their votes. Instead of a reform of ownership the socialists contemplate the traceless disappearance of ownership.

of any argument as to the equity of distribution, and it is this major premise that is being forgotten by the classes among whom socialistic sentiment is gaining. Equity in this connexion seems not to belong in the repertory of socialist concepts. It is at this point—the point of a common ground of argument—that the discrepancy occurs which stands in the way, not only of an eventual agreement between the socialists and their conservative critics, but even of their meeting one another's reasoning with any substantial effect. In the equipment of common-sense ideas on the basis of which the conservatives reason on this matter, there is included the conventional article of ownership, as a prime fact; in the common-sense basis of socialistic thinking this conventional premise has no secure place. There is, therefore, a discrepancy in respect of the metaphysics underlying the knowledge and reasoning of the two parties to the controversy, and the outlook for a common understanding is accordingly vain. No substantial agreement upon a point of knowledge or conviction is possible between persons who proceed from disparate preconceptions.

Still the conservative reformers and the iconoclasts have a good deal in common. The prevalent habit of mind of both classes is a hybrid product of conventional principles and matter-of-fact insight. But these two contrasted grounds of opinion and aspiration are present in unequal degrees in the two contrasted classes; in the conservatives the conventional grounds of finality dominate and bear down the matter-of-fact knowledge of things, while the converse is true of the iconoclasts. Contrasted with earlier times and other cultural regions the consensus, the general drift, of the modern western culture as a whole is of an iconoclastic character; while the class contrast here in question lies only within the range of this western cultural consensus. As one or the other of the two contrasted proclivities—recourse to conventional precedents and recourse to matter-of-fact insight—gains and overbalances the other, the general cultural movement will drift toward a more conservative (archaic), conventional position or toward a more iconoclastic, materialistic position. During modern times the cultural drift has set in the latter direction. With due but not large exceptions, the effective body of the modern population has been growing more matter-of-fact in their thinking, less romantic, less idealistic in their aspirations, less bound by metaphysical considerations in their view of human relations, less mannerly, less devout.

The discrepancy between the conservatives and the iconoclasts need not be taken to mean that the two contrasted classes are moving in opposite directions, nor even in widely divergent directions. Neither class can properly be said to be reactionary.[20] Taken generally, both wings have been moving in the direction of a more

---

[20] Unless it be in the latest extremes of conservatism, such as is shown in the recent success of dynastic politics in Germany, Tory policy in England, and predatory political ideals in America.

impersonal, more matter-of-fact, less conventional point of view. In this composite cultural growth the matter-of-fact habit of mind has on the whole been gaining at the expense of the conventional, and the conventional premises that have been retained have also come to bear more of a matter-of-fact character—as, e.g., in the supersession of feudalistic or theocratic principles of law by natural rights. So that the position for which the effective body of conservatives now stand is not in substance a very archaic one. It is a more matter-of-fact position, less closely bound by authentic conventions, than the position effectively occupied by the iconoclastic wing a hundred years ago.

Throughout the modern cultural complex there is a somewhat variable, scattering shifting of ground to a more matter-of-fact basis. The direction of spiritual growth or change is much the same throughout the general body of the population; but the rate of change, the rate at which matter-of-fact ideals are superseding ideals of conventional authenticity, is not the same for all classes. Hence the class discrepancy here spoken of. The coefficient of change is so much larger in the vulgar, industrial classes as progressively to widen the cultural interval between them and the conservatives in the respect which is here in question. And the resulting discrepancy of institutional aims and ideals may have none the less serious consequences for being due to a differential rate of movement rather than to a divergent cultural trend.

In this differential rate of movement the departure from the ancient landmarks has now gone so far (or is reaching such a point) among the socialistic vulgar as to place their thinking substantially on a plane of material matter-of-fact, particularly as regards economic institutions. Whereas in the conservative classes the change is not yet large enough to take them off the plane of received conventional truth, particularly as regards economic institutions and such social questions as are of an economic complexion. In the case of the former this change in habit of mind has been so considerable as, in effect, to constitute a change in kind; crude matter-of-fact has come to be the dominant note of their attitude, and conventional authenticity has been relegated to a subsidiary place; that is to say, the change is of a revolutionary character. In the case of the conservative classes, so far as touches the institutional notions here under inquiry, the corresponding change has not yet gone so far as to amount to a change in kind; it is not of a revolutionary nature. The views current among the respectable classes on these matters still, in effect, run on the ancient levels on which were built up the pecuniary institutions about which the controversy circles. For the present there need be no apprehension that the more respectable classes will reach a mature revolutionary frame of mind. The discipline of their daily life does not, on the whole, favour such a result.

This, in substance, is also the view taken by the socialistic revolutionaries, particularly by those that are of Marxian antecedents. It is a point of conviction with them, though not wholly of reasoned conviction, that the socialistic movement is, in the nature of the case, a proletarian movement, in which the respectable, that is to say the pecuniarily competent, classes can have no organic part even if they try. It is held, in effect, that the well-to-do are, by force of their economic circumstances, incapable of assimilating the socialist ideas. The argument here set forth may serve to enforce this view, but with a difference. Instead of contrasting the well-to-do with the indigent, the line of demarcation between those available for the socialist propaganda and those not so available is rather to be drawn between the classes employed in the industrial and those employed in the pecuniary occupations. It is a question not so much of possessions as of employments; not of relative wealth, but of work. It is a question of work because it is a question of habits of thought, and work shapes the habits of thought. The socialists themselves construe the distinction to be a distinction in respect of habits of thought; and habits of thought are made by habits of life rather than by a legal relation to accumulated goods. This legal relation may count materially in shaping the animus of the several economic classes; but it appears not to be competent of itself to explain the limitations observable in the spread of socialistic sentiment.

The socialistic disaffection shows a curious tendency to overrun certain classes and to miss certain others. The men in the skilled mechanical trades are peculiarly liable to it, while at the extreme of immunity is probably the profession of the law. Bankers and other like classes of business men, together with clergymen and politicians, are also to be held free of serious aspersion; similarly, the great body of the rural population are immune, including the population of the country towns, and in an eminent degree the small farmers of the remoter country districts; [21] so also the delinquent classes of the cities and the populace of half-civilized and barbarous countries. The body of unskilled labourers, especially those not associated with the men in the skilled mechanical trades, are not seriously affected. The centres of socialistic disaffection are the more important industrial towns, and the effective nucleus of the socialistic malcontents is made up of the more intelligent body of workmen in the highly organized and specialized industries. Not that socialism does not spread in virulent form outside this narrow range, but at a farther remove from the centre of dispersion it appears rather sporadically and uncertainly, while within this field it is fairly endemic. As regards the educated classes, socialistic views are particularly likely to crop out among the men in the material sciences.

The advocates of the new creed have made little headway among the rural classes of Europe, whether peasant

---

[21] Socialistic notions are apparently making some inroads among the rural population of the American prairie region, where a mechanically organized and standardized method of farming prevails, with a large use of mechanical appliances.

farmers or farm labourers. The rural proletariat has hitherto proved virtually impermeable.[22] The discipline of their daily life leaves their spirit undisturbed on the plane of conventionality and anthropomorphism, and the changes to which they aspire lie within the scope of the conventionalities which have grown out of these circumstances of their life and which express the habit of mind enforced by these circumstances.

Without claiming that this explanation is competent to cover the case of socialism in all its bearings, it may be pointed out that this socialistic bias has effectively spread among the people only within the last quarter of a century, which is also approximately the period since which the machine process and the mechanical standardization of industry has reached its fuller development, both as regards the extent of its field and as regards the extent of its technological requirements; that it is found in vigorous growth only in those communities and particularly among those classes whose life is closely regulated by the machine technology; and that the discipline of this machine technology is peculiarly designed

---

[22] So striking has been the failure of the German socialists, for instance, in their attempts upon the integrity of the farming community, that they have latterly changed their tactics, and instead of attempting to convert the peasants to a full socialistic programme, they have turned to measures of compromise, in which the characteristic and revolutionary features of the socialistic programme are softened beyond recognition, if not suppressed. The habits of life, and therefore the habits of thought, of the peasant farmers move on the ancient levels of handicraft, pecuniary management, personal consequence, and prescriptive custom.

to inculcate such iconoclastic habits of thought as come to a head in the socialistic bias. Socialism, in so far as the term means the subversion of the economic foundations of modern culture, occurs only sporadically and dubiously outside the limits, in time and space, of the discipline of the machine technology. While among those classes whose everyday life schools them to do their habitual serious thinking in terms of material cause and effect, the preconceptions of ownership are apparently becoming obsolescent through disuse and through supersession by other methods of apprehending things.[23]

[23] If this account of the class limitation of the socialist bias is accepted, it has an immediate bearing upon a question which is latterly engaging the attention of the advocates of socialism. The question is as to the part played by propertyless office employees and by the business men whom the modern consolidations of business reduce to the position of salaried managers and superintendents. With a faith prompted by their own hopes rather than by observed facts or by the logic of events, the spokesmen for socialism are strongly inclined to claim this "business proletariat" as a contingent which the course of economic development is bound to throw into the socialist camp. The facts do not in any appreciable degree countenance such an expectation. The unpropertied classes employed in business do not take to socialistic vagaries with such alacrity as should inspire a confident hope in the advocates of socialism or a serious apprehension in those who stand for law and order. This pecuniarily disfranchised business population, in its revulsion against unassimilated facts, turns rather to some excursion into pragmatic romance, such as Social Settlements, Prohibition, Clean Politics, Single Tax, Arts and Crafts, Neighborhood Guilds, Institutional Church, Christian Science, New Thought, or some such cultural thimblerig. The work of the captain of industry in curtailing the range of individual discretion in business and in reducing the lesser undertakers to the rank of clerks and subalterns need not be looked upon as unavoidably furthering

But the machine technology not only trains the work-men into materialistic iconoclasm, it has also a selective effect. Persons endowed with propensities and aptitudes of a materialistic, matter-of-fact kind are drafted into the mechanical employments, and such are also peculiarly available socialistic material. Aptitude for the matter-of-fact work of the machine technology means, in a general way, ineptitude for an uncritical acceptance of institutional truths. It is probable, therefore, that the apparent facility with which the mechanical employments (and the material sciences) induce a socialistic or iconoclastic bent is to be set down in part to the fact that the human material in these employments is picked material, peculiarly amenable to this discipline. There is a sifting of the working classes, whereby the socialistic and mechanically capable are roughly segre-

---

the spread of the socialistic bias, except in so far as the change results in throwing the men affected by it out of the pecuniary or business occupations and subjecting them to the discipline of the mechanical industry. At the most, apparently, the change from an independent to a dependent business life serves to weaken the men's interest in the question of property; it does not appear that it throws them into an attitude of substantial distrust or iconoclasm. Their interest in this particular institution slackens through the loss of that emulative motive on which pecuniary endeavour proceeds, but their faith in its intrinsic fitness is not thereby shaken, nor are they thrown into the ranks of the chronic dissentients. The training given by their life continues prevailingly to run on conventional grounds; that is to say, on grounds of legal relation, solvency, and the like. Accountants and office employees are nearly as conservative as clergymen and lawyers, and their being so is apparently due to the fact that their experience runs on much the same ground of conventional finality.

gated out from the rest and subjected to the iconoclastic discipline of the mechanical employments and matter-of-fact thinking; while the residue, which is on the whole made up of the persons that are relatively least capable of revolutionary socialism, is at the same time less exposed to the discipline that might fit them for the socialistic movement. This sifting is, of course, a rough one, and leaves many exceptions both ways.

In the light of this consideration, then, it is to be noted: (1) that the dominance of the machine process in modern industry is not so potent a factor for the inculcation of socialistic notions—it does not so irresistibly shape men's habit of mind in the socialistic sense—as the first survey of the facts would suggest; and (2) that the differentiation of occupations involved in modern industrial methods selectively bunches the socialistic elements together, and so heightens their sense of class solidarity and acts to accentuate their bias, gives consistency to their ideals, and induces that boldness of conviction and action which is to be had only in a compact body of men.

But in either case, whether the visible outcome is chiefly due to their selective or to their disciplinary effect, the bearing of the industrial occupations upon the growth of socialism seems equally close and undeniable. The two modes of influence seem to converge to the outcome indicated above, and for the purpose of the present inquiry a detailed tracing out of the two

strands of sequence in the case neither can nor need be
undertaken.[24]

With such generality as commonly holds in statements of this kind, it may be said that the modern socialistic disaffection is loosely bound up with the machine industry—spreading where this industry spreads
and flourishing where this industry gives the dominant
note of life. The correlation between the two phenomena is of such a kind as to leave no doubt that they

---

[24] Connected with this apparent selective action which the modern
specialization of occupations exerts, there is a further, and at first sight
more singular, point of disparity between the socialists and the conservatives; and this difference has also a curious correlation with the
distribution of the machine industry. In a degree—slight and uncertain, perhaps, but scarcely to be mistaken—the socialists and the
conservatives are apparently of different racial antecedents. It has
been seen above that the propaganda is most vital and widespread in
the industrial towns, as contrasted with the agricultural country. But
if the researches of such students as Ammon, Ripley, Lapouge, Clos-
son, and others that might be named are taken at their face value, it
appears that the towns differ perceptibly from the open country in
point of race; and that the migration from the country into the industrial towns has a selective effect of such a kind that a larger proportion of one racial stock than of another resorts to the towns. The
towns, in those countries where data are available, show a larger
admixture of the dolicho-blond stock than the open country. This
seems to argue that the dolicho-blond stock, or the racial mixture of
the towns in which there is a relatively large admixture of the dolicho-
blond, is perceptibly more efficient in the machine industries, more
readily inclined to think in materialistic terms, more given to radical
innovation, less bound by convention and prescription. This generalization is strengthened by the fact that the more dolicho-blond regions
are also, on the whole, more socialistic than those in which this element is less in evidence. At the same time they are industrially in
advance of the latter in the matter of machine industry; and they are
also Protestant (irreligious) rather than Catholic.

are causally connected; which means either that the machine industry, directly or indirectly, gives rise to socialism, or that the two are expressions of the same complex of causes. The former statement probably expresses the truth of the case in great part, but the latter need not therefore be false. Wherever and in so far as the increase and diffusion of knowledge has made the machine process and the mechanical technology the tone-giving factor in men's scheme of thought, there modern socialistic iconoclasm follows by easy consequence.

The socialistic bias primarily touches economic institutions proper. But that is not the whole of it. When the term is used without modifying phrase it carries a certain implication touching other than primarily economic matters. The political bias of this unmitigated socialism is always radically democratic, to the extent that these socialists are in a high degree intolerant of any monarchical, aristocratic, or other prescriptive government. The state is doomed in the socialistic view.[25] The socialist antagonism to the state takes various forms and goes to varying degrees of intemperance, but it is consistently negative. Except in their destructively hostile attitude to existing political organizations, the socialists have nothing consistent to offer on the head of

[25] This, of course, does not hold for the inoffensive pseudo-socialistic diversions set afoot by various well-meaning politicians and clergymen, known by various qualifying designations, such as "State," "Christian," "Catholic," etc., and designed to act as correctives of the socialistic distemper.

political institutions, less, indeed, latterly than in the earlier days of the propaganda. There seems to be a growing shiftlessness of opinion on this head; one gets the impression that the sense of the socialist malcontents, as near as it may be permissible to use that word in this connexion, is that the community can best get along without political institutions.

There is a like departure from the ancient norms touching domestic relations. This is not confined to those portions of the community that avowedly affect socialistic views, although it has, on the whole, gone farthest among the classes among whom the socialistic views prevail. There is a visible weakening of the family ties, a disintegration of the conventions of household life, throughout large classes. The defection is even felt, by sensitive and solicitous persons, to be of such grave proportions as to threaten the foundations of domestic life and morality. This disintegration of the family ties shows itself most alarmingly among the socialistic classes, with whom it all wears such an air of unconcern as argues that in this respect they are incorrigible. To these the conventional form of the household has in good part ceased to appeal as something sacred. It is no longer one of their secure spiritual assets.

What appears to be in jeopardy, should this socialistic defection gain ground, is the headship of the male in the household economy. The family, as it has come down from the medieval past, under the shelter of the church, is of a patriarchal constitution, at least in theory.

The man has been vested with discretionary control in domestic affairs. In the earlier days his discretion was very direct and full, comprising corporal coercion. Latterly, after and so far as mastery and servitude have passed off the field and natural rights have come to rule, this direct coercive control has been superseded by a pecuniary discretion; so that the male head of the household is alone competent to exercise a proprietary control of household affairs. This latter-day conventional headship of the man is now in its turn beginning to lose the respect of a good share of the populace. The disintegration of the patriarchal tradition has gone farthest among those industrial classes who are at the same time inclined to socialistic views.

At this point in the institutional structure, as well as at other points where the industrial classes are giving evidence of a loss of spiritual ground, there is little indication of a constructive movement toward any specific arrangement to take the place of the institution whose existence is threatened. There is a loosening of the bonds, a weakening of conviction as to the full truth and beauty of the received domestic institutions, without much of a consensus as to what is to be done about it, if anything. In this, as at other junctures of a similar kind, the mechanically employed classes, trained to matter-of-fact habits of thought, show a notable lack of spontaneity in the construction of new myths or conventions as well as in the reconstruction of the old.

All this disintegration of the spiritual foundations of

our domestic institutions spreads with the most telling effect, because most heedlessly, among the population of the industrial towns. But it spreads also outside the limits of the industrial classes; for the habits of life and of thought inculcated by the machine technology are not limited to them, even if these classes are the ones who suffer most and most severely from the machine discipline. The disintegration shows itself, in varying degree, in all modern industrial communities, and it is visible somewhat in proportion as the community is modern and industrial. The machine is a leveller, a vulgarizer, whose end seems to be the extirpation of all that is respectable, noble, and dignified in human intercourse and ideals.

What happens within the narrow range of the institutions of domestic life repeats itself in substance in the larger field of national life and ideals. Fealty to a superior installed by law or custom suffers under the discipline of a life which, as regards its most formative exigencies, is not guided by conventional grounds of validity. And the transmuted form of fealty called patriotism is in much the same insecure case. The new ground of class solidarity and antagonism, for which these extreme spokesmen of the industrial regime stand, is neither ecclesiastic, dynastic, territorial, nor linguistic; it is industrial and materialistic. But in their attitude of heedlessness toward the dynastic and national conventions the socialists are merely the extreme exponents of the spirit of the age in the modern industrial communities.

So, again, as regards the religious life. Men trained by the mechanical occupations to materialistic, industrial habits of thought are beset with a growing inability to appreciate, or even to apprehend, the meaning of religious appeals that proceed on the old-fashioned grounds of metaphysical validity. The consolations of a personal relation (of subservience) to a supernatural master do not appeal to men whose habit of life is shaped by a familiarity with the relations of impersonal cause and effect, rather than by relations of personal dominance and fealty. It does not come as a matter of course for such men to give the catechism's answer to the question, What is the chief end of man? Nor do they instinctively feel themselves to be sinners by virtue of a congenital, hereditary taint or obliquity. Indeed, they can only with great difficulty be seriously persuaded that they are sinners at all. They are in danger of losing the point of view of sin. The relation of status or fealty involved in the concept of sin is becoming alien to their habit of mind. They are therefore slow to realize that their past life has violated such a relation of fealty, on the one hand, and that it is of vital consequence to re-establish such a relation of status by a work of salvation or redemption. The kindly ministrations of the church and the clergy grate on the sensibilities of men so trained, as being so much ado about nothing. The machine, their master, is no respecter of persons and knows neither morality nor dignity nor prescriptive right, divine or human; its teaching is training them into insensibility of the whole range of concepts on which these ministrations proceed.[26]

Not alone in the direction of growth given to vulgar sentiment and to the vulgar insight into facts is the matter-of-fact discipline of the machine technology apparent, but also in the scope and method of that scientific knowledge that has had the vogue since the advent of the machine industry. Scientific inquiry is directed to a different end and carried out under the guidance of a different range of principles or preconceptions in the modern industrial communities than in earlier days or in cultural centres lying outside the machine's dominion. Modern science is single-minded in its pursuit of impersonal relations of causal sequence in the phenomena with which it is occupied.

The line of descent of this matter-of-fact modern science is essentially British, as is that of the machine technology and of the characteristically modern civil and political institutions. It is true, beginnings of the modern scientific movement were made in Italy in the days of the Renaissance, and central Europe had its share in the

---

[26] The cultural era of Natural Rights, Natural Liberty, and Natural Religion reduced God to the rank of a "Great Artificer," and the machine technology is, in turn, relegating Him to that fringe of minor employments and those outlying industrial regions to which the handicraftsmen have been retired.

enlightenment; but these early modern risings of the scientific spirit presently ran into the sand, when war, politics, and religion reasserted their sway in the south of Europe. Similar tentative stirrings of matter-of-fact thought were had in Spain and France before and during the early phases of the state-making era; but here, again, war and politics rendered these onsets nearly nugatory, so that the intellectual output was more speculation than science. In the Low Countries something similar holds true, with a larger qualification. The British community made a later and slow start, coming out of barbarism at a later date and with a heavier handicap of physical obstructions. But being, relatively, sheltered from war and politics, the British were able to take up the fund of scientific gains made by the south-European men of workday insight, to turn it to account, and to carry it over the era of state-making and so prepare the way for the modern scientific, technological era.

Of course, nothing but the most meagre and sketchiest outline of this matter is practicable in this place, and even that only in its relation to the machine industry during the past one hundred years or so. What is said above of the British lead in modern science may perhaps be questioned, and it is not necessary for the present purpose to insist on its truth; but so much seems beyond hazard as that the lead in the material sciences lay with the British through the early machine age, and that the provenance of this modern scientific research today does not extend, in any pronounced degree, beyond those communities that lie within the area of the modern machine industry.

In time and space the prevalence of the modern materialistic science is roughly coextensive with that of the machine process. It is, no doubt, related to it both as cause and as effect; but that its relation to modern industry is more that of effect than cause seems at least broadly suggested by the decay which presently overtook scientific research, e.g., in the south of Europe when those peoples turned their attention from material to spiritual and political affairs.[27]

What is of immediate interest is the change that has come over the scope and method of scientific research since the dominance of the machine process, in comparison with what preceded the coming of the machine age. The beginnings of modern science are older than the industrial revolution; the principles of scientific research (causal explanation and exact measurement) antedate the regime of the machine process. But a change has taken place in the postulates and animus of scientific research since modern science first began, and this change in the postulates of scientific knowledge is related to the growth of the machine technology.

It is unnecessary here to hark back to that scholastic science or philosophy that served as an intellectual ex-

---

[27] There is a similar suggestion in the relative (slight but perceptible) decline of scientific animus in England since the English community has turned its attention and aspirations to imperialistic feats of prowess more than to industrial matters.

pression of the ecclesiastical and political culture of the Middle Ages. Its character, as compared with later science, is sufficiently notorious. By the change from scholastic knowledge to modern science, to the extent to which the change was carried through, the principle (habit of mind) of adequate cause was substituted for that of sufficient reason. The law of causation as it is found at work, in the maturer science of the eighteenth and early nineteenth centuries, comprises two distinguishable postulates: (1) equality (quantitative equivalence) of cause and effect; and (2) similarity (qualitative equivalence) of cause and effect. The former may, without forcing it, be referred to commercial accountancy as its analogue in practical life and as the probable cultural ground out of which the habit of insisting on an inviolable quantitative equivalence gathered consistency. The ascendancy of the latter seems in a similar manner to be referable to the prevalence of handicraft as its cultural ground. Stated negatively, it asserts that nothing appears in the effect but what was contained in the cause, in a manner which suggests the rule that nothing appears in the product of handicraft but what was present in the skill of the artificer. "Natural causes," which are made much of in this middle period of modern science, are conceived to work according to certain "natural laws." These natural laws, laws of the "normal course" of things, are felt to tend to a rational end and to have something of a coercive force. So that Nature makes no mistakes, Nature does nothing in vain, Nature takes the most economical course to its end, Nature makes no jumps, etc. Under this law of natural causation every effect must have a cause which resembles it in the particular respect which claims the inquirer's attention. Among other consequences of this view it follows that, since the details as well as the whole of the material universe are construed to show adaptation to a preconceived end, this "natural order" of things must be the outcome of pre-existent design residing in the "first cause," which is postulated by virtue of this imputed design and is designated the "Great Artificer." There is an element of conation in this original modern postulate of cause and effect. The shadow of the artificer, with his intelligence and manual skill, is for ever in the background of the concepts of natural law. The "cause" dealt with in a given case is not thought of as an effect; and the effect is treated as a finality, not as a phase of a complex sequence of causation. When such a sequence is under inquiry, as in the earlier, pre-Darwinian theories of evolution, it is not handled as a cumulative sequence whose character may blindly change from better to worse, or conversely, at any point; but rather as an unfolding of a certain prime cause in which is contained, implicitly, all that presently appears in explicit form.

In the conception of the causal relation as it may be seen at work a hundred years ago, cause and effect are felt to stand over against one another, so that the cause controls, determines the effect by transmitting its own character to it. The cause is the producer, the effect the product. Relatively little emphasis or interest falls upon the process out of which the product emerges; the interest being centred upon the latter and its relation to the efficient cause out of which it has come. The theories constructed under the guidance of this conception are generalizations as to an equivalence between the producing cause and the effect-product. The cause "makes" the effect, in much the same sense as the craftsman is apprehended to make the article on which he is engaged. There is a felt distinction between the cause and the environing circumstances, much as there is between the workman on the one hand and his tools and materials on the other hand. The intervening process is simply the manner of functioning of the efficient cause, much as the workman's work is the functioning of the workman in the interval between the inception and the completion of the product. The effect is subsequent to the cause, as the workman's product is subsequent to and consequent upon his putting forth his productive efficiency. It is a relation of before and after, in which the process comes in for attention as covering and accounting for the time interval which, in analogy with workmanlike endeavour, is required for the functioning of the efficient cause.[28]

---

[28] Compare, however, Sombart, *Kapitalismus*, especially vol. I, chaps. 8 and 15. Sombart finds the modern scientific concept of cause and effect to be essentially an outcome of the discipline of accountancy enforced by business traffic. So that he makes business enterprise rather than mechanical industry accountable for the rise of modern science and for the matter-of-fact character which distinguishes this science. In this view there is, no doubt, a large and valuable element of truth. To the end of a mathematical formulation

But as time passes and habituation to the exigencies of the machine technology gains in range and consistency, the quasi-personal, handicraft conception of causation decays—first and most notably in those material, inorganic sciences that stand in the closest relation to the mechanical technology, but presently also in the organic sciences, and even in the moral sciences. The machine technology is a mechanical or material process, and requires the attention to be centred upon this process and the exigencies of the process. In such a process no one factor stands out as unequivocally the efficient cause in the case, whose personal character, so to speak, is transfused into the product, and to whose workings the rest of the complex of causes are related only as subsidiary or conditioning circumstances. To the technologist the process comes necessarily to count, not simply as the

---

of causal phenomena as well as a tenacious grasp of the principle of quantitative equivalence, the accountancy enforced by the petty trade of early modern times, as well as by commercial traffic proper, appears to have given the most effective training. In so far as this element of quantitative equivalence, simply, has dominated the growth of science, it has given, as its most perfect product, Positivism. Positivism flourished at its best and freest in France, where the modern economic culture was commercial rather than mechanical. And when the machine discipline seriously invaded France, Positivism languished and died. But modern science is not a calculus simply. It deals not with calculations of quantitative equivalence only, but with efficient causes, active relations, creative forces. The concept of efficient cause is not a derivative of accountancy, nor is it formed in the image of accountancy. But this generic concept of efficient cause, the kinetic concept, antedates Positivism and has outlived it. In its earlier (eighteenth-century) phase this concept shows close relationship with the notion of workmanship, in its later (nineteenth-century) use it has much in common with the notion of mechanical efficiency.

interval of functioning of an initial efficient cause, but
as the substantial fact that engages his attention. He
learns to think in terms of the process, rather than in
terms of a productive cause and a product between which
the process intervenes in such a manner as to afford a
transition from one to the other. The process is always
complex; always a delicately balanced interplay of forces
that work blindly, insensibly, heedlessly; in which any
appreciable deviation may forthwith count in a cumulative manner, the further consequences of which stand
in no organic relation to the purpose for which the
process has been set going. The prime efficient cause
falls, relatively, into the background and yields precedence to the process as the point of technological interest.

   This machine technology, with its accompanying discipline in mechanical adaptations and object-lessons,
came on gradually and rose to a dominating place in the
cultural environment during the closing years of the
eighteenth and the course of the nineteenth century;
and as fast as men learned to think in terms of technological process, they went on at an accelerated pace in
the further invention of mechanical processes, so that
from that time the progress of inventions has been of a
cumulative character and has cumulatively heightened
the disciplinary force of the machine process. This early
technological advance, of course, took place in the British
community, where the machine process first gained headway and where the discipline of a prevalent machine
industry inculcated thinking in terms of the machine

process. So also it was in the British community that modern science fell into the lines marked out by technological thinking and began to formulate its theories in terms of process rather than in terms of prime causes and the like. While something of this kind is noticeable relatively early in some of the inorganic sciences, as, e.g., Geology, the striking and decisive move in this direction was taken toward the middle of the century by Darwin and his contemporaries.[29] Without much preliminary exposition and without feeling himself to be out of touch with his contemporaries, Darwin set to work to explain species in terms of the process out of which they have arisen, rather than out of the prime cause to which the distinction between them may be due.[30] Denying nothing as to the substantial services of the Great Artificer in the development of species, he simply and naïvely left Him out of the scheme, because, as being a personal factor, He could not be stated and handled in terms of process. So Darwin offered a tentative account of the descent of man, without recourse to divine or human directive endeavour and without inquiry as to whence man ultimately came and why, or as to what fortune would ultimately overtake him. His inquiry characteristically confines itself to the process of

[29] Darwin, of course, does not stand alone. He is the great exponent of a mass movement which involves a shifting of the point of view and of the point of interest in scientific research and speculation.

[30] This is the substance of Darwin's advance over Lamarck, for instance.

cumulative change. His results, as well as his specific determination of the factors at work in this process of cumulative change, have been questioned; perhaps they are open to all the criticisms levelled against them as well as to a few more not yet thought of; but the scope and method given to scientific inquiry by Darwin and the generation whose spokesman he is has substantially not been questioned, except by that diminishing contingent of the faithful who by force of special training or by native gift are not amenable to the discipline of the machine process. The characteristically modern science does not inquire about prime causes, design in nature, desirability of effects, ultimate results, or eschatological consequences.

Of the two postulates of earlier modern science—the quantitative equivalence and the qualitative equivalence of cause and effect—the former has come practically to signify the balanced articulation of the process of cumulative change; the endeavour of the Positivists to erect this canon of quantitative equivalence into the sole canon of scientific truth, and so to reduce scientific theory to a system of accountancy, having failed. The latter thesis, that like causes produce like effects, or that the effect is, in some sense, of the same character as the cause, has fallen into decay as holding true only in such tenuously general terms as to leave it without particular force. The scientists are learning more and more consistently to think in the opaque, impersonal terms of strains, mechanical structures, displacement, and the like; terms which are convertible into the working drawings and specifications of the mechanical engineer.

The older preconceptions are, of course, not wholly eliminated from the intellectual apparatus of scientific research and generalization. The cultural situation whose discipline gives the outcome is made up of inherited traditional notions at least as much as of the notions brought in by the machine process. Even among the scientific adepts there has been no complete break with the past; necessarily not, since they are, after all, creatures of their own generation. Many of them, but more especially those who are engaged in upholding the authentic results of scientific research, are somewhat prone to make much of the definitive results achieved, rather than of the process of research in which these results are provisional appliances of work. And many of these, together with the great part of those well-meaning persons who exploit the sciences for purposes of edification, such as clergymen and naturalistic myth-makers, still personify the process of cause and effect and find in it a well-advised meliorative trend. But that work of research which effectually extends the borders of scientific knowledge is nearly all done under the guidance of highly impersonal, mechanical, morally and æsthetically colourless conceptions of causal sequence. And this scientific work is carried out only in those communities which are in due contact with the modern mechanically organized industrial system—only under the shadow of the machine technology.

In the nature of the case the cultural growth dominated by the machine industry is of a sceptical, matter-of-fact complexion, materialistic, unmoral, unpatriotic, undevout. The growth of habits of thought, in the industrial regions and centres particularly, runs in this direction; but hitherto there has enough of the ancient norms of western Christendom remained intact to make a very respectable protest against that deterioration of the cultural tissues which the ferment of the machine industry unremittingly pushes on. The machine discipline, however, touches wider and wider circles of the population, and touches them in an increasingly intimate and coercive manner. In the nature of the case, therefore, the resistance opposed to this cultural trend given by the machine discipline on grounds of received conventions weakens with the passage of time. The spread of materialistic, matter-of-fact preconceptions takes place at a cumulatively accelerating rate, except in so far as some other cultural factor, alien to the machine discipline, comes in to inhibit its spread and keep its disintegrating influence within bounds.

# THE CASE OF AMERICA [1]

✿

## THE SELF-MADE MAN

AMERICA is the oldest and maturest of the colonies founded by the English-speaking peoples, or by any of those Continental peoples which fall into the same class with the English in this connexion, as, e.g., the Dutch or the Scandinavians. And the foundation and impetus date back to that period of west-European culture when the principles of self-help, free contract, and net gain achieved their ascendancy, and before these principles had been pruned back by legal definition to fit a more conservative manner of thinking. It is, indeed, a point of distinction for the American case that here the pruning back of these popular principles of conduct was carried out to fit the working-out of these principles themselves, under such conditions of single-minded conviction that other institutional holdovers of the older order have not seriously troubled the outcome. It was the fortune of the American people to have taken their point of departure from the European situation during a period when the system of Natural Liberty was still "obvious and simple," fresh and crude, and consequently

[1] Reprinted from *Absentee Ownership and Business Enterprise in Recent Times*, 1923, pp. 119–65.

amenable to growth and adaptation on its own premises under the direct impact of the new material circumstances offered by the New World. Whereas later enterprises in colonization have had their institutional point of departure blurred with a scattering of the holdovers that were brought in again by the return wave of reaction in Europe, as well as by those later-come stirrings of radical discontent that have questioned the eternal fitness of the system of Natural Liberty itself. The difference is not wide, and the American advantage is not a great one; nor need it make or mar the outcome in the end, since the colonists and the later-come inhabitants of these other new countries are, after all, the same thing over again in respect of their permanent traits of character. They are all made up of substantially the same hybrid mixture of races, so that by heredity they are all substantially the same people.[2]

In this matter those other, south-European or "Latin," peoples who have had a share in the colonization of the new continents fall somewhat to one side. In this matter of absentee ownership after the pattern set by the system of Natural Rights, these others carry a serious handicap. It is their fortune, not their fault. At that period, when they were taking the lead in the winning of the New World, these south-Europeans were still living very busily in a more archaic and barbarian phase of the European culture, which belongs at a point in the se-

---

[2] Of course, in point of nationality they are, each and several, eternally distinct for the time being.

quence antedating the natural rights that make democracy. Their ideals and motives were, on the whole, of a visibly different order and have worked out in time to a different effect. Their enterprise in colonization, as, e.g., the Spanish and in a degree the Portuguese, was an enterprise in pillage, inflamed and inflated by religious fanaticism and martial vanity; and it has worked out in the erection of a class of colonial nations which have hitherto scarcely proved fit to survive under this newer order of things that has been imposed by the mechanical industry and the business enterprise which makes use of the mechanical industry.

In effect, the English-speaking peoples, on the other hand, colonized with a view to the orderly exploitation of the natural resources; driven, on the whole, by motives and ideals of self-help, equal opportunity, and net gain. The difference may not be wide or substantial, nor is there by any means a sharp contrast between the English-speaking colonial pioneers and the south-Europeans on these heads; not nearly so wide and sharp as this blunt phrasing of it will imply. But, in effect, a difference of this character is visible, and in its working-out this initial difference has told cumulatively in the outcome. And in the outcome the English-speaking colonial nations turn out to be addicted to democratic institutions, the mechanical industries, and business enterprise. It will not do to say that the English-speaking colonization to which America owes its beginnings and its character was untouched by the spirit of plunder or unfamiliar with religious atrocities and warlike vanity; but while the difference may be one of degree rather than of kind, such measure of initial difference as there was appears to have made the outcome. And the difference in the outcome is too obvious to be overlooked by any but statesmen and lawyers.

America is the most mature of these English-speaking colonies. And in all of these colonial nations the mainspring of the enterprise and the enduring preoccupation of the people has been the exploitation of natural resources for private gain. In all of them the natural resources have progressively been taken over into private ownership on a reasoned plan of legalized seizure. It has been a sober and orderly-advancing seizure of these resources, conducted under rules designed to safeguard a democratically equal opportunity of seizure, and advancing as fast as the available resources have successively become, or have promised to become, valuable. The rules governing this progressive subreption have been drawn on lines that constantly call to mind the rules governing games of skill, where a formally even chance is prescribed for all players who "sit in." And these rules of equitable "grab" have also, on the whole, been lived up to with about the same degree of scruple that is commonly to be had in games of luck and skill. In either case, whether in the standard games of chance and dexterity or in the business of taking over natural resources and turning them to account, it is understood that any formally blameless evasion of the rules will rightly inure to the benefit of any competitor who so has been able to "beat the game." It is a principle of self-help. But in either case, too, there is a formal limit on profitable evasion, beyond which tact and salesmanship cease to be sportsmanlike finesse or businesslike ambiguity and become sharp practice or swindle.[3]

So there has been incorporated in American common-sense and has grown into American practice the presumption that all the natural resources of the country must of right be held in private ownership, by those persons who have been lucky enough or shrewd enough to take them over according to the rules in such cases made and provided, or by those who have acquired title from these original impropriators.

With the (partial) exception of the agricultural lands, the ownership of these natural resources is always absentee ownership, and it has always been absentee ownership that has been aimed at in the efforts made to come into possession of them. And they are always acquired and held with a view to getting a larger benefit from them than their cost; that is to say, with a view to getting a margin of something for nothing at the cost of the rest of the community. These are commonplaces, of

---

[3] It is not easy in any given case—indeed it is at times impossible until the courts have spoken—to say whether it is an instance of praiseworthy salesmanship or a penitentiary offence. All that may turn on a point of legal verbiage, and it may also depend somewhat on the magnitude of the transaction and the business rating of the parties in interest; a large transaction is, on the whole, less likely to be found reprehensible.

course, which it should scarcely be necessary to call to mind.

The natural resources of America are, or have been, unexampled in abundance and availability, and they have always been the main factor on which the life and comfort of the inhabitants have depended. They are the indispensable means of life of the population at large, so that the livelihood of all the inhabitants from day to day is unavoidably bound up in their daily use. So long and so far as these resources can be turned to use without hindrance, the American population will always be assured an abundant and easy livelihood. So much so that with free and full use of its unexampled natural resources and an unhindered employment of its workmanship this people may, or rather might, come in for an unexampled material abundance on unexampled easy terms. What stands in the way of this climax of material good fortune, immediately and directly, is the absentee ownership of these natural resources. And what stands in the way of discontinuing this absentee ownership of the country's resources is the moral sense of the American body of citizens; and in this they are in close accord with the working bias of their constituted authorities, whose chief care it is to safeguard and augment all rights of absentee ownership at all points.

Doubtless the discontinuance of absentee ownership in the country's resources would not of itself set the industrial system free to run at full capacity and so make the most of the country's workmanship; business considerations could not permit that, so long as business considerations continue to control the industrial system— and there is other business to be taken care of than that which is occupied with the control of natural resources. But it remains true that absentee ownership of the country's resources stands first and obviously in the way of a continued full run of the country's productive industry.

Should it occur to anyone to take exception to this broad statement, it should suffice to call attention to the fact that the raw materials drawn from these natural resources command a price beyond the cost of the workmanship that goes to bring out the supply. Should this, again, be questioned, there is the fact that the absentee owners of the country's coal, ore, oil, water-power, timber, quarries, water frontage, building sites, and the like, continue to hold these properties as a valued possession from which they derive a revenue. This is free income payable to the absentee owners of these things and constitutes an overhead charge on the country's productive industry; it goes into the cost of the goods produced, and is that much of a burden and restriction on the output. This should also be sufficiently obvious; but the moral sense of the body of citizens will tolerate no disallowance of this right of the absentee owners to get this legalized margin of something for nothing.

Natural resources are valuable to their owners not because the owners have produced these things nor because they have invested their "savings" in them, but

because the community has use for them and is willing
to pay something for their use—because they are an
indispensable means of living. Failing either the industrial usefulness which these things now have, or
failing the continued willingness to allow the absentee
owners a usufruct in these resources as a source of free
income, they will no longer have value as assets, whatever they may have cost.[4] Natural resources are acquired, owned, and valued as a source of free income;
income for which no equivalent in useful work is given,
whatever the cost at which these assets may have been
acquired. At the same time they will be of no use, and
so will have no value as assets, except as they are turned
to use by the workmanship of the population. It is the
state of the industrial arts that makes them natural resources, not the funds invested in their ownership. In
the language of mathematics, the value of these things
as a source of free income to their owners is a "function"
of the workmanship of the population at large. And for
the completeness of statement it should be added that
the workmanship of the population is a "function" of
the state of the industrial arts; which is a joint stock of
technical knowledge and workmanlike habits ingrained
in the population and carried on jointly by the country's

---

[4] A classic illustration of the first point are the flint deposits of
Denmark, which were of first-rate consequence as natural resources
in the stone age; while the second point is covered by the case of the
Negro man-power of the Southern States, which ceased to be assets as
soon as the consent to its usufruct by absentee ownership was withdrawn.

man-power, which in this respect carries on as an indivisible going concern.

The absentee owner of natural resources is enabled to make them a source of free income, that is to say make them assets, by the power legally conferred on him to withhold them from use until his charge for their use is allowed him. What this charge will be is always a question of what the traffic will bear; which is the same as what will yield him the largest net return. But what the traffic will bear will vary indefinitely according to the circumstances of the case, and the value of given resources as assets will vary accordingly.[5] Aside from changes in the industrial arts, the most considerable and most widely effective of these varying circumstances is

---

[5] E.g., certain copper properties have varied greatly in their value as assets, with the continued discovery of further copper deposits, on the one hand, and with the increased requirements of electrical material, on the other hand. So also have nickel properties responded to changing circumstances of the same order. And both, but particularly nickel, considered as a means of free income for absentee owners, have been greatly helped out from time to time by a protective tariff designed to safeguard and augment the free income of vested interests of this class. It is the whole wisdom of a protective tariff that when the charges so imposed by the absentee owners are so protected by a protective duty the traffic can be made to bear a heavier charge. In further illustration of the general statement above, it may be recalled that the discovery of the Minnesota iron ores and the gradual perfecting of the steel smelting processes incontinently cut down the value as assets of those Cuban ore bodies whose American absentee owners were to have been safeguarded in their free income by the Spanish-American War. But there are no end of illustrative instances, since the whole use and value of these natural resources, as well as variations in their value as assets, turn on the state of technological knowledge, with which the owners of them have nothing to do.

the varying degree in which competition prevails among the owners of such assets.[6]

In the usual course, in the case of such staple resources as coal, oil, or the ores, the business of exploitation has at the outset commonly been competitive in a pronounced degree; that is, the owners have competed in the market by speeding up the output and underbidding on the price. The result has been low prices for the time being, and a rapid exhaustion, with waste, of the natural supply. Presently, as the holdings have been drawn together into the ownership of a smaller and more manageable number of absentee owners, these owners have more and more consistently acted in collusion, and in time have drawn together into combinations which have taken on a corporate character, at least in effect, and so have ceased to compete among themselves.[7]

The result is not that competition ceases or declines when the business of a given line of natural supply so outgrows what is called the competitive stage and passes under the control of a collusive or corporate combination of absentee owners, but only that it takes a new turn, commonly with an increased vigour and persistence. Instead of competing against one another, to their own mutual defeat, the absentee owners now turn their

---

[6] Compare, e.g., the case of the Texas oil fields with that of the anthracite coal field.

[7] The salt business, e.g., shows a very fair instance of this gradual shifting from a competitive to a monopolistic footing.

undivided competitive efforts against the consumers. It becomes a competition not within the business but between this business as a whole and the rest of the community. This stage of business maturity, which may be called the stage of vested interest, has progressively been reached in a very passable fashion by the generality of that absentee ownership that controls the necessary supply of raw materials used in the leading industries—in what are sometimes called the "key industries."

There is, of course, the large exception of agricultural food products, and the partial exception of such a natural staple as crude oil, where the continued opening of new deposits and the continued growth of an undersupplied market continues still to trouble the business and its vested interests with a weedy crop of upstart competitors for the market. The agricultural soil, the natural resource from which the food products are drawn, is not amenable to absentee ownership except in a partial measure, at least not yet; and agricultural food products have accordingly not yet been successfully handled on the non-competitive or collusive plan, so far as concerns their production; although there are typical cases of collusion and absentee control to be found among the concerns that own the business of milling, packing, and marketing many of these food products. And while crude oil is still troubled with irresponsible competitive production for an open market, of the kind sometimes called "wild-catting," the efforts toward a collusive stability of the business have, after all, been as successful as might reasonably be looked for. So that, on the whole, the owners and distributors are already engaged on a fairly secure and consistent collusive competition against the rest of the community.

The farmers who have to do with the great staples have, for some time past and repeatedly, endeavoured to establish a collusive control of their market, with a view to narrowing and stabilizing the margin between the prices they get and the prices which the consumers pay; but so far with no substantial results. It has quite uniformly worked out in nothing better than gestures of desperation. Their markets are controlled, but not by the farmers. Absentee ownership in farming has yet reached neither the extent nor the scale which would enable a collusive combination of farm-owners to determine what the traffic will bear and arrange the volume of output accordingly. All that matter is now taken care of by those massive vested interests that move obscurely in the background of the market and decide for themselves what the traffic will bear for their benefit at the cost of the farmers on the one side and the consumers of farm products on the other.

## II. THE INDEPENDENT FARMER

The case of the American farmer is conspicuous; though it can scarcely be called singular, since in great part it is rather typical of the fortune which has overtaken the underlying populations throughout Christendom under the dominion of absentee ownership in its later developed phase. Much the same general run of conditions recurs elsewhere in those respects which engage the fearsome attention of these farmers. By and large, the farmer is so placed in the economic system that both as producer and as consumer he deals with business concerns which are in a position to make the terms of the traffic, which it is for him to take or leave. Therefore the margin of benefit that comes to him from his work is commonly at a minimum. He is commonly driven by circumstances over which he has no control, the circumstances being made by the system of absentee ownership and its business enterprise. Yet he is, on the whole, an obstinately loyal supporter of the system of law and custom which so makes the conditions of life for him.

His unwavering loyalty to the system is in part a holdover from that obsolete past when he was the Independent Farmer of the poets; but in part it is also due to the still surviving persuasion that he is on the way, by hard work and shrewd management, to acquire a "competence"; such as will enable him some day to take his due place among the absentee owners of the land and so come in for an easy livelihood at the cost of the rest of the community; and in part it is also due to the persistent though fantastic opinion that his own present interest is bound up with the system of absentee ownership, in that he is himself an absentee owner by so much as he owns land and equipment which he works with hired help—always presuming that he is such an owner, in effect or in prospect.

It is true, the farmer-owners commonly are absentee owners to this extent. Farming is team work. As it is necessarily carried on by current methods in the great farming sections, farm work runs on such a scale that no individual owner can carry on by use of his own personal work alone, or by use of the man-power of his own household alone—which makes him an absentee owner by so much. But it does not, in the common run, make him an absentee owner of such dimensions as are required in order to create an effectual collusive control of the market, or such as will enable him, singly or collectively, to determine what charges the traffic shall bear. It leaves him still effectually in a position to take or leave what is offered at the discretion of those massive absentee interests that move in the background of the market.[8]

Always, of course, the farmer has with him the abiding comfort of his illusions, to the effect that he is in some occult sense the "Independent Farmer," and that he is somehow by way of achieving a competence of absentee ownership by hard work and sharp practice, some day; but in practical effect, as things habitually work out, he is rather to be called a quasi-absentee owner, or perhaps a pseudo-absentee owner, being too

[8] Cf. Wallace, *Farm Prices*.

small a parcel of absentee ownership to count as such in the outcome. But it is presumably all for the best, or at least it is expedient for business-as-usual, that the farmer should continue to nurse his illusions and go about his work; that he should go on his way to complete that destiny to which it has pleased an all-seeing and merciful Providence to call him.

From colonial times and through the greater part of its history as a republic America has been in the main an agricultural country. Farming has been the staple occupation and has employed the greater part of the population. And the soil has always been the chief of those natural resources which the American people have taken over and made into property. Through the greater part of its history the visible growth of the country has consisted in the extension of the cultivated area and the increasing farm output, farm equipment, and farm population. This progressive taking-over and settlement of the farming lands is the most impressive material achievement of the American people, as it is also the most serviceable work which they have accomplished hitherto. It still is, as it ever has been, the people's livelihood; and the rest of the industrial system has, in the main, grown up, hitherto, as a subsidiary or auxiliary, adapted to and limited by the needs and the achievements of the country's husbandry. The incentives and methods engaged in this taking-over of the soil, as well as the industrial and institutional consequences that have followed, are accordingly matters of prime considera-

tion in any endeavour to understand or explain the
national character and the temperamental bent which
underlies it.

The farm population—that farm population which
has counted substantially toward this national achievement—has been a ready, capable, and resourceful body
of workmen. And they have been driven by the incentives already spoken of in an earlier passage as being
characteristic of the English-speaking colonial enterprise
—individual self-help and cupidity. Except transiently
and provisionally, and with doubtful effect, this farm
population has nowhere and at no time been actuated
by a spirit of community interest in dealing with any of
their material concerns. Their community spirit, in material concerns, has been quite notably scant and precarious, in spite of the fact that they have long been
exposed to material circumstances of a wide-sweeping uniformity, such as should have engendered a spirit of
community interest and made for collective enterprise,
and such as could have made any effectual collective
enterprise greatly remunerative to all concerned. But
they still stand sturdily by the timeworn make-believe
that they still are individually self-sufficient masterless
men, and through good report and evil report they have
remained Independent Farmers, as between themselves,
which is all that is left of their independence—Each for
himself, etc.

Of its kind, this is an admirable spirit, of course; and
it has achieved many admirable results, even though the

results have not all been to the gain of the farmers. Their self-help and cupidity have left them at the mercy of any organization that is capable of mass action and a steady purpose. So they have, in the economic respect—and incidentally in the civil and political respect —fallen under the dominion of those massive business interests that move obscurely in the background of the market and buy and sell and dispose of the farm products and the farmers' votes and opinions very much on their own terms and at their ease.

But all the while it remains true that they have brought an unexampled large and fertile body of soil to a very passable state of service, and their work continues to yield a comfortably large food supply to an increasing population, at the same time that it yields a comfortable run of free income to the country's kept classes. It is true, in the end the farm population find themselves at work for the benefit of business-as-usual, on a very modest livelihood. For farming is, perhaps necessarily, carried on in severalty and on a relatively small scale, even though the required scale exceeds what is possible on a footing of strict self-ownership of land and equipment by the cultivators; and there is always the pervading spirit of self-help and cupidity, which unavoidably defeats even that degree of collusive mass action that might otherwise be possible. Whereas the system of business interests in whose web the farmers are caught is drawn on a large scale, its units are massive, impersonal, imperturbable, and, in effect, irresponsible, under the established order of law and custom, and they are interlocked in an unbreakable framework of common interests.

By and large, the case of America is as the case of the American farm population, and for the like reasons. For the incentives and ideals, the law and custom and the knowledge and belief, on which the farm population has gone about its work and has come to this pass, are the same as have ruled the growth and shaped the outcome for the community at large. Nor does the situation in America differ materially from the state of things elsewhere in the civilized countries, in so far as these others share in the same material civilization of Christendom.

In the American tradition, and in point of historical fact out of which the tradition has arisen, the farmer has been something of a pioneer. Loosely it can be said that the pioneering era is now closing, at least provisionally and as regards farming. But while the pioneer-farmer is dropping out of the work of husbandry, his pioneer soul goes marching on. And it has been an essential trait of this American pioneering spirit to seize upon so much of the country's natural resources as the enterprising pioneer could lay hands on—in the case of the pioneer-farmer, so much of the land as he could get and hold possession of. The land had, as it still has, a prospective use and therefore a prospective value, a "speculative" value as it is called; and the farmer-pioneer was concerned with seizing upon this prospective value and turning it into net gain by way of absentee ownership, as much as the pioneer-farmer was concerned with turning the fertile soil to present use in the creation of a livelihood for himself and his household from day to day.

Habitually and with singular uniformity the American farmers have aimed to acquire real estate at the same time that they have worked at their trade as husbandmen. And real estate is a matter of absentee ownership, an asset whose value is based on the community's need of this given parcel of land for use as a means of livelihood, and the value of which is measured by the capitalized free income which the owner may expect to come in for by holding it for as high a rental as the traffic in this need will bear. So that the pioneering aim, in American farming, has been for the pioneer-farmers, each and several, to come in for as much of a free income at the cost of the rest of the community as the law would allow; which has habitually worked out in their occupying, each and several, something more than they could well take care of. They have habitually "carried" valuable real estate at the same time that they have worked the soil of so much of their land as they could take care of, in as effectual a manner as they could under these circumstances. They have been cultivators of the main chance as well as of the fertile soil; with the result that, by consequence of this intense and unbroken habituation, the farm population is today imbued with that penny-wise spirit of self-help and cupidity that now leaves them and their work and holdings at the disposal of those massive vested interests that know the uses of collusive mass action, as already spoken of above.

But aside from this spiritual effect which this protracted habituation to a somewhat picayune calculation of the main chance has had on the farmers' frame of mind, and aside from their consequent unfitness to meet the businesslike manœuvres of the greater vested interests, this manner of pioneering enterprise which the farmers have habitually mixed into their farming has also had a more immediate bearing on the country's husbandry, and, indeed, on the industrial system as a whole. The common practice has been to "take up" more land than the farmer could cultivate, with his available means, and to hold it at some cost. Which has increased the equipment required for the cultivation of the acres cultivated, and has also increased the urgency of the farmer's need of credit by help of which to find the needed equipment and meet the expenses incident to his holding his idle and semi-idle acres intact. And farm credit has been notoriously usurious. All this has had the effect of raising the cost of production of farm products; partly by making the individual farm that much more unwieldy as an instrument of production, partly by further enforcing the insufficiency and the make-shift character for which American farm equipment is justly famed, and partly also by increasing the distances over which the farm supplies and the farm products have had to be moved.

This last point marks one of the more serious handicaps of American farming, at the same time that it has contributed materially to enforce that "extensive," "superficial," and exhausting character of American farming which has arrested the attention of all foreign observers. In American practice the "farm area" has always greatly exceeded the "acreage under cultivation," even after all due allowance is made for any unavoidable inclusion of waste and half-waste acreage within the farm boundaries. Even yet, at the provisional close of the career of the American pioneer-farmer, the actual proportion of unused and half-used land included within and among the farms will materially exceed what the records show, and it greatly exceeds what any inexperienced observer will be able to credit. The period is not long past—if it is past—when, taking one locality with another within the great farming sections of the country, the idle and half-idle lands included in and among the farms equalled the acreage that was fully employed, even in that "extensive" fashion in which American farming has habitually been carried on.

But there is no need of insisting on this high proportion of idle acreage, which none will credit who has not a wide and intimate knowledge of the facts in the case. For more or less—for as much as all intelligent observers will be ready to credit—this American practice has counted toward an excessively wide distribution of the cultivated areas, excessively long distances of transport, over roads which have by consequence been excessively bad—necessarily and notoriously so—and which have hindered communication to such a degree as in many instances to confine the cultivation to such crops as can be handled with a minimum of farm buildings and will bear the crudest kind of carriage over long distances and with incalculable delays. This applies not only to the farm-country's highways, but to its railway facilities as well. The American practice has doubled the difficulty of transportation and retarded the introduction of the more practicable and more remunerative methods of farming; until make-shift and haphazard have in many places become so ingrained in the habits of the farm population that nothing but abounding distress and the slow passing of generations can correct it all.[9] At the same time, as an incident by the way, this same excessive dispersion of the farming communities over long distances, helped out by bad roads, has been perhaps the chief factor in giving the retail business communities of the country towns their strangle-hold on the underlying farm population.

And it should surprise no one if a population which has been exposed to unremitting habituation of this kind has presently come to feel at home in it all; so that the

[9] As a side issue to this arrangement of magnificent distances in the fertile farm country, it may be called to mind that the education of the farm children has on this account continually suffered from enforced neglect, with untoward results. And there are those who believe that the noticeably high rate of insanity among farmers' wives in certain sections of the prairie country is traceable in good part to the dreary isolation enforced upon them by this American plan of "country life."

bootless chicanery of their self-help is rated as a masterly fabric of axiomatic realities, and sharp practice has become a matter of conscience. In such a community it should hold true that "An honest man will bear watching," that the common good is a by-word, that "Everybody's business is nobody's business," that public office is a private job, where the peak of aphoristic wisdom is reached in that red-letter formula of democratic politics, "Subtraction, division, and silence." So it has become a democratic principle that public office should go by rotation, under the rule of equal opportunity—equal opportunity to get something for nothing—but should go only to those who value the opportunity highly enough to make a desperate run for it. Here men "run" for office, not "stand" for it. Subtraction is the aim of this pioneer cupidity, not production; and salesmanship is its line of approach, not workmanship; and so, being in no way related quantitatively to a person's workmanlike powers or to his tangible performance, it has no "saturation point." [10]

---

[10] This civilized-man's cupidity is one of those "higher wants of man" which the economists have found to be "indefinitely extensible," and like other spiritual needs it is self-authenticating, its own voucher.

The Latin phrase is *auri sacra fames*, which goes to show the point along the road to civilization reached by that people. They had reached a realization of the essentially sacramental virtue of this indefinitely extensible need of more; but the *aurum* in terms of which they visualized the object of their passion is after all a tangible object, with physical limitations of weight and space, such as to impose a mechanical "saturation point" on the appetite for its accumulation. But the civilized peoples of Christendom at large, and more particularly America, the most civilized and most Christian of

The spirit of the American farmers, typically, has been that of the pioneer rather than the workman. They have been efficient workmen, but that is not the trait which marks them for its own and sets them off in contrast with the common run. Their passion for acquisition has driven them to work, hard and painfully, but they have never been slavishly attached to their work; their slavery has been not to an imperative bent of workmanship and human service, but to an indefinitely extensible cupidity which drives to work when other expedients fail; at least so they say. So they have been somewhat footloose in their attachment to the soil as well as somewhat hasty and shiftless in its cultivation. They have always, in the typical case, wanted something more than their proportionate share of the soil; not because they were driven by a felt need of doing more than their fair share of work or because they aimed to give the community more service than would be a fair equivalent of their own livelihood, but with a view to cornering something more than their proportion of the community's indispensable means of life and so getting a little something for nothing in allowing their holdings to be turned to account, for a good and valuable consideration.

---

them all, have in recent times removed this limitation. The object of this "higher want of man" is no longer specie, but some form of credit instrument which conveys title to a run of free income; and it can accordingly have no "saturation point," even in fancy, inasmuch as credit is also indefinitely extensible and stands in no quantitative relation to tangible fact.

The American farmers have been footloose, on the whole, more particularly that peculiarly American element among them who derive their traditions from a colonial pedigree. There has always been an easy shifting from country to town, and this steady drift into the towns of the great farming sections has in the main been a drift from work into business. And it has been the business of these country towns—what may be called their business-as-usual—to make the most of the necessities and the ignorance of their underlying farm population. The farmers have on the whole been ready to make such a shift whenever there has been an "opening"; that is to say, they have habitually been ready to turn their talents to more remunerative use in some other pursuit whenever the chance has offered, and indeed they have habitually been ready to make the shift out of husbandry into the traffic of the towns even at some risk whenever the prospect of a wider margin of net gain has opened before their eager eyes.

In all this pursuit of the net gain the farm population and their country-town cousins have carried on with the utmost good nature. The business communities of the country towns have uniformly got the upper hand. But the farmers have shown themselves good losers; they have in the main gracefully accepted the turn of things and have continued to count on meeting with better luck or making a shrewder play next time. But the upshot of it so far has habitually been that the farm population find themselves working for a very modest livelihood and the country towns come in for an inordinately wide margin of net gains; that is to say, net gain over necessary outlay and over the value of the services which they render their underlying farm populations.

To many persons who have some superficial acquaintance with the run of the facts it may seem, on scant reflection, that what is said above of the inordinate gains that go to the country towns is a rash overstatement, perhaps even a malicious overstatement. It is not intended to say that the gains *per capita* of the persons currently engaged in business in the country towns, or the gains per cent on the funds invested, are extraordinarily high; but only that as counted on the necessary rather than the actual cost of the useful work done, and as counted on the necessary rather than the actual number of persons engaged, the gains which go to the business traffic of the country towns are inordinately large.[11]

---

[11] It may be added, though it should scarcely be necessary, that a good part of the gains which are taken by the country-town business community passes through their hands into the hands of those massive vested interests that move obscurely in the background of the market, and to whom the country towns stand in a relation of feeders, analogous to that in which the farm population stands to the towns. In good part the business traffic of the country towns serves as ways and means of net gain to these business interests in the background. But when all due allowance is made on this and other accounts, and even if this element which may be called net gains in transit be deducted, the statement as made above remains standing without material abatement: the business gains which come to the country towns in their traffic with their underlying farm populations are inordinately large, as counted on the necessary cost and use-valve of the service rendered, or on the necessary work done. But whether these net gains, in so far as they are "inordinate"—that is in so far

## III. THE COUNTRY TOWN

The country town of the great American farming region is the perfect flower of self-help and cupidity standardized on the American plan. Its name may be Spoon River or Gopher Prairie, or it may be Emporia or Centralia or Columbia. The pattern is substantially the same, and is repeated several thousand times with a faithful perfection which argues that there is no help for it, that it is worked out by uniform circumstances over which there is no control, and that it wholly falls in with the spirit of things and answers to the enduring aspirations of the community. The country town is one of the great American institutions; perhaps the greatest, in the sense that it has had and continues to have a greater part than any other in shaping public sentiment and giving character to American culture.

The location of any given town has commonly been determined by collusion between "interested parties" with a view to speculation in real estate, and it continues through its life-history (hitherto) to be managed as a real-estate "proposition." Its municipal affairs, its civic pride, its community interest, converge upon its real

as they go in under the caption of Something for Nothing—are retained by the business men of the town or are by them passed on to the larger business interests which dominate them, that is an idle difference for all that concerns the fortunes of the underlying farm population or the community at large. In either case it is idle waste, so far as concerns the material well-being of any part of the farm population.

estate values, which are invariably of a speculative character, and which all its loyal citizens are intent on "boom-
ing" and "boosting"—that is to say, lifting still farther
off the level of actual ground-values as measured by the
uses to which the ground is turned. Seldom do the current (speculative) values of the town's real estate exceed
the use-value of it by less than 100 per cent; and never
do they exceed the actual values by less than 200 per
cent, as shown by the estimates of the tax assessor; nor
do the loyal citizens ever cease their endeavours to lift
the speculative values to something still farther out of
touch with the material facts. A country town which
does not answer to these specifications is "a dead one,"
one that has failed to "make good," and need not be
counted with, except as a warning to the unwary
"boomer." [12] Real estate is the one community interest
that binds the townsmen with a common bond; and it
is highly significant—perhaps it is pathetic, perhaps admirable—that those inhabitants of the town who have
no holdings of real estate and who never hope to have
any will commonly also do their little best to inflate the
speculative values by adding the clamour of their unpaid
chorus to the paid clamour of the professional publicity-

---

[12] "The great American game," they say, is Poker. Just why
Real Estate should not come in for honourable mention in that way
is not to be explained off hand. And an extended exposition of the
reasons why would be tedious and perhaps distasteful, besides calling
for such expert discrimination as quite exceeds the powers of a layman in these premises. But even persons who are laymen on both heads
will recognize the same family traits in both.

agents, at the cost of so adding a little something to their own cost of living in the enhanced rentals and prices out of which the expenses of publicity are to be met.

Real estate is an enterprise in "futures," designed to get something for nothing from the unwary, of whom it is believed by experienced persons that "there is one born every minute." So, farmers and townsmen together throughout the great farming region are pilgrims of hope looking forward to the time when the community's advancing needs will enable them to realize on the inflated values of their real estate, or looking more immediately to the chance that one or another of those who are "born every minute" may be so ill advised as to take them at their word and become their debtors in the amount which they say their real estate is worth. The purpose of country-town real estate, as of farm real estate in a less extreme degree, is to realize on it. This is the common bond of community interest which binds and animates the business community of the country town. In this enterprise there is concerted action and a spirit of solidarity, as well as a running business of mutual manœuvring to get the better of one another. For eternal vigilance is the price of country-town real estate, being an enterprise in salesmanship.

Aside from this common interest in the town's inflated real estate, the townsmen are engaged in a vigilant rivalry, being competitors in the traffic carried on with the farm population. The town is a retail trading-station, where farm produce is bought and farm supplies are sold, and there are always more traders than are necessary to take care of this retail trade. So that they are each and several looking to increase their own share in this trade at the expense of their neighbours in the same line. There is always more or less active competition, often underhand. But this does not hinder collusion between the competitors with a view to maintain and augment their collective hold on the trade with their farm population.

From an early point in the life-history of such a town collusion habitually becomes the rule, and there is commonly a well-recognized ethical code of collusion governing the style and limits of competitive manœuvres which any reputable trader may allow himself. In effect, the competition among business concerns engaged in any given line of traffic is kept well in hand by a common understanding, and the traders as a body direct their collective efforts to getting what can be got out of the underlying farm population. It is on this farm trade also, and on the volume and increase of it, past and prospective, that the real-estate values of the town rest. As one consequence, the volume and profit of the farm trade is commonly overstated, with a view to enhancing the town's real-estate values.

Quite as a matter of course the business of the town arranges itself under such regulations and usages that it foots up to a competition, not between the business concerns, but between town and country, between traders and customers. And quite as a matter of course, too, the number of concerns doing business in any one town greatly exceeds what is necessary to carry on the traffic; with the result that while the total profits of the business in any given town are inordinately large for the work done, the profits of any given concern are likely to be modest enough. The more successful ones among them commonly do very well and come in for large returns on their outlay, but the average returns per concern or per man are quite modest, and the less successful ones are habitually doing business within speaking-distance of bankruptcy. The number of failures is large, but they are habitually replaced by others who still have something to lose. The conscientiously habitual overstatements of the real-estate interests continually draw new traders into the town, for the retail trade of the town also gets its quota of such persons as are born every minute, who then transiently become supernumerary retail traders. Many fortunes are made in the country towns, often fortunes of very respectable proportions, but many smaller fortunes are also lost.

Neither the causes nor the effects of this state of things have been expounded by the economists, nor has it found a place in the many formulations of theory that have to do with the retail trade; presumably because it is all, under the circumstances, so altogether "natural" and unavoidable. Exposition of the obvious is a tedious employment, and a recital of commonplaces does not hold the interest of readers or audience. Yet, for completeness of the argument, it seems necessary here to go a little farther into the details and add something on the reasons for this arrangement. However obvious and natural it may be, it is after all serious enough to merit the attention of anyone who is interested in the economic situation as it stands, or in finding a way out of this situation; which is just now (1923) quite perplexing, as the futile endeavours of the statesmen will abundantly demonstrate.

However natural and legitimate it all undoubtedly may be, the arrangement as it runs today imposes on the country's farm industry an annual overhead charge which runs into ten or twelve figures, and all to the benefit of no one. This overhead charge of billions, due to duplication of work, personnel, equipment, and traffic, in the country towns is, after all, simple and obvious waste. Which is perhaps to be deprecated, although one may well hesitate to find fault with it all, inasmuch as it is all a simple and obvious outcome of those democratic principles of self-help and cupidity on which the commonwealth is founded. These principles are fundamentally and eternally right and good—so long as popular sentiment runs to that effect—and they are to be accepted gratefully, with the defects of their qualities. The whole arrangement is doubtless all right and worth its cost; indeed it is avowed to be the chief care and most righteous solicitude of the constituted authorities to maintain and cherish it all.

To an understanding of the country town and its place in the economy of American farming it should be noted that in the great farming regions any given town has a virtual monopoly of the trade within the territory tributary to it. This monopoly is neither complete nor indisputable; it does not cover all lines of traffic equally nor is outside competition completely excluded in any line. But the broad statement is quite sound, that within its domain any given country town in the farming country has a virtual monopoly of trade in those main lines of business in which the townsmen are chiefly engaged. And the townsmen are vigilant in taking due precautions that this virtual monopoly shall not be broken in upon. It may be remarked by the way that this characterization applies to the country towns of the great farming country, and only in a less degree to the towns of the industrial and outlying sections.

Under such a (virtual) monopoly the charge collected on the traffic adjusts itself, quite as a matter of course, to what the traffic will bear. It has no other relation to the costs or the use-value of the service rendered. But what the traffic will bear is something to be determined by experience and is subject to continued readjustment and revision, with the effect of unremittingly keeping the charge close up to the practicable maximum. Indeed, there is reason to believe that the townsmen are habitually driven by a conscientious cupidity and a sense of equity to push the level of charges somewhat over the maximum; that is to say, over the rate which would yield them the largest net return. Since there are too many of them, they are so placed as habitually to feel that they come in for something short of their just deserts, and their endeavour to remedy this state of things is likely to lead to overcharging rather than the reverse.

What the traffic will bear in this retail trade is what the farm population will put up with, without breaking away and finding their necessary supplies and disposing of their marketable products elsewhere, in some other town, through itinerant dealers, by recourse to brokers at a distance, through the mail-order concerns, and the like. The two dangerous outside channels of trade appear to be the rival country towns and the mail-order houses, and of these the mail-order houses are apparently the more real menace as well as the more dreaded. Indeed they are quite cordially detested by right-minded country-town dealers. The rival country towns are no really grave menace to the usurious charges of any community of country-town business men, since they are all and several in the same position, and none of them fails to charge all comers all that the traffic will bear.

There is also another limiting condition to be considered in determining what the traffic will bear in this retail trade, though it is less, or at least less visibly, operative; namely, the point beyond which the charges cannot enduringly be advanced without discouraging the farm population unduly; that is to say, the point beyond which the livelihood of the farm population will be cut into so severely by the overcharging of the retail trade that they begin to decide that they have nothing more to lose, and so give up and move out. This critical point appears not commonly to be reached in the ordinary retail trade—as, e.g., groceries, clothing, hardware—possibly because there still remains, practicable in an extremity, the recourse to outside dealers of one sort or another. In the business of country-town banking, however, and similar money-lending by other persons than the banks, the critical point is not infrequently reached and passed. Here the local monopoly is fairly complete and rigorous, which brings on an insistent provocation to overreach.

And then, too, the banker deals in money-values, and money-values are for ever liable to fluctuate; at the same time that the fortunes of the banker's farm clients are subject to the vicissitudes of the seasons and of the markets; and competition drives both banker and client to base their habitual rates, not on a conservative anticipation of what is likely to happen, but on the lucky chance of what may come to pass barring accidents and the acts of God.' And the banker is under the necessity—"inner necessity," as the Hegelians would say—of getting all he can and securing himself against all risk, at the cost of any whom it may concern, by such charges and stipulations as will ensure his net gain in any event.

It is the business of the country-town business community, one with another, to charge what the traffic will bear; and the traffic will bear charges that are inordinately high as counted on the necessary cost or the use-value of the work to be done. It follows, under the common-sense logic of self-help, cupidity, and business-as-usual, that men eager to do business on a good margin will continue to drift in and cut into the traffic until the number of concerns among whom the gains are to be divided is so large that each one's share is no more than will cover costs and leave a "reasonable" margin of net gain. So that while the underlying farm population continues to yield inordinately high rates on the traffic, the business concerns engaged, one with another, come in for no more than what will induce them to go on; the reason being that in the retail trade as conducted on this plan of self-help and equal opportunity the stocks, equipment, and man-power employed will unavoidably exceed what is required for the work, by some 200 to 1000 per cent—those lines of the trade being the more densely over-populated which enjoy the nearest approach to a local monopoly, as e.g., groceries, or banking.[13]

---

[13] The round numbers named above are safe and conservative, particularly so long as the question concerns the staple country towns of the great farming regions. As has already been remarked, they are only less securely applicable in the case of similar towns in the industrial and outlying parts of the country. To some they may seem large and loose. They are based on a fairly exhaustive study of statistical materials gathered by special inquiry in the spring of 1918 for the Statistical Division of the Food Administration, but not published hitherto.

There has been little detailed or concrete discussion of the topic. See, however, a very brief paper by Isador Lubin on "The Economic Costs of Retail Distribution," published in the *Twenty-Second Re-*

It is perhaps not impertinent to call to mind that the retail trade throughout, always and everywhere, runs on very much the same plan of inordinately high charges and consequently extravagant multiplication of stocks, equipment, work, personnel, publicity, credits, and costs. It runs to the same effect in city, town, and country. And in city, town, or country town it is in all of these several respects the country's largest business enterprise in the aggregate; and always something like three-fourths to nine-tenths of it is idle waste, to be cancelled out of the community's working efficiency as lag, leak, and friction. When the statesmen and the newspapers—and other publicity-agencies—speak for the security and the meritorious work of the country's business men, it is something of this sort they are talking about. The bulk of the country's business is the retail trade, and in an eminent sense the retail trade is business-as-usual.

The retail trade, and therefore in its degree the country town, have been the home ground of American culture and the actuating centre of public affairs and public sentiment throughout the nineteenth century, ever more securely and unequivocally as the century advanced and drew toward its close. In American parlance "The Pub-

---

*port of the Michigan Academy of Science,* which runs in great part on the same material.

It is, or should be, unnecessary to add that the retail trade of the country towns is neither a unique nor an extravagant development of business-as-usual. It is in fact very much the sort of thing that is to be met with in the retail trade everywhere, in America and elsewhere.

lic," so far as it can be defined, has meant those persons who are engaged in and about the business of the retail trade, together with such of the kept classes as draw their keep from this traffic. The road to success has run into and through the country town, or its retail-trade equivalent in the cities, and the habits of thought engendered by the preoccupations of the retail trade have shaped popular sentiment and popular morals and have dominated public policy in what was to be done and what was to be left undone, locally and at large, in political, civil, social, ecclesiastical, and educational concerns. The country's public men and official spokesmen have come up through and out of the country-town community, on passing the test of fitness according to retail-trade standards, and have carried with them into official responsibility the habits of thought induced by these interests and these habits of life.

This is also what is meant by democracy in American parlance, and it was for this country-town pattern of democracy that the Defender of the American Faith once aspired to make the world safe. Meantime democracy, at least in America, has moved forward and upward to a higher business level, where larger vested interests dominate and bulkier margins of net gain are in the hazard. It has come to be recognized that the country-town situation of the nineteenth century is now by way of being left behind; and so it is now recognized, or at least acted on, that the salvation of twentieth-century democracy is best to be worked out by making the world safe for Big Business and then let Big Business take care of the interests of the retail trade and the country town, together with much else. But it should not be overlooked that in and through all this it is the soul of the country town that goes marching on.

Toward the close of the century, and increasingly since the turn of the century, the trading community of the country towns has been losing its initiative as a maker of charges and has by degrees become tributary to the great vested interests that move in the background of the market. In a way the country towns have in an appreciable degree fallen into the position of toll-gate keepers for the distribution of goods and collection of customs for the large absentee owners of the business. Grocers, hardware dealers, meat-markets, druggists, shoe-shops, are more and more extensively falling into the position of local distributors for jobbing houses and manufacturers. They increasingly handle "package goods" bearing the brand of some (ostensible) maker, whose chief connexion with the goods is that of advertiser of the copyright brand which appears on the label. Prices, and margins, are made for the retailers, which they can take or leave. But leaving, in this connexion, will commonly mean leaving the business—which is not included in the premises. The bankers work by affiliation with and under surveillance of their correspondents in the sub-centres of credit, who are similarly tied in under the credit routine of the associated banking-houses in the great centres.

And the clothiers duly sell garments under the brand of "Cost-Plus," or some such apocryphal token of merit.

All this reduction of the retailers to simpler terms has by no means lowered the overhead charges of the retail trade as they bear upon the underlying farm population; rather the reverse. Nor has it hitherto lessened the duplication of stocks, equipment, personnel, and work that goes into the retail trade; rather the reverse, indeed, whatever may yet happen in that connexion. Nor has it abated the ancient spirit of self-help and cupidity that has always animated the retail trade and the country town; rather the reverse; inasmuch as their principals back in the jungle of Big Business cut into the initiative and the margins of the retailers with "package goods," brands, advertising, and agency contracts; which irritates the retailers and provokes them to retaliate and recoup where they see an opening, that is at the cost of the underlying farm population. It is true, the added overcharge which so can effectually be brought to rest on the farm population may be a negligible quantity; there never was much slack to be taken up on that side.

The best days of the retail trade and the country town are past. The retail trader is passing under the hand of Big Business and so is ceasing to be a masterless man ready to follow the line of his own initiative and help to rule his corner of the land in collusion with his fellow-townsmen. Circumstances are prescribing for him. The decisive circumstances that hedge him about have been changing in such a way as to leave him no longer fit to do business on his own, even in collusion with his fellow-townsmen. The retail trade and the country town are an enterprise in salesmanship, of course, and salesmanship is a matter of buying cheap and selling dear; all of which is simple and obvious to any retailer, and holds true all around the circle from grocer to banker and back again. During the period while the country town has flourished and grown into the texture of the economic situation, the salesmanship which made the outcome was a matter of personal qualities, knack, and skill that gave the dealer an advantage in meeting his customers man to man, largely a matter of tact, patience, and effrontery; those qualities, in short, which have qualified the rustic horse-trader and have cast a glamour of adventurous enterprise over American country life. In this connexion it is worth recalling that the personnel engaged in the retail trade of the country towns has in the main been drawn by self-selection from the farm population, prevailingly from the older-settled sections where this traditional animus of the horse-trader is of older growth and more untroubled.

All this was well enough, at least during the period of what may be called the masterless country town, before Big Business began to come into its own in these premises. But this situation has been changing, becoming obsolete, slowly, by insensible degrees. The factors of change have been such as: increased facilities of transport and communication; increasing use of advertising, largely made possible by facilities of transport and communica-

tion; increased size and combination of the business
concerns engaged in the wholesale trade, as packers,
jobbers, warehouse-concerns handling farm products; increased resort to package-goods, brands, and trade-marks,
advertised on a liberal plan which runs over the heads
of the retailers; increased employment of chain-store
methods and agencies; increased dependence of local
bankers on the greater credit establishments of the financial centres. It will be seen, of course, that this new
growth finally runs back to and rests upon changes of a
material sort, in the industrial arts, and more immediately on changes in the means of transport and communication.

In effect, salesmanship, too, has been shifting to the
wholesale scale and plane, and the country-town retailer
is not in a position to make use of the resulting wholesale
methods of publicity and control. The conditioning circumstances have outgrown him. Should he make the
shift to the wholesale plan of salesmanship, he will cease
to be a country-town retailer and take on the character
of a chain-store concern, a line-yard lumber syndicate, a
mail-order house, a Chicago packer instead of a meat-
market, a Reserve Bank instead of a county-seat banker,
and the like; all of which is not contained in the premises
of the country-town retail trade.

The country town, of course, still has its uses, and its
use so far as bears on the daily life of the underlying
farm population is much the same as ever; but for the
retail trade and for those accessory persons and classes

who draw their keep from its net gains the country town is no longer what it once was. It has been falling into the position of a way-station in the distributive system, instead of a local habitation where a man of initiative and principle might reasonably hope to come in for a "competence"—that is a capitalized free livelihood— and bear his share in the control of affairs without being accountable to any master-concern "higher-up" in the hierarchy of business. The country town and the townsmen are by way of becoming ways and means in the hands of Big Business. Barring accidents, Bolshevism, and the acts of God or of the United States Congress, such would appear to be the drift of things in the calculable future; that is to say, in the absence of disturbing causes.

This does not mean that the country town is on the decline in point of population or the volume of its traffic; but only that the once masterless retailer is coming in for a master, that the retail trade is being standardized and reparcelled by and in behalf of those massive vested interests that move obscurely in the background, and that these vested interests in the background now have the first call on the "income stream" that flows from the farms through the country town. Nor does it imply that that spirit of self-help and collusive cupidity that made and animated the country town at its best has faded out of the mentality of this people. It has only moved upward and onward to higher duties and wider horizons. Even if it should appear that the self-acting collusive

storekeeper and banker of the nineteenth-century country town "lies a-mouldering in his grave," yet "his soul
goes marching on." It is only that the same stock of men
with the same traditions and ideals are doing Big Business on the same general plan on which the country town
was built. And these men who know the country town
"from the ground up" now find it ready to their hand,
ready to be turned to account according to the methods
and principles bred in their own bone. And the habit of
mind induced by and conducive to business-as-usual is
much the same whether the balance sheet runs in four
figures or in eight.

It is an unhappy circumstance that all this plain speaking about the country town, its traffic, its animating spirit,
and its standards of merit unavoidably has an air of finding fault. But even slight reflection will show that this
appearance is unavoidable even where there is no inclination to disparage. It lies in the nature of the case,
unfortunately. No unprejudiced inquiry into the facts
can content itself with anything short of plain speech,
and in this connexion plain speech has an air of disparagement because it has been the unbroken usage to avoid
plain speech touching these things, these motives, aims,
principles, ways and means and achievements, of these
substantial citizens and their business and fortunes. But
for all that, all these substantial citizens and their folks,
fortunes, works, and opinions are no less substantial and
meritorious, in fact. Indeed one can scarcely appreciate

the full measure of their stature, substance, and achievements, and more particularly the moral costs of their
great work in developing the country and taking over its
resources, without putting it all in plain terms, instead
of the salesmanlike parables that have to be employed
in the make-believe of trade and politics.

The country town and the business of its substantial
citizens are and have ever been an enterprise in salesmanship; and the beginning of wisdom in salesmanship
is equivocation. There is a decent measure of equivocation which runs its course on the hither side of prevarication or duplicity, and an honest salesman—such "an
honest man as will bear watching"—will endeavour to
confine his best efforts to this highly moral zone where
stands the upright man who is not under oath to tell the
whole truth. But "self-preservation knows no moral
law"; and it is not to be overlooked that there habitually enter into the retail trade of the country towns many
competitors who do not falter at prevarication and who
even do not hesitate at outright duplicity; and it will not
do for an honest man to let the rogues get away with
the best—or any—of the trade, at the risk of too narrow
a margin of profit on his own business—that is to say a
narrower margin than might be had in the absence of
scruple. And then there is always the base-line of what
the law allows; and what the law allows cannot be far
wrong. Indeed, the sane presumption will be that who-
ever lives within the law has no need to quarrel with his
conscience. And a sound principle will be to improve the

hour today and, if worse comes to worst, let the courts determine tomorrow, under protest, just what the law allows, and therefore what the moral code exacts. And then, too, it is believed and credible that the courts will be wise enough to see that the law is not allowed to apply with such effect as to impede the volume or narrow the margins of business-as-usual.

"He either fears his fate too much, Or his deserts are small, Who dare not put it to the touch" and take a chance with the legalities and the moralities for once in a way, when there is easy money in sight and no one is looking, particularly in case his own solvency—that is his life as a business concern—should be in the balance. Solvency is always a meritorious work, however it may be achieved or maintained; and so long as one is quite sound on this main count one is sound on the whole, and can afford to forget peccadilloes, within reason. The country-town code of morality at large as well as its code of business ethics, is quite sharp, meticulous; but solvency always has a sedative value in these premises, at large and in personal detail. And then, too, solvency not only puts a man in the way of acquiring merit, but it makes him over into a substantial citizen whose opinions and preferences have weight and who is therefore enabled to do much good for his fellow-citizens—that is to say, shape them somewhat to his own pattern. To create mankind in one's own image is a work that partakes of the divine, and it is a high privilege which the substantial citizen commonly makes the most of. Evidently this salesmanlike pursuit of the net gain has a high cultural value at the same time that it is invaluable as a means to a competence.

The country-town pattern of moral agent and the code of morals and proprieties, manners and customs, which come up out of this life of salesmanship is such as this unremitting habituation is fit to produce. The scheme of conduct for the business man and for "his sisters and his cousins and his aunts" is a scheme of salesmanship, seven days in the week. And the rule of life of country-town salesmanship is summed up in what the older logicians have called *suppressio veri* and *suggestio falsi*. The dominant note of this life is circumspection.[14] One must avoid offence, cultivate good-will, at any reasonable cost, and continue unfailing in taking advantage of it; and, as a corollary to this axiom, one should be ready to recognize and recount the possible short-comings of one's neighbours, for neighbours are (or may be) rivals in the trade, and in trade one man's loss is another's gain, and a rival's disabilities count in among one's assets and should not be allowed to go to waste.

One must be circumspect, acquire merit, and avoid offence. So one must eschew opinions, or information, which are not acceptable to the common run of those whose good-will has or may conceivably come to have any commercial value. The country-town system of knowledge and belief can admit nothing that would annoy the

---

[14] It might also be called salesmanlike pusillanimity.

prejudices of any appreciable number of the respectable townsfolk. So it becomes a system of intellectual, institutional, and religious holdovers. The country town is conservative; aggressively and truculently so, since any assertion or denial that runs counter to any appreciable set of respectable prejudices would come in for some degree of disfavour, and any degree of disfavour is intolerable to men whose business would presumably suffer from it. Whereas there is no (business) harm done in assenting to, and so in time coming to believe in, any or all of the commonplaces of the day before yesterday. In this sense the country town is conservative, in that it is by force of business expediency intolerant of anything but holdovers. Intellectually, institutionally, and religiously, the country towns of the great farming country are "standing pat" on the ground taken somewhere about the period of the Civil War; or according to the wider chronology, somewhere about mid-Victorian times. And the men of affairs and responsibility in public life, who have passed the test of country-town fitness, as they must, are men who have come through and made good according to the canons of faith and conduct imposed by this system of holdovers.

Again it seems necessary to enter the caution that in so speaking of this system of country-town holdovers and circumspection there need be no hint of disparagement. The colloquial speech of our time, outside of the country-town hives of expedient respectability, carries a note of disallowance and disclaimer in all that it has to say of holdovers; which is an unfortunate but inherent defect of the language, and which it is necessary to discount and make one's peace with. It is only that outside of the country towns, where human intelligence has not yet gone into abeyance and where human speech accordingly is in continued process of remaking, sentiment and opinion run to the unhappy effect which this implicit disparagement of these holdovers discloses.

Indeed, there is much, or at least something, to be said to the credit of this country-town system of holdovers, with its canons of salesmanship and circumspection. It has to its credit many deeds of Christian charity and Christian faith. It may be—as how should it not?—that many of these deeds of faith and charity are done in the businesslike hope that they will have some salutary effect on the doer's balance sheet; but the opaque fact remains that these business men do these things, and it is to be presumed that they would rather not discuss the ulterior motives.

It is a notorious commonplace among those who get their living by promoting enterprises of charity and good deeds in general that no large enterprise of this description can be carried through to a successful and lucrative issue without due appeal to the country towns and due support by the businesslike townsmen and their associates and accessory folks. And it is likewise notorious that the country-town community of business men and substantial households will endorse and contribute to virtually any enterprise of the sort, and ask few questions.

The effectual interest which prompts to endorsement of and visible contribution to these enterprises is a salesmanlike interest in the "prestige value" that comes to those persons who endorse and visibly contribute; and perhaps even more insistently there is the loss of "prestige value" that would come to anyone who should dare to omit due endorsement and contribution to any ostensibly public-spirited enterprise of this kind that has caught the vogue and does not violate the system of prescriptive holdovers.

Other interest there may well be, as, e.g., human charity or Christian charity—that is to say solicitude for the salvation of one's soul—but without due appeal to salesmanlike respectability the clamour of any certified solicitor of these good deeds will be but as sounding brass and a tinkling cymbal. One need only try to picture what would be the fate, e.g., of the campaigns and campaigners for Red Cross, famine relief, Liberty Bonds, foreign missions, Inter-Church fund, and the like, in the absence of such appeal and of the due response. It may well be, of course, that the salesmanlike townsman endorses with the majority and pays his contribution as a mulct, under compunction of expediency, as a choice between evils, for fear of losing good-will. But the main fact remains. It may perhaps all foot up to this with the common run, that no man who values his salesmanlike well-being will dare follow his own untoward propensity in dealing with these certified enterprises in good deeds, and speak his profane mind to the certified campaigners. But it all

comes to the same in the upshot. The substantial townsman is shrewd perhaps, or at least he aims to be, and
it may well be that with a shrewd man's logic he argues
that two birds in the bush are worth more than one in
the hand; and so pays his due peace-offering to the certified solicitor of good deeds somewhat in the spirit of
those addicts of the faith who once upon a time bought
Papal indulgences. But when all is said, it works; and
that it does so, and that these many adventures and adventurers in certified mercy and humanity are so enabled
to subsist in any degree of prosperity and comfort is to
be credited, for the major part, to the salesmanlike tact
of the substantial citizens of the country towns.

One hesitates to imagine what would be the fate of
the foreign missions, e.g., in the absence of this salesmanlike solicitude for the main chance in the country
towns. And there is perhaps less comfort in reflecting
on what would be the terms of liquidation for those many
churches and churchmen that now adorn the land, if
they were driven to rest their fortunes on unconstrained
gifts from *de facto* worshippers moved by the first-hand
fear of God, in the absence of that more bounteous sub-
vention that so comes in from the quasi-consecrated respectable townsmen who are so constrained by their
salesmanlike fear of a possible decline in their prestige.

Any person who is seriously addicted to devout observances and who takes his ecclesiastical verities at their
face might be moved to deprecate this dependence of
the good cause on these mixed motives. But there is no

need of entertaining doubts here as to the ulterior good-
ness of these businesslike incentives. Seen in perspective
from the outside—as any economist must view these matters—it should seem to be the part of wisdom, for the
faithful and for their businesslike benefactors alike, to
look steadfastly to the good end and leave ulterior questions of motive on one side. There is also some reason
to believe that such a view of the whole matter is not
infrequently acted upon. And when all is said and allowed for, the main fact remains, that in the absence of
this spirit of what may without offence be called salesmanlike pusillanimity in the country towns, both the
glory of God and the good of man would be less boun-
tifully served, on all these issues that engage the certified
solicitors of good deeds.

This system of innocuous holdovers, then, makes up
what may be called the country-town profession of faith,
spiritual and secular. And so it comes to pass that the
same general system of holdovers imposes its bias on
the reputable organs of expression throughout the community—pulpit, public press, courts, schools—and dominates the conduct of public affairs; inasmuch as the constituency of the country town, in the main and in the
everyday run, shapes the course of reputable sentiment
and conviction for the American community at large.
Not because of any widely prevalent aggressive preference for that sort of thing, perhaps, but rather because
it would scarcely be a "sound business proposition" to

run counter to the known interests of the ruling class; that is to say, the substantial citizens and their folks. But the effect is much the same and will scarcely be denied.

It will be seen that in substantial effect this country-town system of holdovers is of what would be called a "salutary" character; that is to say, it is somewhat intolerantly conservative. It is a system of professions and avowals, which may perhaps run to no deeper ground than a salesmanlike pusillanimity, but the effect is much the same. In the country-town community and its outlying ramifications, as in any community of men, the professions made and insisted on will unavoidably shape the effectual scheme of knowledge and belief. Such is the known force of inveterate habit. To the young generation the prescriptive holdovers are handed down as self-evident and immutable principles of reality, and the (reputable) schools can allow themselves no latitude and no question. And what is more to the point, men and women come to believe in the truths which they profess, on whatever ground, provided only that they continue stubbornly to profess them. Their professions may have come out of expedient make-believe, but, all the same, they serve as premises in all the projects, reflections, and reveries of these folks who profess them. And it will be only on provocation of harsh and protracted exposure to material facts running unbroken to the contrary that the current of their sentiments and convictions can be brought to range outside of the lines drawn for them by these professed articles of truth.

The case is illustrated, e.g., by the various and widely varying systems of religious verities current among the outlying peoples, the peoples of the lower cultures, each and several of which are indubitable and immutably truthful to their respective believers, throughout all the bizarre web of their incredible conceits and grotesqueries, none of which will bear the light of alien scrutiny.[15] Having come in for these professions of archaic make-believe, and continuing stubbornly to profess implicit faith in these things as a hopeful sedative of the wrath to come, these things come to hedge about the scheme of knowledge and belief as well as the schemes of what is to be done or left undone. In much the same way the country-town system of prescriptive holdovers has gone into action as the safe and sane body of American common-sense; until it is now self-evident to American public sentiment that any derangement of these hold-

---

[15] There is, of course, no call in this Christian land to throw up a doubt or question touching any of the highly remarkable verities of the Christian confession at large. While it will be freely admitted on all hands that many of the observances and beliefs current among the "non-Christian tribes" are grotesque and palpable errors of mortal mind; it must at the same time, and indeed by the same token, be equally plain to any person of cultivated tastes in religious superstition, and with a sound bias, that the corresponding convolutions of unreason in the Christian faith are in the nature of a divine coagulum of the true, the beautiful, and the good, as it was in the beginning, is now, and ever shall be: World without end. But all the while it is evident that all these "beastly devices of the heathen," just referred to, are true, beautiful, and good to their benighted apprehension only because their apprehension has been benighted by their stubborn profession of these articles of misguided make-believe through the generations; which is the point of the argument.

overs would bring the affairs of the human race to a disastrous collapse. And all the while the material conditions are progressively drawing together into such shape that this plain country-town common-sense will no longer work.

# THE CAPTAINS OF FINANCE

# AND THE ENGINEERS[1]

✿

IN the beginning, that is to say during the early growth
of the machine industry, and particularly in that new
growth of mechanical industries which arose directly
out of the Industrial Revolution, there was no marked
division between the industrial experts and the business
managers. That was before the new industrial system
had gone far on the road of progressive specialization
and complexity, and before business had reached an ex-
actingly large scale; so that even the business men of
that time, who were without special training in technological matters, would still be able to exercise something of an intelligent oversight of the whole, and to
understand something of what was required in the mechanical conduct of the work which they financed and
from which they drew their income. Not unusually the
designers of industrial processes and equipment would
then still take care of the financial end, at the same time
that they managed the shop. But from an early point
in the development there set in a progressive differentiation, such as to divide those who designed and administered the industrial processes from those others who

[1] Reprinted from *The Engineers and the Price System*, 1921, pp.
58–82.

designed and managed the commercial transactions and took care of the financial end. So there also set in a corresponding division of powers between the business management and the technological experts. It became the work of the technologist to determine, on technological grounds, what could be done in the way of productive industry, and to contrive ways and means of doing it; but the business management always continued to decide, on commercial grounds, how much work should be done and what kind and quality of goods and services should be produced; and the decision of the business management has always continued to be final, and has always set the limit beyond which production must not go.

With the continued growth of specialization the experts have necessarily had more and more to say in the affairs of industry; but always their findings as to what work is to be done and what ways and means are to be employed in production have had to wait on the findings of the business managers as to what will be expedient for the purpose of commercial gain. This division between business management and industrial management has continued to go forward, at a continually accelerated rate, because the special training and experience required for any passably efficient organization and direction of these industrial processes has continually grown more exacting, calling for special knowledge and abilities on the part of those who have this work to do and requiring their undivided interest and their undivided attention to the work in hand. But these specialists in technological knowledge, abilities, interest, and experience, who have increasingly come into the case in this way—inventors, designers, chemists, mineralogists, soil experts, crop specialists, production managers, and engineers of many kinds and denominations—have continued to be employees of the captains of industry, that is to say, of the captains of finance, whose work it has been to commercialize the knowledge and abilities of the industrial experts and turn them to account for their own gain.

It is perhaps unnecessary to add the axiomatic corollary that the captains have always turned the technologists and their knowledge to account in this way only so far as would serve their own commercial profit; not to the extent of their ability, or to the limit set by the material circumstances, or by the needs of the community. The result has been, uniformly and as a matter of course, that the production of goods and services has advisedly been stopped short of productive capacity, by curtailment of output and by derangement of the productive system. There are two main reasons for this, and both have operated together throughout the machine era to stop industrial production increasingly short of productive capacity: (a) The commercial need of maintaining a profitable price has led to an increasingly imperative curtailment of the output, as fast as the advance of the industrial arts has enhanced the productive capacity. And (b) the continued advance of the mechanical technology has called for an ever-increasing volume and diversity of special knowledge, and so has left the businesslike captains of finance continually farther in arrears, so that they have been less and less capable of comprehending what is required in the ordinary way of industrial equipment and personnel. They have therefore, in effect, maintained prices at a profitable level by curtailment of output rather than by lowering production-cost per unit of output, because they have not had such a working acquaintance with the technological facts in the case as would enable them to form a passably sound judgment of suitable ways and means for lowering production-cost; and at the same time, being shrewd business men, they have been unable to rely on the hired-man's-loyalty of technologists whom they do not understand. The result has been a somewhat distrustful blindfold choice of processes and personnel and a consequent enforced incompetence in the management of industry, a curtailment of output below the needs of the community, below the productive capacity of the industrial system, and below what an intelligent control of production would have made commercially profitable.

Through the earlier decades of the machine era these limitations imposed on the work of the experts by the demands of profitable business and by the technical ignorance of the business men appears not to have been a heavy handicap, whether as a hindrance to the continued development of technological knowledge or as an obstacle to its ordinary use in industry. That was before the mechanical industry had gone far in scope, complexity, and specialization; and it was also before the continued work of the technologists had pushed the industrial system to so high a productive capacity that it is for ever in danger of turning out a larger product than is required for a profitable business. But gradually, with the passage of time and the advance of the industrial arts to a wider scope and a larger scale, and to an increasing specialization and standardization of processes, the technological knowledge that makes up the state of the industrial arts has called for a higher degree of that training that makes industrial specialists; and at the same time any passably efficient management of industry has of necessity drawn on them and their special abilities to an ever-increasing extent. At the same time and by the same shift of circumstances, the captains of finance, driven by an increasingly close application to the affairs of business, have been going farther out of touch with the ordinary realities of productive industry; and, it is to be admitted, they have also continued increasingly to distrust the technological specialists, whom they do not understand, but whom they can also not get along without. The captains have perforce continued to employ the technologists, to make money for them, but they have done so only reluctantly, tardily, sparingly, and with a shrewd circumspection; only because and so far as they have been persuaded that the use of these technologists was indispensable to the making of money.

One outcome of this persistent and pervasive tardi-

ness and circumspection on the part of the captains has
been an incredibly and increasingly uneconomical use
of material resources, and an incredibly wasteful organization of equipment and man-power in those great industries where the technological advance has been most
marked. In good part it was this discreditable pass, to
which the leading industries had been brought by these
one-eyed captains of industry, that brought the regime
of the captains to an inglorious close, by shifting the
initiative and discretion in this domain out of their hands
into those of the investment bankers. By custom the investment bankers had occupied a position between or
overlapping the duties of a broker in corporate securities and those of an underwriter of corporate flotations—
such a position, in effect, as is still assigned them in the
standard writings on corporation finance. The increasingly large scale of corporate enterprise, as well as the
growth of a mutual understanding among these business
concerns, also had its share in this new move. But about
this time, too, the "consulting engineers" were coming
notably into evidence in many of those lines of industry
in which corporation finance has habitually been concerned.

So far as concerns the present argument the ordinary
duties of these consulting engineers have been to advise
the investment bankers as to the industrial and commercial soundness, past and prospective, of any enterprise
that is to be underwritten. These duties have comprised
a painstaking and impartial examination of the physical

properties involved in any given case, as well as an equally impartial auditing of the accounts and appraisal of the commercial promise of such enterprises, for the guidance of the bankers or syndicate of bankers interested in the case as underwriters. On this ground working arrangements and a mutual understanding presently arose between the consulting engineers and those banking-houses that habitually were concerned in the underwriting of corporate enterprises.

The effect of this move has been twofold: experience has brought out the fact that corporation finance, at its best and soundest, has now become a matter of comprehensive and standardized bureaucratic routine, necessarily comprising the mutual relations between various corporate concerns, and best to be taken care of by a clerical staff of trained accountants; and the same experience has put the financial houses in direct touch with the technological general staff of the industrial system, whose surveillance has become increasingly imperative to the conduct of any profitable enterprise in industry. But also, by the same token, it has appeared that the corporation financier of nineteenth-century tradition is no longer of the essence of the case in corporation finance of the larger and more responsible sort. He has, in effect, come to be no better than an idle wheel in the economic mechanism, serving only to take up some of the lubricant.

Since and so far as this shift out of the nineteenth century into the twentieth has been completed, the corporation financier has ceased to be a captain of industry and has become a lieutenant of finance; the captaincy having been taken over by the syndicated investment bankers and administered as a standardized routine of accountancy, having to do with the flotation of corporation securities and with their fluctuating values, and having also something to do with regulating the rate and volume of output in those industrial enterprises which so have passed under the hand of the investment bankers.

By and large, such is the situation of the industrial system today, and of that financial business that controls the industrial system. But this state of things is not so much an accomplished fact handed on out of the recent past; it is only that such is the culmination in which it all heads up in the immediate present, and that such is the visible drift of things into the calculable future. Only during the last few years has the state of affairs in industry been obviously falling into the shape so outlined, and it is even yet only in those larger and pace-making lines of industry which are altogether of the new technological order that the state of things has reached this finished shape. But in these larger and underlying divisions of the industrial system the present posture and drift of things is unmistakable. Meantime very much still stands over out of that regime of rule-of-thumb, competitive sabotage, and commercial log-rolling, in which the businesslike captains of the old order are so altogether well at home, and which has been the best that the captains have known how to contrive for the management of that industrial system whose captains they have been. So that wherever the production experts are now taking over the management, out of the dead hand of the self-made captains, and wherever they have occasions to inquire into the established conditions of production, they find the ground cumbered with all sorts of incredible make-shifts of waste and inefficiency —such make-shifts as would perhaps pass muster with any moderately stupid elderly laymen, but which look like blindfold guesswork to these men who know something of the advanced technology and its working-out.

Hitherto, then, the growth and conduct of this industrial system presents this singular outcome. The technology—the state of the industrial arts—which takes effect in this mechanical industry is in an eminent sense a joint stock of knowledge and experience held in common by the civilized peoples. It requires the use of trained and instructed workmen—born, bred, trained, and instructed at the cost of the people at large. So also it requires, with a continually more exacting insistence, a corps of highly trained and specially gifted experts, of divers and various kinds. These, too, are born, bred, and trained at the cost of the community at large, and they draw their requisite special knowledge from the community's joint stock of accumulated experience. These expert men, technologists, engineers, or whatever name may best suit them, make up the indispensable General Staff of the industrial system; and without their immediate and unremitting guidance and correction the industrial system will not work. It is a mechanically organized structure of technical processes designed, installed, and conducted by these production engineers. Without them and their constant attention the industrial equipment, the mechanical appliances of industry, will foot up to just so much junk. The material welfare of the community is unreservedly bound up with the due working of this industrial system, and therefore with its unreserved control by the engineers, who alone are competent to manage it. To do their work as it should be done these men of the industrial general staff must have a free hand, unhampered by commercial considerations and reservations; for the production of the goods and services needed by the community they neither need nor are they in any degree benefited by any supervision or interference from the side of the owners. Yet the absentee owners, now represented, in effect, by the syndicated investment bankers, continue to control the industrial experts and limit their discretion, arbitrarily, for their own commercial gain, regardless of the needs of the community.

Hitherto these men who so make up the general staff of the industrial system have not drawn together into anything like a self-directing working force; nor have they been vested with anything more than an occasional, haphazard, and tentative control of some disjointed sector of the industrial equipment, with no direct or decisive relation to that personnel of productive industry that may be called the officers of the line and the rank and file. It is still the unbroken privilege of the financial management and its financial agents to "hire and fire." The final disposition of all the industrial forces still remains in the hands of the business men, who still continue to dispose of these forces for other than industrial ends. And all the while it is an open secret that with a reasonably free hand the production experts would to-day readily increase the ordinary output of industry by severalfold—variously estimated at some 300 per cent to 1200 per cent of the current output. And what stands in the way of so increasing the ordinary output of goods and services is business-as-usual.

Right lately these technologists have begun to become uneasily "class-conscious" and to reflect that they together constitute the indispensable general staff of the industrial system. Their class-consciousness has taken the immediate form of a growing sense of waste and confusion in the management of industry by the financial agents of the absentee owners. They are beginning to take stock of that all-pervading mismanagement of industry that is inseparable from its control for commercial ends. All of which brings home a realization of their own shame and of damage to the common good. So the engineers are beginning to draw together and ask themselves, "What about it?"

This uneasy movement among the technologists set in, in an undefined and fortuitous way, in the closing years of the nineteenth century; when the consulting engineers, and then presently the "efficiency engineers," began to make scattered corrections in detail, which showed up the industrial incompetence of those elderly laymen who were doing a conservative business at the cost of industry. The consulting engineers of the standard type, both then and since then, are commercialized technologists, whose work it is to appraise the industrial value of any given enterprise with a view to its commercial exploitation. They are a cross between a technological specialist and a commercial agent, beset with the limitations of both and commonly not fully competent in either line. Their normal position is that of an employee of the investment bankers, on a stipend or a retainer, and it has ordinarily been their fortune to shift over in time from a technological footing to a frankly commercial one. The case of the efficiency engineers, or scientific-management experts, is somewhat similar. They too have set out to appraise, exhibit, and correct the commercial shortcomings of the ordinary management of those industrial establishments which they investigate, to persuade the business men in charge how they may reasonably come in for larger net earnings by a more closely shorn exploitation of the industrial forces at their disposal. During the opening years of the new century a lively interest centred on the views and expositions of these two groups of industrial experts; and not least was the interest aroused by their exhibits of current facts indicating an all-pervading lag, leak, and

friction in the industrial system, due to its disjointed
and one-eyed management by commercial adventurers
bent on private gain.

During these few years of the opening century the
members of this informal guild of engineers at large
have been taking an interest in this question of habitual
mismanagement by ignorance and commercial sabotage,
even apart from the commercial imbecility of it all. But
it is the young rather than the old among them who
see industry in any other light than its commercial value.
Circumstances have decided that the older generation
of the craft have become pretty well commercialized.
Their habitual outlook has been shaped by a long and
unbroken apprenticeship to the corporation financiers
and the investment bankers; so that they still habitually
see the industrial system as a contrivance for the roundabout process of making money. Accordingly, the established official Associations and Institutes of Engineers, which are officered and engineered by the elder
engineers, old and young, also continue to show the
commercial bias of their creators, in what they criticize
and in what they propose. But the new generation which
has been coming on during the present century are not
similarly true to that tradition of commercial engineering that makes the technological man an awestruck lieutenant of the captain of finance.

By training, and perhaps also by native bent, the
technologists find it easy and convincing to size up men
and things in terms of tangible performance, without

commercial afterthought, except so far as their apprenticeship to the captains of finance may have made commercial afterthought a second nature to them. Many of
the younger generation are beginning to understand that
engineering begins and ends in the domain of tangible
performance, and that commercial expediency is another
matter. Indeed, they are beginning to understand that
commercial expediency has nothing better to contribute
to the engineer's work than so much lag, leak, and friction. The four years' experience of the war has also been
highly instructive on that head. So they are beginning
to draw together on a common ground of understanding,
as men who are concerned with the ways and means of
tangible performance in the way of productive industry,
according to the state of the industrial arts as they know
them at their best; and there is a growing conviction
among them that they together constitute the sufficient
and indispensable general staff of the mechanical industries, on whose unhindered team work depends the due
working of the industrial system and therefore also the
material welfare of the civilized peoples. So also, to
these men who are trained in the stubborn logic of technology, nothing is quite real that cannot be stated in
terms of tangible performance; and they are accordingly
coming to understand that the whole fabric of credit
and corporation finance is a tissue of make-believe.

Credit obligations and financial transactions rest on
certain principles of legal formality which have been
handed down from the eighteenth century, and which

therefore antedate the mechanical industry and carry no secure conviction to men trained in the logic of that industry. Within this technological system of tangible performance corporation finance and all its works and gestures are completely idle; it all comes into the working scheme of the engineers only as a gratuitous intrusion which could be barred out without deranging the work at any point, provided only that men made up their mind to that effect—that is to say, provided the make-believe of absentee ownership were discontinued. Its only obvious effect on the work which the engineers have to take care of is waste of materials and retardation of the work. So the next question which the engineers are due to ask regarding this time-worn fabric of ownership, finance, sabotage, credit, and unearned income is likely to be: Why cumbers it the ground? And they are likely to find the scriptural answer ready to their hand.

It would be hazardous to surmise how, how soon, on what provocation, and with what effect the guild of engineers are due to realize that they constitute a guild, and that the material fortunes of the civilized peoples already lie loose in their hands. But it is already sufficiently plain that the industrial conditions and the drift of conviction among the engineers are drawing together to some such end.

Hitherto it has been usual to count on the interested negotiations continually carried on and never concluded between capital and labour, between the agents of the

investors and the body of workmen, to bring about whatever readjustments are to be looked for in the control of
productive industry and in the distribution and use of
its product. These negotiations have necessarily been,
and continue to be, in the nature of business transactions,
bargaining for a price, since both parties to the negotia-
tion continue to stand on the consecrated ground of
ownership, free bargain, and self-help; such as the commercial wisdom of the eighteenth century saw, approved,
and certified it all, in the time before the coming of this
perplexing industrial system. In the course of these endless negotiations between the owners and their workmen
there has been some loose and provisional syndication
of claims and forces on both sides; so that each of these
two recognized parties to the industrial controversy has
come to make up a loose-knit vested interest, and each
speaks for its own special claims as a party in interest.
Each is contending for some special gain for itself and
trying to drive a profitable bargain for itself, and
hitherto no disinterested spokesman for the community
at large or for the industrial system as a going concern
has seriously cut into this controversy between these
contending vested interests. The outcome has been businesslike concession and compromise, in the nature of
bargain and sale. It is true, during the war, and for the
conduct of the war, there were some half-concerted
measures taken by the Administration in the interest of
the nation at large, as a belligerent; but it has always
been tacitly agreed that these were extraordinary war

measures, not to be countenanced in time of peace. In time of peace the accepted rule is still business-as-usual; that is to say, investors and workmen wrangling together on a footing of business-as-usual.

These negotiations have necessarily been inconclusive. So long as ownership of resources and industrial plant is allowed, or so long as it is allowed any degree of control or consideration in the conduct of industry, nothing more substantial can come of any readjustment than a concessive mitigation of the owners' interference with production. There is accordingly nothing subversive in these bouts of bargaining between the federated workmen and the syndicated owners. It is a game of chance and skill played between two contending vested interests for private gain, in which the industrial system as a going concern enters only as a victim of interested interference. Yet the material welfare of the community, and not least of the workmen, turns on the due working of this industrial system, without interference. Concessive mitigation of the right to interfere with production, on the part of either one of these vested interests, can evidently come to nothing more substantial than a concessive mitigation.

But owing to the peculiar technological character of this industrial system, with its specialized, standardized, mechanical, and highly technical interlocking processes of production, there has gradually come into being this corps of technological production specialists, into whose keeping the due functioning of the industrial system has

now drifted by force of circumstance. They are, by force
of circumstance, the keepers of the community's material
welfare; although they have hitherto been acting, in
effect, as keepers and providers of free income for the
kept classes. They are thrown into the position of responsible directors of the industrial system, and by the
same move they are in a position to become arbiters of
the community's material welfare. They are becoming
class-conscious, and they are no longer driven by a commercial interest, in any such degree as will make them
a vested interest in that commercial sense in which the
syndicated owners and the federated workmen are
vested interests. They are, at the same time, numerically and by habitual outlook, no such heterogeneous
and unwieldy body as the federated workmen, whose
numbers and scattering interest has left all their endeavours substantially nugatory. In short, the engineers
are in a position to make the next move.

By comparison with the population at large, including the financial powers and the kept classes, the technological specialists which come in question here are a very
inconsiderable number; yet this small number is indispensable to the continued working of the productive
industries. So slight are their numbers, and so sharply
defined and homogeneous is their class, that a sufficiently
compact and inclusive organization of their forces should
arrange itself almost as a matter of course, so soon as
any appreciable proportion of them shall be moved by
any common purpose. And the common purpose is not

far to seek, in the all-pervading industrial confusion, obstruction, waste, and retardation which business-as-usual continually throws in their face. At the same time they are the leaders of the industrial personnel, the workmen, of the officers of the line and the rank and file; and these are coming into a frame of mind to follow their leaders in any adventure that holds a promise of advancing the common good.

To these men, soberly trained in a spirit of tangible performance and endowed with something more than an even share of the sense of workmanship, and endowed also with the common heritage of partiality for the rule of Live and Let Live, the disallowance of an outworn and obstructive right of absentee ownership is not likely to seem a shocking infraction of the sacred realities. That customary right of ownership by virtue of which the vested interests continue to control the industrial system for the benefit of the kept classes belongs to an older order of things than the mechanical industry. It has come out of a past that was made up of small things and traditional make-believe. For all the purposes of that scheme of tangible performance that goes to make up the technologist's world, it is without form and void. So that, given time for due irritation, it should by no means come as a surprise if the guild of engineers are provoked to put their heads together and, quite out of hand, disallow that large absentee ownership that goes to make the vested interests and to unmake the industrial system. And there stand behind them the

massed and rough-handed legions of the industrial rank
and file, ill at ease and looking for new things. The
older commercialized generation among them would,
of course, ask themselves: Why should we worry? What
do we stand to gain? But the younger generation, not so
hard-bitten by commercial experience, will be quite as
likely to ask themselves: What do we stand to lose?
And there is the patent fact that such a thing as a general strike of the technological specialists in industry
need involve no more than a minute fraction of one per
cent of the population; yet it would swiftly bring a
collapse of the old order and sweep the time-worn fabric
of finance and absentee sabotage into the discard for
good and all.

# THE DYNASTIC STATE[1]

✿

IT is only with the new departure of 1870 that Germany has come to take its place in the general apprehension as a singularly striking, not to say unique, instance of exuberant growth. The history of its unfolding power, of course, is not contained in this brief interval that lies within the memory of men still living; but the new departure by force of which the life-history of the German nation has come to diverge so notably from the commonplace run of events in modern Europe can after all not be pushed back far beyond that epoch. Anyone who seeks a precise period from which to date this epoch of German history will have difficulty in deciding on any given point earlier than the year named. And what had taken place in the way of an unfolding of national forces before that date is of great significance only for its bearing on what has taken place since then.

The visible achievements of the German people during this historical period, so far as they are amenable to statistical statement, are a gain in population, in industrial efficiency, and in military force. Other gains are claimed, perhaps even of greater moment in the apprehension of the spokesmen, and there is no inclination here to discount or minimize their achievements out-

---

[1] Reprinted from *Imperial Germany and the Industrial Revolution*, 1915, pp. 58–84.

side of this material domain; but the magnitude of the
advance in these other lines is in some degree a matter
of estimate and opinion, which may in that degree be
influenced by sentiments of self-complacency or of de-
preciation, whereas the gains in the material respect
spoken for above are beyond cavil. But judged by these
physical measurable marks of excellence, the historical
period within which this modern onset of the German
people runs will have to be dated somewhat back of the
French-Prussian war. In each of the three respects
named the advance was well under way before that date.
It is, however, safe to say that this beginning of the
current era falls within the second quarter of the nineteenth century.[2] It is also safe to say that the prime
mover among these factors of the nation's unfolding
power has been its increased industrial efficiency, rather
than either of the other two. While their increasing
efficiency has doubtless been conditioned by the growth
in population, the initiative, as between these two, has
doubtless vested in the former rather than in the latter.
In the correlation between industrial advance and population the primacy belongs to the former. The like
is true, of course, as regards the growth in military
strength. Also, doubtless, a large place among the causes
of growth and efficiency is believed to be due to a wise

---

[2] Cf., e.g., W. H. Dawson, *The Evolution of Modern Germany*,
chap. 3; also more at large, von Sybel, *The Founding of the German
Empire*, vol. I; and Sombart, *Die deutsche Volkswirtschaft im XIX.
Jahrhundert*, Book II.

governmental policy and a shrewd administration, but opinion counts for much in the appraisal of this governmental policy, and opinion on such a matter is liable to partiality, for or against. The unfolding of warlike power has unequivocally been a work of governmental policy, and the same policy has unquestionably sought to further the industrial advance; the question that presents itself in the latter connexion is not as to the faithful intentions and endeavour of the government—or "State," to use the German concept—but only as to the probable degree of efficacy of these good intentions and endeavour; and on this head opinions will not coincide, and the proposition will therefore best be left out of the premises.

As is well known, the practical movement for German union, which came to a successful issue in the eventual formation of the Empire, owed its beginnings and its earlier success to the economic needs of the German countries—or it may be said to have been provoked by the grievous burden of artificial evils created by the governments of the small states among which the country was divided. So, as a practical measure, it begins with the formation of a Tariff Union, designed to remove certain of the obstacles which the particularist policies of these states had erected. And this union and uniformity of economic policy within the Empire is still one of the chief assets of its strength, particularly the absence of internal tariff restrictions.

The place and relation of Germany to the industrial development of modern Europe, therefore, will necessarily be the point of departure for any inquiry into the fortunes and achievements of the German people in this modern era. On this head, then, its natural resources available for modern industrial use are of the same kind and range as those found in the neighbouring countries; there is substantially nothing to distinguish the German lands from those of north Europe at large, unless it be that the resources of the country are slightly under grade in quality and slightly scant in quantity, at least as compared with the most fortunate of the neighbouring countries. Again, in point of native proclivity and aptitude the German population is virtually identical with its neighbours. In respect of hereditary endowment—racial character—it is the same people as the population of the neighbouring nations—more particularly identical with the Dutch, Belgian, and British. By virtue of its hybrid extraction it is, like these others, gifted with a large capacity for acquiring and turning to account a wide range of technological knowledge; and by virtue of the same hereditary bias of workmanship that animates these others it is, like its neighbours, assiduously and sagaciously addicted to industry and thrift. What chiefly distinguishes the German people from these others in this connexion, and more particularly from the British, is that the Germans are new to this industrial system; and the distinctive traits of the German case are in the main traceable to this fact that they are still in their novitiate.

When the current era in the life-history of the German people began, in the second quarter of the nineteenth century, Germany was far in arrears, as compared with its neighbours to the west, but more particularly as contrasted with the British. This is historical commonplace, of course. It may be taken with such allowance and qualification as seem needful; the main fact remains, that in certain decisive, or at least substantial, respects Germany was in an anachronistic state, particularly as seen from the station occupied by the English-speaking peoples. There is no call to depreciate the merits of the German culture of that time in those respects in which it excelled, as there would also be no use in attempting an undervaluation of it; it is too large a fact in the heritage of mankind to suffer seriously from an assault of words. However, those genial respects in which the civilization characteristic of Germany excelled—in which, indeed, Germany triumphed—were not in the line of efficiency that counted materially toward fitness for life under the scheme of things then taking shape in Europe. It may have been better or it may have been worse than what came to take its place, but in any case it was not an articulate part of the working scheme; as is proven in the sequel, which was worked out with only negligible contributions from the accumulated wisdom of the German people.

Germany was in arrears in the industrial arts and in its political institutions, as well as in such features of its civil and domestic scheme of life as come intimately into correlation with, or under the dominant influence of, these fundamental agencies in the scheme of institutions. This is the visible difference between the case of the German and of the British peoples at the time, apart from superficial peculiarities of usage and the decorative elements of culture. In industrial matters Germany was still at the handicraft stage, with all that is implied in that description in the way of institutional impedimenta and meticulous standardization of trifles. Measured by the rate of progression that had brought the English community to the point where it then stood, the German industrial system was some two and a half or three centuries in arrears—somewhere in Elizabethan times; its political system was even more archaic; and use and wont governing social relations in detail was of a character such as this economic and political situation would necessarily foster.

The characterization so offered applies to the industrial organization as a working system. It does not overlook the fact that many alien details had been intruded into this archaic system by force of Germany's unavoidable contact with the more modern industrial communities of western Europe. But it was not until the second half of the nineteenth century that the alien elements seriously began to derange the framework of the archaic scheme. Politically much the same will hold, except that fewer modernisms had found their way over the frontiers in this domain, nor had such modernisms effected

an equally secure and disturbing lodgment in the tissues
of the body politic, Germany being still consistently organized on the pattern of the "Territorial State"—a
peculiarly petty and peculiarly irresponsible autocracy,
which has come to its best maturity only among the Germanic peoples, and which has held its place with remarkable tenacity within the limits of the Fatherland.
The "Territorial State," or its less finished replica under
another designation, has not been unknown elsewhere
in the north-European country, but it passed out by
obsolescence some time ago among the other north-
European peoples; so that even the Scandinavian countries, which would appear by geographical necessity to
have been designed for petty things, had lost this archaic
fashion of state policy and political control by the time
when the question of its supersession began to attract an
(ineffectual) speculative interest in Germany. The territorial state is in effect a territorial aggregate, with its
population conceived as an estate belonging in usufruct
to a given prince; the concept is visibly of feudal derivation, and the habit of mind which makes it a practicable
form of political organization is the feudal habit of personal subservience to a personal master. In such a polity
subordination, personal allegiance, is the prime virtue,
the chief condition precedent to its carrying on; while
insubordination is the fatal vice, incompatible with such
a coercive system. As seen from the standpoint of the
political interests in such a state, the spirit of abnegation
is by apologetic euphemism spoken of as "duty," while

insubordination is called "contumacy." The former is the habit of mind engendered by continued and consistent suppression, and is the basis of a servile political organization, such as the territorial state; the latter, if allowed a free course, will eventuate in an anarchistic autonomy, such as appears to have been the constitution of Germanic society in the prehistoric ages before the barbarian invasions established a coercive rule in what is now the Fatherland. The latter appears to coincide with the natural bent of these peoples; but the former has that secure hold on their spirit that results from fifteen centuries of submission to a masterful discipline of coercion. The spirit of "duty" in these people is apparently not "nature," in the sense of native proclivity; but it is "second nature" with the people of the Fatherland, as being the ingrained traditional attitude induced by consistent and protracted experience.

In speaking of these things in the terms current among modern civilized men it is nearly impossible to avoid the appearance of deprecating this servile or submissive attitude of "duty"; particularly will this difficulty beset anyone using the English language—the fringe of derogatory suggestion carried by the available words and phrases is appreciably less embarrassing, e.g., in German, although even there the commonplace vocabulary lends itself with greater facility to the dispraise of servility and irresponsible rule than to the commendation of these elements of modern patriotism. That such should be the case is doubtless due to the drift of institutional development in western Europe in modern times, which has on the whole set somewhat consistently in the direction of a gradual loosening of the grip of dynastic autocracy. This drift has perhaps not so much created or initiated the growth of an anarchistic (that is to say, non-servile) spirit, but rather has permissively harboured it and so allowed the naturally anarchistic bent of these peoples to reassert itself in a measure, by force of the indefeasible resiliency that characterizes all hereditary proclivities.[3] Any, even a very cursory, scrutiny of the historical growth of free, or popular, institutions in modern Europe should satisfy all parties in interest that this growth

---

[3] . . . The folk-tales, and other folklore, of Germany testify to the tenacious hold which this archaic, small-scale scheme of neighbourhood autonomy still has on the spirit of the German people. These folk-tales have lived obscurely in the hand-to-mouth legendary lore transmitted through generations of illiterate and commonplace idealists held in subjection, and doubtless in loyal allegiance, under the coercive rule of the dynastic territorial state; but the ideals to which they give expression still are those of that quasi-anarchistic neighbourhood life that has not come within the horizon of these people's experience, or even of their narratives of reality, since long before the close of the pagan era. This state of the folk-tales is all the more remarkable in view of the fact that the tales have undergone a fairly complete revision in all that relates to the religious cult, where the church, the cross, the priest, and the monk come in with all the air of being well at home. These "cult objects," as one might call them, are of the medieval, or even of the modern pattern; whereas the social and political life and apparatus still is typically idealized after the pre-Christian fashion. The preservation of this homely folklore of the archaic type has been the work of the submerged classes. The corresponding legendary lore of the ruling classes is of another and later spirit, though this, too, is archaic as tested by comparison with current actualities, turning to the medieval rather than to the modern scheme in its ideal creations.

has come about not because the authorities vested with discretion and power have not taken thought to defeat it wherever a chance has offered, but because the conditioning circumstances have not enabled them to discourage it sufficiently. And by virtue of the close and facile communication of ideas among modern peoples the anarchistic penchant has, by channels of education and neighbourly intercourse, come to infect even the subject populations of the better preserved territorial states; so that even there, under the shadow of the masterful system, the current vocabulary shows a weakness for free institutions and the masterless man.

While the exigencies of the language, therefore, almost unavoidably give a colour of deprecation to any discussion of this surviving habit of abnegation in the people of the Fatherland, there is no intention here to praise or to blame this spirit of subordination that underlies so much of German culture and German achievement. It is one of the larger factors that have gone to the creation of the modern era in that country, and this era and its "system" will have to count with whatever strength or weakness this animus of feudalism contributes to the outcome. Now, it happens that this surviving feudalistic animus of fealty and subservience has visibly been a source of strength to the German state hitherto, as it presumably also has to the economic system, apart from the political ends to be served by the community's economic efficiency. This is to be recognized and taken account of quite apart from any question as to the ultimate merits of such a popular temper in any other connexion, or even as to its ulterior value for the ends of the state. For all that concerns the present inquiry it may or may not appear, as doubtless would appear to the mind of most English-speaking persons, that this spirit of subservient alacrity on which the Prussian system of administrative efficiency rests is beneath the human dignity of a free man; that it is the spirit of a subject, not of a citizen; that except for dynastic uses it is a defect and a delinquency; and that in the end the exigencies of civilized life will not tolerate such an anachronistic remnant of medievalism, and the habit of it will be lost. For all that can be made to appear today, it may also be true that it has only a transient value even for the uses of the dynastic state; but all that does not derange the fact that hitherto it has visibly been a source of strength to the German state, and presumably to the German people at large as an economic body.

In the second quarter of the nineteenth century there began a complex movement of readjustment and rehabilitation in German affairs. At least on its face this movement is primarily of an economic character, the immediate provocation to practical activity being the needs of trade and of the princely exchequers. Much genial speculation, of an academic kind, and much edifying popular exposition and agitation of national ideals ran along beside these practical measures, and this intellectual and spiritual disturbance may have had more or less to do with the measures taken and with the general drift of national policy. It is not easy to say whether this spiritual disturbance is to be rated as a cause or a concomitant of the practical changes going forward during this period, but it should seem reasonable to give it place on both of these grounds. The fashion among historians of the period, particularly among patriotic historians, has been to construe this complex movement of forces, material and immaterial, that makes German history through the middle half of the century, as a movement of the German spirit, initiated by the exuberant national genius of the race. Such is the tradition, but the tradition comes out of the Romantic era; out of which no tradition of a more matter-of-fact character could conceivably come.

A matter-of-fact view of such an historical movement will necessarily look to the factors which may have had a part in shaping habits of thought at the time, and here there are only two lines of derivation to which the analysis can securely run back—discounting, as is the current fashion, any occult agencies, such as manifest destiny, national genius, Providential guidance, and the like. There is no call to undervalue these occult agencies, of course, but granting that these and their like are the hidden springs, it is also to be called to mind that it is their nature to remain hidden, and that the tangible agencies through which these presumed hidden prime movers work must be sufficient for the work without recourse to the hidden springs, which can have an effect only by force of a magical efficacy. Their relation to the course of events is of the nature of occult or magical efficacy, not of causal efficiency; and under the modern materialistic prejudice in these matters of scientific inquiry, the causal sequence in which an explanation of events is sought must be complete in all elements that touch the motivation and the outcome, without drawing on any but tangible fact, on matters that are of the nature of "data." To the modern preconception in favour of efficient cause, as contrasted with the Romantic postulate of efficacious guidance, any attempt to set up a logical finality in any terms other than matter-of-fact is quite nugatory. It may be a genial work of futility, and it may have its value as dramatic art or homiletical discourse; but in the house of scientific inquiry such premises, and generalizations in such terms, are but as sounding brass and a tinkling cymbal.

There are two lines of agency visibly at work shaping the habits of thought of the people in the complex movement of readjustment and rehabilitation spoken of above. These are the received scheme of use and wont, and the new state of the industrial arts; and it is not difficult to see that it is the latter that makes for readjustment; nor should it be any more difficult to see that the readjustment is necessarily made under the surveillance of the received scheme of use and wont. The latter is modified in the course of this new range of habituation enforced by the new state of the industrial arts, but the changes taking place in use and wont are, here as elsewhere, made in the way of tardy concession under the impact of exigencies that tangibly will not tolerate usage that has passed out of date. The complex movement in question is a movement of readjustment in the arts of life to meet the requirements of new technological conditions, and of rehabilitation of the received scheme of princely policy to make it workable under the new technological conditions. The changes which appear in the outcome, therefore, come about on the initiative of the new technological advance, and by expedient concessions and shrewd endeavours on the part of the constituted authority to turn the new-won efficiency to use for its own ends; the conscious directive management in the case being under the hands of the governmental organization and directed to such a rehabilitation of the territorial state as would enable it to do business on the increased scale imposed by the new state of the industrial arts, and adequately to handle the forces which the new industrial system so placed at its disposal.

Much had already been done during the preceding hundred years to take advantage of technological improvements, so far as these improvements contributed directly to the military strength of the prince, and much had been done, incidentally to the extension of territorial control and of fiscal administration, in the way of improved means of communication and intercourse; but the modern industrial system, as such, and except as an outside and essentially alien factor, had not seriously touched the German population, particularly not the Prussian dominions which take the central place in the rehabilitation of Germany in the nineteenth century. But the industrial state of Germany was after all medieval rather than modern, and the state of the industrial arts, therefore, still continued on the whole favourable to the maintenance of the old regime, particularly since this old regime was securely lodged in the interests and traditional ideals of the dynastic rulers and of the privileged classes.

There is a side line of influence from the technological side in the growth of German culture prior to its modernization, which requires to be noted in any attempt to realize what has taken place in the unfolding of the modern era. The art of printing and the consequent use of printed matter had always been at home among the German people since that technological advance first was made. From the outset and down into the nineteenth century the printer's art was a handicraft process, and was well developed in Germany. But the institutional consequences, the effect on use and wont, on the habit of consuming printed matter, need not therefore be of the handicraft order. A free consumption of printed matter means a free intercourse of ideas and therefore an exposure of the consumers to contact with ideas current beyond the circle of their immediate personal contact. The habitual consumption of print has much the same order of disciplinary effect as habituation to the wide-reaching standardization of the arts of life brought on by the machine industry; but it goes without saying that the effect so wrought by the use of print will not extend much beyond the class of persons addicted to it; the illiterate, and the classes who make little use of print anyway, will not be seriously or extensively disturbed—what may be called the extravasation of printed literature is not a matter of large consequence, although it is not to be denied that the diffusion of ideas conveyed by print, among the illiterate, will always amount to something. Whereas the disciplinary value of life under the standardization regime of the machine industry touches the illiterate perhaps more immediately and intimately, and almost as comprehensively, as it touches the classes who habitually read. It is worth noting in this immediate connexion, although it is a proposition of general validity, that in the nature of the case no profound or massive revolutionary disturbance of the established order, in any respect, can be carried through by the medium of printed matter alone, or in the absence of other, materially more exacting and peremptory factors of habituation working to the same general effect. So in the case of Germany, although that fraction of the population that were given to reading had long been in contact with the intellectual movement in Europe at large and had, indeed, from time to time, taken effective part in the shaping of current ideas, yet this fraction made up so small a class, was so little in touch with the mass of the population, and held its intellectual convictions on such "academic" tenure—that is to say, so uniformly without reinforcement from their own experience of mechanical fact —that with the best intentions they never succeeded in in-

fecting the people at large with their own ideals of a
new order, or in disturbing the incumbents of office in
their tenure and usufruct of the old order.[4] At the same

---

[4] The disturbances of 1848 may serve to show how things run on
this head. The enlightened conceptions and impulses of the literate
minority here joined hands with the irritation of the illiterate due
to intolerable conditions of physical discomfort, with a transient appearance of success, and with the net result that in the end both parties
to the misunderstanding were convicted of contumacy.

By the same token, the meticulous vigilance of the keepers of political antiquities in such an archaic state as Russia, e.g., should
be rated as supererogation, particularly as regards the circulation
of obnoxious literature that purveys excessively modern ideas. In
spite of all efforts the diffusion of the ideas that come in by way of
print scarcely extends beyond the readers; and of these, again, it is
only a fraction that are seriously deranged by what they read; and
the readers are, fortunately, but a negligible percentage of the mass.
The alien ways of thinking that come in in this way, without treading
the ground of the workday routine of industry, may flutter the birds
of plumage that roost in the upper branches of the tree of knowledge,
but all the disturbance will go on over the heads of that multitude the
usufruct of which is of value to the ruling class. The habits of thought
of the latter are made by the workday routine, and provided the routine of the system is not seriously deranged, these will continue in the
same frame of mind, such that any goose-girl can still lead them con-
tentedly to the plucking-sheds. On the other hand the substitution of
a new industrial system, enforcing a workday routine of a different
trend, might easily breed mischief. But, judging by the German example as an object lesson, the wiser precaution against a fatal derangement of the system of irresponsible mastery would apparently
be so far to engender the habit of reading as to make the assimilation
of the new industrial order an easy matter, resulting in a marked advance in efficiency and physical comfort, and then to temper coercion
with a well-conceived cajolery.

The encouragement of illiteracy and the exclusion of obnoxious
literature with a view to maintenance of the *status quo* in religious
concerns may be quite another matter. The derangement to be hedged
against in this case being of a somewhat superficial kind—a change
in the colour-scheme of current superstitions—it is conceivable that

time printed matter is a highly efficient vehicle for the
spread, assimilation, and standardization of habits of
thought that are otherwise consonant with the workday
exigencies of the arts of life; and then, too, the habit
of reading is a nearly indispensable auxiliary of that
machine technology that invaded the German community
in the nineteenth century—less so, of course, at that date
(middle of the century) than at any later time, but
sufficiently so even then to count seriously in the outcome.[5] Now, literacy, both in the higher potency of
"learning" and in the homelier fashion of ability fluently
to read print, was relatively common among the German
people at the time when the new era came on; and the
movement for improving and extending the means of
popular education was already in good practicable shape,
so that deficiencies in this respect could be made good as
fast as they visibly required a remedy. It used to be one
of the stock aspersions on the German community that
it was top-heavy with a redundance of learned men. Fault-
finding on this score has ceased since the latter part of
the century, the learned class having been found useful

heretical teachings might work mischief even in the absence of discrepancies of a technological kind.

[5] It should need no insistence or amplification to gain assent to
the proposition, e.g., that illiteracy is a serious, perhaps the decisive,
obstacle to the present reorganization of the Russian community (or
communities) on the lines of the modern industrial system; nor need
there be any doubt entertained that the higher percentage and higher
range of literacy among the Germans or the English-speaking peoples
accounts for much of their superior industrial efficiency. Under the
old regime of handicraft and household industry, illiteracy was by
comparison a trivial deficiency if any.

and the demand for men proficient in the sciences having fully caught up. Meantime the character of this learning, or rather the direction of it, has changed somewhat, the change resulting on the whole in a pronounced shift toward those branches of knowledge that have some technological or commercial value.[6]

As regards the logical relation between the modern industrial advance and the modernized dynastic state in Germany, it may be held that the makers of this state, the policy of the Hohenzollern dynasty from Frederick the Great to William II, have made use of all available

[6] The supererogatory character of German learning under the old regime is doubtless connected with the absence of a large-scale technology of such a kind as to obtrude questions of wide theoretical bearing. The organization of social life on class lines and the standardization of it in terms of putative worth and authenticity, birth and antecedents, will also have contributed to a bias in favour of putative theoretical constructions and an interest in the lore of intrinsic, that is to say metaphysical, creatures and characters rather than in matter-of-fact. While those classes whose conventional standard of propriety would not admit their employment in useful or gainful occupations were prevented by their ubiquitous poverty from going consistently into a life of sports and standardized dissipation, at least on such a scale and with such generality as to take up the slack of the respectable classes; learning, being a form of dissipation within the reach of this very numerous and very impecunious gentry, came in for a larger share of attention at their hands and came to be rated more confidently as a mark of gentility than in England, e.g., or even in France. But learning that is or may be gainful, or that concerns itself with matters germane to the quest of a livelihood or to the ways and means of vulgar industry, cannot well be genteel, more particularly in a community where industry typically is of the vulgar nature of manual labour, and manual labour is conventionally taboo to a gentleman.

technological improvements to extend the dominion and improve the efficiency of the state; or it may be held, on the other hand, that the technological advance which enforced a larger scale of industry and trade, as well as a larger and more expensive equipment and strategy in the art of war, also drove the dynastic state to reorganization on a new and enlarged plan, involving an increased differentiation of the administrative machinery and a more detailed and exacting control of the sources of revenue. Either view appears to be equally true. German students of the case have commonly adopted the former, somewhat to the neglect of what force there is in the latter view. It should be evident that the minuscular territorial state of the high tide of German particularism, with its crepuscular statesmanship, would have no chance of survival under the conditions prevailing in Europe in the nineteenth century. It is equally evident that those dynastic statesmen within this circle of particularism who, either by force of insight or by force of special exigencies and tentative expedients, were led to take advantage of the larger and mechanically more efficient devices of the new age would enjoy a differential advantage as against their conservative neighbours, and would in the end supplant them in the domain of statecraft and presently take over their substance—the dynastic state being necessarily of a competitive, or rapacious, character, and free to use any expedient that comes to hand. It is a case of selective survival working out through the competitive manœuvres of those who had the administration of the one and the other policy in hand. When the state of the industrial arts had so extended the physical reach of civil administration and political strategy as definitively to make a large-scale national organization practicable, the old order of self-sufficient petty principalities became impossible. This change reached the German territories at a later date than the rest of western Europe, and it did not take effect in a reorganization of national life until so late a date that the retardation is a matter of surprise in spite of all the explanations offered by the historians. But in consequence of this retardation the magnitude of the reorganization when it came was also such as to leave the historians somewhat at a loss to account for it without recourse to race characteristics imputed *ad hoc* and the magical effects of a nepotic predilection on the part of Providence.

By wise management on the part of the dynastic statesmen who have had the direction of policy and the control of the administrative machinery, the rapidly increasing material efficiency of the German community, due to the introduction of the modern state of the industrial arts, has successfully been turned to the use of the state, in a degree not approached elsewhere in western Europe; so that in effect the community stands to the Hohenzollern state somewhat in the relation of a dynastic estate, a quasi-manorial demesne or domain, to be administered for dynastic ends, very much after the fashion of the cameralistic administration of fiscal affairs in the territorial states of Germany a hundred years ago. This

subservience of the community to dynastic ends and
dynastic management has been secured in the gross by a
policy of warlike aggression, and in detail by a system
of bureaucratic surveillance and unremitting interference
in the private life of subjects. It goes without saying
that there is no secure ground for such a scheme of
dynastic usufruct and control except in the loyal support
of popular sentiment; and it likewise goes without saying that such a state of popular sentiment can be maintained only by unremitting habituation, discipline sagaciously and relentlessly directed to this end. More
particularly must the course of habituation to this end be
persistent and unwavering if it is to hold the personal
allegiance of a body of subjects exposed to the disintegrating discipline of modern life; where the machine
industry constantly enforces the futility of personal force
and prerogative in the face of wide-sweeping inanimate
agencies and mechanical process, and where the ubiquitous haggling of the price system constantly teaches that
every man is his own keeper. It is a matter of common
notoriety that all this has been taken care of with unexampled thoroughness and effect under the Prussian
rule.[7]

Chief of the agencies that have kept the submissive
allegiance of the German people to the state intact is,

---

[7] Perhaps the most concise and yet the most illuminating presentation of this Prussian economic policy, typically as pursued by Frederick the Great, is that of Professor Schmoller, *The Mercantile System.* (Translation reprinted in *Economic Classics*, ed. Ashley.)

of course, successful warfare, seconded by the disciplinary effects of warlike preparation and indoctrination with warlike arrogance and ambitions. The attention deliberately given to these concerns is also a fact of common notoriety; so much so, indeed, that the spokesmen of the system have come to take it for granted as a matter of course, and so are apt to overlook it. The experience of war induces a warlike frame of mind; and the pursuit of war, being an exercise in the following of one's leader and execution of arbitrary orders, induces an animus of enthusiastic subservience and unquestioning obedience to authority. What is a military organization in war is a servile organization in peace. The system is the same, and the popular animus requisite to its successful working is the same in either case. It reaches its best efficiency in either case, in war or peace, only when the habit of arbitrary authority and unquestioning obedience has been so thoroughly ingrained that subservience has become a passionate aspiration with the subject population, where the habit of allegiance has attained that degree of automatism that the subject's ideal of liberty has come to be permission to obey orders—somewhat after the fashion in which theologians interpret the freedom of the faithful, whose supreme privilege it is to fulfil all the divine commands. Such an ideal growth of patriotic sentiment appears to have been attained, in a tolerable degree of approximation, in the German case, if one is to credit the popular encomiasts, who explain that "duty," in the sense indicated, combined with "freedom," makes up the goal to which the German spirit aspires. "Duty," of course, comprises the exercise of arbitrary command on the part of the superior as well as the obedience of the inferior, but such arbitrary authority is exercised only in due submission to higher authority, until it traces back to the dynastic head—who, it would appear, in turn exercises only a delegated authority, vested in his person by divine grace.

The phrase, "dynastic state," is here used in preference to "patrimonial state," not because there is any substantial difference between the two conceptions, but rather because the later German spokesmen for the German state, as it is seen at work during the Imperial era, appear to have an aversion to the latter term, which they wish to apply to the territorial state of the pre-imperial time, in contradistinction to the state as rehabilitated in the adoption of a constitution comprising a modicum of representative institutions and parliamentary forms. The designation "dynastic" is still applicable, however; and in effect the constitutional rehabilitation has not taken the German state out of the category of patrimonial monarchies. The difference resulting from the Imperial constitution is in large part a difference in form and in administrative machinery; it does not greatly circumscribe the effectual powers, rights, and discretion of the Imperial crown; still less does it seriously limit the powers of the Prussian crown, or the dynastic claims of suzerainty vested in the Prussian succession. Even under the constitution it is a government resting on the suzerainty of the crown, not on the discretion of a parliamentary body. It is, in other words, a government of constitutionally mitigated absolutism, not of parliamentary discretion tempered with monarchy.

In the shift from particularism to the Empire no revolutionary move was made, comparable with the change initiated in the United Kingdom by the revolution of 1688; if such a shift to a democratic constitution is to overtake the German state, that move lies still in the future. The changes introduced with the constitution of the Empire, in so far as they have been effectual, were such as were made necessary by the larger scale on which the new national jurisdiction was required to work, and involved only such a modicum of delegated jurisdiction to parliamentary and local organizations as would be expedient for the control and usufruct of territory and resources, population, trade, and industry, that exceed the effectual reach of the simpler bureaucracy character-istic of the small territorial state. The economic policy of the Imperial era has still continued to be a "cameralis-tic" policy, with such concessive adaptations as the mod-ern scale and complexity of economic affairs necessitate. It is true, under the administration of Bismarck there was a perceptible drift in the direction of those "liberal" pre-conceptions that subconsciously biased the endeavours of all European statesmen through much of the latter half of the century; but this drift, which showed itself in the Bismarckian policies of trade, colonies, and incipient min-isterial responsibility, never came to anything conclusive under his hands; nor had it gone so far as in any appreciable degree to embarrass the endeavours of the later emperor directed to the complete revendication of the imperial suzerainty. The paramount authority, under the Imperial constitution, vests in the crown, not in any representative body, although this holds with even less qualification in the Prussian than in the Imperial government; but Germany has, in these respects, been progressively "Prussianized" during the Imperial era, while Prussia has not been drawing toward the lines of that democratic autonomy that holds the rest of north and central Europe, at least on a qualified and provisional tenure.

Imperial Germany does not depart sensibly from the pattern of Prussia under Frederick the Great, in respect of its national policies or the aims and methods of government control, nor do the preconceptions of its statesmen differ at all widely from those prevalent among the dynastic jobbers of that predaceous era of state-making. The difference touches mainly the machinery of politics and administration, and it is mainly of such a character as is dictated by an endeavour to turn the results of modern industry and commerce to account for the purposes that once seemed good to the pragmatists of that earlier era. That such is the case need give no occasion for dispraise. At least there is nothing of the kind implied here. It may be an untoward state of things, perhaps, though sufficient proof of such a contention has not yet come in sight. It is specifically called to mind here because it is one of the main factors in the case of Imperial Germany considered as a phase of the development of institutions in the western culture.

This modern state of the industrial arts that so has led to the rehabilitation of a dynastic state in Germany on a scale exceeding what had been practicable in earlier times —this technological advance was not made in Germany but was borrowed, directly or at the second remove, from the English-speaking peoples, primarily, and in the last resort almost wholly, from England. What has been insisted on above is that British use and wont in other than the technological respect was not taken over by the German community at the same time. The result being that Germany offers what is by contrast with England an anomaly, in that it shows the working of the modern state of the industrial arts as worked out by the English, but without the characteristic range of institutions and convictions that have grown up among English-speaking peoples concomitantly with the growth of this modern state of the industrial arts. Germany combines the results of English experience in the development of modern technology with a state of the other arts of life more nearly equivalent to what prevailed in England before the modern industrial regime came on; so that the German people have been enabled to take up the technological heritage of the English without having paid for it in the habits of thought, the use and wont, induced in the English community by the experience involved in achieving it. Modern technology has come to the Germans ready-made, without the cultural consequences which its gradual development and continued use has entailed among the people whose experience initiated it and determined the course of its development.

The position of the Germans is not precisely unique in this respect; in a degree the same general proposition will apply to the other western nations,[8] but it applies to none with anything like the same breadth. The case of Germany is unexampled among western nations both as regards the abruptness, thoroughness, and amplitude of its appropriation of this technology, and as regards the archaism of its cultural furniture at the date of this appropriation.

It will be in place to call to mind in this connexion . . . the advantage of borrowing the technological arts rather than developing them by home growth. In the transit from one community to another the technological elements so borrowed do not carry over the fringe of other cultural elements that have grown up about them in the course of their development and use. The new expedients come to hand stripped of whatever has only a putative or conventional bearing on their use. On the lower levels of culture this fringe of conventional or putative exactions bound up with the usufruct of given technological devices would be mainly of the nature of magical or religious observances; but on the higher levels, in cases of the class

---

[8] It applies with at least equal cogency to the case of Japan, and indeed the Japanese case is strikingly analogous to that of Germany in this connexion.

here in question, they are more likely to be conventionalities embedded in custom and to some extent in law, of a secular kind, but frequently approaching the mandatory character of religious observances, as e.g., the requirement of a decently expensive standard of living.

# ON THE STATE
# AND ITS RELATION
# TO WAR AND PEACE[1]

To many thoughtful men ripe in worldly wisdom it is known of a verity that war belongs indefeasibly in the Order of Nature. Contention, with manslaughter, is indispensable in human intercourse, at the same time that it conduces to the increase and diffusion of the manly virtues. So, likewise, the unspoiled youth of the race, in the period of adolescence and aspiring manhood, also commonly share this gift of insight and back it with a generous commendation of all the martial qualities; and women of nubile age and no undue maturity gladly meet them half-way.

On the other hand, the mothers of the people are commonly unable to see the use of it all. It seems a waste of dear-bought human life, with a large sum of nothing to show for it. So also many men of an elderly turn, prematurely or otherwise, are ready to lend their countenance to the like disparaging appraisal; it may be that the spirit of powess in them runs at too low a tension, or they may have outlived the more vivid appreciation of the spiritual values involved. There are many, also, with a turn for exhortation, who find employment for their

---

[1] Reprinted from *On the Nature of Peace and the Terms of Its Perpetuation*, 1917, pp. 1–30.

best faculties in attesting the well-known atrocities and
futility of war.

Indeed, not infrequently such advocates of peace will
devote their otherwise idle powers to their work of exhortation without stipend or subsidy. And they uniformly
make good their contention that the currently accepted
conception of the nature of war—General Sherman's formula—is substantially correct. All the while it is to be
admitted that all this axiomatic exhortation has no visible
effect on the course of events or on the popular temper
touching warlike enterprise. Indeed, no equal volume of
speech can be more incontrovertible or less convincing
than the utterances of the peace advocates, whether subsidized or not. "War is Bloodier than Peace." This would
doubtless be conceded without argument, but also without prejudice. Hitherto the pacifists' quest of a basis for
enduring peace, it must be admitted, has brought home
nothing tangible—with the qualification, of course, that
the subsidized pacifists have come in for the subsidy. So
that, after searching the recesses of their imagination,
able-bodied pacifists whose loquacity has never been at
fault hitherto have been brought to ask: "What Shall
We Say?"

Under these circumstances it will not be out of place
to inquire into the nature of this peace about which swings
this wide orbit of opinion and argument. At the most,
such an inquiry can be no more gratuitous and no more
nugatory than the controversies that provoke it. The

intrinsic merits of peace at large, as against those of war-like enterprise, it should be said, do not here come in question. That question lies in the domain of precon-ceived opinion, so that for the purposes of this inquiry it will have no significance except as a matter to be in-quired into; the main point of the inquiry being the na-ture, causes, and consequences of such a preconception favouring peace, and the circumstances that make for a contrary preconception in favour of war.

By and large, any breach of the peace in modern times is an official act and can be taken only on initiative of the governmental establishment, the state. The national au-thorities may, of course, be driven to take such a step by pressure of warlike popular sentiment. Such, e.g., is pre-sumed to have been the case in the United States' attack on Spain during the McKinley administration; but the more that comes to light of the intimate history of that episode, the more evident does it become that the popular war sentiment to which the administration yielded had been somewhat sedulously "mobilized" with a view to such yielding and such a breach. So also in the case of the Boer War, the move was made under sanction of a popular war spirit, which, again, did not come to a head without shrewd surveillance and direction. And so again in the current European war, in the case, e.g., of Ger-many, where the initiative was taken, the state plainly had the full support of popular sentiment, and may even be said to have precipitated the war in response to this urgent popular aspiration; and here again it is a matter of notoriety that the popular sentiment had long been sedulously nursed and "mobilized" to that effect, so that the populace was assiduously kept in spiritual readiness for such an event. The like is less evident as regards the United Kingdom, and perhaps also as regards the other Allies.

And such appears to have been the common run of the facts as regards all the greater wars of the last one hundred years—what may be called the "public" wars of this modern era, as contrasted with the "private" or administrative wars which have been carried on in a corner by one and another of the Great Powers against hapless barbarians, from time to time, in the course of administrative routine.

It is also evident from the run of the facts as exemplified in these modern wars that, while any breach of the peace takes place only on the initiative and at the discretion of the government, or state,[2] it is always requisite in furtherance of such warlike enterprise to cherish and eventually to mobilize popular sentiment in support of any warlike move. Due fomentation of a warlike animus is indispensable to the procuring and maintenance of a suitable equipment with which eventually to break the peace, as well as to ensure a diligent prosecution of such enterprise when once it has been undertaken. Such a spirit of militant patriotism as may serviceably be mobilized in support of warlike enterprise has accordingly

---

[2] A modern nation constitutes a state only in respect of or with ulterior bearing on the question of international peace or war.

been a condition precedent to any people's entry into the modern Concert of Nations. This Concert of Nations is a Concert of Powers, and it is only as a Power that any nation plays its part in the concert, all the while that "power" here means eventual warlike force.

Such a people as the Chinese, e.g., not pervaded with an adequate patriotic spirit, comes into the Concert of Nations not as a Power but as a bone of contention. Not that the Chinese fall short in any of the qualities that conduce to efficiency and welfare in time of peace, but they appear, in effect, to lack that certain "solidarity of prowess" by virtue of which they should choose to be (collectively) formidable rather than (individually) fortunate and upright; and the modern civilized nations are not in a position, nor in a frame of mind, to tolerate a neighbour whose only claim on their consideration falls under the category of peace on earth and good-will among men. China appears hitherto not to have been a serviceable people for warlike ends, except in so far as the resources of that country have been taken over and converted to warlike uses by some alien power working to its own ends. Such have been the several alien dynasties that have seized upon that country from time to time and have achieved dominion by usufruct of its unwarlike forces. Such has been the nature of the Manchu empire of the recent past, and such is the evident purpose of the prospective Japanese usufruct of the same country and its populace. Meantime the Chinese people appear to be incorrigibly peaceable, being scarcely willing to fight in any

concerted fashion even when driven into a corner by un-
provoked aggression, as in the present juncture. Such a
people is very exceptional. Among civilized nations there
are, broadly speaking, none of that temper, with the sole
exception of the Chinese—if the Chinese are properly to
be spoken of as a nation.

Modern warfare makes such large and direct use of
the industrial arts, and depends for its successful prosecution so largely on a voluminous and unremitting supply
of civilian services and wrought goods, that any inoffensive and industrious people, such as the Chinese, could
doubtless now be turned to good account by any warlike power that might have the disposal of their working
forces. To make their industrial efficiency count in this
way toward warlike enterprise and imperial dominion,
the usufruct of any such inoffensive and unpatriotic populace would have to fall into the hands of an alien
governmental establishment. And no alien government
resting on the support of a home population trained in
the habits of democracy or given over to ideals of common honesty in national concerns could hopefully undertake the enterprise. This work of empire-building out of
unwarlike materials could apparently be carried out only
by some alien power hampered by no reserve of scruple,
and backed by a servile populace of its own, imbued with
an impeccable loyalty to its masters and with a suitably
bellicose temper, as, e.g., Imperial Japan or Imperial
Germany.

However, for the commonplace national enterprise the

common run will do very well. Any populace imbued with a reasonable measure of patriotism will serve as ways and means to warlike enterprise under competent management, even if it is not habitually prone to a bellicose temper. Rightly managed, ordinary patriotic sentiment may readily be mobilized for warlike adventure by any reasonably adroit and single-minded body of statesmen—of which there is abundant illustration. All the peoples of Christendom are possessed of a sufficiently alert sense of nationality, and by tradition and current usage all the national governments of Christendom are warlike establishments, at least in the defensive sense; and the distinction between the defensive and the offensive in international intrigue is a technical matter that offers no great difficulty. None of these nations is of such an incorrigibly peaceable temper that they can be counted on to keep the peace consistently in the ordinary course of events.

Peace established by the state, or resting in the discretion of the state, is necessarily of the nature of an armistice, in effect terminable at will and on short notice. It is maintained only on conditions, stipulated by express convention or established by custom, and there is always the reservation, tacit or explicit, that recourse will be had to arms in case the "national interests" or the punctilios of international etiquette are traversed by the act or defection of any rival government or its subjects. The more nationally minded the government or its subject populace, the readier the response to the call of any such

opportunity for an unfolding of prowess. The most peaceable governmental policy of which Christendom has experience is a policy of "watchful waiting," with a jealous
eye to the emergence of any occasion for national resentment; and the most irretrievably shameful dereliction
of duty on the part of any civilized government would
be its eventual insensibility to the appeal of a "just war."
Under any governmental auspices, as the modern world
knows governments, the keeping of the peace comes at
its best under the precept, "Speak softly and carry a big
stick." But the case for peace is more precarious than the
wording of the aphorism would indicate, in as much as
in practical fact the "big stick" is an obstacle to soft
speech. Evidently, in the light of recent history, if the
peace is to be kept it will have to come about irrespective of governmental management—in spite of the state
rather than by its good offices. At the best, the state, or
the government, is an instrumentality for making peace,
not for perpetuating it.

Anyone who is interested in the nature and derivation
of governmental institutions and establishments in Europe, in any but the formal respect, should be able to
satisfy his curiosity by looking over the shoulders of the
professed students of Political Science. Quite properly
and profitably that branch of scholarship is occupied
with the authentic pedigree of these institutions, and
with the documentary instruments in the case; since Political Science is, after all, a branch of theoretical juris-

prudence and is concerned about a formally competent analysis of the recorded legal powers. The material circumstances from which these institutions once took their beginning, and the exigencies which have governed the rate and direction of their later growth and mutation, as well as the *de facto* bearing of the institutional scheme on the material welfare or the cultural fortunes of the given community—while all these matters of fact may be germane to the speculations of Political Theory, they are not intrinsic to its premises, to the logical sequence of its inquiry, or to its theoretical findings. The like is also true, of course, as regards that system of habits of thought, that current frame of mind, in which any given institutional scheme necessarily is grounded, and without the continued support of which any given scheme of governmental institutions or policy would become nugatory and so would pass into the province of legal fiction. All these are not idle matters in the purview of the student of Political Science, but they remain after all substantially extraneous to the structure of political theory; and in so far as matters of this class are to be brought into the case at all, the specialists in the field cannot fairly be expected to contribute anything beyond an occasional *obiter dictum*. There can be no discourteous presumption, therefore, in accepting the general theorems of current political theory without prejudice, and looking past the received theoretical formulations for a view of the substantial grounds on which the governmental establishments have grown into shape, and the circumstances, material and spiritual, that surround their continued working and effect.

By lineal descent the governmental establishments and the powers with which they are vested, in all the Christian nations, are derived from the feudal establishments of the Middle Ages; which, in turn, are of a predatory origin and of an irresponsible character.[3] In nearly all instances, but more particularly among the nations that are accounted characteristically modern, the existing establishments have been greatly altered from the medieval pattern, by concessive adaptation to later exigencies or by a more or less revolutionary innovation. The degree of their modernity is (conventionally) measured, roughly, by the degree in which they have departed from the medieval pattern. Wherever the unavoidable concessions have been shrewdly made with a view to conserving the autonomy and irresponsibility of the governmental establishment, or the "state," and where the state of national sentiment has been led to favour this work of conservation, as, e.g., in the case of Austria, Spain, or Prussia, there the modern outcome has been what may be called a Dynastic State. Where, on the other hand, the run of national sentiment has departed notably from the ancient holding-ground of loyal abnegation, and has enforced a measure of revolutionary innovation, as in the case of France or of the English-speaking peoples, there the modern outcome has been an (ostensibly) democratic

---

[3] The partial and dubious exception of the Scandinavian countries or of Switzerland need raise no question on this head.

commonwealth of ungraded citizens. But the contrast so indicated is a contrast of divergent variants rather than of opposites. These two type-forms may be taken as the extreme and inclusive limits of variation among the governmental establishments with which the modern world is furnished.[4]

The effectual difference between these two theoretically contrasted types of governmental establishments is doubtless grave enough, and for many purposes it is consequential, but it is after all not of such a nature as need greatly detain the argument at this point. The two differ less, in effect, in that range of their functioning which comes in question here than in their bearing on the community's fortunes apart from questions of war and peace. In all cases there stand over in this bearing certain primary characteristics of the ancient regime, which all these modern establishments have in common, though not all in an equal degree of preservation and effectiveness. They are, e.g., all vested with certain attributes of "sovereignty." In all cases the citizen still proves on closer attention to be in some measure a "subject" of the state, in that he is invariably conceived to owe a "duty" to the constituted authorities in one respect and another. All civilized governments take cognizance of Treason, Sedition, and the like; and all good citizens are not only content but profoundly insistent on the clear duty of the

---

[4] Cf., e.g., Eduard Meyer, *England: Its Political Organisation and Development*, chap. 2.

citizen on this head. The bias of loyalty is not a matter on which argument is tolerated. By virtue of this bias of loyalty, or "civic duty"—which still has much of the colour of feudal allegiance—the governmental establishment is within its rights in coercively controlling and directing the actions of the citizen, or subject, in those respects that so lie within his duty; as also in authoritatively turning his abilities to account for the purposes that so lie within the governmental discretion, as, e.g., the Common Defence.

These rights and powers still remain to the governmental establishment even at the widest democratic departure from that ancient pattern of masterful tutelage and usufruct that marked the old-fashioned patrimonial state—and that still marks the better preserved ones among its modern derivatives. And so intrinsic to these governmental establishments are these discretionary powers, and by so unfailing a popular bias are they still accounted a matter of course and of axiomatic necessity, that they have invariably been retained also among the attributes of those democratic governments that trace their origin to a revolutionary break with the old order.

To many, all this will seem a pedantic taking note of commonplaces—as if it were worth while remarking that the existing governments are vested with the indispensable attributes of government. Yet history records an instance at variance with this axiomatic rule, a rule which

is held to be an unavoidable deliverance of common-
sense. And it is by no means an altogether unique instance.
It may serve to show that these characteristic and unimpeachable powers that invest all current governmental
establishments are, after all, to be rated as the marks of a
particular species of governments, and not characteristics
of the genus of governmental establishments at large.
These powers answer to an acquired bias, not to an underlying trait of human nature; a matter of habit, not of
heredity.

Such an historical instance is the so-called Republic, or
Commonwealth, of Iceland—tenth to thirteenth centuries. Its case is looked on by students of history as a
spectacular anomaly, because it admitted none of these
primary powers of government in its constituted authorities. And yet, for contrast with these matter-of-course preconceptions of these students of history, it is well to note
that in the deliberations of those ancients who installed
the Republic for the management of their joint concerns,
any inclusion of such powers in its competency appears
never to have been contemplated, not even to the extent
of its being rejected. This singularity—as it would be
rated by modern statesmen and students—was in no degree a new departure in state-making on the part of the
founders of the Republic. They had no knowledge of
such powers, duties, and accountabilities, except as un-
wholesome features of a novel and alien scheme of irresponsible oppression that was sought to be imposed on
them by Harald Fairhair, and which they incontinently

made it their chief and immediate business to evade. They also set up no joint or collective establishment with powers for the Common Defence, nor does it appear that such a notion had occurred to them.

In the history of its installation there is no hint that the men who set up this Icelandic Commonwealth had any sense of the need, or even of the feasibility, of such a coercive government as would be involved in concerted preparation for the common defence. Subjection to personal rule, or to official rule in any degree of attenuation, was not comprised in their traditional experience of citizenship; and it was necessarily out of the elements comprised in this traditional experience that the new structure would have to be built up. The new commonwealth was necessarily erected on the premises afforded by the received scheme of use and wont; and this received scheme had come down out of pre-feudal conditions, without having passed under the discipline of that regime of coercion which the feudal system had imposed on the rest of Europe, and so had established as an "immemorial usage" and a "second nature" among the populations of Christendom. The resulting character of the Icelandic Commonwealth is sufficiently striking when contrasted with the case of the English commonwealth of the seventeenth century, or the later French and American republics. These, all and several, came out of a protracted experience in feudalistic state-making and state policy; and the common defence—frequently on the offensive— with its neccessary coercive machinery and its submissive loyalty, consequently would take the central place in the resulting civic structure.

To close the tale of the Icelandic commonwealth it may be added that their republic of insubordinate citizens presently fell into default, systematic misuse, under the disorders brought on by an accumulation of wealth, and that it died of legal fiction and constitutional formalities after some experience at the hands of able and ambitious statesmen in contact with an alien government drawn on the coercive plan. The clay vessel failed to make good among the iron pots, and so proved its unfitness to survive in the world of Christian nations—very much as the Chinese are today at the mercy of the defensive rapacity of the Powers.

> And the mercy that we gave them
> Was to sink them in the sea,
> Down on the coast of High Barbarie.

No doubt, it will be accepted as an axiomatic certainty that the establishment of a commonwealth after the fashion of the Icelandic Republic, without coercive authority or provision for the common defence, and without a sense of subordination or collective responsibility among its citizens, would be out of all question under existing circumstances of politics and international trade. Nor would such a commonwealth be workable on the scale and at the pace imposed by modern industrial and commercial conditions, even apart from international jealousy and ambitions, provided the sacred rights of ownership were to be maintained in something like their current shape. And yet something of a drift of popular sentiment, and indeed something of deliberate endeavour, setting in the direction of such a harmless and helpless national organization is always visible in western Europe, throughout modern times; particularly through the eighteenth and the early half of the nineteenth centuries; and more particularly among the English-speaking peoples and, with a difference, among the French. The Dutch and the Scandinavian countries answer more doubtfully to the same characterization.

The movement in question is known to history as the Liberal, Rationalistic, Humanitarian, or Individualistic departure. Its ideal, when formulated, is spoken of as the System of Natural Rights; and its goal in the way of a national establishment has been well characterized by its critics as the Police State, or the Night-Watchman State. The gains made in this direction, or perhaps better the inroads of this animus in national ideals, are plainly to be set down as a shift in the direction of peace and amity; but it is also plain that the shift of ground so initiated by this strain of sentiment has never reached a conclusion and never has taken effect in anything like an effectual working arrangement. Its practical consequences have been of the nature of abatement and defection in the pursuit of national ambitions and dynastic enterprise, rather than a creative work of installing any institutional furniture suitable to its own ends. It has in effect gone no farther than what would be called an incipient correction of abuses.

The highest rise, as well as the decline, of this movement lie within the nineteenth century.

In point of time, the decay of this amiable conceit of *laissez-faire* in national policy coincides with the period of great advance in the technology of transport and communication in the nineteenth century. Perhaps, on a larger outlook, it should rather be said that the run of national ambitions and animosities had, in the eighteenth and nineteenth centuries, suffered a degree of decay through the diffusion of this sentimental predilection for Natural Liberty, and that this decline of the manlier aspirations was then arrested and corrected by help of these improvements in the technological situation; which enabled a closer and more coercive control to be exercised over larger areas, and at the same time enabled a more massive aggregate of warlike force to strike more effectively at a greater distance. This whole episode of the rise and decline of *laissez-faire* in modern history is perhaps best to be conceived as a transient weakening of nationalism, by neglect; rather than anything like the growth of a new and more humane ideal of national intercourse. Such would be the appraisal to be had at the hands of those who speak for a strenuous national life and for the arbitrament of sportsmanlike contention in human affairs. And the latter-day growth of more militant aspirations, together with the more settled and sedulous attention to a development of control and of formidable armaments, such as followed on through the latter half of the nineteenth century, would then be rated as a resumption of those older aims and ideals that had been falling somewhat into abeyance in the slack-water days of Liberalism.

There is much to be said for this latter view; and, indeed, much has been said for it, particularly by the spokesmen of imperialist politics. This bias of Natural Liberty has been associated in history with the English-speaking peoples, more intimately and more extensively than with any other. Not that this amiable conceit is in any peculiar degree a race characteristic of this group of peoples; nor even that the history of its rise and decline runs wholly within the linguistic frontiers indicated by this characterization. The French and the Dutch have borne their share, and at an earlier day Italian sentiment and speculation lent its impulsion to the same genial drift of faith and aspiration. But, by historical accident, its centre of gravity and of diffusion has lain with the English-speaking communities during the period when this bias made history and left its impress on the institutional scheme of the western civilization. By grace of what may, for the present purpose, be called historical accident, it happens that the interval of history during which the bias of Natural Liberty made visible headway was also a period during which these English-speaking peoples, among whom its effects are chiefly visible, were relatively secure from international disturbance, by force of inaccessibility. Little strain was put upon their sense of national solidarity or national prowess; so little, indeed, that there was some danger of their patriotic animosity falling into decay by disuse; and then they were also busy with other things. Peaceable intercourse, it is true, was relatively easy, active, and far-reaching—eighteenth and nineteenth centuries—as compared with what had been the case before that time; but warlike intercourse on such a scale as would constitute a substantial menace to any large nation was nearly out of the question, so far as regards the English-speaking peoples. The available means of aggression, as touches the case of these particular communities, were visibly and consciously inadequate as compared with the means of defence. The means of internal or intra-national control or coercion were also less well provided by the state of the arts current at that time than the means of peaceable intercourse. These means of transport and communication were, at that stage of their development, less well suited for the purposes of far-reaching warlike strategy and the exercise of surveillance and coercion over large spaces than for the purposes of peaceable traffic.

But the continued improvement in the means of communication during the nineteenth century presently upset that situation, and so presently began to neutralize the geographical quarantine which had hedged about these communities that were inclined to let well enough alone. The increasing speed and accuracy of movement in shipping, due to the successful introduction of steam, as well as the concomitant increasing size of the units of equipment, all run to this effect and presently set at naught the peace barriers of sea and weather. So also the development of railways and their increasing availability for strategic uses, together with the far-reaching coordination of movement made possible by their means and by the telegraph; all of which is further facilitated by the increasing mass and density of population. Improvements in the technology of arms and armament worked to the like effect, of setting the peace of any community on an increasingly precarious footing, through the advantage which this new technology gave to a ready equipment and a rapid mobilization. The new state of the industrial arts serviceable for warlike enterprise put an increasingly heavy premium on readiness for offence or defence, but more particularly it all worked increasingly to the advantage of the offensive. It put the Fabian strategy out of date, and led to the doctrine of a defensive offence.

Gradually it came true, with the continued advance in those industrial arts that lend themselves to strategic uses, and it came also to be realized, that no corner of the earth was any longer secure by mere favour of distance and natural difficulty, from eventual aggression at the hands of any provident and adventurous assailant—even by help of a modicum of defensive precaution. The fear of aggression then came definitively to take the place of international good-will and became the chief motive in public policy, so fast and so far as the state of the industrial arts continued to incline the balance of advantage to the side of the aggressor. All of which served greatly to strengthen the hands of those statesmen who, by interest or temperament, were inclined to imperialistic enterprise. Since that period all armament has conventionally been accounted defensive, and all statesmen have professed that the common defence is their chief concern. Professedly all armament has been designed to keep the peace; so much of a shadow of the peaceable bias there still stands over.

Throughout this latest phase of modern civilization the avowed fear of aggression has served as apology, possibly as provocation in fact, to national armaments; and throughout the same period any analysis of the situation will finally run the chain of fear back to Prussia as the, putative or actual, centre of disturbance and apprehension. No doubt, Prussian armament has taken the lead and forced the pace among the nations of Christendom; but the Prussian policy, too, has been diligently covered with the same decorous plea of needful provision for the common defence and an unremitting solicitude for international peace—to which has been added the canny afterthought of the "defensive offence."

It is characteristic of this era of armed peace that in all these extensive preparations for breaking the peace any formal avowal of other than a defensive purpose has at all times been avoided as an insufferable breach of diplomatic decorum. It is likewise characteristic of the same era that armaments have unremittingly been increased, beyond anything previously known; and that all men have known all the while that the inevitable outcome of this avowedly defensive armament must eventually be

war on an unprecedented scale and of unexampled fe-
rocity. It would be neither charitable nor otherwise to the
point to call attention to the reflection which this state of
the case throws on the collective sagacity or the good
faith of the statesmen who have had the management of
affairs. It is not practicable to imagine how such an outcome as the present could have been brought about by any
degree of stupidity or incapacity alone, nor is it easier to
find evidence that the utmost sagacity of the statecraft
engaged has had the slightest mitigating effect on the
evil consummation to which the whole case has been
brought. It has long been a commonplace among observers of public events that these professedly defensive
warlike preparations have in effect been preparations for
breaking the peace; against which, at least ostensibly, a
remedy had been sought in the preparation of still heavier
armaments, with full realization that more armament
would unfailingly entail a more unsparing and more disastrous war—which sums up the statecraft of the past
half-century. . . .

It may well be that the plea of defensive preparation
advanced by the statesmen, Prussian and others, in apology for competitive armaments is a diplomatic subterfuge
—there are indications that such has commonly been the
case; but even if it commonly is visibly disingenuous, the
need of making such a plea to cover more sinister designs
is itself an evidence that an avowedly predatory enterprise no longer meets with the requisite popular approval.

Even if an exception to this rule be admitted in the recent attitude of the German people, it is to be recalled that the exception was allowed to stand only transiently, and that presently the avowal of a predatory design in this case was urgently disclaimed in the face of adversity. Even those who speak most fluently for the necessity of war, and for its merits as a needed discipline in the manly virtues, are constrained by the prevailing sentiment to deprecate its necessity.

Yet it is equally evident that when once a warlike enterprise has been entered upon so far as to commit the nation to hostilities, it will have the cordial support of popular sentiment even if it is patently an aggressive war. Indeed, it is quite a safe generalization that when hostilities have once been got fairly under way by the interested statesmen, the patriotic sentiment of the nation may confidently be counted on to back the enterprise irrespective of the merits of the quarrel. But even if the national sentiment is in this way to be counted on as an incidental matter of course, it is also to be kept in mind in this connexion that any quarrel so entered upon by any nation will forthwith come to have the moral approval of the community. Dissenters will of course be found, sporadically, who do not readily fall in with the prevailing animus; but as a general proposition it will still hold true that any such quarrel forthwith becomes a just quarrel in the eyes of those who have so been committed to it.

A corollary following from this general theorem may be worth noting in the same connexion. Any politician who succeeds in embroiling his country in a war, however nefarious, becomes a popular hero and is reputed a wise and righteous statesman, at least for the time being. Illustrative instances need perhaps not, and indeed cannot gracefully, be named; most popular heroes and reputed statesmen belong in this class.

Another corollary, which bears more immediately on the question in hand, follows also from the same general proposition: Since the ethical values involved in any given international contest are substantially of the nature of afterthought or accessory, they may safely be left on one side in any endeavour to understand or account for any given outbreak of hostilities. The moral indignation of both parties to the quarrel is to be taken for granted, as being the statesman's chief and necessary ways and means of bringing any warlike enterprise to a head and floating it to a creditable finish. It is a precipitate of the partisan animosity that inspires both parties and holds them to their duty of self-sacrifice and devastation, and at its best it will chiefly serve as a cloak of self-righteousness to extenuate any exceptionally profligate excursions in the conduct of hostilities.

Any warlike enterprise that is hopefully to be entered on must have the moral sanction of the community, or of an effective majority in the community. It consequently becomes the first concern of the warlike statesman to put this moral force in train for the adventure on which he is bent. And there are two main lines of motivation by which the spiritual forces of any Christian nation may so be mobilized for warlike adventure: (1) the preservation or furtherance of the community's material interests, real or fancied, and (2) vindication of the national honour. To these should perhaps be added as a third, the advancement and perpetuation of the nation's "Culture"; that is to say, of its habitual scheme of use and wont. It is a nice question whether, in practical effect, the aspiration to perpetuate the national Culture is consistently to be distinguished from the vindication of the national honour. There is perhaps the distinction to be made that "the perpetuation of the national Culture" lends a readier countenance to gratuitous aggression and affords a broader cover for incidental atrocities, since the enemies of the national Culture will necessarily be conceived as an inferior and obstructive people, falling beneath the rules of commonplace decorum.

Those material interests for which modern nations are in the habit of taking to arms are commonly of a fanciful character, in that they commonly have none but an imaginary net value to the community at large. Such are, e.g., the national trade or the increase of the national territory. These and the like may serve the warlike or dynastic ambitions of the nation's masters; they may also further the interests of office-holders, and more particularly of certain business houses or business men who stand to gain some small advantage by help of the powers in control; but it all signifies nothing more to the common man than an increased bill of governmental expense and a probable increase in the cost of living.

That a nation's trade should be carried in vessels owned by its citizens or registered in its ports will doubtless have some sentimental value to the common run of its citizens, as is shown by the fact that disingenuous politicians always find it worth their while to appeal to this chauvinistic predilection. But it patently is all a completely idle question, in point of material advantage, to anyone but the owners of the vessels; and to these owners it is also of no material consequence under what flag their investments sail, except so far as the government in question may afford them some preferential opportunity for gain—always at the cost of their fellow-citizens. The like is equally true as regards the domicile and the national allegiance of the business men who buy and sell the country's imports and exports. The common man plainly has no slightest material interest in the nationality or the place of residence of those who conduct this traffic; though all the facts go to say that in some puzzle-headed way the common man commonly persuades himself that it does make some occult sort of difference to him; so that he is commonly willing to pay something substantial toward subsidizing business men of his own nationality, in the way of a protective tariff and the like.

The only material advantage to be derived from such a preferential trade policy arises in the case of international hostilities, in which case the home-owned vessels and merchants may on occasion count toward military readiness; although even in that connexion their value is contingent and doubtful. But in this way they may contribute in their degree to a readiness to break off peaceable relations with other countries. It is only for warlike purposes, that is to say for the dynastic ambitions of warlike statesmen, that these preferential contrivances in economic policy have any substantial value; and even in that connexion their expediency is always doubtful. They are a source of national jealousy, and they may on occasion become a help to military strategy when this national jealousy eventuates in hostilities.

The run of the facts touching this matter of national trade policy is something as follows: At the instance of business men who stand to gain by it, and with the cordial support of popular sentiment, the constituted authorities sedulously further the increase of shipping and commerce under protection of the national power. At the same time they spend substance and diplomatic energy in an endeavour to extend the international market facilities open to the country's business men, with a view always to a preferential advantage in favour of these business men, also with the sentimental support of the common man and at his cost. To safeguard these commercial interests, as well as property-holdings of the nation's citizens in foreign parts, the nation maintains naval, military, consular, and diplomatic establishments, at the common expense. The total gains derivable from these commercial and investment interests abroad, under favourable circumstances, will never by any chance equal the cost of the governmental apparatus installed to further and safeguard them. These gains, such as they are, go to the investors and business men engaged in these enterprises; while the costs incident to the adventure are borne almost wholly by the common man, who gets no gain from it all. Commonly, as in the case of a protective tariff or a preferential navigation law, the cost to the common man is altogether out of proportion to the gain which accrues to the business men for whose benefit he carries the burden. The only other class, besides the preferentially favoured business men, who derive any material benefit from this arrangement is that of the office-holders who take care of this governmental traffic and draw something in the way of salaries and perquisites; and whose cost is defrayed by the common man, who remains an outsider in all but the payment of the bills. The common man is proud and glad to bear this burden for the benefit of his wealthier neighbours, and he does so with the singular conviction that in some occult manner he profits by it. All this is incredible, but it is everyday fact.

In case it should happen that these business interests of the nation's business men interested in trade or investments abroad are jeopardized by a disturbance of any kind in these foreign parts in which these business interests lie, then it immediately becomes the urgent concern of the national authorities to use all means at hand for maintaining the gainful traffic of these business men undiminished, and the common man pays the cost. Should such an untoward situation go to such sinister lengths as to involve actual loss to these business interests or otherwise give rise to a tangible grievance, it becomes an affair of the national honour; whereupon no sense of proportion as between the material gains at stake and the cost of remedy or retaliation need longer be observed, since the national honour is beyond price. The motivation in the case shifts from the ground of material interest to the spiritual ground of the moral sentiments.

In this connexion "honour" is of course to be taken in the euphemistic sense which the term has under the *code duello* governing "affairs of honour." It carries no connotation of honesty, veracity, equity, liberality, or unselfishness. This national honour is of the nature of an intangible or immaterial asset, of course; it is a matter of prestige, a sportsmanlike conception; but that fact must not be taken to mean that it is of any the less substantial effect for purposes of a *casus belli* than the material assets of the community. Quite the contrary: "Who steals my purse, steals trash," etc. In point of fact, it will commonly happen that any material grievance must first be converted into terms of this spiritual capital, before it is effectually turned to account as a stimulus to warlike enterprise.

Even among a people with so single an eye to the main chance as the American community it will be found true, on experiment or on review of the historical evidence, that an offence against the national honour commands a profounder and more unreserved resentment than any infraction of the rights of person or property simply. This has latterly been well shown in connexion with the manœuvres of the several European belligerents, designed to bend American neutrality to the service of one side or the other. Both parties have aimed to intimidate and cajole; but while the one party has taken recourse to effrontery and has made much and ostentatious use of threats and acts of violence against person and property, the other has constantly observed a deferential attitude toward American national self-esteem, even while engaged on a persistent infraction of American commercial rights. The first-named line of diplomacy has convicted itself of miscarriage and has lost the strategic advantage, as against the none too adroit finesse of the other side. The statesmen of this European war power were so ill advised as to enter on a course of tentatively cumulative intimidation, by threats and experimentally graduated crimes against the property and persons of American citizens, with a view to coerce American cupidity and yet to avoid carrying these manœuvres of terrorism far enough to arouse an unmanageable sense of outrage. The experiment has served to show that the breaking-point in popular indignation will be reached before the terrorism has gone far enough to raise a serious question of pecuniary caution.

This national honour, which so is rated a necessary of life, is an immaterial substance in a peculiarly high-wrought degree, being not only not physically tangible but also not even capable of adequate statement in pecuniary terms—as would be the case with ordinary immaterial assets. It is true, where the point of grievance out of which a question of the national honour arises is a pecuniary discrepancy, the national honour cannot be satisfied without a pecuniary accounting; but it needs no argument to convince all right-minded persons that even at such a juncture the national honour that has been compromised is indefinitely and indefinably more than what can be made to appear on an accountant's page. It is a highly valued asset, or at least a valued possession, but it is of a metaphysical, not of a physical nature, and it is not known to serve any material or otherwise useful end apart from affording a practicable grievance consequent upon its infraction.

This national honour is subject to injury in divers ways, and so may yield a fruitful grievance even apart from offences against the person or property of the nation's business men; as, e.g., through neglect or disregard of the conventional punctilios governing diplomatic intercourse, or by disrespect or contumelious speech touching the Flag, or the persons of national officials, particularly of such officials as have only a decorative use, or the costumes worn by such officials, or, again, by failure to observe the ritual prescribed for parading the national honour on stated occasions. When duly violated the national honour may duly be made whole again by similarly immaterial instrumentalities; as, e.g., by recital of an appropriate formula of words, by formal consumption of a stated quantity of ammunition in the way of a salute, by "dipping" an ensign, and the like—procedure which can, of course, have none but a magical efficacy. The national honour, in short, moves in the realm of magic, and touches the frontiers of religion.

Throughout this range of duties incumbent on the national defence, it will be noted, the offences or discrepancies to be guarded against or corrected by recourse to arms have much of a ceremonial character. Whatever may be the material accidents that surround any given concrete grievance that comes up for appraisal and redress, in bringing the case into the arena for trial by combat it is the spiritual value of the offence that is played up and made the decisive ground of action, particularly in so far as appeal is made to the sensibilities of the common man, who will have to bear the cost of the adventure. And in such a case it will commonly happen that the common man is unable, without advice, to see that any given hostile act embodies a sacrilegious infraction of the national honour. He will at any such conjuncture scarcely rise to the pitch of moral indignation necessary to float a warlike reprisal, until the expert keepers of the Code come in to expound and certify the nature of the transgression. But when once the lesion to the national honour has been ascertained, appraised, and duly exhibited by those persons whose place in the national economy it is to look after all that sort of thing, the common man will be found nowise behindhand about resenting the evil usage of which he so, by force of interpretation, has been a victim.